THE SPLINTERED CROSS

Exploring the Origins of Christian Denominations:
A Step toward Understanding One Another

THE SPLINTERED CROSS

Exploring the Origins of Christian Denominations:
A Step toward Understanding One Another

Jeffrey Richards

KwestWorks
KW

Cover Image:
© 2020

Published by: KwestWorks LLC
Bountiful, Utah

Edited by: Scarlett Lindsay

Please send comments or questions about this work to: support@KwestWorks.com

Printed on Demand in the United States

Library of Congress Control Number: 2020936640

Paperback ISBN 13: 978-1-7343818-2-5
e-Book ISBN 13: 978-1-7343818-4-9

Contents

Preface

I celebrate with all Christians who have found peace, stability, and purpose through their Christian beliefs and practices. A Christian life is a good life! These wonderful fruits of Christian living become a safe haven, like a protective fort, against the challenges and pitfalls of our time. Indeed, there is comfort and clarity by remaining safely within our denomination's walls. Staying protected usually means sticking with the denominational status quo—to perceive, believe, and do the things that were perceived, believed, and done last week and the week before.

My purpose with this book is to be the catalyst that motivates you to take a wider view, one that investigates the roots of belief and considers a broader context.

Consider the downsides and opportunities lost by never looking beyond our individual denominational safe havens. We remain isolated from Christians of other denominations and shortchange the opportunity for all Christians to influence the world as a unified body. We don't understand others' beliefs and practices and too often view them with suspicion or even derision. Without the context and history of broader Christianity, we are too willing to assert the "rightness" of the flavor of Christianity we believe in. We too easily adopt an us-versus-them mindset and thus miss an opportunity to associate with and support fellow Christians in their journey of faith. We often don't understand the roots of our own beliefs and have never challenged them; as a result, we might not realize that our beliefs and the faith they inspire may be fragile. Or worse, our beliefs could be misguided.

This book is a challenge to each Christian to step outside the safety of his or her "denominational fort" to take a much wider view of Christianity. The intent of this book is to instill a perspective that is informed, balanced, and mature. It is not to accuse or exonerate, not to criticize or extol. The book does not intend to destroy faith but rather to elevate and celebrate it.

The broader view starts with an understanding of today's Christian landscape, even though the picture is confusing, fractured, and chaotic. The title of this book, *The Splintered Cross*, attempts to capture the tension between the idyllic view of a unified body of Christ symbolized by the cross and the reality of a highly divided religion. Christianity's many denominations with their competing claims can be as much faith-destroying as they are faith-inspiring! Thus, taking a broader view is not just an academic exercise. It puts personal faith at risk! But I sincerely believe that gaining a more complete and mature perspective is worth that risk.

The fractured landscape of Christianity is, of course, the direct result of Christian history. The wide variety of beliefs and practices is the fruit of seeds planted long ago. Christian history is the starting point of our individual Christian story. In other words, we really can't take this journey without diving into history!

History gives us awareness that we are part of something much bigger. The novelist Michael Crichton expressed this well:

> If you don't know history, then you don't know anything.
> You are a leaf that doesn't know it is part of a tree.

I have not written this book for scholars (although they may find it interesting). My goal is to communicate with average Christians by creating a tapestry that is interesting and enlightening—a tapestry with rich details that I hope will avoid the tedium so often associated with history. I am not a religious scholar, a member of the trained clergy, or a professional historian. In fact, my background is in engineering and business. I was an executive for many years in a *Fortune* 500 firm. My qualifications for writing this book are my personal journey and perspectives gained from it, a passion for the subject, and years of attempting to communicate complicated things in intelligible and interesting ways.

The lessons I learned in my personal journey are a preview of the perspective I hope to instill in each reader, and so I start with those lessons.

Lesson 1: Simplistic stories of the past leave us vulnerable.

The seed for my interest in Christian "splintering" was planted in college when I took a course on the history of primitive Christianity. Prior to that class, I had a dangerously simplistic understanding of early Christian history. The version I had learned in Sunday School reinforced my own beliefs and the position of my own denomination. My simplistic Sunday School understanding was not wrong, per se, but because it left out the messiness and ambiguity of true history, I was left with a fragile faith and was ill-prepared to relate to my fellow Christians. The college course introduced me to the "rest of the story."[1] What I learned challenged but did not crush my Christian faith. In the end, a more robust understanding matured my faith and helped me see all Christians differently. I have felt an inner passion to help others take the same journey of discovery relative to the origins of denominations within Christianity.

Lesson 2: "Seek first to understand, then to be understood."[2]

I grew up in Salt Lake City, Utah—the "capital" of The Church of Jesus Christ of Latter-day Saints. Members are often called Mormons,[3] Latter-day Saints, or LDS for short. My ancestors were converts to the young church in the early 1800s. They suffered terrible persecution because of their new faith, being driven from homes in Missouri and Illinois at the hand of militias and mobs comprised of other Christians. They became part of the great Mormon pioneer exodus seeking refuge in the desert lands of the Great Salt Lake Valley. My family has often recounted the stories of our ancestors' courage in the face of overwhelming adversity. Their legacy inspired my own faith and commitment. But I was unaware that it also shaded my perspective of the Christian world. The common thread to these true and harrowing stories of persecution and exile was the notion that Latter-day Saints were destined as a people to be misunderstood.

In my youth, I could not easily perceive this belief. After all, I was immersed in a Latter-day Saint community. My friends were members the Church, and the vast majority of my neighbors were as well. But when I left Utah to pursue my career, I lived in eight different cities from coast to coast, from the Midwest to the Southwest, and my career required me to travel extensively around the United States. In short, until recently, all of my adult life was lived outside of Utah. Few of my adult friends, neighbors, colleagues, professional advisers, customers, and so on, belonged to my church. I was a minority in the midst of every imaginable Christian denomination. This new context revealed to me my inner expectation that my faith was bound to be misunderstood.

Some aspects of my experience reinforced this belief. In one of our Midwest stops, Baptist neighbors did not let their daughter play with our children because we were Latter-day Saints. Our neighbors had deep biases against our church that they had gained from annual anti-Mormon sessions held in the local Baptist church. But these biases were against theoretical Mormons. There we were in the flesh—real neighbors. Our normalness perplexed our neighbors and eventually eroded their resistance. We became good friends. Similarly, in a rare moment of personal candor in a professional setting, my boss of over ten years shared that he struggled to reconcile the view of Mormons he had gained from the anti-Mormon preaching in his church with the person that I was. How could I be a man of integrity and Christian goodness and yet believe in a religion characterized by his pastor as a cult? Many times through the years I have been asked whether I am a Christian. These and similar situations reinforced the belief developed in my childhood and buried deep in my psyche that as a member of The Church of Jesus Christ of Latter-day Saints I was bound to be misunderstood. A related corollary of this belief was that, if given the opportunity in a rare discussion about religion, I needed to explain my religion, that is, to *give to* rather than *receive from* other Christians.

Another belief, this one not so subtle, also played a role in my relationship with other Christians. The Church of Jesus Christ of Latter-day Saints believes that the Christian church apostatized from the primitive Christianity established by Jesus Christ. Furthermore, Latter-day Saints believe that Jesus Christ restored His gospel in the "latter-days" through a prophet. I have come to believe in this claim along with its corollary, that if the restored Church of Jesus Christ uniquely has the true gospel, then other Christian denominations do not. Clearly, this belief reinforces the notion that if given the opportunity in a religious discussion, I should *give to* rather than *receive from* other Christians.

Gratefully, during my decades of living in many parts of the United States, I came to understand just how limiting this bias was. I was privileged to associate with many wonderful Christians who were examples to me of faith and Christlike love. It became painfully clear that just as members of other denominations misunderstood my beliefs, I misunderstood theirs. I had no more knowledge of their denominations' principle beliefs than they did of mine. We mutually had so little cross-denominational understanding that we didn't know what we had in common and lacked sufficient background to put in perspective the differences. Mutual ignorance has too often been the ingredient for polarization, distrust, and even outright contention. Thus, one purpose for this book grew from the notion of applying the sage advice of a well-known business book, "Seek first to understand, then to be understood,"[4] to the context of Christianity. I developed a passionate awareness that I had to rectify my own paltry knowledge of other denominations.

Lesson 3: Contrast reveals unnoticed details.

The children's program *Sesame Street* often had small segments introduced with a cute song with the lyrics, "One of these things is not like the other . . ." *Sesame Street* used an effective teaching technique of comparing and contrasting to teach children to observe even the finest details. We intuitively know that contrast, such as in pictures, allows us to see boundaries and recognize objects. We experience the value of contrast when we are outside as the sun sets and twilight envelopes us. As the light fades, details are lost and objects run together. The children's book *Where's Waldo* is an example of the opposite of contrast. Waldo blends in with the visual noise of the picture, which makes him hard to see.

Comparisons are a figurative way to create contrast. I have observed that learning the origin and doctrines of other denominations creates contrast and reveals new aspects and depth to the doctrines of my own denomination.

Lesson 4: Christian "splintering" reveals profound truths about Jesus's intent and priorities.

Knowing the extent of Christian splintering forces one to deal with the disconnect between Jesus's stated aspiration for unity and the reality of a bewildering array of Christian denominations. In today's Western world where we can buy anything at the click of a button, we expect a full range of choices in any category: cars of all shapes, colors, and functions; fashion of every variety; infinite food choices. In short, choice is our normal! Thus, when we see tens of thousands of Christian denominations delivering virtually every combination of doctrine and practice, it may feel totally compatible with our modern world. However, this book reminds us that the initial intent expressed by Jesus was unity in truth. Modern Christian diversity should feel dissonant, not normal! In fact, my business training and experience tells me that the ideal of unity would have been the outcome of a well-designed, robustly established, and well-run organization, and through this lens, Christianity has failed!

My precollege understanding of Christianity left me inclined to blame the failure of unity on generations of postapostolic misguided leaders; however, that view of history was uninformed. This book makes it clear that unity evaporated within the first generation of Christians. In fact, if we were to judge primitive Christianity through the lens of management best-practices, we would find ample reasons to criticize Jesus Himself and the first generation of apostolic leaders.

Jesus left much of the church's organizational detail and doctrine undefined, and it seems that there was so much more that Jesus could have done to establish a robust organization, define doctrine, establish practices, and implement processes for dealing with change, uncertainty, and disagreement. Not doing so left the space for varied interpretations and inevitable schisms. Why didn't He do more?

The answer to this question requires us to view Christian history through the paradigm of faith. We have to start with the belief that the omniscient and perfect Lord Jesus accomplished exactly what He intended to do. He didn't start an experimental church that failed. He omnisciently must have known of divisive forces, and so whatever He did or didn't do to inoculate the church was done in perfect divine wisdom. At best, I am left to speculate why He gave the church what He did. Some of my possible answers may resonate as truth, but none are sure answers: Perhaps He gave the church what it was prepared to absorb in its infancy, expecting His inspired leaders to use judgment, seek additional revelation, and counsel together to mature the church. Perhaps He wanted it to be clear that the religion He started was less about the establishment and perfection of an organization; rather, the purpose of the church was and always has been to convey the gospel— and to provide salvation for individuals. Perhaps He needed us to recognize that in spite of disagreements and divisions sincere and truth-seeking individuals can still find Christ and gain degrees of truth according to individual circumstance. Perhaps it is essential to the shaping of each Christian that he or she be committed to Christ based on faith, even in the face of myriad reasons to criticize Christianity's flaws.

Lesson 5: Christian divisions require us to examine our personal beliefs about unity.

Intertwined with the story of Christianity's splintering is the story of attempts to enforce unity. Generations of Christian leaders believed that they were pursuing God's will in preserving unity through coercion. Their motivations and justifications are every bit as relevant to Christians today. There are profound things to consider and tough questions to answer relative to promoting modern Christian unity. I dedicate a chapter to "Counterfeit Unity" to challenge us to form individual conclusions about church-state alliances, tolerance, and unity.

Any work dealing with history is subject to the challenges of reconstructing the past. Indeed, piecing together history, particularly ancient history, has pitfalls. Often, historians have only scattered pieces of a much larger puzzle, so they must paint the picture of the entire puzzle by making reasonable assumptions about the gaps. Additionally, I am not a scholar or a professional historian, as I noted earlier, and so I am limited to secondary sources. Finally, unintentional biases can creep into any historical work as facts are woven together into a narrative. Undoubtedly, the historical portions of this work are not immune from these challenges.

I ask that you keep a couple of things in mind as you read. First, I have written this book as objectively as possible without denominational bias. I am in no way trying to prove the validity of one denomination over another! If the facts as I've portrayed them offend you, or if you disagree with what you read in the book, I apologize for my unintended offense and encourage you to independently dig deeper to discover the truth as best as it can be known. Second, the Christian history in this book is a means to an end—the end being a more informed, balanced, and mature perspective. Thus, if there are errors found relative to historical particulars, they are unintentional, isolated, and not intended to bias the history toward any particular conclusion. Most importantly, if found, errors need not undermine the principle goal of gaining perspective.

I have used online resources liberally. Not only does online searchability greatly facilitate research, it gives you the opportunity to go directly to my sources and dig in more deeply if interested. Given my audience and my purpose, I have liberally availed myself of Wikipedia. I take confidence from the findings of independent studies that have found that Wikipedia is generally as reliable as trusted long-standing encyclopedias.[5] In topic after topic, I turned to multiple sources and repeatedly found that Wikipedia offered depth and details that were simply too invaluable to ignore.

Hopefully, you're motivated to come on this journey with me. You will undoubtedly learn things that challenge and maybe even offend your current understanding. This risk is expressed well by the theologian and historian Rev. S. Baring-Gould:

> English Churchmen have long gazed with love on the Primitive Church as the ideal of Christian perfection, the Eden wherein the first fathers of their faith walked blameless before God, and passionless towards each other. To doubt, to dissipate in any way this pleasant dream, may shock and pain certain gentle spirits. Alas! the fruit of the tree of γνώσεις [knowledge], if it opens the eyes, saddens also and shames the heart.[6]

My belief is that gaining a more robust understanding of your denomination's Christian origin and its place in the Christian landscape will ultimately mature your faith.

It's time to start the journey. I hope you join me.

---

1 Paul Harvey, an American broadcaster, famously shared stories with an unexpected twist and then concluded by saying, "Now you know the *rest* of the story."

2 Habit 5 in *7 Habits of Highly Effective People*. Covey 1989, 235.

3 *Mormon* is a reference to belief in an additional book of scripture to the Bible called the Book of Mormon, believed to be an ancient record of a branch of the Israelites in the Americas.

4 Covey 1989.

5 Terdiman 2016.

6 Baring-Gould M.A. 1874, vi.

Chapter 1

From One to Many

We live in a world of immense diversity. The natural world surrounds us with amazing complexity and variety. Humankind has matched natural diversity in every facet of our creations: in our cultures, food, languages, buildings, tools, entertainment, transportation, professions, fashion, and so on. Many in the world today are blessed with the freedom to choose among diverse options. It is perhaps fitting then that we have a myriad of choices relative to religion. At the macro level, there are numerous major world religions: Christianity, Islam, Hinduism, Buddhism, Taoism, and more. Christianity is the largest of these with approximately 2.5 billion adherents.[1] However, given a world population exceeding 7 billion people, even Christianity is not a majority. The study of world religions is a worthy journey in its own right. However, this book is about Christianity alone. Within Christianity, there is incredible variation with an estimated forty-eight thousand denominations![2]

In the natural world, *variation* is called *diversity*. Christian variation might seem as normal to our modern sensibilities as natural diversity. Through the lens of "normal," we might be tempted to call forty-eight thousand denominations "Christian diversity." However, in the context of Christianity, in which the intent of its founder was a unified faith, variation could be considered a sign of dysfunction and a deviation from the ideal. Hence, the title of this book, *The Splintered Cross,* conveys what arguably should be the unsettling reality of a highly divided religion.

Within Christianity's forty-eight thousand denominations, beliefs and practices have been interpreted and molded in every imaginable way. About the only thing common among Christians is a belief in Jesus. In almost every aspect of worship, including doctrine, governance and authority, worship practices, and holy writ, there are stark differences among denominations.

Many believe that Jesus, the Father, and the Holy Ghost are an inseparable Trinity, while others believe that Jesus is the mortal Messiah, not equal to the Father.

Some regularly go to a sanctuary to pray and participate in rituals, while for others the extent of their religious observance is to watch Christian broadcast television.

Many recite creeds or refer to respective "confessions of faith," and others reject any directives other than the Bible.

Some have an altar in their home with the Virgin Mary or the crucified Christ on it, while others have literally no identifiable tokens of their Christianity.

Some pray while fingering beads. Others pray with raised arms and face, and yet others pray with folded arms and a bowed head.

Some dress in plain clothing and drive carriages, while others live in the most luxurious homes, drive the most expensive cars, and travel in private aircraft.

Some go to church on Sunday, while others observe the Jewish Sabbath of Saturday, and still others reject the Sabbath as a bygone requirement.

Some strictly observe Torah, the law of the Jews, while others would limit the law to the Ten Commandments, and others reject any commandment from the Old Testament.

Some embrace and practice prophecy, speaking in tongues, and gifts of the Spirit, while others are very circumspect about these Spiritual gifts. Some regard certain living persons as oracles of God, while others reject any notion that someone today has the authority to speak God's words.

Some participate actively in the governance of their local church, and others leave governance to full-time clergy.

Some claim to be saved in the instant in which they were "born again," and others express hope that through a lifetime of obedient and righteous living they can qualify for salvation. Some assert that every person has the potential to be saved, and others claim that only a small group of "the elect" are saved.

Some believe that Jesus's return will mark the end of the millennium, others believe the millennium is figurative, and yet others believe Jesus will come to usher in the millennium.

Clearly, there are myriad differences in the places of worship, priestly roles, rituals, sacraments, expectations, doctrines, social practices, and so on, within Christianity.

Consider the magnitude of 48,000 different denominations. By the year 1900, the major branches of Christianity had been formed, with the major schisms already in the past. Yet, at that time, there were about 1,600 denominations, a modest number by today's comparison. Between 1900 and 1970, denominations grew by about 245 per year. Between 1970 and 2000, the annual growth more than doubled to over 500 per year. Since 2000, the rate has increased by another 50 percent to nearly 800 new denominations per year.[3]

Why has there been a virtual explosion in the number of denominations? One explanation can be found in the foundational principles of the sixteenth-century Reformation. The premise of the Reformation was that the centralized authority of the church was corrupt and could be challenged. Rejecting the authority of clergy, Reformers espoused the doctrine of the "priesthood of all believers." The Reformed branch of Zwingli and Calvin rejected a bishop-centric (episcopal) hierarchy and established a priest-centric (presbyterian) governance. Offshoots from Calvinism took it one step further and established congregational churches with no hierarchy outside the local congregation. The rejection of centralized authority became so ingrained in the Reformation that, over time, belief in a central authority, as in a pope or a prophet, became a defining characteristic of a cult.[4] In short, as centralized authority waned, the seeds of variation sprouted. Within the fertile soil of religious freedom created by the Enlightenment, the American Revolution, and democratization across the world, Christian variation blossomed.

To get a sense for the variation that has resulted from Christian splintering, let's take a virtual tour of the world. On our tour, we will find that one out of every three people we meet are Christian.[5] One out of every four are Muslim.[6] One out of every seven to eight will be Hindu.[7] One out of every ten will claim to reject or will be entirely skeptical about religion.[8] In short, the single most common religion we'll find is Christianity. As on any journey, it is useful to have a map. Figure 1 is one version of a high-level map of Christianity. From left to right, it illustrates the schisms of Christianity over time. In future chapters, we'll take a chronological journey and refer back to this figure. We'll see all of the denominational branches listed in Figure 1 as we figuratively travel around the world.

We'll find that some denominations are much more common than others. Five out of every ten Christians we meet will be Catholic, and one out of every ten will be Orthodox. Three out of ten will come from a Protestant tradition,[9] and one out of every one hundred or so belongs to a Christian denomination not descending from one of these three traditions, including Christians from groups such as Jehovah's Witnesses, The Church of Jesus Christ of Latter-day Saints, and Messianic Jews.[10] Unlike the Catholic and Orthodox Christians, which belong to relatively homogeneous communions, the Protestants and other Christians belong to literally tens of thousands of denominations. On our journey, we might be surprised to find that more Protestant Christians identify as Pentecostal or Charismatic than as any other Protestant denominational family.[11]

We'll find geographic enclaves in which the Christians are not diverse at all. We might get a mistaken sense that members of a dominant denomination in that area are dominant in the world. For example, in the UK we'll find Anglicans who belong to the Church of England at every turn. But, globally, Anglicans account for less than 4 percent of all Christians.[12] We'll meet many Lutherans in Germany but find relatively few outside the country. Lutherans account for 2.6 percent of total Christians.[13] If we travel through the Intermountain West of the United States, we'll see the chapels of The Church of Jesus Christ of Latter-day Saints in nearly every neighborhood, but the members of the church, often called Mormons, account for just 0.7 percent of total Christians—about one in every 150 Christians.[14]

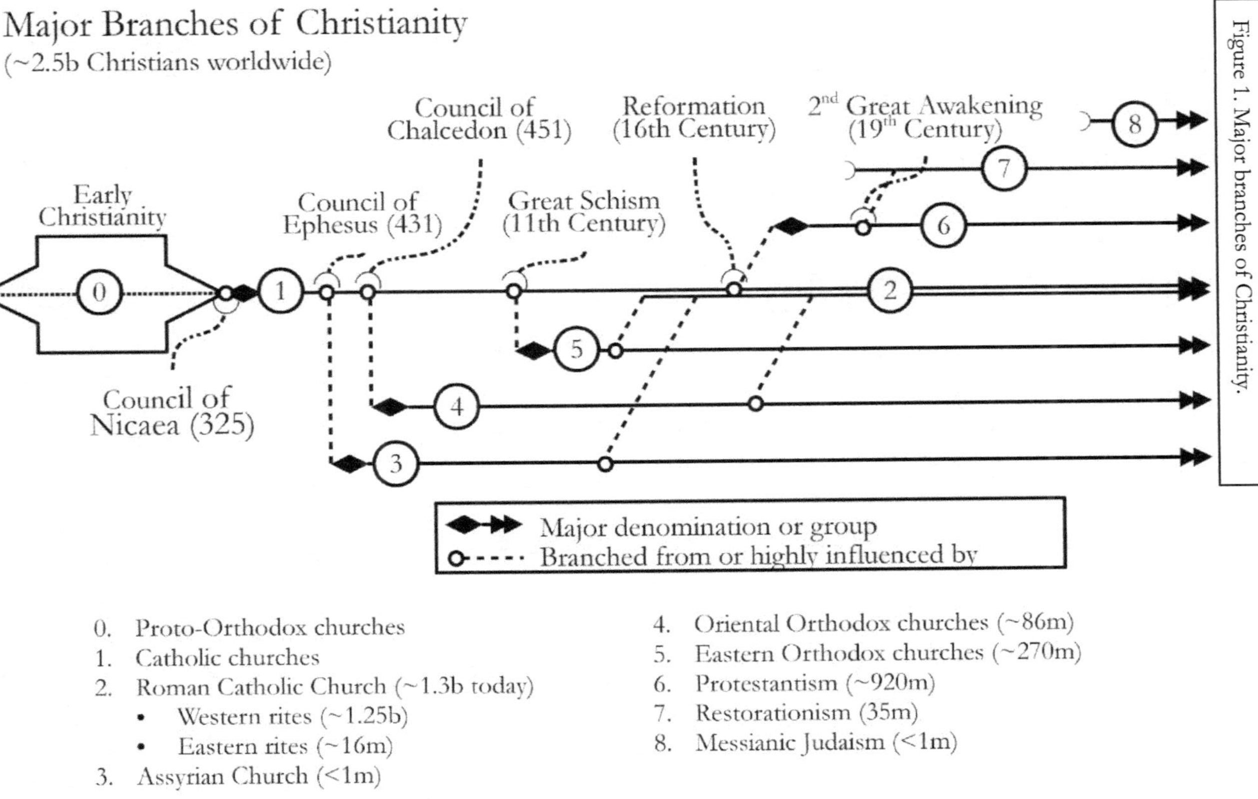

Major Branches of Christianity
(~2.5b Christians worldwide)
Early Christianity
Council of Nicaea (325)
Council of Ephesus (431)
Council of Chalcedon (451)
Great Schism (11th Century)
Reformation (16th Century)
2nd Great Awakening (19th Century)
Major denomination or group
Branched from or highly influenced by
0. Proto-Orthodox churches
1. Catholic churches
2. Roman Catholic Church (~1.3b today)
• Western rites (~1.25b)
• Eastern rites (~16m)
3. Assyrian Church (<1m)
4. Oriental Orthodox churches (~86m)
5. Eastern Orthodox churches (~270m)
6. Protestantism (~920m)
7. Restorationism (35m)
8. Messianic Judaism (<1m)
Figure 1. Major branches of Christianity.

If we travel in a slightly arced line from Athens, Greece, through the Eastern European countries of Bulgaria, Romania, Moldova, Ukraine, Belarus, and on to Russia, we'll find very similar churches. Four out of every five people will be Christian, and nearly every Christian will belong to the Eastern Orthodox communion. Christians in each country belong to their respective state church and look to a different patriarch, but they have similar worship, rites, or liturgy to their fellow Eastern Orthodox churches.[15]

If we turn west and leave the homogenous Eastern Orthodox Christianity of Russia and Belarus and head across Europe toward the United Kingdom, we'll find an alternating patchwork of denominations. In Poland, nearly everyone will be Christian and Catholic.[16] Nearly three out of four Germans will nominally be Christians, but these will be a fifty-fifty split between Catholics and Protestants.[17] As we cross into France, 63 percent of the population there will be Christian and virtually all Catholic.[18] In the UK, Protestants, specifically Anglicans, will account for 75 percent of the Christian majority.[19] In our trip across Europe, the diversity will still be relatively tame in terms of total denominations. We'll find Catholics, Lutherans, Reformed (Calvinists), Anglicans, and a smattering of less than 1 percent each of Orthodox and "other" denominations.

In contrast, in the United States we'll see a vast array of denominations. In the Northeast, we'll find that 50 percent of the Christians are Catholic and the rest are a diverse smattering of every conceivable denomination.[20] In the upper Midwest, we'll find that 73 percent are Christian. Of these, 63 percent are Protestant, with an even split between evangelical and mainline Protestants. To illustrate how pockets of denominations exist, we could stop in Minnesota, where we'll find a large concentration of Lutherans, tilting the scales toward mainline Protestants in that area.[21] In the Southern states, known as the Bible Belt, we'll be immersed in evangelical Christianity, with nearly 60 percent of Christians characterizing themselves as evangelical.[22] We'll find every possible Protestant denomination and many large nondenominational megachurch congregations. One out of every three Christians we'll meet will be a Baptist.[23] On the west side of the Rockies, up and down the valleys of Idaho, Utah, and Arizona, we'll find members of The Church of Jesus Christ of Latter-day Saints. In Utah, 75 percent of the predominantly Christian state will be

Mormon.[24] But in the West overall, we'll find a broad mix of all denominations, with Protestants modestly outnumbering Catholics.[25]

In our journey through South America, we will find that 92 percent of the population is Christian,[26] and, other than in Brazil, nearly 90 percent of South American Christians are Catholic[27]—a legacy of the Spanish colonization of South America. We may be amazed at how indigenous people have meshed their cultural traditions with Catholicism, a blending called *syncretism*.[28] In Brazil, we will still find a Catholic majority, but we'll also find a large community of twenty-five million Pentecostals, members of the Assemblies of God, equating to 15 percent of all Christians and the majority of non-Catholics in Brazil.[29]

Perhaps one of our biggest surprises as we traverse the world will be finding more Christians in Africa than in any other continent. Even though Christianity is not the dominant religion on the African continent—about 45 percent Africa's population is Christian—there are 631 million Christians there.[30] In northern Africa, although the dominant religion is Islam, we will find a significant Christian community in Egypt, Ethiopia, and Eritrea. Most of these Christians belong to the communion of Oriental Orthodox churches, including the Coptic Orthodox Church in Egypt.[31] In sub-Saharan Africa, we'll find a dizzying variety of denominations, many of which are offshoots of Protestant branches first brought to Africa by colonizers and missionaries.[32] We'll see that flavors of Pentecostalism are prevalent;[33] the denomination's beliefs in healing, prophecy, and exorcism resonate with traditional African religions. We will see polygamy practiced in many homegrown independent African churches and will come to understand that polygamy, long practiced in African culture, was one of the most compelling causes for the splintering of African churches from their European predecessors.[34] Many of the denominations we'll encounter are not known in the West because they are syncretic combinations of Protestantism and traditional African religions.[35] We'll see the legacy of colonization by European powers. Anglicans will be common in countries colonized by Britain, such as Ghana, Kenya, and Malawi, and Catholics will be common in countries colonized by France, Belgium, and Portugal, such as Angola and Mozambique. In the Democratic Republic of the Congo, we will find a balanced mix of Catholics and Protestants; however, in this country all of the sixty-two diverse Protestant denominations are united under one governing church, the Church of Christ in the Congo.[36] Throughout Africa, we'll find growing communities of Seventh-day Adventists, Jehovah's Witnesses, and members of The Church of Jesus Christ of Latter-day Saints.[37]

If we take a journey and travel eastward from the birthplace of Christianity in the Holy Land, we'll see shadows of a rich Christian history, even if the density of Christians is very low. Throughout the countries of the Middle East, we will find a potentially confusing mix of Orthodox and Catholic churches. We'll see that denominations in that area not only separated into distinct entities based on the Orthodox schisms shown in Figure 1 and explored later in this book but also remained segregated into different churches due to differences in liturgical rites and ethnicity. Some churches originated within an Orthodox branch but then split off from the branch to become an autonomous church in communion with the Roman Catholic Church. We might be surprised to find twenty-four Catholic churches in the Middle East. By far the largest and most commonly known is the Roman Catholic Church. The other twenty-three are Eastern Catholic churches, most of them splitting off from the Orthodox branches that had themselves branched from Catholicism.

Israel provides a useful example of the overlapping origins of Orthodox and Catholic churches. The country is only 2 percent Christian but officially recognizes ten Christian churches. Of these, six are Catholic, including the Roman Catholic Church and five autonomous Eastern Catholic churches. Israel's Christian churches are listed in table 1. A close examination of the table reveals how the churches remain distinct based on a combination of factors. For example, the Armenian Apostolic and Syriac Orthodox both originated from the Oriental Orthodox schism but remained separate based on different ethnic backgrounds, liturgical rites, and allegiance to different patriarchs. The Armenian Catholic Church split from the Armenian Apostolic Church to become an autonomous Eastern Catholic Church in communion with the Roman Catholic Church. Thus, even though it is of the same ethnicity and still uses the same rites as its fellow Armenian predecessor, it now honors a separate patriarch and is in communion with Roman Catholicism.

This Catholic and Orthodox splintering would be acutely apparent if we were to swing north and travel through Antakya, Turkey, the ancient city of Antioch located between Syria and the Mediterranean. The city is home to *five* different patriarchs heading up distinct churches of Eastern Catholic, Eastern Orthodox, and Oriental Orthodox Christianity![38]

Table 1. Recognized Churches in Israel

Recognized church in Israel	Ethnic origin	Rite	Original branch	Current communion
Roman Catholic	Various	Latin or Western	Catholic	Catholic
Maronite	Lebanese	Antiochian or "West Syriac"	Catholic	Eastern Catholic
Chaldean Catholic	Assyrian	East Syriac	Assyrian Church	Eastern Catholic
Armenian Apostolic	Armenian	Armenian	Oriental Orthodox	Oriental Orthodox
Armenian Catholic	Armenian	Armenian	Oriental Orthodox	Eastern Catholic
Syriac Orthodox	Assyrian	Antiochian or "West Syriac"	Oriental Orthodox	Oriental Orthodox
Syriac Catholic	Assyrian	Antiochian or "West Syriac"	Oriental Orthodox	Eastern Catholic
Greek Catholic Melkite	Mostly Arab	Byzantine or Constantinople	Eastern Orthodox	Eastern Catholic
Eastern Orthodox (e.g., Greek Orthodox)	Various	Byzantine or Constantinople	Eastern Orthodox	Eastern Orthodox
Protestant				

Source: Israel 2015 International Religious Freedom Report 2015.

The pattern of Catholic and Orthodox splintering we found in Israel will be common as we travel through the sparse Christian lands of Iraq and Iran.[39] We will also see the pattern in India where there are thirty million Christians, although given the large population of India, the density of Christians is still less than 3 percent.[40] In Kerala, where the Nasrani, or St. Thomas Christians, belong to a variety of Catholic and Orthodox churches with different rites and allegiances to different patriarchs, reflecting the influence from the Assyrian Church, the Oriental Orthodox Church, and the Catholic Church.[41] On the other side of the country in the northeastern states of Meghalaya, Mizoram, and Nagaland, Christians are the majority of the population, a result of Protestant missionary success. Perhaps, we'll be surprised that in the heart of India, in one of its most sizable cities, Hyderabad, we will find one of the largest nondenominational megachurches in the world, Calvary Temple Church. It has a sanctuary that holds eighteen thousand worshipers, a Bible college, and approximately two hundred thousand members. Its size compares with the large megachurches that dot the southern United States.[42]

As we travel around Asia, Christians will be few and far between. In China, estimates range from thirty million to over one hundred million Christians out of a population of 1.4 billion.[43] We will find three officially sanctioned Christian churches that have historical roots in Western Christianity but today have no external ties. Most Protestants will belong to the Three-Self Patriotic Church, a unified nondenominational Protestant church. It was named Three-Self Church to reassure the Chinese government that it is independent of Western influence. Its name encapsulates its threefold independence from the West: self-governing, self-supporting, and self-propagating.[44] We will encounter millions of Catholics who belong to the Chinese Patriotic Catholic Church, a church organized by the Chinese government in 1957 with the express purpose of severing Chinese Catholics from the authority of Rome.[45] We will have to be very careful not to talk about nonsanctioned denominations and not to proselyte native Chinese people because these activities are banned. Nevertheless, we will likely find "hidden" Christians who practice their faith outside the state-sanctioned churches. Their numbers are hard to measure but are estimated to be in the tens of millions. They worship in small, covert, unregistered, and illegal groups called "house churches."[46] We may witness official government persecution of Christians, which by some accounts is increasing.[47] If we end our journey through Asia with a visit to South Korea, we will find one of the largest Pentecostal megachurches in the world, the Yoido Full Gospel Church, with its nearly five hundred thousand members, a considerable sanctuary, and extensive campus with education and mission buildings.

—————————————— ❧ ❧ ——————————————

Our virtual worldwide tour gives us an appreciation for the vast diversity of Christian denominations. With so much splintering, a complete study of every denomination would be nearly impossible and beyond the interest of most of us. This book attempts to find a balance between superficiality and completeness. Size and influence both factored into the decision to include certain denominations. Undoubtedly, some will argue that certain denominations were covered that should not have been, while some will ask why others were not included. Admittedly, our exploration of Christian splintering in the chapters that follow is disproportionately focused on Western Christianity. African and Asian Christianity, while vibrant and diverse, are not covered in depth in this book.

Notes

---

[1] Johnson and Zurlo 2018.

[2] Johnson and Zurlo 2018.

[3] Johnson and Zurlo 2018.

[4] What is the definition of a cult? n.d. Discussed in Chapter 11: Counterfeit Unity—Coerced Belief.

[5] Johnson and Zurlo 2018.

[6] Johnson and Zurlo 2018.

[7] Johnson and Zurlo 2018.

[8] Johnson and Zurlo 2018.

[9] The Center for the Study of Global Christianity separates "independents" from the mainline Protestant bucket. As such, Protestants account for 22 percent and Independents 17 percent of total Christians Johnson and Zurlo 2018. The Pew Forum groups the majority of these two buckets together given the historical common heritage. In the Pew accounting, Protestants represent 36.7 percent. Pew has a small bucket for truly non-Protestant-derived denominations such as the Church of Christ, The Church of Jesus Christ of Latter-day Saints, and Jehovah's Witnesses. This bucket accounts for just 1.3 percent of Christianity.

[10] Hackett and Grim 2011.

[11] Center for the Study of Global Christianity 2018.

[12] Center for the Study of Global Christianity 2018.

[13] Center for the Study of Global Christianity 2018.

[14] Center for the Study of Global Christianity 2018.

[15] Hackett and Grim 2011.

[16] Hackett and Grim 2011.

[17] Hackett and Grim 2011.

[18] Hackett and Grim 2011.

[19] Hackett and Grim 2011.

[20] Pew n.d.

[21] Pew n.d.

[22] This includes historical white evangelical churches and historically black Protestant churches, which tend to fit the characteristics of evangelical Pew n.d.

[23] Pew n.d.

[24] Pew n.d.

[25] Pew n.d.

[26] Center for the Study of Global Christianity 2018.

[27] 87 percent derived from data from Pew Forum Hackett and Grim 2011.

[28] Syncretism involves the merging or assimilation of several originally discrete traditions, especially in the theology and mythology of religion, thus asserting an underlying unity and allowing for an inclusive approach to other faiths Wikipedia, Syncretism 2018. In Bolivia, for example, indigenous people who are Catholic continue to make offerings to Mother Earth. The market for llama fetuses and related indigenous offering ingredients is thriving Popper 2007.

[29] Center for the Study of Global Christianity 2018.

[30] Center for the Study of Global Christianity 2018.

[31] Oriental Orthodox churches are often lumped into one Orthodox bucket in religious surveys; however, Oriental Orthodox are a distinct religious group apart

from Eastern Orthodox. Just as the Greek Orthodox Church is often the "face" of the Eastern Orthodox communion, the Coptic Orthodox Church in Egypt is the face of the Oriental Orthodox communion.

[32] Examples include Kimbanguism in the DR Congo, in which the doctrine is based on Baptist beliefs and they recite the Trinitarian formula; however, they believe Father Simon Kimbangu is the Holy Spirit. Alongside Simon Kimbangu, the Trinity are Father Kisolokele (first son of Kimbangu) as God the Father, Father Salomon Diangani Dialungana (the reincarnated Jesus and second son of Kimbangu), Father Diangienda Kuntima (last son, reincarnation of Kimbangu and second human form of the Holy Spirit), and Father Simon Kimbangu Kiangani (grandson of Kimbangu, third human form of the Holy Spirit, and current spiritual leader of the Church since 2001) Wikipedia, Kimbanguism 2018. The Zion Christian Church founded in 1924 in South Africa is one of the largest local denominations. It believes its founder, Engenas Lekganyane, is the mediator between the faithful and God.

[33] M. Harper 1984.

[34] Falaye 2016. Most European denominations refused to baptize polygamists. Some of these polygamists used their influence and standing to start new denominations. Examples include Isaiah Shembe, messiah of the Nazarite Baptist Church in South Africa, who had four wives; Josiah Oshitelu, founder of the Aladura (Church of the Lord), who had seven wives; and Johane Maranke, founder of the African Apostolic Church in Zambia and Zimbabwe, who had sixteen wives before he died in 1963 Muthengi 1995.

[35] Wikipedia, Christianity in Africa 2018.

[36] Wikipedia, Church of Christ in the Congo 2018.

[37] Wikipedia, Christianity in Africa 2018.

[38] Patriarchs in Antioch, each claiming succession from Peter are Maronite Church, Syriac Catholic Church, Melkite Catholic Church, Antiochian Orthodox Church (Eastern Orthodox), and Syriac Orthodox (Oriental Orthodox).

[39] Wikipedia, Christianity in Iraq 2018., Wikipedia, Christianity in Iran 2018.

[40] Center for the Study of Global Christianity 2018.

[41] Wikipedia, Christianity in India 2018.

[42] Wikipedia, List of the largest evangelical churches 2018.

[43] The low end of the estimates comes from official state census, which counts members of the sanctioned churches. Pew Research estimates 67 million as of 2010 Hackett and Grim 2011. and Center for Study of Global Christianity estimates over 100 million including unregistered house churches Center for the Study of Global Christianity 2018.

[44] Wikipedia, Christianity in China 2018.

[45] Wikipedia, Christianity in China 2018.

[46] Wikipedia, Christianity in China 2018.

[47] Mikelionis 2018.

Chapter 2

Unity—The Unfulfilled Aspiration

By mid-1941, the world had descended into the deadliest conflict in its history. The Nazis, rising from the lands of the Protestant Reformation, had joined forces with the Fascist army from Italy, the center of the Roman Catholic Church.[1] This "Christian army" of axis powers had quickly overwhelmed other countries with their "lightning war" and had invaded and captured European Poland, Czechoslovakia, Denmark, Norway, Holland, Belgium, and France. Countries in areas bordering the Mediterranean, including Greece, northern Africa, and the Baltic regions, had also fallen. England's independence was far from certain as it faced a constant barrage against its major cities. Hundreds of thousands of Jews had been rounded up in captured territories and locked into ghettos or sent to concentration camps.[2] It's difficult to fully appreciate the severity of the existential crisis that the world faced at that time.

It was against this backdrop that on August 9, 1941, the HMS *Prince of Wales* slipped into Placentia Bay in remote Newfoundland. Awaiting the *Prince of Wales* was the USS *Augusta*. This was a dangerous time to be on the Atlantic waters, thus the rendezvous was in secret. Aboard the two ships were Winston Churchill, aboard the *Prince of Wales*, and Franklin Roosevelt, aboard the *Augusta*.[3] At stake was nothing less than the preservation of the free world.[4]

Here were two of the most powerful men in the world—they commanded armies and led nations. But in an act of reverence and humility, they held a church service with the men gathered on the deck of the *Prince of Wales*. Winston Churchill chose the hymn "Onward

Christian Soldiers." He described his overwhelming emotion at seeing the gathered men and explained the motivation for his choice of hymn:

> When I looked upon that densely packed congregation of fighting men of the same language, of the same faith, of the same fundamental laws, of the same ideals . . . it swept across me that here was the only hope, but also the sure hope, of saving the world from measureless degradation.[5]

That body of men was a small portion of another Christian army—this one raising their voices in the truest spirit of goodness. Their song was less a statement of fact than a prayer of hope—that they could be a saintly army unified with a common hope and belief in the freedom of humanity and a common motivating love:

> Like a mighty army
> Moves the Church of God;
> Brothers, we are treading
> Where the Saints have trod.
> *We are not divided;*
> *All one body we:*
> *One in hope and doctrine,*
> *One in charity.* [6]

This story is included here because it encapsulates many of the broader realities that we will see throughout this book: the allied leaders had a keen awareness of overwhelming and impending evil and recognized the powerful role that faith in God and His goodness could play to combat it. Their many differences, including the men's nationalities and denominations, faded compared to the gravity of the situation. Their pleas for unity were intense and heartfelt and superseded denominations, creeds, and confessions. Their Christian values inspired them with purpose and courage; yet, they could see that their enemy had twisted their common religion into a tool of power to unify the forces of tyranny. This paradox of two Christian armies arrayed in mortal combat against each other reveals a theme that we will revisit later in this book. Namely, that the disposition of people's hearts and the fruits of those intents are far more important than denominational affiliation.

Now, let us shift time and place to another intense plea for unity—this one in a quiet, intimate setting by a humble leader with eleven of his closest associates.

On the eve of His capture, Jesus gathered with His apostles for one last meal. Jesus knew full well what lay ahead for Him personally and for the disciples He loved. It was with this keen awareness of the intensity of the experiences soon to come that Jesus ended the solemn gathering with a prayer to the Father. Rather than a swelling chorus of voices, it was His voice alone that spoke quietly and reverently. Nevertheless, surely his single plea was every bit as intense and heartfelt as the one sung by the chorus of men gathered on the ships during World War II. With an omniscient awareness of the evil that would attack and subvert believers, He prayed,

> I pray for them [the gathered apostles]: . . . I pray not that thou shouldest take them out of the world, but that thou shouldest keep them from the evil. . . . thy word is truth . . . that they also might be sanctified *through the truth*. Neither pray I for these alone, but for them also which shall believe on me through their word; That they *all may be one*; as thou, Father, art in me, and I in thee, that they *also may be one in us*.[7]

These were not idle words in a rote prayer. Jesus knew the evil His followers would face in the world, and He knew the value of truth. With these two precedent thoughts, protection against evil and retaining the truth, He prayed for oneness—for unity. He prayed for the eleven apostles gathered with Him and for all those who would believe their words.

Like Jesus, Paul aspired to unity within the body of Christ, as evidenced by his words to the Ephesians:

> Endeavoring to keep the *unity of the Spirit in the bond of peace*. . . . And he gave some, apostles; and some, prophets; and some, evangelists; and some, pastors and teachers; For the perfecting of the saints, for the work of the ministry, for the edifying of the body of Christ: *Till we all come in the unity of the faith, and of the knowledge of the Son of God*, unto a

perfect man, unto the measure of the stature of the fulness of Christ: That we henceforth be no more children, tossed *to and fro, and carried about with every wind of doctrine, by the sleight of men, and cunning craftiness, whereby they lie in wait to deceive.*[8]

Importantly, Paul's aspiration for unity was not just about everyone believing the same thing. Paul aspired to unity based on the truth of the gospel, including the knowledge of the Son of God. Nevertheless, Paul acknowledged the evil forces full of deceit and craftiness that would threaten unity.

Truth was to be a fundamental purpose for and ingredient of unity. Jesus promised, "If ye continue in my word, then are ye my disciples indeed; and ye shall know the truth, and the truth shall make you free."[9] Paul echoed the essence of Jesus's words when he wrote to Timothy, "Our Savior . . . will have all men . . . come unto the knowledge of the truth."[10]

For a few short years, with the apostles closely tending the flock, there was incredible harmony and unity, as described in the New Testament:

> These all continued with *one accord* in prayer and supplication, with the women, and Mary the mother of Jesus, and with his brethren.[11]

> And they continued steadfastly in the apostles' doctrine and fellowship, and in breaking of bread, and in prayers. . . . And all that believed were together, and had all things common; And sold their possessions and goods, and parted them to all men, as every man had need. And they, continuing daily with one accord in the temple, and breaking bread from house to house, did eat their meat with gladness and *singleness of heart* . . .[12]

> And the multitude of them that believed *were of one heart and of one soul*: neither said any of them that ought of the things which he possessed was his own; but they had all things common. And with great power gave the apostles witness of the resurrection of the Lord Jesus: and great grace was upon them all. Neither was there any among them that lacked: for as many as were possessors of lands or houses

sold them, and brought the prices of the things that were sold, And laid them down at the apostles' feet: and distribution was made unto every man according as he had need.[13]

Then had the churches rest throughout all Judaea and Galilee and Samaria, and were edified; and walking in the fear of the Lord, and in the comfort of the Holy Ghost, were multiplied.[14]

The simplistic version of Christian history jumps from these early days of the apostolic ministry with its idyllic unity to the "unified" Catholic Church that emerged in the fourth century, giving the impression that the splintering of Christianity happened centuries after the apostles' deaths. Simplistic history gives the impression of an idyllic primitive church. This simplistic view is not reality. Divisions emerged within the lifetime of the apostles. Doctrinal wanderings, whether innocent or malicious, began soon after Jesus's death. This reality is clear from the repeated warnings and admonitions in New Testament epistles. Nearly every epistle preserved in the New Testament warns against deviations *already* taking root in the primitive church. Some prophesied of a complete falling away.

Near the end of his traveling ministry in about the year 58,[15] Paul journeyed to Jerusalem and on the way called the elders from Ephesus to him for one final council. He prophetically warned them,

For I know this, that after my departing shall grievous wolves enter in among you, not sparing the flock. Also of your own selves shall men arise, speaking perverse things, to draw away disciples after them.[16]

In addition to meeting and warning a group of elders from Ephesus, Paul sought to further protect the saints there by appointing the young and stalwart Timothy as bishop. Nevertheless, the prophetic Paul could see the coming flood of deceit and deviation from true doctrine:

But evil men and seducers shall wax worse and worse, deceiving, and being deceived. But continue thou in the things which thou hast learned and hast been assured of,

> knowing of whom thou hast learned them; . . . For the time will come when they will not endure sound doctrine; but after their own lusts shall they heap to themselves teachers, having itching ears; And they shall turn away their ears from the truth, and shall be turned unto fables.[17]

Perhaps it was with a longer view beyond Timothy's own ministry that he could see an even more dire impact on the believers:

> Now the Spirit speaketh expressly, that in the latter times some shall depart from the faith, giving heed to seducing spirits, and doctrines of devils; Speaking lies in hypocrisy; having their conscience seared with a hot iron; Forbidding to marry, and commanding to abstain from meats, which God hath created to be received with thanksgiving of them which believe and know the truth.[18]

The saints in Thessalonica were caught up in a debate about the timing of the second coming of Jesus Christ. Paul addressed the debate by reminding them of an earlier prophecy he had made, namely, that Christ would not come again until there had been a "falling away" led by the "man of sin" who would act and behave as if he were appointed by God.

> Let no man deceive you by any means: for that day [the second coming of the Lord] shall not come, except there *come a falling away first, and that man of sin be revealed,* the son of perdition; Who opposeth and exalteth himself above all that is called God, or that is worshipped; so that he as God sitteth in the temple of God, shewing himself that he is God. Remember ye not, that, when I was yet with you, I told you these things? And now ye know what withholdeth that he might be revealed in his time. *For the mystery of iniquity doth already work.*[19]

In Corinth, Paul addressed a number of divisive forces already affecting the church, including competing claims for authority, intellectual sophistry, and Judaizers who would have new converts become Jewish Christians. Several leader-missionaries had been influential in converting Corinthian saints. Consequently, the saints divided themselves up according to the leader-missionary who had converted them. Paul waded into the confusion:

> Now I beseech you, brethren, by the name of our Lord Jesus Christ, that ye all speak the same thing, and that there be no divisions among you; but that ye be perfectly joined together in the same mind and in the same judgment. For it hath been declared unto me of you, my brethren, by them which are of the house of Chloe, that there are contentions among you. Now this I say, that every one of you saith, I am of Paul; and I of Apollos; and I of Cephas; and I of Christ. Is Christ divided? was Paul crucified for you? or were ye baptized in the name of Paul?[20]

Influential teachers claiming to be apostles were among the people of Corinth teaching a perverted gospel. Paul warned the Corinthians,

> But I fear, lest by any means, as the serpent beguiled Eve through his subtilty, so your minds should be corrupted from the simplicity that is in Christ. For if he that cometh preacheth another Jesus, whom we have not preached, or if ye receive another spirit, which ye have not received, or another gospel, which ye have not accepted, ye might well bear with him. . . . For such are *false apostles*, deceitful workers, transforming themselves into the apostles of Christ. And no marvel; for Satan himself is transformed into an angel of light. Therefore it is no great thing if his ministers also be transformed as the ministers of righteousness; whose end shall be according to their works.[21]

To Titus, believed to be appointed by Paul as the bishop of Crete, Paul wrote against the influence of Judaizers. Not only did the Judaizers seek to impose the Law along with circumcision, they incited contention relative to the superiority of Jewish ancestry:

> For there are *many unruly and vain talkers and deceivers, specially they of the circumcision* [Jewish Christians]: Whose mouths

> must be stopped, who subvert whole houses, teaching things which they ought not, for filthy lucre's sake.[22]

> But avoid foolish questions, and *genealogies*, and contentions, and strivings *about the law [of Moses]*; for they are unprofitable and vain. A man that is an heretick after the first and second admonition reject.[23]

The Galatians faced the same issue. Judaizers were coming among the new converts and urging them to be circumcised and follow the Law of Moses.[24] Paul frankly confronts the Galatians: "I am afraid of you, lest I have bestowed upon you labour in vain."[25] He adds,

> I marvel that ye are so soon removed from him that called you into the grace of Christ unto another gospel: Which is not another; but *there be some that trouble you* [Judaizers sent from Jerusalem], and would pervert the gospel of Christ. But though we, or an angel from heaven, preach any other gospel unto you than that which we have preached unto you, let him be accursed. As we said before, so say I now again, If any man preach any other gospel unto you than that ye have received, let him be accursed. For do I now persuade men, or God? or do I seek to please men? for if I yet pleased men, I should not be the servant of Christ. But I certify you, brethren, that the gospel which was preached of me is not after man. For I neither received it of man, neither was I taught it, but by the revelation of Jesus Christ.[26]

The Colossians, in the heart of Greek influence, faced the challenge of sophistry born of philosophy. We don't know whether Greek-influenced doctrines that stripped Jesus of divinity had already surfaced or whether Paul was speaking prophetically; nevertheless, his epistle to the Colossians presaged the doctrinal debate about Jesus's nature that would grip Christianity for centuries. How could a mortal Jesus be divine?

> Beware lest any man spoil you through philosophy and vain deceit, after the tradition of men, after the rudiments of the

world, and not after Christ. *For in him dwelleth all the fulness of the Godhead bodily.*[27]

Peter likewise prophesied plainly of heresies on the very doorstep of the early church:

> But there were false prophets also among the people [ancient Israel], even as there shall be *false teachers among you, who privily shall bring in damnable heresies,* even denying the Lord that bought them, and bring upon themselves swift destruction. And *many shall follow* their pernicious ways; by reason of whom the way of truth shall be evil spoken of.[28]

John recorded in Revelations that Ephesus was already dealing with false apostles:

> I know thy works, and thy labour, and thy patience, and how thou canst not bear them which are evil: and thou hast tried *them which say they are apostles, and are not,* and hast found them liars.[29]

John warned his "children" to be alert to false teachers that were countering simple Christian truths relative to Jesus:

> Little children, it is the last time: and as ye have heard that antichrist shall come, *even now are there many antichrists;* whereby we know that it is the last time. . . . These things have I written unto you *concerning them that seduce you.*[30]

> Beloved, believe not every spirit, but try the spirits whether they are of God: because *many false prophets are gone out into the world.*[31]

> For *many deceivers are entered into the world, who confess not that Jesus Christ is come in the flesh.* This is a deceiver and an antichrist.[32]

Jude, though not an apostle, echoed Peter's concerns about heresies that twisted the doctrine of grace to justify lustful (lascivious) behavior. He wrote,

> For there are *certain men crept in unawares,* who were before
> of old ordained to this condemnation, ungodly men,
> turning the grace of our God into lasciviousness,[33] and
> denying the only Lord God, and our Lord Jesus Christ.[34]

Our limited and finite minds can hardly grasp the intensity and urgency with which Jesus must have pled with the Father that His apostles could be kept from evil, be sanctified by truth, and become completely unified.[35] He surely had the breadth and depth of understanding about the nature of the evil they and other believers would face and its fruits of confusion, corruption, and division.

It is with this perspective that we can appreciate how important His aspiration was. It is through this perspective of unity so intensely desired, needed, and lost that we should consider the history of Christian splintering. Without this perspective, we may very well be indifferent to the contests, rivalries, debates, and divisions that splintered believers in Christ. Without this perspective, we may very well see splintering through our twenty-first-century sensibilities and see it as diversity—the fruits of creativity and innovation—an outcome to celebrate rather than a failed attempt to fulfill Jesus's aspiration.

This book challenges each of us to consider what Jesus hoped for us as Christians and ask whether His aspirations still apply to us as a collective body of Christians. There are no easy or pat answers. Unity without truth, unity in evil, and unity by coercion were clearly not Jesus's intent. The fact that Jesus's able and empowered apostles could not preserve unity during the apostolic period is a testament to the challenges that they faced and evidence of the inherent difficulty of being unified in truth.

The next chapter is all about many of the divisive forces that confronted the church. These forces were like headwinds confronting a sailing vessel. They caused the church to veer and ultimately to splinter.

Notes

[1] Nazi Germany and Fascist Italy joined together in 1939 under the Pact of Steel, an agreement that included commitments of mutual support in war and agreement to an anti-Semitic Manifesto of Race, which stripped Jews of citizenship and removed them from government posts Wikipedia, Pact of Steel 2018.

[2] Robinson 2011.

[3] Klein 2016.

[4] The two leaders signed the Atlantic Charter on August 14, 1941, agreeing to a set of eight ideals that would govern the postwar world. The charter committed signatories to not seek territorial expansion as a result of war; to give all people the right of self-determination, global cooperation, and advancement of social welfare; and to pursue a world free of want and fear 1941: The Atlantic Charter n.d.

[5] Wikipedia, Onward Christian Soldiers 2017.

[6] Wikipedia, Onward Christian Soldiers 2017. (emphasis added).

[7] John 17:9, 15, 17, 19–21.

[8] Ephesians 4:3, 11–14 (emphasis added).

[9] John 8:31–32.

[10] 1 Timothy 2:3–4.

[11] Acts 1:14.

[12] Acts 2:42, 44–46 (emphasis added).

[13] Acts 4:32–35 (emphasis added).

[14] Acts 9:31.

[15] Marotta 2016.

[16] Acts 20:29–30.

[17] 2 Timothy 3:13–14; 4:3–4.

[18] 1 Timothy 4:1–3.

[19] 2 Thessalonians 2:3–7 (emphasis added).

[20] 1 Corinthians 1:10–13.

[21] 2 Corinthians 11:3–4, 13–15 (emphasis added).

[22] Titus 1:10–11 (emphasis added).

[23] Titus 3:9–10 (emphasis added).

[24] Galatians 6:12 (emphasis added).

[25] Galatians 4:11.

[26] Galatians 1:6–12 (emphasis added).

[27] Colossians 2:8–9 (emphasis added).

[28] 2 Peter 2:1–2.

[29] Revelations 2:2 (emphasis added).

[30] 1 John 2:18, 26 (emphasis added).

[31] 1 John 4:1 (emphasis added).

[32] 2 John 1:7 (emphasis added).

[33] Sexual depravity.

[34] Jude 1:4 (emphasis added).

[35] See John 17:9, 15, 17, 19–21.

Chapter 3

Headwinds

The fledgling body of Christians was unified at the start, as described in the previous chapter. The apostles intimately cared for the flock and showed the early converts many miraculous signs, just as Jesus had done.[1] Undoubtedly, the apostles were not average men. Jesus had selected them after spending the entire night in prayer to the Father.[2] He commissioned them and patiently tutored them[3] for their daunting responsibilities, which included to testify and spread the gospel,[4] to organize the church,[5] to perform ordinances,[6] and to preserve true doctrine.[7] Their qualifications were that they had been taught directly by Jesus,[8] had witnessed Jesus's miraculous ministry and resurrection,[9] were entitled to ongoing inspiration and guidance, and were empowered to act in the Lord's name.[10] Nevertheless, deviation and division took root and infected the church during their lifetimes. We'll see in this chapter that this reality was not evidence of incompetent leadership; rather, it was the result of powerful forces that confronted the church. Like headwinds confronting a sailing ship, these forces caused the church to veer, accommodate, hunker down, and ultimately splinter.

Some of these forces were contextual; that is, they were specific to the time and place in which Christianity was born. C. S. Lewis captured the essence of context when he said, "What you see and hear depends a good deal on where you are standing; it also depends on what sort of person you are."[11] Early converts brought with them their culture and heritage. Non-Judean converts brought with them Greek culture and philosophy. Jewish converts brought their legalism and rigorous worship. Furthermore, the slow travel and difficult communication of that time limited the direct influence of the apostles.

Other forces were structural; that is, they were timeless challenges associated with imparting truth to a group of organized believers. Even if Christianity were born today, it would face the timeless challenges of knowing and imparting spiritual truth, dealing with an evolving body of scripture, navigating questions of authority and governance, and recognizing and responding to purposeful corruption by deceivers and evildoers. In the sections that follow, we will examine both the context-specific and structural headwinds.

Geographic Separation of the Apostles

In the previous chapter, excerpts from the book of Acts referred to the first years of the church, when the apostles were still gathered with converts in the Jerusalem area. The apostles personally led the early converts and were directly engaged in the spiritual and temporal challenges of the growing church. The apostles were still gathered as a body when the first council was held (covered in the next chapter). Unfortunately, Acts records only the first years of the apostles' ministry—that period in which they were still centrally gathered and unified in a communal order. From chapter 13 on, the book of Acts is singularly focused on Paul. Thus, our understanding of the far-reaching assignments of the apostles is generally from tradition rather than scripture.

John's geography likely covered the seven churches of Asia Minor referred to in the book of Revelations. Peter likely oversaw the areas surrounding Palestine, including what is today Syria, Lebanon, and northern Egypt, until he traveled to Rome. Tradition holds that James the son of Zebedee evangelized in Spain before his martyrdom in the year 44. Bartholomew and James, son of Alpheus, purportedly evangelized Armenia. By tradition, Thomas went to India and perhaps even to China. There are similar traditions for all the apostles.

There is no record of the apostles gathering again as a central body to govern the church after they left the Jerusalem area. Even within each geographic ministry, it simply wasn't possible for an apostle to be constantly among the dispersed congregations of his own proselytes. The very existence of apostolic epistles written to various congregations is evidence of the necessity to minister to the fledgling congregations from afar.

Greek Philosophy

Within the Greek philosophical tradition into which Christianity was born, successive generations of philosophers adopted and then adapted ideas from their predecessors. This was the intellectual "job" of a philosopher. There was no preconceived notion that all truth had been discovered. It was not heresy to adopt and adapt. Plato did it with ideas he gleaned from Socrates and Pythagoras. Aristotle did it with Plato's ideas. Not surprisingly, the Greek-trained intellectuals who became Christian demonstrated the same pattern relative to the doctrines of the gospel. It was inevitable that doctrines such as the nature of God would be subject to the intellectual rigor of religious philosophers and thereby evolve through successive generations.

Christian theologians and church fathers believed that Christianity and Greek philosophy were but two manifestations of the same truth. Philosophy was not a corrupting influence to be shunned but rather another lens through which to see the same eternal truths found in Hebrew scripture. Truth could not contradict truth, and so with optimism borne of a deep commitment to Greek philosophy, Christian theologians committed themselves to integrate the two worlds of belief in pursuit of a more complete understanding of God.[12]

Platonism played a particularly important role in theologians' attempt to understand God. Plato taught that there are immaterial and invisible "perfect forms." Everything material is inherently imperfect and is only an approximate representation of an immaterial perfect form. He conceived of levels in the universe with ultimate Goodness being in the highest level and material humans trapped in the lowest level. Christians perceived that Plato had described the fundamental truths of God and His relationship with humankind.[13] Henry Blumenthal, a scholar of Greek philosophy noted:

> The first Christian to use Greek philosophy in the service
> of the Christian faith was Justin Martyr (martyred c. 65),
> whose passionate rejection of Greek polytheism, combined
> with an open and positive acceptance of the essentials of

Platonic religious philosophy and an unshakable confidence in its harmony with Christian teaching, was to remain characteristic of the Christian Platonist tradition. This was carried on in the Greek-speaking world by Clement of Alexandria (c. 150–c. 215), a persuasive Christian humanist, and by the greatest of the Alexandrian Christian teachers, Origen (c. 185–254). Although Origen was consciously more hostile to and critical of Platonic philosophy than either Justin or Clement, he was, nonetheless, more deeply affected by it. He produced a synthesis of Christianity and late Middle Platonism of remarkable originality and power, which is the first great Christian philosophical theology. In spite of subsequent condemnations of some of his alleged views, his influence on Christian thought was strong and lasting. The Greek philosophical theology that developed during the Trinitarian controversies over the relationships among the persons of the Godhead, which were settled at the ecumenical councils of Nicaea (325) and Constantinople (381), owed a great deal to Origen on both sides, orthodox and heretical. Its most important representatives on the orthodox side were the three Christian Platonist theologians of Cappadocia, Basil of Caesarea (c. 329–379), Gregory of Nazianzus (c. 330–c. 389), and Basil's brother Gregory of Nyssa (c. 335–c. 394). Of these three, Gregory of Nyssa was the most powerful and original thinker (as well as the closest to Origen). He was the first great theologian of mystical experience, at once Platonic and profoundly Christian, and he exerted a strong influence on later Greek Christian thought.[14]

Eusebius, one of the earliest church historians, believed that most of the "church fathers" of the first three centuries believed that the Greek philosophers, lawgivers, and poets had obtained their wisdom from the ancient Hebrews. The assertion was made especially in the case of Plato and Pythagoras, who were said to have become acquainted with the books of the Hebrews upon their journey to Egypt.[15] Eusebius used the example of Philo of Alexandria (15–10 BC;

died 45–50), a Jewish philosopher living in Alexandria, Egypt, to demonstrate that the truth of Christianity was revealed by God through multiple channels.[16] By all accounts, Philo was not Christian.[17] Nevertheless, by merging Greek philosophy with Hebrew theology, Philo reached many conclusions that anticipated Christian doctrines. One of the most profound was his doctrine of Logos:

> Philo saw the cosmos as a great chain of being presided over by the Logos, a term going back to pre-Socratic philosophy, which is the mediator between God and the world, though at one point he identifies the Logos as a second God. . . . He called the Logos the first-begotten Son of God, the man of God, the image of God, and second to God.[18]

Perhaps Greek-inspired Christian theologians felt justified in part by the Gospel of John,[19] which unabashedly opens by using the Greek concept of Logos to introduce Jesus:

> In the beginning was the Word [Logos], and the Word [Logos] was with God, and the Word [Logos] was God. The same was in the beginning with God. All things were made by him; and without him was not any thing made that was made. . . . And the Word [Logos] was made flesh, and dwelt among us, (and we beheld his glory, the glory as of the only begotten of the Father,) full of grace and truth.[20]

Logos literally translates to "word," "reason," or "plan." However, in Greek philosophy and theology, it meant much more. It referred to "the divine reason implicit in the cosmos, ordering it and giving it form and meaning."[21] Why would John, an apostle from the Jewish tradition, use a term so deep with meaning to the Greeks? In all likelihood, the author of the Gospel of John was tailoring the gospel to the understanding of its intended audience. By the close of the first century when the Gospel of John was written, John's ministry was to the Greek churches in Asia Minor.[22] The author undoubtedly intended to integrate the glorious message of Jesus Christ with his flock's formative Greek-inspired belief in Logos. The implicit message to the converted Greeks was that they did not need to abandon the essentials of their belief in the Greek divine to accept Christianity because all that the

Greek Christians believed about Logos wonderfully applied to Jesus Christ. However, by equating Jesus with Logos, the Gospel of John tacitly endorsed fusing Christian doctrine with Greek philosophy.

In the chapters that follow, we'll see Greek philosophy factor heavily into Christian splintering, particularly related to doctrines of the Godhead, Christ, and salvation. The influence of Greek philosophy was not limited to a specific era; it affected the first doctrinal creeds and the doctrines of the Reformation.

Traditions of the Jews

Jewish traditions, including religious practices and beliefs, had a profound influence on doctrine and worship in the early church. Two aspects are worthy of mention here.

First, the Jews were staunchly monotheistic and had been reprimanded by God repeatedly throughout their history for turning from the one and only God, Yahweh: "Hear, O Israel: The LORD our God is *one* LORD."[23] Thus, Jesus's claims of divinity and equality with God simply didn't fit this framework. As we will learn in more depth later, the monotheism of the Jews was a predefined requirement in their definition of God.

Second, the bulwark of Jewish civil society was the Law of Moses. The Gospel of Matthew records Jesus saying,

> Think not that I have come to destroy the law, or the prophets; I am not come to destroy, but to fulfill. For verily I say unto you, Till heaven and earth pass, one jot or one tittle shall in no wise pass from the law, till all be fulfilled.[24]

Few things polarized the early church like the varied interpretations of these words. On one extreme were those who believed the Law of Moses was still operative. These were largely Jewish converts, but there were some gentiles who adopted the Law as they converted to Christianity. Collectively, they continued to practice the Law of Moses after accepting Jesus. They interpreted Jesus's words "to fulfill" as confirming the importance of the Law and believed that "every jot and tittle" had not yet passed away. To this group, Jesus did not supersede the Law, replace it, or render it obsolete. At the other extreme were those largely gentile converts who had never been under the Law. To a fault, some in this group interpreted Paul's teachings relative to the Law to mean freedom from *all* law. A figurative battle between these extremes played out in the early church, affecting the resulting doctrine. We'll see this battle play out in the next chapter. We will also see the disagreement about Law-inspired practices divide Christians relative to the role of rituals and ordinances, the ongoing observance of a Sabbath, the celebration of Easter, the wearing of vestments, and so on.

Nature of Spiritual Truth

The poet and philosopher Ralph Waldo Emerson captured what we all know intuitively to be true: "People only see what they are prepared to see."[25] This is acutely so in the case of spiritual matters. By its very nature, spiritual truth is conditionally knowable, defies proof by natural means, and is therefore difficult to transmit. Two people can hear the same words, see the same manifestation, and be side by side in the same religious events and yet reach very different conclusions and hold very different beliefs. One may know and understand truth, and one may not, and yet without an objective external measure both people may be totally confident that they perceived the truth perfectly. Jesus attested to this reality when He said,

> Therefore speak I to them in parables: because they seeing see not; and hearing they hear not, neither do they understand . . . and their ears are dull of hearing, and their eyes they have closed. . . . But blessed are your eyes, for they see: and your ears, for they hear.[26]

Paul echoed the same sentiment:

> The things of God knoweth no man, but the Spirit of God. Now we have received, not the spirit of the world, but the spirit which is of God; that we might know the things that are freely given to us of God. Which things also we speak, not in the words which man's wisdom teacheth, but which the Holy Ghost teacheth; comparing spiritual things with spiritual. *But the natural man receiveth not the things of the Spirit of God: for they are foolishness unto him: neither can he know them, because they are spiritually discerned.*[27]

What a conundrum! Gospel truths appear as foolishness according to the natural means of learning. Indeed, the precious truths of the gospel were committed to the humble, weak, and largely uneducated. To those who were learned and wise, the gospel truth was foolishness, as Paul attested:

> For after that in the wisdom of God the world by wisdom knew not God, it pleased God by the foolishness of preaching to save them that believe. For the Jews require a sign, and the Greeks seek after wisdom: But we preach Christ crucified, unto the Jews a stumblingblock, and unto the Greeks foolishness. . . . For ye see your calling, brethren, how that not many wise men after the flesh, not many mighty, not many noble, are called.[28]

Ironically, Paul's teachings, which contain such rich insight into spiritual truth, as just illustrated, were themselves hard to understand by many and apt to be misunderstood and twisted. Peter cautioned the saints about Paul's "hard-to-understand" teaching:

> Our beloved brother Paul also according to the wisdom given unto him hath written unto you; As also in all his epistles, speaking in them of these things; in which are *some things hard to be understood, which they that are unlearned and unstable wrest, as they do also the other scriptures, unto their own destruction.*[29]

The conflict of the nature of spiritual truth versus the truth embodied in the laws of nature is illustrated by the story of Pythagoras. Ask any teenage mathematics student about the Pythagorean theorem and he or she will spout $A^2 + B^2 = C^2$. Pythagoras, the Greek-born namesake of this famous theorem, is possibly one of the most familiar names in mathematics due to the famous theorem that bears his name. What most of us don't know is that Pythagoras was a philosopher.[30] Pythagoras founded a philosophical community based on mystical ideas that harmonized spiritual beliefs related to the destiny of the soul with numbers and mathematics.[31] Like many mystics, Pythagoras did not commit his ideas to writing. Rather, they were passed along verbally within Pythagorean communities that proliferated and persisted for over one hundred years. Plato's ideas about the soul and perfect forms represented by numbers were influenced by Pythagoras.[32] Plato, in turn, strongly influenced Aristotle, one of Plato's students. In short, Pythagorean ideas persisted through generations of Greek philosophers.

The mystical elements of Pythagoras's teachings became faint shadows as subsequent generations of philosophers repurposed and reshaped them. In contrast, Pythagoras's teachings related to mathematics and music harmonics persisted intact through time and became foundational knowledge in these disciplines.[33] Why were the mystical elements of his teachings transitory while the other elements persisted? Because the natural laws underpinning Pythagorean mathematics and harmonics were provable and therefore transferable with integrity from one generation to the next.

As with Pythagoras's mystical teachings, there is no way to prove or perfectly preserve the spiritual truth or doctrines of Christianity as they are passed from one generation to the next. Spiritual truth is "only known by the Spirit," as Paul put it, and the Spirit's tutelage is to individuals and is subtle. Each learner is left to decipher truth through his or her own filters created from individual backgrounds and biases. Thus, doctrines of the gospel were, and always will be, potentially malleable as they are interpreted and transmitted.

The chapters that follow tell the story of many theologians and biblical scholars attempting to decipher spiritual truth through their own biases and experiences.

Limitations of Scripture

To understand the challenge facing the early church relative to maintaining consistent doctrine and practice, we must not naively hold the existing New Testament in our hands and imagine the apostles, church leaders, and converts holding the same published scriptures in theirs. Indeed, during its critical formative years, the church lacked a consistent body of scripture. Even after the New Testament was codified, the scriptures failed to be the singular unifying source of truth for Christians.

The early congregations of the new church had sparse and inconsistent fragments of the story of Jesus's life. The historian

Reverend S. Baring-Gould gives us a sense for the fragmentary nature of early scripture:

> No sooner was a Church founded by an apostle than there rose a demand for this sort of instruction, and it was supplied by the jottings-down of reminiscences of the Lord and his teaching, orally given by those who had companied with him. Thus there sprang into existence an abundant crop of memorials of the Lord, surrounded by every possible guarantee of their truth. And these fragmentary records passed from one Church to another. The pious zeal of an Antiochian community furnished with the memorials of Peter would borrow of Jerusalem the memorials of James and Matthew. One of the traditions of John found its way into the Hebrew Gospel—that of the visit of Nicodemus; but it never came into the possession of the compiler of the first Gospel or of St. Luke. After a while, each Church set to work to string the anecdota it possessed into a consecutive story, and thus the Synoptical Gospels came into being.[34]

The letters of Paul started circulating in the middle of the first century and were the first widely circulated written works of the church. Paul wrote his first epistle to the Thessalonians from Corinth around the year 50. His other epistles were written within a short time frame with the book of Romans written in about the year 56. By the end of the first century, Paul's epistles were widely circulated.[35] The gospels we recognize in the New Testament emerged late in the first century. The Gospel of Mark was likely the compiled collection of Peter's stories written soon after Peter's death around the year 63.[36] The Gospel of Matthew was likely compiled using Mark's narrative of Jesus's acts and from other sources of Jesus's teachings. Scholars date it after the fall of Jerusalem to about 70–80.[37] The Gospel of Luke and the book of Acts were written about the year 80.[38] The Gospel of John appears to have been written from Ephesus by John or one of his disciples at the end of the first century.[39] Importantly, Paul's epistles and the four commonly accepted gospels were not the only "scriptures" circulating throughout the church as it exited the apostolic era!

Evidence of many circulating gospels is found in existing fragments of noncanonical gospels and references to them by early church fathers. The influential bishop Clement of Alexandria (c. 150–c. 215), for example, quoted liberally from the Gospel of the Hebrews, the Gospel of the Egyptians, the Letter of Barnabas, and the Didache—none of which are considered canonical today.[40] Irenaeus, a bishop in what is now France, illustrated the challenge of defining canon. He was a staunch advocate for defining a set of canonical scriptures and condemned the Gospel of Truth in his work, *Against Heresies* (c. 180). However, he, like many others of his time, accepted the *Shepherd of Hermas*—a book that was ultimately rejected as canonical.[41]

Some circulating gospels were the catalyst for unique doctrinal beliefs. An important example is that of the Gospel of the Clementines and its companion documents, the Clementine Recognitions and Homilies. These documents were purportedly the sayings and doings of St. Peter. They taught that Christians were first and foremost Jews who also believed that Jesus was the Messiah. Again, the historian Baring-Gould provides valuable insight:

> There is another storehouse of texts and references to a Gospel regarded as canonical at a very early date by the Nazarene or Ebionite Church [Christian churches in Palestine]. This storehouse is that curious collection of the sayings and doings of St. Peter, the Clementine Recognitions and Homilies. . . . To believe in the mission of Christ is, in the Clementine Homilies, to become a Jew. The convert from Gentiledom by passing into the Church passes under the Law, becomes, as we are told, a Jew. But the convert is made subject not to the Law as corrupted by the traditions of the elders, but to the original Law as re-proclaimed by Christ. The author of the Recognitions twice makes St. Peter say that the only difference existing between him and the Jews is in the manner in which they view Christ.[42]

Another poignant example of a gospel with profound doctrinal implications was that of the Gospel of St. Peter. This gospel, like that of Mark, was supposedly a collection of the teachings of Peter. However, a new bishop in Antioch learned the pitfalls of relying on the assumed authority of a gospel based on the purported sponsoring apostle:

> Serapion, Bishop of Antioch, in 190, on entering his see, learned that there was a Gospel attributed to St. Peter read in the sacred services of the church of Ehosus, in Cilicia. Taking it for granted, as he says, that all in his diocese held the same faith, without perusing this Gospel, he sanctioned its use, saying, "If this be the only thing that creates difference among you, let it be read." But he was speedily made aware that this Gospel was not orthodox in its tendency. It favoured the opinions of the Docetse.[43] It was whispered that if it had an apostolic parentage, it had heretical sponsors. Serapion thereupon borrowed the Gospel, read it, and found it was even as had been reported. "Peter," said he, "we receive with the other apostles as Christ himself," but this Gospel was, if not apocryphal as to its facts, at all events heretical as to its teaching. Thereupon Serapion, regretting his precipitation in sanctioning the use of the Gospel, wrote a book upon it, "in refutation of its false assertions."[44]

It was not lost on early church fathers that inconsistent scripture across the church was a problem, but for centuries, attempts at creating a common canon fell short.[45] Eastern and western churches disagreed on many circulating texts, including Hebrews, Revelations, and various epistles. In 365, Athanasius, the bishop of Alexandria and influential participant in the Council of Nicaea, published a compromise list of twenty-seven books of the New Testament and referred to them as "canonized."[46] Later councils held near the end of the century ratified his list.[47]

Undoubtedly, the Bible is an invaluable reservoir of truth, and we as Christians cherish it, some to the point of asserting its inerrancy.[48] However, it is undeniable that even the general acceptance of a common canon in the fourth century did not resolve all the questions facing the young church. It was far from a comprehensive manual containing guidance on all needed doctrine and practice. In large part, this was due to the very nature of the Bible—it is a compilation of independent works written to specific audiences and tailored to the culture, preparation, biases, and capacity of each audience. Consider examples of how the audience influenced the content:

- Paul's harsh criticisms of the Law of Moses were direct reflections of "battles" with Judaizers in certain gentile congregations.

- The lack of maturity of early Christians limited the doctrines that Paul could teach—he lamented that he needed to continue to offer gospel "milk" rather than offer the "meat" of deeper doctrines.[49]

- Jesus taught opaquely using parables describing the majority of listening Jews as "this people's heart is waxed gross, and their ears are dull of hearing."[50]

- The doctrine of Jesus's relationship with the Father differed between gospels according to the audience. The Gospel of John emphasized Jesus's immortality and oneness with the Father and associated Jesus with the Greek Logos—an understandable approach given his audience of Greek Christians in Asia Minor. The Gospel of Matthew, written to Jews, emphasized Jesus's mortality and separateness from the Father as the heir of the Davidic throne (through Joseph) and as fulfillment of the promised messenger and Messiah sent by God.

It is true that a compilation of multiple works written by independent authors to distinct audiences creates breadth and a richer gospel tapestry. However, audience-specific writings are bound to treat some topics more completely, others lightly, and others not at all. Furthermore, where there is overlap between authors or even between epistles from the same author, there may appear to be contradictions.[51] Where there is no overlap, we are left to accept and interpret profound doctrines from just one source.[52] Of course, differences of interpretation arising from translation and transcription issues only made matters worse through the centuries.[53]

We'll see in the next chapter how the early church dealt with the question of gentiles and the Law of Moses. It illustrates how the church faced unresolved questions after Jesus's departure. Although this particular issue was partially resolved as recorded in scripture, there were myriad other relevant questions without clear answers in canonized scripture: Who had authority in the church? Could it be passed on? How should the church be organized and administered? How should the Sabbath day be honored, if at all? How should baptism be administered? How should the Lord's Supper be extended to believers? In a world dominated by servitude, could the gospel be taught to slaves? The questions went on and on. Although the New Testament hinted at answers to some of these questions, there was ample room for interpretation and innovation. The very fact that denominations have created nonbiblical, canon-like texts to supplement scripture[54] is evidence of the limitation of the scriptures themselves to be the complete guide for the church.

Ambiguous Authority

Relative to any defined group we could ask common questions such as the following: What is its purpose? What are its goals and ideology? How is it governed? Is there a formal organization with formal authority? What are the norms and expectations? How are they enforced? Is participation voluntary? These and similar questions are the heart of organizational design.

It is through the lens of organizational design that we recognize another major headwind facing early Christianity; namely, the organization of and authority within the church as described in the New Testament were largely undefined. Jesus not only minimally established an organization but also emphasized servant-leadership, which left the inevitable issue of authority inconclusive. Furthermore, in the apostolic period, offices or roles, to the extent they existed, were given titles that had corresponding general meanings, leaving Christians uncertain about whether the use of such terms referred to general responsibilities or to specific offices of authority. Unquestionably, such ambiguity was fertile ground for inevitable disagreements.

According to the gospels, Jesus appointed two different groups and gave to each a degree of authority. Foremost of these groups was the twelve apostles.[55] At times, the gospels use the words *disciples* and *apostles* interchangeably, but context often clarifies when Jesus is specifically traveling with, teaching, or empowering the twelve apostles versus a broader group of disciple-followers. The second group was a body of seventy men that He sent out as emissaries to prepare for future visits to various cities.[56] Like the apostles, these men received delegated power to heal, preach, condemn, and cast out devils.[57] Notably, the seventy are only mentioned once as a group and are never mentioned during the apostolic period. Given that the gospels tell us only of these two commissioned groups, we have to take on faith Paul's assertion that He, meaning Jesus, established other roles in the church:

> And he gave some, *apostles*; and some, *prophets*; and some, *evangelists*; and some, *pastors* and *teachers*; For the perfecting of the saints, for the work of the ministry, for the edifying of the body of Christ.[58]

It is certainly possible that the gospel authors did not record all of Jesus's administrative actions that created other leadership positions. After all, the author of the Gospel of John explains that he had to be very selective about what to include and uses some hyperbole to suggest that all of Jesus's works would fill so many volumes that "the world itself could not contain" them all.[59] Or, perhaps Paul included offices established by the apostles acting by inspiration from the resurrected Lord. This latter possibility is not without precedent. In the earliest days of the apostolic church, the apostles found themselves overwhelmed as they attempted to preside over both the temporal and the spiritual affairs of the rapidly growing church. Consequently, they appointed seven men of "honest report, full of the Holy Ghost and wisdom" to assist in the temporal affairs of the church.[60] Clearly, the apostles delegated some authority to these men when they were ordained, but such authority was limited. Acts records that Stephen was "full of faith and power" and "did great wonders and miracles."[61] Philip, likewise, performed miracles of healing and casting out devils.[62] He was authorized to baptize but was not authorized to bestow the Holy Ghost by the laying on of hands. That was evidently reserved for the apostles.[63]

The initial purpose for appointing the seven was to offload temporal matters from the apostles; however, if Stephen and Philip are any indication of the role, the seven also preached the gospel or evangelized. In fact, Luke, the author of Acts, refers to Philip as "the evangelist, one of the seven."[64] Notably, the fate of the office held by the seven is unclear in scripture. Stephen suffered a martyr's death of stoning soon after being appointed,[65] yet there is no record in Acts of the apostles appointing another to fill his place.

Luke was a disciple of Paul's, and it is possible that they both used the term *evangelist* in the same way. Perhaps, then, Paul was referring to the seven called by the apostles when he included *evangelist* in the enumeration of positions quoted earlier. If so, Paul included the offices established directly by Jesus as well as those established by His appointed apostles. Nevertheless, reconciling Paul's list to what Jesus did as recorded in the gospels requires speculation.

While it is abundantly clear that the original twelve apostles (eleven after Judas) had a special commission and position of leadership, many aspects of their role are unclear in the New Testament. Was there seniority among the apostles? Was there to be a "quorum" of twelve apostles perpetually? Were they to act as a unified body to preside over a unified church, or were they twelve independent leaders commissioned to evangelize different lands and preside over their respective flocks? Did they singularly or collectively have authority over other leaders? Was the apostleship an office to which one was ordained, or was it a description of a messenger, one called to preach or evangelize new flocks? Could others be apostles without being one of the twelve? What was the source of their authority? This book won't attempt to answer all these and related questions. At best, there are only clues to *some* of the answers, but the absence of clear answers reinforces the profound reality—the role of the apostles as a group and the authority of the individuals within the group were not clearly defined! We'll look at a just a few examples to illustrate the point.

Judas, one of the original twelve, betrayed Jesus and then committed suicide.[66] Soon thereafter, the remaining eleven apostles considered two qualified candidates and selected a man named Matthias to replace Judas.[67] This might very well be evidence of the importance of a *quorum of twelve* and of the intent to perpetuate the group. However, about ten years later, while the apostles were still centralized, James the brother of John was killed by Herod.[68] Importantly, there is no recorded gathering of the apostles to appoint a replacement. Of course, the absence of a record does not mean it didn't happen, but asserting that it did would be speculation. The apostles eventually dispersed to many different lands, effectively ensuring the ultimate dissolution of the twelve.

Within the group of twelve, seniority was implied by several events but was not explicitly established. The Gospel of Mark uniquely lists the first three apostles as Peter, James, and John.[69] About the end of the first year of Jesus's ministry, a ruler named Jarius pleaded with Jesus to heal his daughter, but by the time Jesus arrived, the girl was dead. All the miracles Jesus had previously performed would pale in comparison to what He was about to do. Raising a dead person back to life would be profoundly glorious, sacred, and intimate. Thus, it was significant that He allowed only Peter, James, and John to accompany Him into the house.[70] Similarly, only Peter, James, and John witnessed the sacred events with Jesus on the Mount of Transfiguration.[71] And again, it was Peter, James, and John who were invited to stay close to Jesus as He retreated into the Garden of Gethsemane the night before His crucifixion.[72] These events suggest the seniority of Peter, James, and John; yet, very late in Jesus ministry, after He prophesied of His impending death, the apostles naturally debated among themselves who was to be the senior leader. Jesus could have used the opportunity to make the hierarchy explicitly clear; instead, He taught the antithesis of power and authority—the principle of servant-leadership: "he that is greatest among you, let him be as the younger; and he that is chief, as he that doth serve."[73] In fact, as Luke records the event, Jesus then warned Peter—presumably in front of his fellow apostles—that "Satan hath desired to have you, that he may sift you as wheat." Did this warning suggest that Peter had been the one arguing for primacy?

The New Testament suggests that early converts did not universally recognize the twelve as *the* final authority. This can be seen in the dynamics of the first recorded council of the leadership of the church, a topic covered in detail in the next chapter. Attending the council were the apostles and elders, including Peter and James, the brother of the Lord.[74] They had gathered to consider whether the Law of Moses applied to the gentiles. It was a controversial issue leading to "much disputing."[75] Peter's leadership was apparent when he rose and successfully calmed the heated debate. He set the stage for Paul and Barnabas to tell their story. Nevertheless, Acts is quite clear that it was James, the brother of the Lord and not an apostle, who rose and rendered the final verdict, saying, "Wherefore my sentence is . . . " As another example of the ambiguous authority of the twelve, Paul asserted apostleship to the Corinthians, who were grappling with split loyalties. Paul claimed to be equal in every respect to the original twelve.[76]

The lack of clarity relative to hierarchy and authority was not just at the highest level of the church. Other roles were described with terms that had existing general meanings. Thus, in our scriptures these words are variably translated. Take the Greek *episkopos*. It meant "overseer" and was thus closely related to shepherding.[77] Thus, when Paul gathered the leaders of Ephesus to him in Miletus one last time, he called them episkopos and reminded them of their pastoral duty to feed the flock.[78] The scholars of the King James Version (KJV) Bible translated *episkopos* in this instance according to its general meaning, rendering, "The Holy Ghost hath made you *overseers*."[79] Peter also connected episkopos with shepherding: "For ye were as sheep going astray; but are now returned unto the Shepherd and [episkopos] of your souls."[80] However, in this instance, the translators translated *episkopos* into a very different word, the Old English word *bishop*. This is significant because Christians generally recognize the meaning of *bishop* as a clerical office rather than as a general description of an overseer or shepherd. Paul's enumeration of the positions of leadership quoted earlier in this chapter included pastor, but not bishop. And yet, Paul appointed Timothy and Titus into the "office of episkopos," or "office of a bishop."[81] We are left to wonder whether Paul equated *pastor* and *bishop* and used the terms synonymously. Jesus never used the term *episkopos*, but He did appoint Peter to be a shepherd, commanding him to "feed my sheep."[82] Although this may suggest that Jesus established Peter as the first episkopos, such a conclusion, like virtually everything else related to church hierarchy and authority, is speculative.

Other terms used to describe roles in the early church are equally vague about their authority and formal position in a hierarchy. The

Greek word *diakonos*[83] was usually translated according to its general meaning of "servant" or "minister," except in Philippians, where it was translated as "deacon," suggesting an office allied with bishops.[84] The terms *prophet, elder,* and *teacher* were also used generally and in reference to leaders with implied authority.

These examples reveal that there was ample room for widely varying interpretation relative to issues of governance, including hierarchy and authority. We'll see in the chapters that follow a repetitive theme that sharp disagreements related to authority divided the church.

Evil Intentions

All the headwinds touched on so far were morally neutral. They were not inherently good or bad. They were impediments regardless of the intents of those involved. Well-intentioned believers bringing with them all of their cultural background and personal biases could unwittingly alter spiritual truth as they sought to understand, apply, and transmit it. Honest converts could have misplaced loyalties, and others could assume unwarranted authority. All this was challenging enough; however, the list of headwinds would be incomplete if it did not include the reality of purposeful corruption by agents of evil.

Christians, like the Jews from which they originated, believe in Satan and his legion of evil angels. According to scripture, Satan, or the devil, is an evil being who seeks to destroy the works of God and ensnare His children:[85]

> And the great dragon was cast out, that old serpent, called the Devil, and Satan, which deceiveth the whole world: he was cast out into the earth, and his angels were cast out with him.[86]

Jesus confronted Satan during a period of temptation[87] and frequently cast devils out of afflicted souls during His ministry.[88] As noted in the previous chapter, Jesus prayed to the Father that His followers could be protected from evil.[89]

The constant barrage by Satan, his angels, and his willing mortal minions has always impeded the progress of believers and corrupted the truth. The early Christian church was not immune.

We see the assault on the early Christian church underway in the epistles. Jude described Satan's agents as "ungodly men."[90] Paul insinuates evil intent when he calls those who are perverting doctrine "unruly and vain talkers and deceivers."[91] Paul is perfectly clear about the source of doctrinal perversion when he describes those whom Timothy would confront in Corinth as "giving heed to seducing spirits, and doctrines of devils."[92] Paul again insinuated malicious motive when he wrote to the Philippians that "some indeed preach Christ even of envy and strife . . . preach Christ of contention, not sincerely."[93] Peter warned, "Be sober, be vigilant; because your adversary the devil, as a roaring lion, walketh about, seeking whom he may devour."[94]

In Acts 8, we learn of a corrupt convert to the church. Phillip had taught the gospel in Samaria and there found a people that had been "bewitched" by the sorcery and influence of a man named Simon. The people of Samaria mistook Simon's power for the power of God. Simon sought to purchase the authority to control the gifts of the Holy Ghost, leading to a direct confrontation with Peter:

> Thy money perish with thee, because thou hast thought that the gift of God may be purchased with money. Thou hast neither part nor lot in this matter: for thy *heart is not right* in the sight of God. Repent therefore of this thy wickedness, and pray God, if perhaps the thought of thine heart may be forgiven thee. For I perceive that thou art in the *gall of bitterness,* and in the *bond of iniquity.*[95]

Other early apocryphal documents tell the story of Simon, called Magus (magician), going to Rome and using his magical arts to claim believers. Some have equated Simon of Acts with Simon called Magus. In some accounts, Simon claimed to be the Messiah.[96] Like others inspired by the devil, Simon Magus was consequential to the Christian faith because he offered a close substitute of true power and doctrine and was therefore able to confuse those who were new in the gospel.[97]

We may not be able to decipher the motives of specific instigators of Christian divisions, but we can be sure that Satan was hard at work confusing, sowing dissent, and corrupting.

The headwinds covered in this chapter created the conditions in which dissent and division were essentially inevitable. We will see schism after schism as we progress through the remainder of this book. Although the actors and specifics of each split were unique, they all shared common themes. Like bread recipes with varying amounts of the same ingredients, divisions within Christianity were usually driven by disagreement over some combination of three "ingredients," or themes: doctrine, governance, and practice.[98] We'll see schisms inspired entirely by disagreement over doctrine. In others, governance will be the leading motivator. But, in general, divisions have been the result of varying combinations of all three. These three themes form a useful lens through which to understand the splintering we are about to explore.

The story of Christian splintering is an interesting historical journey in its own right. However, we will gain insights relevant to our own Christian experience if we personalize the journey by asking tough questions of ourselves: What is my own Christian heritage? How is it similar to and different from other Christian denominations? What did Jesus intend when He organized Christianity? Ideally, what should have happened at each point of division? What is the truth that Jesus claimed would make us free? Where is it found? Should Christians be united, and, if so, by what means and at what cost? And so on.

The stories in the pages that follow will hopefully help us understand our own Christian heritage and better understand the heritage of our fellow Christians. With an understanding of similarities *and differences*, perhaps we will be more prone to dialogue and respect, which will allow us to see past denominational differences to our common faith and purpose.

Notes

---

[1] See Acts 2:42 and Acts 5:12–17.

[2] See Luke 6:12–13. Later in a prayer to the Father, Jesus acknowledges that the apostles were given to Him by the Father. See John 17:6.

[3] This tutoring included the lessons recorded in the gospels during Jesus's mortal ministry and during the forty days of personal visits after Jesus's resurrection (see Acts 1:2–3) The gospels contain a fraction of all that Jesus did and taught (see John 21:25).

[4] See Mark 16:14–15.

[5] Acts 6:1–6 tells of the twelve apostles creating a new leadership office to deal with the temporal affairs of the church. Seven faithful men were called and ordained.

[6] See Acts 8:12–17. Not all missionaries were authorized to perform all ordinances. The apostles needed to go to Samaria to confer the Holy Ghost through laying on of hands.

[7] See 2 Peter 1:18–21.

[8] The apostles were with Jesus for about three years during His mortal ministry. Importantly, after His ascension, Jesus instructed the apostles for forty days (see Acts 1:3).

[9] See John 20:19–31.

[10] See Luke 9:1–2.

[11] Wise Old Sayings n.d.

[12] This is an example of syncretism. See endnote 28 to chapter 1.

[13] Blumenthal and Armstrong 2017.

[14] Blumenthal and Armstrong 2017.

[15] See footnote 48 in Eusebius n.d., 103.

[16] See Eusebius n.d., 153-154, particularly footnote 299.

[17] Although he traveled to Palestine and wrote about Jewish sects there, he made no mention of the contemporary Jesus and the rise of the band of Jewish Christians. Furthermore, he represented the persecuted Jews, not the Christians, before the Roman Emperor Caligula.

[18] Editors, Philo Judaeus 2017.

[19] Scholars debate whether John the Apostle wrote the gospel or if one of his disciples did. It is generally believed to have been written late in the first century from the city of Ephesus Bruce, Davis and Others 2018.

[20] John 1:1–3, 14.

[21] Editors, Logos 2012.

[22] The seven churches referred to in Revelations are all in Asia Minor. See Revelations 1:4.

[23] Deuteronomy 6:4 (emphasis added).

[24] Matt 5:17–18.

[25] Wise Old Sayings n.d.

[26] Matthew 13:13–16.

[27] 1 Corinthians 2:11–14 (emphasis added).

[28] 1 Corinthians 1:21–27.

[29] 2 Peter 3:15–16 (emphasis added).

[30] It should be noted that Pythagoras's life and teachings are only surmised through excerpts of other writers, which in most cases were written well after Pythagoras's

death. Thus, much of his story is as much legend as precise history. The uncertainty is treated in great detail by Huffman Huffman 2014. Nevertheless, his story is still useful to illustrate the point being made here about spiritual versus natural truth.

[31] Thesleff 2013.

[32] Wikipedia, Plato 2018.

[33] Thesleff 2013.

[34] Baring-Gould M.A. 1874, xxvi.

[35] Sander, et al. 2017.

[36] Sander, et al. 2017.

[37] Sander, et al. 2017.

[38] Sander, et al. 2017.

[39] Sander, et al. 2017.

[40] Sander, et al. 2017.

[41] Sander, et al. 2017.

[42] Baring-Gould M.A. 1874, 193,199.

[43] Those claiming that Jesus had not actually come in the flesh.

[44] Baring-Gould M.A. 1874, 219.

[45] Wikipedia, Development of the New Testament canon 2019.

[46] Wikipedia, Development of the New Testament canon 2019.

[47] Wikipedia, Development of the New Testament canon 2019.

[48] Meaning that all that the Bible is free of any errors.

[49] See Hebrews 5:11–14 and 1 Corinthians 3:1–3.

[50] Matthew 13:15.

[51] Consider the faith-works debate that has divided Christians. Scriptures from different books appear to contradict each other. Paul's teachings in Ephesians 2:8–9 and Titus 3:5–7 seem clear enough that salvation does not depend at all on works; however, other scriptures seem to contradict this binary formula. James 2:14–26 is often considered a counterweight to Paul. The Gospel of Matthew records Jesus teaching that we will be rewarded according to works (Matthew 16:27). Even Paul, to a different audience echoed Jesus's teaching of a reward based on works (Romans 2:6).

[52] Consider several examples of deeper doctrines taught by just one person: John alone includes the exchange between Jesus and the Jews when Jesus expressly referred to Himself as "I am" (see John 8:58), a reference to Jehovah of the Old Testament, the great I AM (see Exodus 3:14). John alone includes Jesus's words, "I and my Father are one" (see John 10:30). Peter alone taught that Jesus visited the spirits in prison after His crucifixion and that the dead were taught the gospel (see 1 Peter 3:18–20 and 1 Peter 4:6). Paul alone refers to the practice of baptism for the dead (see 1 Corinthians 15:29). Paul alone compared the glory of resurrected bodies to the glories of the sun, moon, and stars (see 1 Corinthians 15:40–42). Paul alone refers to more than one heaven (see 2 Corinthians 12:2). Paul alone refers to what many Christians call the rapture (see 1 Thessalonians 4:17). John alone refers to the sealing of twelve thousand from each of the twelve tribes (see Revelations 7:4–8).

[53] Sander, et al. 2017.

[54] Examples include the canons and creeds of ecumenical councils and the various books of religious standards, such as liturgical rites, catechisms, the Book of

Concord (Lutheran), Westminster Confession (Presbyterian), and Book of
Common Prayer (Anglican).

55 See Matthew 10:1–5 or Luke 6:13–16.

56 See Luke 10:1.

57 See Luke 10:9, 11, 17–19.

58 Ephesians 4:11–12 (emphasis added).

59 See John 21:25.

60 See Acts 6:1–7.

61 Acts 6:8.

62 See Acts 8:6–7.

63 See Acts 8:13–17.

64 Acts 21:8.

65 See Acts 7:54–60.

66 See Acts 1:16–18.

67 See Acts 1:23–26.

68 See Acts 12:2.

69 Compare Mark 3:16–17 to Matthew 10:2. The books of Matthew and Luke include
Peter's brother Andrew. James was John's brother, not to be confused with the
other prominent James, who was the brother of Jesus.

70 See Mark 5:37.

71 See Matt 17:1.

72 See Mark 14:33.

73 See Luke 22:21–27.

74 James the brother of Jesus, also known as James the Just, was not an apostle.
However, he was clearly a senior leader. See Acts 12:17, Acts 15:13, and Acts 21:18.
In the apocryphal Clementines, James is identified as the bishop of the church, and
Clement addresses James as bishop of Jerusalem The Clementine Homilies 1870, 1,
6.

75 See Acts 15:4–30.

76 See 2 Corinthians 12:11–12.

77 1985. episkopos n.d.

78 See Acts 20:28.

79 Acts 20:28 (emphasis added).

80 1 Peter 2:25; with original Greek word *episkopos*.

81 1 Timothy 3:1; also see Titus 1:7.

82 See John 21:15–17.

83 1249. diakonos n.d.

84 Compare Philippians 1:1 with Ephesians 3:7 and Romans 13:4.

85 The Hebrew Old Testament refers to Satan in verses such as 1 Chronicles 21:1, Job
1:6–12, Psalms 109:6, and Zechariah 3:1–2.

86 Revelations 12:9.

87 See Matthew 4:1–11.

88 See, for example, Matthew 9:32–33, Mark 5:6–16.

89 See John 17:15.

90 Jude 1:4.

91 Titus 1:10.

92 1 Timothy 4:1–2.

[93] Philippians 1:15–16.
[94] 1 Peter 5:8.
[95] Acts 8: 20–23 (emphasis added).
[96] Kirsch, Simon Magus 1912.
[97] Kirsch, Simon Magus 1912.
[98] The formal terms for these three could be *theology*, *polity*, and *liturgy*, respectively.

The First Schism—The Law of Moses

In the sermon on the mount, Jesus taught, "Think not that I am come to destroy the law, or the prophets: I am not come to destroy but to fulfill. For verily I say unto you, Till heaven and earth pass, one jot or one tittle shall in no wise pass from the law, till all be fulfilled."[1] Few statements have been so variably interpreted. The range of interpretations vexed the church and led to the first schism within it.

The first followers of Jesus were Jews. The initial chapters in Acts paint the picture of unity and harmony. The saints had all things in common.[2] They ate together and met in the temple together.[3] Importantly, these were things that Jews did only with other Jews. The converts' new beliefs meshed with their Jewish beliefs. The good news of the gospel—that Jesus was the Son of God, the heir of David, and had broken the hold of death—was not incompatible with the religion of their fathers. Jewish converts believed that Jesus had called them to pursue an even higher law while not abandoning the Law they had always lived. Thus, the "jots and tittles" of the Law of Moses were to still govern their lives.

Luke, the author of Acts, did not elaborate on the religious observance of the early converts, but he gave clues. These clues, along with clues from various epistles and evidence found in the apocrypha, reveal that the Law of Moses was alive and well among the Jewish converts to Christianity. Extending the gospel to the gentiles was the seismic event that required the church to challenge its early beliefs and practices relative to the Law. Therefore, we will start our journey with that event.

The Great Commission

The Gospels of Mark and Matthew record a final commandment from Jesus: "Go ye into all the world, and preach the gospel to every creature."[4] This command to preach to the entire world is known as the *great commission* and seems clear enough as recorded in our New Testament. We reasonably conclude that the apostles' mission immediately after Jesus's ascension was to evangelize all the known world and to teach "every creature," including non-Jews. Why, then, for over a decade after Jesus's death did the apostles continue to act in accordance with the commission at the time of their calling, "Go *not* into the way of the Gentiles and into any city of the Samaritans enter ye not"?[5] The contradiction between the great commission as recorded in two of the gospels of the New Testament and the apostles' actions in the first decade of the church requires us to seek an alternate and perhaps more nuanced understanding.

It is unlikely that the apostles received the great commission from Jesus and simply ignored it. There are too many examples recorded in Acts of the apostles demonstrating great courage and boldness. The events explored in this chapter suggest that the commission as reported in the two gospels was a composite of multiple commissions received from the Lord during *and* after His mortal ministry. We all know that recollections evolve as time passes. It is important for us to recognize that the gospels were written many decades after Jesus's personal instruction to the apostles—well after additional revelation extended the gospel to the gentiles.[6] It is certainly reasonable to surmise that the verbal retelling of Jesus's parting commission to the apostles evolved to incorporate the commission received much later to extend the gospel to the gentiles. In addition to the evidence of the apostles' actions during the first decade, consider that John's gospel records Jesus's final commission very differently: Speaking to Peter, the Lord commanded, "feed my sheep."[7] Rather than a commission to evangelize the entire world, Peter was commanded to care for those already converted—which at the time would have meant the Jews.

If the great commission to teach all the world had been clearly taught by Jesus and understood by the apostles during His mortal ministry or during the forty days He spent with them after His resurrection,[8] what would we expect to see in the actions of the apostles? We would expect the apostles to welcome gentiles into the church without hesitation. We would expect them to appoint and set apart missionaries to preach to the gentiles. We would expect them to proactively define the relationship between gentiles and the Law of Moses and its associated ordinances and commandments. If the observance of the Law of Moses were to change, we would expect the leadership to be exemplars of that change.

What we see in the earliest days of the church is the exact opposite of all that we would expect. We see years pass after Jesus's death with the gospel being taught only to Jews. We see the need for God to prod Peter through revelation to meet with a gentile. We see reluctance among the Jewish leadership to extend the gospel to the gentiles. We see the calling and setting apart of missionaries to go unto the broader gentile world by *local* leaders in Antioch without apostolic sanction. We see uncertainty about whether gentiles should observe the Law of Moses. We see the Jewish leadership and members continuing to observe the Law. We see contention among the leadership about the Law. Finally, we see a division of the church into factions while the apostles are still alive.

On the day of Pentecost,[9] thousands of Jews from all over the civilized world were gathered for the Feast of Weeks.[10] Many of the gathered Jews witnessed the outpouring of the Holy Ghost upon the assembled Jewish Christians. Even the unconverted felt the Spirit and were "pricked in their hearts" and were compelled to ask Peter, "Men and brethren, what shall we do?"[11] On that day, thousands of additional Jews became Christian. Believers continued to gather at the temple, and their worship remained intertwined with the temple.[12] Even many priests believed, and there is no indication that in doing so they had to leave their position in the temple.[13] As the days, weeks, and years unfolded, Peter, James,[14] and John ministered in Jerusalem and in the regions immediately adjacent to it. During the first fifteen years or so of the church, a period in which Acts still includes Peter in the narrative, there is no mention of the apostles leaving the Jewish heartland of Judaea.

Saul

Naturally, the growth of the church raised the ire of the chief priests. They repeatedly subjected the leading apostles to trials,[15] and they enlisted a zealous young man named Saul to squash the new sect. Saul had proven his brutality in the trial and stoning of Stephen and had become the primary persecutor of the Jewish converts.[16] Stephen's stoning was but a preview of the horrors Saul inflicted. He was ruthless! In Saul's own words,

> I persecuted this way unto the death, binding and delivering into prisons both men and women. . . . I imprisoned and beat in every synagogue them that believed on thee: And when the blood of thy martyr Stephen was shed, I also was standing by, and consenting unto his death, and kept the raiment of them that slew him.[17]

> Many of the saints did I shut up in prison, having received authority from the chief priests; and when they were put to death, I gave my voice against them. And I punished them oft in every synagogue, and compelled them to blaspheme; and being exceedingly mad against them, I persecuted them even unto strange cities.[18]

In an apocryphal account, Saul led a riled mob to stop James the brother of Jesus, also known as James the Just, from preaching in the temple. According to the account, Saul pushed James the Just down a set of stone steps and left him for dead at the bottom.

> While he [Saul] was thus speaking, and adding more to the same effect, and while James the bishop was refuting him, he began to excite the people and to raise a tumult, so that the people might not be able to hear what was said. Therefore he began to drive all into confusion with shouting, and to undo what had been arranged with much labour, and at the same time to reproach the priests, and to enrage them with revilings and abuse, and, like a madman, to excite every one to murder, saying, "What do ye? Why do ye hesitate? Oh, sluggish and inert, why do we not lay hands upon them, and pull all these fellows to pieces?"

When he had said this, he first, seizing a strong brand from the altar, set the example of smiting. Then others also, seeing him, were carried away with like madness. Then ensued a tumult on either side, of the beating and the beaten. Much blood is shed; there is a confused flight, in the midst of which that enemy attacked James, and threw him headlong from the top of the steps; and supposing him to be dead, he cared not to inflict further violence upon him.[19]

Saul had an incredible conversion experience a few years after the death of the Savior, in about 36.[20] He was on the road to Damascus while carrying out his duties to suppress the Christian sect.[21] After his conversion, he taught in the synagogues in Damascus and "confounded the Jews."[22] He traveled through nearby areas of Arabia before returning to Damascus.[23] In all, three years passed before he ventured to Jerusalem to meet with church leaders.[24] For reasons not expounded in the scriptures, Barnabas was Saul's advocate. Perhaps he had been in Damascus and had seen Saul's zealous commitment to the new faith and Saul's oratorial talents that were capable of "confounding the Jews." Regardless, Barnabas steadfastly vouched for Saul to Peter and James the Just.[25] In contrast to Saul's reputation of persecution, Barnabas was trusted even though he was a non-Palestinian Jew from the island of Cyprus. He was known as "a good man, and full of the Holy Ghost and of faith"[26] and had demonstrated his selflessness and commitment by joining the early saints in selling all that he had.[27]

Saul met with Peter for fifteen days.[28] We know nothing of what transpired between the two men, but during this time Saul went and worshiped in the temple.[29] While there, he had a vision in which the Lord told him, "Make haste, and get thee quickly out of Jerusalem: for they [Judaean saints] will not receive thy testimony concerning me. . . . Depart: for I will send thee far hence *unto the Gentiles.*"[30] Saul left abruptly and alone for Syria. According to the Lord's command, he avoided the "churches of Judaea which were in Christ."[31] He headed back home via Syria to Tarsus,[32] laying low, as it were. He understood from the Lord's warning that he was to stay out of the heart of the church, where he was not trusted or wanted. We can understand from the glimpses presented earlier into Saul's severe persecution of Christ's followers why he was so unwelcome in Judaean churches. It would be hard for anyone to forgive such cruelty. Early Jewish converts who had lived under the law of an "eye for an eye" for their entire lives would have found it particularly difficult to exercise the higher law of unconditional Christian forgiveness.

Importantly, we are left to speculate whether Saul told Peter about his temple vision and the Lord's promise that Saul would be sent to the gentiles. It appears that he did not, or, if he did, it appears that Peter did not accept the vision as applicable to the church in general because, years later, the Lord had to prod Peter to accept the gentile Cornelius into the church. Peter's reluctance suggests that, as of Saul's departure from Jerusalem, Peter still didn't understand that the gospel was to be preached to the gentiles. Acts is silent as to whether Saul received any appointment or ordination from Peter during his visit. He returned to Tarsus and fell off the radar for about a decade, patiently waiting upon the Lord for the fulfillment of his revelatory but private mission call to the gentiles.

After Saul ceased persecuting the church, the harmonious state of the Jewish Christian church was described by Luke: "Then had the churches rest throughout all Judaea and Galilee and Samaria, and were edified; and walking in the fear of the Lord, and in the comfort of the Holy Ghost, were multiplied."[33] It is important to recognize two important aspects of the scope of the church at this point in about 37:[34] the converts were all Jews, and the official church was contained within greater Palestine. Later in Acts, there is a retrospective comment that some Jews who had scattered because of Saul's persecutions had begun proselyting farther north in Antioch and the islands of Cyprus and Crete (Phoenicia); however, the way this fact is included in the narrative suggests that the introduction of the gospel into these far-flung cities was an organic outcome of persecution and its accompanying migration of individual members rather than a purposeful expansion of the ministry by the apostles.[35] Notably, even in the northern outposts of Antioch, Cyprus, and Crete, the converts to the gospel were still strictly Jews.

His historic persecution of the Judaean Christians naturally led to initial distrust of the converted Saul. However, in the history that follows, we need to understand that there was another perhaps more significant factor that undermined the Judaean leadership's trust in him. Saul was a Jew like Peter and the other apostles. But, unlike them, he had been born in Tarsus outside of Palestine. The Jews outside of Palestine were Hellenized Jews. Whereas Palestinian Jews followed the rabbinical tradition and relentlessly pursued increasingly rigorous compliance of the Law of Moses, Hellenized Jews (such as Philo of Alexandria, who was previously introduced in this book) believed that Greek philosophy was another fountain of truth. The very fact that Saul was by birth a Hellenized Jew and by training a student of both Greek and Jewish traditions, just as his teacher Gamaliel was,[36] cast him as a proponent of a different Jewish worldview as explained by the historian Baring-Gould:

> St. Paul [Saul], an accomplished Greek scholar, brought up at Tarsus amidst Hellenistic Jews, adopted the theology and exegesis in vogue at Alexandria, and on both these accounts excited the suspicion and dislike of the national party at Jerusalem. The Nazarenes[37] were imbued with the prejudices they had acquired in their childhood, in the midst of which they had grown up, and they could not but regard Paul with alarm when he turned without disguise to the Greeks, and introduced into the Church the theological system and scriptural interpretations of a Jewish community they had always regarded as of questionable orthodoxy.[38]

The Gospel to the Gentiles

When the door to the gentiles was opened by revelation around the year 45 it was a seismic event that rocked the church. Cornelius, a gentile centurion living in Palestine, and Peter, the senior apostle, received sequential visions that meshed into one divine message that the gospel was open to the gentiles. Peter dreamed that he was instructed to eat meat deemed "unclean" to the Jews.[39] In the dream, Peter resisted eating the meat, based on his obedience to the customs of the Jews, saying "Not so, Lord; for I have never eaten any thing that is common or unclean."[40] Clearly, nothing that the Lord had taught him to that point had prepared Peter to think differently about the Law of

Moses, the rabbinical hedges that had been built up around it, or the equality of the gentiles in the sight of God. The Lord thereupon made it clear that He had cleansed the meat and Peter was to eat it. Perhaps anticipating Peter's reluctance arising from the deepest fibers of his Jewish soul, the Lord repeated the message three times! Emissaries from Cornelius arrived at Peter's door while he was still pondering the vision. Cornelius had sent them because of his own heavenly revelation received earlier. To Peter's credit, he accepted the gentile emissaries and accompanied them to Cornelius's house, where a gentile group of Cornelius's friends and family were gathered.[41]

Peter's first words to Cornelius reveal just how momentous it was for him as a Jew to meet and eat with a group of gentiles: "Ye know how that it is an unlawful thing for a man that is a Jew to keep company, or come unto one of another nation; but God hath shewed me that I should not call any man common or unclean."[42] We can sense the conflict in Peter. Clearly, the rabbinical hedge separating Jew and gentile was deeply ingrained in him. It's important to note that the Law recorded in scripture did not prohibit eating or being with gentiles. The prohibition was part of the rabbinical hedge about the Law called by Jesus the "tradition of the elders."[43] Peter and his companions courageously pushed past their inhibitions and enjoyed a spiritual feast with the gathered gentiles that culminated in the gentiles' baptisms.[44]

If the Lord had indeed given the great commission and clarified the role of the Mosaic Law for Jews and gentiles during His mortal ministry, we would not expect to see the events recorded in Acts 10. Peter would not have needed additional revelation. He would not have honored the Law by anchoring his opening comments to Cornelius in it. He would have *known* beforehand that "God is no respecter of persons" rather than merely *perceiving* it to be so.[45] We would not expect the Jews who had accompanied Peter to be so astonished that the Holy Ghost would descend on the assembled gentiles just as it had on the Jews on the day of Pentecost.[46] We would expect that the Jewish converts in Jerusalem would have anticipated and welcomed the gentiles. But they did not. Instead, when Peter returned to Jerusalem, the Jewish leadership confronted him. Their condemnation illustrates their ongoing commitment to the Law of Moses. They accused Peter, "Thou wentest in to men uncircumcised, and didst eat with them."[47] In rebuttal, Peter recounted the sequence of events in detail in a way that convinced those present to accept his revelation as genuine and the receipt of the Holy Ghost by Cornelius as evidence that the door was open to the gentiles.

The word of Cornelius's baptism spread quickly through the church and soon reached Barnabas. We can imagine that the news had particular importance to Barnabas, who had been raised in the gentile nation of Cyprus and who had spent so much time outside of the Jewish majority in Palestine. Barnabas headed immediately to Tarsus to find Saul.[48] Why go to Saul? After all, as Saul's escort to Jerusalem many years earlier, Barnabas had seen firsthand the distrust that many of the leaders in Jerusalem had toward Saul.[49] Furthermore, for about ten years Saul had been in virtual exile, living outside the geography of established Christianity. Perhaps Barnabas knew of Saul's temple revelation and the promise the Lord made to Saul about preaching to the gentiles. We simply don't know for sure. But it is clear that Barnabas' first priority after hearing the news was to inform Saul.

Barnabas took Saul to Antioch. It was the closest city to Tarsus with an organized church, and it was reasonably far from the Judaean churches where Saul was unwelcome. Also, the Antioch church, while still comprised strictly of Jews, courageously viewed themselves as a separate faith from Judaism. They were the first to call themselves Christians.[50]

There were "prophets and teachers" in Antioch.[51] Their titles indicate that they were persons of authority, but they were definitely not apostles. The term *prophet* is ambiguously used in the New Testament, so it is not clear what specific office these leaders had; evidently their office was sufficient for them to set apart and ordain Saul and Barnabas. The Holy Ghost sanctioned their choice to send the two as missionaries for the "work whereunto I have called them."[52] It is notable that the leaders in Antioch did not seek the approval of the apostles in Jerusalem prior to setting apart Saul and Barnabas. Did the local leaders understand that the "work whereunto I have called them" was the mission to the gentiles privately revealed to Saul in the temple? Did they understand that from their satellite congregation in Antioch, far from the center of the church, they were sending out missionaries to burst open the door to the gentiles? We are left to wonder whether the apostles and elders in Jerusalem were aware of the goings-on in Antioch. Yes, the door to the gentiles had been opened a sliver with the conversion of Cornelius and a pocket of gentiles in the Judaean lands of Caesarea. But were the Jerusalem-based leaders of the church directing and anticipating the seismic change that was about to happen as waves of gentiles accepted the gospel of Jesus Christ?

The companionship of Barnabas and Saul set out on their mission to the gentile world in about 46,[53] starting in Barnabas's home country of Cyprus.[54] As Saul journeyed deep into the former Greek city-states of Cyprus, Corinth, Ephesus, and so on, he understandably decided to use his Greek name Paul rather than Saul, his Hebrew name.[55] From this point forward, the narrative will also refer to him as Paul.

The Council

The addition of gentiles into the church in Antioch led someone in authority, most likely James the Just,[56] to send Judaizers[57] to Antioch from Judaea to ensure that new converts were dutifully adopting the Law of Moses. Acts records the message of the Judaizers as follows, "Certain men which came down from Judaea taught the brethren and said, Except ye be circumcised after the manner of Moses, ye cannot be saved."[58] To the new gentile converts, the message was chilling— salvation required that one become a Jew and live by the Law of Moses. Clearly, Paul and Barnabas had not been teaching this doctrine, and the book of Acts likely understates the intensity of the argument that followed: "Paul and Barnabas had no small dissension and disputation with them [the Judaizers]."[59] This confrontation exposed undefined doctrine. Up to that point, Jesus had left the question of the Law open to widely varying interpretation. There had been no prior guidance from the apostles and no agreement as to the treatment of gentiles within the community of Jewish Christians. The opposing parties, the Judaizers on one side and Paul and Barnabas on the other, wisely recognized that without the apostles and senior elders of the church they couldn't resolve the dispute, so they determined to send Paul, Barnabas, and others to the center of the church in Jerusalem to settle the question. The church was approximately seventeen years old at that point, in about the year 49.[60]

Paul tells us that the council was a "private" affair, including only senior leaders of "reputation."[61] Perhaps the leaders in Jerusalem considered it unwise to advertise the many controversial aspects of the council, including Paul's unwelcome presence in Judaea and the sensitive questions related to the Law. Nevertheless, the apostles and other elders were in attendance.[62] James the Just was there and appears to have presided.[63] Importantly, at least one gentile was there. Paul had invited a young gentile convert named Titus.[64] Perhaps he brought Titus simply to showcase the goodness of a gentile Christian. Perhaps it was to force the assembled apostles and elders to confront their prejudices against gentiles by having one in their midst. Perhaps it was to force their doctrinal hand as a litmus test of sorts to see if they would compel Titus to be circumcised before joining the council. Notably, Titus was not compelled to be circumcised, a fact that Paul later used as evidence that the leaders agreed to exclude gentiles from the requirements of the Law.[65]

The question being considered was profound: When gentiles accepted the gospel, were they also accepting Judaism? Many of those gathered in the council, particularly those who were once Pharisees, passionately believed that gentile converts must obey the Law of Moses.[66] There were impassioned arguments on both sides, or, as the scriptures say, "There was much disputing."[67] Peter calmed the debate when he stood and argued in favor of excluding gentiles from the Law.[68] Paul and Barnabas provided evidence of the hand of God in their ministry, which by implication suggested that God accepted the gentiles without the ordinances of the Law of Moses.[69] Finally, James the Just arose and rendered a "sentence," or a ruling, that the gentile believers were not required to follow the Law of Moses, albeit with some exceptions.[70] The council produced a letter, addressing it to the "Gentiles of Antioch and Syria and Cilicia."[71]

Did the council resolve the issue that had arisen in Antioch? Yes and no. Yes, in the sense that the gentile saints in Antioch had clear guidance that they did not need to be circumcised and were not subject to the Law of Moses. No, in the sense that many related questions were left unanswered. The council's letter was geographically restricted, addressed to Antioch and nearby provinces. Did the letter apply outside of Antioch, Syria, and Cilicia? As we will see, based on the fact that Judaizers continued to preach circumcision in other areas, some took the geographic restriction literally. The letter was also demographically restricted, addressed only to the gentiles. Did that mean that the Jewish Christians were still expected to observe the Law? As we will see, many believed that Jewish Christians were to zealously follow the Law. The letter was silent about the relationship within the church between Jew and gentile. Were the rabbinical hedges that prohibited Jews from meeting and eating with gentiles still operative among a congregation made up of both Jews and gentiles? As we will soon see, some certainly believed that the hedge was still operative.

The Jewish and Gentile Branches

The decision of the council in about the year 49 effectively created two churches: the main branch of Jewish Christians that grafted Christian beliefs onto their Jewish faith, which included their observance of the Law of Moses, and the small but growing gentile branch beside it. Both churches believed in Jesus, but their forms of worship, doctrine of Jesus, and doctrines of salvation were bound to diverge based on the role of the Law in their daily lives and worship. The Jewish branch looked to Peter and James the Just as the leading authorities, and the gentile faction looked to Paul as the leading apostle.

This schism in the early church does not jump off the pages of the New Testament, but evidence of it is there. The clues are obscure because by the time the New Testament was canonized in the fourth century the gentile church had become dominant and the Jewish church had slipped into the obscurity of sectarian Judaism. Accordingly, writings such as the Gospel of the Clementines and the Gospel of the Hebrews that had been widely used by the Jewish Christians in and around Jerusalem and that supported the ongoing observance of the Law were excluded from the canon. Instead, the writings of Paul dominated the New Testament canon.

The book of Acts disproportionately dwells on Paul, evidence that it is not a comprehensive retelling of early church history. Very few of the apostles are even mentioned in Acts. Peter falls out of the narrative after the council of Jerusalem! This is particularly noteworthy given the fact that Acts was written sometime after 85,[72] and by that time, Peter and Paul had contemporaneously ministered in Rome, died in Rome, and had both been replaced by other bishops, as we will discuss later. Also, by the time Luke wrote the book of Acts, Jerusalem had fallen, the temple had been destroyed, and the Jewish Christians had been exiled. None of these important events in Jewish Christian history are in Acts. The only glimpses we get of the Jewish Christian church after the council are when Paul visited Jerusalem and from Paul's epistles opposing the influence of Judaizers. The bottom line is that the history of the Jewish Christian church, including the ministries of Peter, the other apostles, and James the Just, is conspicuously absent.

We can only speculate about the motive for this absence of Jewish Christian history. Luke is believed to have been a disciple and ofttimes companion of Paul, so perhaps it was a matter of recording the events closer to his personal experience.[73] However, given how Luke recorded many events that he had not personally witnessed, it is also very possible and perhaps likely that he focused entirely on Paul after the Jerusalem council because he believed that Paul's ministry was comparatively more important than that of the other apostles, and in a related way, that the gentile branch of the church was the true vine of Christianity.

In the rest of this chapter we'll consider the evidences of the schism that existed in the early church. Most of these evidences will be clues from the New Testament; however, we will also consider supplemental evidence from scholars. To organize the clues, we'll consider the following: Paul's ambiguous commission and authority, the ongoing contention with Judaizers, a confrontation between Peter and Paul at Antioch, and the ongoing practice of the Law by Jewish Christians.

Paul's Ambiguous Commission and Authority

Paul retrospectively recorded that he left the council believing that he and Peter were co-heads over two branches of Christians. He viewed himself as the apostle over the uncircumcised, or gentiles, and Peter the apostle over the circumcised, or Jews. Paul recorded this understanding about four years after the council in an epistle to the Galatians,

> When they [the council] saw that the gospel of the uncircumcision was committed unto me, as the gospel of the circumcision was unto Peter; (For he that wrought

> effectually in Peter to the apostleship of the circumcision, the same was mighty in me toward the Gentiles:) And when James [the brother of the Lord], Cephas [Peter], and John, who seemed to be pillars, perceived the grace that was given unto me, they gave to me and Barnabas the right hands of fellowship; that we should go unto the heathen, and they unto the circumcision.[74]

He affirmed his belief about the scope of his apostleship to the Romans: "For I speak to you Gentiles, inasmuch as *I am the apostle of the Gentiles*, I magnify mine office."[75] He urged the Corinthians to accept him as an equal to the other apostles and reminded them that he had demonstrated the same signs and deeds of the apostles, "for in nothing am I behind the very chiefest apostles though I be nothing. Truly the signs of an apostle were wrought among you in all patience, in signs, and wonders, and mighty deeds."[76]

Today's Christians associate the title of apostle with Paul just as readily as with Peter; however, this association is due to Paul's own assertions and is not based on an act of ordination recorded in scripture. Interestingly, although Luke dedicated much of the book of Acts to Paul, he was notably silent on Paul's ordination as an apostle. Yes, he referred to Paul as an apostle,[77] but he also included Barnabas in that reference, leading us to question whether it was a generic reference to them as the first evangelists to that area. The only physical ordination of Paul that Luke recorded was when Paul and Barnabas were first set apart by the "laying on of hands" by the local leaders in Antioch.[78] The second epistle of Peter is the only non-Pauline epistle preserved in the New Testament that refers to Paul. In it, Peter refers to Paul simply as a "brother."[79]

Arguably, Paul's own view of his authority evolved. As we learned earlier in this chapter, after his visit to Jerusalem, he went into exile for about a decade in Tarsus. He didn't challenge the authority of the known pillars of the church. His first missionary journey with Barnabas started with an ordination by local leaders in Antioch, and there is no indication in Acts that he viewed himself as an apostle at that time. After the council in Jerusalem, we see the first glimpse of his changing view. In his first epistle after the council, written to the Thessalonians while on his *second* mission in about 50, he referred to himself *and Silas*[80] as apostles of the Lord.[81] In this epistle, there was no hint of contention with Judaizers and no overt defense of his authority, so his use of the term *apostles* appears to be akin to "first evangelists," or the ones who first introduced the gospel and who are the shepherds of the new flock.

Fast forward three years to about 53. By then, Judaizers were actively going out from Jerusalem, as we will learn in more detail later. Also, by this time, Paul had seen firsthand in an incident at Antioch how Jewish customs still influenced even the most senior leaders—again, this is something we will dive into later. Therefore, his epistle to the Galatians takes an entirely different tone. We should appreciate how significant his opening statement was: "Paul, an apostle, (not of men, neither by man, but by Jesus Christ, and God the Father, who raised him from the dead)."[82] He was boldly asserting that he was an apostle, establishing up-front his authority to challenge the Judaizers being sent into Galatia. This was itself a bold claim, but to this he added that his apostleship was not the result of man's ordination. Rather, he was directly called as an apostle by Jesus. Paul did not give details about how Jesus called him, nor did he clarify by what definition he considered himself an apostle. Paul, like the other apostles commissioned by the mortal Jesus, was a firsthand witness to Jesus's resurrection.[83] He had heard the voice of the Lord on the road to Damascus and had seen the Lord in the temple.[84] However, unlike the twelve called by Jesus whose calling and ordination were specifically conveyed in the gospels, there is no record of Paul being selected or ordained by the surviving twelve apostles as Matthias had been in the first year of the church.[85] In fact, Paul's apostolic status was evidently not widely known or accepted. Otherwise, Paul's assertion would not have been coupled with such defensive statements. To the Corinthians he wrote just a few years later,

> Am I not an apostle? am I not free? have I not seen Jesus Christ our Lord? are not ye my work in the Lord? If I be not an apostle unto others, yet doubtless I am to you: for the seal of mine apostleship are ye in the Lord. Mine answer to them that do examine me is this, Have we not power to eat and to drink? Have we not power to lead about a sister, a wife, as well as other apostles, and as the brethren of the Lord, and Cephas?[86]

He clearly was defending against those who would "examine him" in his apostolic claim. He accepts that others didn't view him as an apostle, but he believes that those he had led to conversion should. He had personally seen Jesus and was thus an apostolic witness of Him. He also argued that in his ministry he had the same freedom and authority to govern the gentile saints' patterns of eating, drinking, and social relations as James the Just and Peter had relative to those still living under the Law.

To Timothy, he similarly asserted his apostleship, "I am ordained a preacher, and an apostle," but then he adds a defensive comment, "I speak the truth in Christ, and lie not."[87] Why would Paul feel compelled to state that he wasn't lying unless he was defending against those who believed he was?

Paul considered himself the "apostle of the gentiles," or as he wrote to the Galatians, the apostle to the "uncircumcised." After the council in Jerusalem, Paul and his new companion, Silas, ventured through Asia Minor to Athens itself. Indeed, they were in "gentile lands," but their pattern was to first teach the Jews that were dispersed in those lands.[88] Thus, Paul's efforts led to both Jewish and gentile converts. Clearly, he had a very broad view of what it meant to be "the apostle of the gentiles." He certainly didn't limit his teaching to non-Jews, which suggests that Paul saw himself as the lead apostle not only to uncircumcised non-Jews but also to all those living in heathen or gentile *nations*. Undoubtedly, this broad scope based on the geography of "gentile nations" was yet another point of contention with the other leaders of the church.

As time passed, other apostles and evangelists taught and converted in the major cities. In Corinth, for example, an eloquent Jew from Alexandria had been so influential in converting souls that some in Corinth considered themselves followers of Apollos, while others considered themselves followers of Peter and some of Paul: "For it hath been declared unto me of you, my brethren, by them which are of the house of Chloe, that there are contentions among you. Now this I say, that every one of you saith, I am of Paul; and I of Apollos; and I of Cephas [Peter]; and I of Christ."[89] Paul pleaded with the Corinthians to ignore the other teachers of Christ and to follow him, "For though ye have ten thousand instructors in Christ . . . I beseech you, be ye followers of me."[90] From these excerpts we get a glimpse into the confusion that existed among the saints relative to leadership. If Paul's status as the lead apostle to all gentile nations had been widely accepted, we would not expect to see such confusion.

The Ongoing Contention with Judaizers

We learned earlier in this chapter that the council in Jerusalem was a direct result of "certain men which came down from Judaea" who taught, "Except ye be circumcised after the manner of Moses, ye cannot be saved." The council settled the matter for the gentile saints in Antioch and the neighboring provinces of Syria and Cilicia (southern Turkey). The geographic and demographic scope of the letter sent out from the council was limited, and it is clear that Judaizers continued to operate in other areas *after* the council.

Galatia appears to have been the first city in which Judaizers gained a foothold. Paul wrote:

> I marvel that ye are so soon removed from him that called you into the grace of Christ unto another gospel: Which is not another; but there be some that trouble you [Judaizers] and would pervert the gospel of Christ.[91]

The nature of the corruption is clear from the rest of the epistle. It was the introduction of the Law of Moses, about which Paul expressed his dismay: "how turn ye again to the weak and beggarly elements, whereunto ye desire again to be in bondage? Ye observe days, and months, and times, and years."[92] He continued, "For I testify again to every man that is circumcised, that he is a debtor to do the whole law."[93]

Crete was evidently afflicted by Judaizers, as Paul warned Titus, the man he had placed in Crete as the bishop:

> For there are many unruly and vain talkers and deceivers, *specially they of the circumcision.* Whose mouths must be stopped, who subvert whole houses, teaching things which they ought not, for filthy lucre's sake.[94]

> But avoid foolish questions, and *genealogies,* and contentions, and strivings *about the law [of Moses]*; for they are unprofitable and vain.[95]

There is not the same passionate defense against Judaizers in Colossae; nevertheless, Paul warns the saints there:

> This I say, lest any man beguile you with enticing words . . . Let no man therefore judge you in meat, or in drink, or in respect of an holyday, or of the new moon, or of the sabbath days.[96]

In the second epistle to the Corinthians, Paul echoes the call to the Galatians to resist another gospel of Christ:

> But I fear, lest by any means, as the serpent beguiled Eve through his subtilty, so your minds should be corrupted from the simplicity that is in Christ. For if he that cometh preacheth another Jesus, whom we have not preached, or if ye receive another spirit, which ye have not received, or another gospel, which ye have not accepted, ye might well bear with him.[97]

It is clear that he is equating Judaizing Jewish Christians to "false apostles"[98] among the Corinthian saints when he identified them as Jews: "Are they Hebrews? So am I. Are they Israelites? So am I. Are they the seed of Abraham? So am I. Are they ministers of Christ? . . . I am more."[99]

The Confrontation at Antioch

Paul concluded his extensive second missionary journey to the "gentile nations" in about 52 and headed to Jerusalem in time for an upcoming feast. He evidently went up and "saluted the church," which most likely means that he greeted the leaders of the church in Jerusalem, and then headed to Antioch.[100] Peter, along with some companions, decided to join Paul in Antioch. It must have been quite the gathering. There was Peter the senior apostle along with other visitors from Jerusalem, Paul's former companion Barnabas, Paul, Silas, and of course the many local leaders and saints of Antioch. They all gathered together as Christians without regard for individual heritage. We can imagine the experience of new converts meeting, mingling, and even eating with Peter the senior apostle—the man who had been by Jesus's side throughout His ministry. We can imagine the spiritual feast and heartfelt love shared between the Antioch saints and Peter.

The idyllic scene was shattered when emissaries sent by James the Just arrived from Jerusalem. Everything changed. Peter "withdrew and separated himself" like a devout Jew.[101] Peter's companions did as well. Even Barnabas, who had been so instrumental in bringing many gentiles into the church, followed Peter's example.[102] Paul was dumbfounded and dismayed by Peter's withdrawal. He put the blame for the shattered harmony among the Antioch saints directly on Peter rather than on James, the one who had sent the Jewish emissaries.[103] After all, Peter had previously boldly defended eating and mingling with Cornelius and had shown the same openness toward the Antioch gentiles prior to the arrival of James's emissaries. Paul was so angry that he berated Peter in front of them all.[104]

Our glimpse into this controversial event is in the Epistle to the Galatians. Paul referenced the Antioch incident with Peter and the Jerusalem council as important related events in the controversy surrounding the Law. However, it's important to note that Paul presented these events as out-of-sequence snippets, which renders the epistle somewhat confusing.[105] Nevertheless, the Epistle to the Galatians sheds significant light on the tension that persisted relative to the Law even after the Jerusalem council.

We are left to wonder just how mutually offended the two leading figures in Antioch were and whether the offense was ever fully resolved. Did Peter and Paul resolve the differences exposed in Antioch and ultimately see eye to eye? We simply don't know, but some clues suggest the opposite. Peter warned the church about Paul's teachings:

> our beloved brother Paul also according to the wisdom given unto him hath written unto you; As also in all his epistles, speaking in them of these things; in which are some things hard to be understood, which they that are unlearned and unstable wrest, as they do also the other scriptures, unto their own destruction.[106]

Scholars believe that in an apocryphal epistle from Peter to James the Just, Peter was likely referring to Paul as the one in opposition to his own teachings:

> For some from among the Gentiles have rejected my legal preaching, attaching themselves to certain lawless and *trifling preaching of the man who is my enemy.* And these things some have attempted while I am still alive, to transform my words by certain various interpretations, in order to the dissolution of the law; as though I also myself were of such a mind, but did not freely proclaim it, which God forbid! For such a thing were to act in opposition to the law of God which was spoken by Moses, and was borne witness to by our Lord in respect of its eternal continuance; for thus He spoke: 'The heavens and the earth shall pass away, but one jot or one tittle shall in no wise pass from the law.'"[107]

The Practice of the Law by Jewish Christians

The decision reached in the council in Jerusalem relieved only the gentiles from the observance of the Law of Moses. This dichotomy between what was expected of Jewish Christians and gentile Christians is reflected in the dramatically different experiences of two young converts close to Paul, both of whom later served as bishops. Titus, a Greek, accompanied Paul to the council and based on its ruling was not required to be circumcised. In contrast, Timothy of Lystra was half Jew. His father was Greek and his mother was a Jew.[108] Prior to enlisting Timothy's service, Paul had Timothy circumcised to establish his bona fides as a Jew *and to comply with the rulings of the council.*[109] Paul knew that Timothy would be ministering among Jews and they would know of his mixed heritage, "because of the Jews which were in those quarters: for they knew that his father was a Greek."[110]

Paul's position on the Law is arguably ambiguous. He railed against Judaizers, as we've already seen. He alternately compared the Law to a variety of negative things, at times calling it "bondage,"[111] "servitude,"[112] "flesh,"[113] "enmity,"[114] a "source of sin,"[115] and so on. He repeatedly taught that the Law did not save and that its purpose was fulfilled. Paul implied that the Law was abrogated when he told the Colossians that the "handwriting of the ordinances" were "nailed to the cross."[116] Similarly, he suggested that saints were no longer under the Law in his message to the Galatians:

> Wherefore the law was our schoolmaster to bring us unto Christ, that we might be justified by faith. But after that faith is come, *we are no longer under a schoolmaster.* For ye are all the children of God by faith in Christ Jesus. For as many of you as have been baptized into Christ have put on Christ. There is neither Jew nor Greek, there is neither bond nor free, there is neither male nor female: for ye are all one in Christ Jesus. And if ye be Christ's, then are ye Abraham's seed, and heirs according to the promise.[117]

Yet, in spite of his generally negative characterization of the Law, Paul didn't outright tell Jewish Christians to stop practicing it and even showed some indication that Jewish Christians should or could continue to observe it. Using circumcision as a symbol for being under the Law, Paul wrote,

> Is any man called being circumcised [a Jew that becomes a Christian]? Let him not become uncircumcised. Is any called in uncircumcision [a gentile that becomes a Christian]? Let him not be circumcised.[118]

If a Jew under the Law joined the church, he should continue to obey the Law. Similarly, to the Romans he wrote,

> Know ye not, brethren, (for I speak to them that know the law,) how that the law hath dominion over a man as long as he liveth?[119]

Perhaps Paul was simply being pragmatic. The justification for Timothy's circumcision mentioned earlier was in part due to consideration of how the Jews would accept him. Timothy's ministry would have been hampered by the Jews' unwillingness to be in his presence had he not been circumcised. Paul followed a similar pattern in his own observance:

> And unto the Jews I became as a Jew, that I might gain the Jews; to them that are under the law, as under the law, that I might gain them that are under the law; To them that are without law, as without law, (being not without law to God, but under the law to Christ,) that I might gain them that are without law.[120]

As another example, Paul urged situational pragmatism to the Corinthians. If meats proscribed by the Law offended a fellow Law-observing Christian and would make him stumble, don't eat the meats:

> But meat [food prohibited by the Law] commendeth us not to God: for neither, if we eat, are we the better; neither, if we eat not, are we the worse. But take heed lest by any means this liberty of yours become a stumblingblock to them that are weak. . . . And through thy knowledge shall the weak brother perish, for whom Christ died? But when ye sin so against the brethren, and wound their weak conscience, ye sin against Christ. Wherefore, if meat make my brother to offend, I will eat no flesh while the world standeth, lest I make my brother to offend.[121]

Apparently for Paul, it was not always one way or the other. Eat your meats free from the restrictions of the Law unless doing so would offend Jewish brethren who are weak in the gospel and continue to observe the Law and thereby cause them to be offended and stumble. It was as if Paul recognized the need to walk a tightrope relative to the Law. With this in mind, let's consider evidence that Paul himself continued to observe the Law.

Paul spent eighteen months, the majority of his second mission, in greater Corinth because the Lord revealed that "I have much people in this city."[122] While there, in about 52, he took upon himself a vow.[123] He doesn't tell us why he took the vow nor does he tell us what the vow was; however, it was most likely the Nazarite vow, a commitment under the Law to separate oneself unto the Lord. If so, the fulfillment of the vow required ritual cleansing, shaving the head, and prescribed sacrifices in the temple.[124] Accordingly, Paul shaved his head as part of the vow and headed purposefully, "by all means," to Jerusalem in time for a feast. Note the timing. This was after the council but *before* the incident at Antioch and *before* the challenges with Judaizers described earlier. We might suggest that this was an interlude during which time Paul's observance of the Law as a Jewish Christian was not wrought with controversy.

About six years later, at the conclusion of his third mission, Paul repeated his journey to Jerusalem; however, by this time controversies abounded relative to the Law. Judaizers had been sent from Judaea, congregations were struggling to navigate the ambiguous rulings of the council, Paul had seen at Antioch just how much influence James the Just had when the likes of Peter and Barnabas withdrew themselves from the gentile converts, and word was circulating in the church that Paul had sharpened his position relative to the Law by telling Jews living in "gentile lands" to abandon the Law and no longer circumcise their children or observe the Jewish customs.[125] It was a much wiser and seasoned Paul who understood that, given the controversies, returning to Jerusalem was fraught with potential conflict. Thus, he described his journey: "I go bound in the spirit unto Jerusalem, not knowing the things that shall befall me there."[126] Paul felt compelled to go to Jerusalem, but he fully understood that whatever happened would eventually take him to Rome.[127]

Paul arrived in Jerusalem and met with James the Just and the assembled elders of the Judaean church.[128] Paul related the success of his ministry and the spread of the gospel among the gentiles. The elders' response was telling. The assembled group "glorified the Lord" but then immediately jumped to what was at the forefront of their minds: "Thou seest, brother, how many thousands of Jews there are which believe; *and they are all zealous of the law*."[129] Their response is one of the clearest and most definitive clues that the Jerusalem-based, predominantly Jewish branch of the church continued to be zealous followers of the Law. The elders anticipated that Paul's presence in Jerusalem among the believing Jews would be controversial. Surely, the wounds of Paul's persecutions were still tender for longtime saints, but the leaders' primary concern was the circulating rumor that in the "gentile lands" Paul had been absorbing converted Jews into the gentile church and teaching them that it was no longer necessary to observe the Law.[130]

The leaders knew they couldn't hide Paul's presence from the local church.[131] Consequently, James devised a way for Paul to demonstrate his faithfulness to the Law and thereby convince the Jewish Christians that the rumors were false. James knew of four Jewish Christians in Jerusalem who were near the completion of their own Nazarite vows. He proposed that Paul join these four in the required seven-day ritual temple purification and pay for the costly offerings required to complete their vows.[132] Paul agreed to the plan and joined the others for seven days in the temple.[133] Was he being a hypocrite, as he had accused Peter of being in Antioch, acting like a Jew when among Jews? Was he just being pragmatic? Or did he sincerely participate in the temple ceremonies of the Law? We don't know the answer to these questions, but we have a clue from Paul's later legal trials. In a trial before Felix, the Roman governor, Paul said that one of the reasons for his journey to Jerusalem was to make "offerings."[134] Taken at face value, his statement to Felix suggests that he still honored the Law and its ritual offerings, even if he recognized that it was not by the Law that salvation came.

Perhaps the Judaean Jewish Christians under James's leadership accepted this token from Paul as evidence of his ongoing support of the Law; however, Jews from Asia Minor were also at the temple and could not tolerate seeing Paul there. These Jews confirmed the circulating rumors—Paul had in fact taught against the Law in their distant synagogues. Also, when they recognized some of Paul's gentile companions in Jerusalem, they accused Paul of being so brazen as to bring gentile Greeks into the temple. They riled up the city against Paul to the point the people swarmed, taking him from the temple with the intent to kill him.[135]

Paul's willingness to take upon himself the Nazarite vow during his second mission and to support the same vow taken by four other Jewish Christians at the end of his third mission is perplexing given that the fulfillment of the vow required multiple offerings, one of which was a sin offering.[136] Paul was not confused about the efficacy of animal sacrifice versus the sacrifice of the Savior. He wrote, "For it is not possible that the blood of bulls and of goats should take away sins . . . we are sanctified through the offering of the body of Jesus Christ once for all."[137] Why would he take a vow that culminated in a sin offering?

Because Paul recognized the purpose and sanctity of ordinances as patterns of the Savior's sacrifice, even if those ordinances themselves did not save. He said, "It was therefore necessary that the *patterns of things* in the heavens should be purified with these [blood sacrifices]; but the heavenly things themselves [Christ's sacrifice] with better sacrifices than these."[138] He taught that, when performed with personal purity and faith, ordinances can be an opportunity to approach God: "By faith, Abel offered unto God a more excellent sacrifice . . . by which he obtained witness that he was righteous."[139]

As a final clue to the practice of the Law and the wedge it created in the early church, we'll consider the day of worship of the early Christians, as described by scholars. The Jewish faction continued to observe the seventh-day Sabbath, while Paul began the practice of taking the Lord's Supper and worshipping on the first day of the week, or the Lord's Day in the "gentile lands" of Asia Minor:[140]

> The Sabbath or Saturday (for so the word sabbatum is constantly used in the writings of the fathers, when speaking of it as it relates to Christians) was held by them in great veneration, and especially in the Eastern parts honoured with all the public solemnities of religion. For which we are to know, that the gospel in those parts mainly prevailing amongst the Jews, they being generally the first converts to the Christian faith, they still retained a mighty reverence for the Mosaic institutions, and especially for the sabbath.[141]

> He [Christ] ate, walked about, taught, and performed miracles on the Sabbath. But though he relaxed the severity of observance, he did not abrogate the institution; and the Nazarene Church [Jewish Christians], after the Ascension, continued to venerate and observe the Sabbath as of divine appointment. The observance of the Lord's-day was apparently due to St. Paul alone, and sprang up in the Gentile churches in Asia Minor and Greece of his founding.[142]

It took centuries for the question of the Sabbath to be resolved through councils. The Catholic Church passed rules in the Synod of

Laodicea, held in 363, that prohibited the seventh-day Sabbath observance:

> Christians must not judaize by resting on the Sabbath, but must work on that day, rather honouring the Lord's Day; and, if they can, resting then as Christians. But if any shall be found to be judaizers, let them be anathema [excommunicated] from Christ.[143]

The First Schism Reflected in Today's Christianity

What became of the two factions resulting from the first schism? The answer differs based on geography. In the western regions including Asia Minor, Greece, and Rome, the gentile church grew and became dominant such that when the gentile and Jewish factions merged to become the Catholic Church, gentile or Pauline practices and doctrines survived, and Jewish customs of the Law were nearly eradicated.[144] Evidence of the merger is found in the succession of leadership in Rome. The official position of the Catholic Church is that Linus succeeded Peter as bishop and Cletus succeeded Linus.[145] However, the historian Baring-Gould suggests that the two bishops ministered simultaneously overseeing the Jewish and gentile factions:

> In Rome, in Greece, in Asia Minor, there were large communities, not of converted Jews only, but of proselytes from Gentiledom, who regarded themselves as constituting the Church of Christ. The existence of this fact is made patent by the Clementines and the Apostolic Constitutions. St. Peter's successors in the see of Rome have been a matter of perplexity. It has impressed itself on ecclesiastical students that Linus and Cletus ruled simultaneously. I have little doubt it was so. The Judaizing Church was strong in Rome. Probably each of the two communities had its bishop set over it, one by Paul, the other by Peter. Whilst the "Catholic" Church, the Church of the compromise, grew and prospered, and conquered the world, the narrow Judaizing Church dwindled till it expired, and with its expiration ceased conversion from Judaism. This Jewish

Church retained to the last its close relationship with Mosaism.[146]

The faction that was centered in Jerusalem, known as the Nazarene sect, never fully separated itself from Judaism. It is notable that historians who were contemporaries of the early Christians, including Josephus, Justus of Tiberias, and Philo of Alexandria, did not mention a separate Christian sect outside of the four major sects of Judaism (Sadducees, Pharisees, Essenes, and Zealots). The book of Acts tells us that the church was communal and likely poor. The members sold all of their possessions and had all things in common. The asceticism and Mosaic observances of the church were evidently so similar to those of the Jewish sect of the Essenes that they were indistinguishable.[147]

The Romans destroyed the temple and expelled the Jews, including the Nazarene faction of the church, from Jerusalem in the year 70. The Jewish Christians worshiped in exile in Pella Syria for a period of time. Scholars believe that this branch of the church emerged from exile as the Ebionite sect, *Ebonite* meaning "the poor."[148] Like the Essenes, this group lived an ascetic life and practiced the Mosaic Law but without animal sacrifices. As believers in Jesus, they considered Jesus to be the Messiah, the true prophet foretold by Moses; however, they did not accept the divinity or virgin birth of Jesus. They believed that He was born of a mortal father and mother, becoming the Messiah through adoption by God. They used as scripture the Gospel of the Hebrews[149] and the Gospel of the Clementines.[150] The Ebionites faded and eventually disappeared in the fourth century.[151]

Today, there is a flourishing community of Jewish believers in Jesus, a movement often referred to as Nazarenes or Messianic Judaism. Messianic Jews believe that the ruling of the Jerusalem council was never rescinded and is still valid today—gentiles are relieved from the requirements of the Law, but Jews are not. Like the Jewish Christians of the first century, Messianic Jews observe the Law, referring to it by its Hebrew name, Torah. They worship on the Sabbath, use the Hebrew version of the Old Testament, consider Jews as the chosen people, and have adopted the Hebrew nomenclature of the early Judaean church, including using Jesus's Aramaic name, Yeshua, rather than His Greek name, Jesus.[152]

The story in this chapter will likely be new for many readers, particularly for Christians who have been taught a simplified "Sunday School" version of a perfectly functioning primitive church. As we've seen, early Christians had to figure many things out, and the journey was messy. Factions developed within the lifetime of the apostles, dashing the hope for unity. We are left with more questions than answers as we exit the apostolic period. Here are just a few questions that scratch the surface of those that could be asked:

- Why did Jesus leave so much undefined, including the authority and administration of the church and the ongoing role of the Law? Was He constrained by the maturity, context, or character of the early saints? Were there patterns that the church needed to learn that were just as important as the doctrines themselves—to rely on ongoing revelation and councils? Did He intend for the church to mature "line upon line, precept upon precept, here a little and there a little"?[153] Did He purposefully leave so much undefined to emphasize the central role of His saving sacrifice versus the secondary aspects of worship practices and organizational administration?

- Christian "camps" seem to gravitate to extremes relative to ritual sacraments. Do Peter's and James's ongoing observance of the Law and Paul's participation late in his ministry in ceremonial vows and offerings suggest that there may be an ongoing purpose for ritual ordinances in Christianity? Do Paul's actions relative to ceremonial vows, including temple purification and offerings after both his second and third missions, counterbalance some of his critical rhetoric in his epistles? Should we moderate Paul's criticism of the Law and related ordinances, recognizing that he was in full combat with Judaizers and that if taken out of context the criticisms may leave us with a distorted view of his beliefs about the Law?

- How should we view the disproportionate place that Paul has in our New Testament and his influence on Christian doctrine? Clearly, Paul was chosen of the Lord and his ministry was guided by divine influence, but was Paul's authority to define doctrine commensurate to or even superior to the apostles that

Jesus had called and commissioned? If not, where are the teachings of the twelve? Did Paul's letters and doctrines crowd out the others because they were more correct or because gentile Christians dominated the church by the time the New Testament was canonized? Is it wise for Christians to base so many foundational doctrines on Paul alone?

Notes

---

[1] Matt 5:17–18.

[2] Acts 4:32–37.

[3] See Acts 2:41–46.

[4] See Mark 16:15 and Matthew 28:19.

[5] Matthew 10:5.

[6] Stefon, Benz and Others, Christianity 2017.

[7] John 21:15–17.

[8] See Acts 1:3.

[9] The Pentecostal feast, sometimes called the Feast of Weeks, was a Jewish holy feast required in Exodus 34:22. It was celebrated fifty days after Passover. After the events transpired that are recorded in Acts 2, it became a sacred day to both Jews and Christians.

[10] See Acts 2.

[11] Acts 2:37.

[12] See Acts 2:46.

[13] See Acts 6:7.

[14] This James refers to James, the brother of John. Acts records that this James was martyred soon after the door to the gentiles was opened. See Acts 12:2.

[15] On the second occasion before the council, the chief priests decided to kill the apostles (Acts 5:33), but they were spared due to the calming advice of Gamaliel, a doctor of the Law (Acts 5:34–40). Ironically, a short time later, Stephen, the first martyr of the new faith, was condemned by Gamaliel's protégé, Saul of Tarsus (Acts 22:3).

[16] See Acts 26:10–12.

[17] Acts 22:4, 19–20.

[18] Acts 26:10–11.

[19] The Clementine Recognitions 1867, 188.

[20] Marotta 2016.

[21] See Acts 9:3–19.

[22] Acts 9:22.

[23] Galatians 1:17.

[24] Galatians 1:18.

[25] See Acts 9:27 and Galatians 1:18.

[26] Acts 11:24.

[27] See Acts 4:36–37.

[28] Galatians 1:18.

[29] Acts 22:17.

[30] Acts 22:18, 21 (emphasis added).

[31] Galatians 1:21–22

[32] See Acts 11:25.

[33] Acts 9:31.

[34] Marotta 2016.

[35] See Acts 11:19–20.

[36] Gamaliel's status as both a Greek and as a Jewish scholar along the tradition of Alexandrian Jews such as Philo is implied in the Talmud and asserted by scholars: "Gamaliel, the teacher of St. Paul, was well versed in Greek literature; that this

37 Jewish Christians are referred to as the "sect of the Nazarenes" in Acts 24:5.

38 Baring-Gould M.A. 1874, xv.

39 See Acts 10:1.

40 Acts 10:14.

41 Acts 10:22–33.

42 Acts 10:28.

43 See Mark 2:7–9 for an example. The rabbinical interpretations of the Law are contained in the Jewish Talmud.

44 See Acts 10:44–48.

45 See Acts 10:34–35.

46 See Acts 10:45.

47 Acts 11:2.

48 Acts 11:25.

49 See Acts 9:26.

50 Acts 11:26.

51 See Acts 13:1.

52 Acts 13:2.

53 Marotta 2016.

54 See Acts 13:4.

55 It is often taught that Saul's name was changed to Paul during his conversion on the road to Damascus. A close examination of Acts reveals that this was not the case. Saul was still called Saul by the Lord (Acts 9:4). Luke, the author of Acts, clarifies in Acts 13:9 that he went by both Saul and Paul Wikipedia, Paul the Apostle 2018.

56 James the Just is the same as James, the brother of the Lord, and by tradition was the bishop of Jerusalem.

57 Judaizers were Jewish Christians who believed that the Law of Moses was still operative and that Christians must become Jews by being circumcised (males) and living the Law of Moses.

58 Acts 15:1.

59 Acts 15:2.

60 Marotta 2016.

61 See Galatians 2:2. Paul dates the visit to Jerusalem in Galatians 2 at seventeen years after his conversion, about 49 AD. Most, but not all, scholars agree that this was the same visit as the visit described in Acts 15:4 Marotta 2016.

62 See Acts 15:6.

63 It was James who rendered the final verdict; see Acts 15:19.

64 See Galatians 2:1.

65 See Galatians 2:3.

66 See Acts 15:5.

67 Acts 15:7.

68 See Acts 15:7–11.

69 See Acts 15:12.

70 See Acts 15:13–20.

71 Acts 15:23.

72 Sander, et al. 2017.

73 The pronouns "we" and "us" in various passages in Acts suggest that Luke, the author of Acts, may have been with Paul on these occasions; see Acts 16:10; 20:5; 21:1, 8; 27:1; 28:16.

74 Galatians 2:7–9.

75 Romans 11:13 (emphasis added).

76 2 Corinthians 12:11–12.

77 See Acts 14:14.

78 See Acts 13:3.

79 2 Peter 3:15.

80 His visit to Thessalonica occurred in his second mission. Paul and Barnabas had a falling out, and Silas was his companion for this mission.

81 See 1 Thessalonians 2:6.

82 Galatians 1:1.

83 See Luke 24:36.

84 Acts 22:17–18.

85 Judas Iscariot was replaced by Matthias in a formal selection and ordination (Acts 1:26).

86 1 Corinthians 9:1–5.

87 1 Timothy 2:7.

88 The story of Paul in Antioch is illustrative. He taught the Jews in their synagogue on a particular Sabbath. Some even believed. On the following Sabbath, the gentiles also gathered to the synagogue to hear the word. The Jews, the bulk of whom did not believe but had tolerated the teaching the week before, were now incensed with the multitude of gentiles in their synagogue. They refused to let Paul preach, claiming blasphemy. Paul said something profound to the Jews before turning to the gentiles: "It was necessary that the word of God should first have been spoken to you." Clearly, God had not rejected the Jews. They were still a favored people to God, and the gospel was open to them. It was necessary for Paul to give them the chance to accept or reject the message (Acts 13:14–15,42–48). This pattern was repeated many times. See Acts 17:2–5, 17; Acts 18:4,6, 7–8, 19.

89 1 Corinthians 1:11–12.

90 1 Corinthians 4:15–16.

91 Galatians 1:6–7.

92 Galatians 4:9–10.

93 Galatians 5:3.

94 Titus 1:10–11 (emphasis added).

95 Titus 3:9 (emphasis added).

96 Colossians 2:4, 16.

97 2 Corinthians 11:3–4.

98 2 Corinthians 11:13.

99 2 Corinthians 11:22–23.

100 See Acts 18:21–22. This visit to Jerusalem must have been short with a very limited audience because it did not cause the stir of his later visit, in which he was taken prisoner.

101 See Galatians 2:12.

102 See Galatians 2:13.

103 See Galatians 2:11.

104 See Galatians 2:14.

105 Galatians tells the story out of sequence. Galatians 2:4 is most likely speaking of the original Judaizers mentioned in Acts 15:1. Galatians 2:1–3 speaks of the journey to the council, and verses 7–10 tell of the council itself. Verses 11–14 are the later incident, about four years later, when Peter withdrew himself.

106 2 Peter 3:15–16.

107 The Clementine Homilies 1870, 2. (emphasis added).

108 See Acts 16:1.

109 See Acts 16:3.

110 See Acts 16:3.

111 See Galatians 4:9.

112 See Galatians 4:7.

113 See Romans 8:3.

114 See Ephesians 2:15.

115 See Romans 7:5, 9.

116 Colossians 2:14.

117 Galatians 3:24–29 (emphasis added).

118 1 Corinthians 7:18.

119 Romans 7:1.

120 1 Corinthians 9:20–21.

121 1 Corinthians 8:8–13.

122 Acts 18:10.

123 See Acts 18:18, 21.

124 See Numbers 6:5–18.

125 See Acts 21:21.

126 Acts 20:22.

127 See Acts 19:21.

128 See Acts 21:18.

129 Acts 21:20 (emphasis added).

130 See Acts 21:21.

131 See Acts 21:22.

132 See Acts 21:23–24.

133 See Acts 21:26–27.

134 Acts 24:17.

135 See Acts 21:27–32.

136 See Numbers 6:13–21.

137 Hebrews 10:4, 10.

138 Hebrews 9:23 (emphasis added).

139 Hebrews 11:4.

140 See Acts 20:7.

141 Cave 1840, 83.

142 Baring-Gould M.A. 1874, 18.
143 Canon 29; Synod of Laodicea 1900.
144 Arguably, vestments and features of Catholic ritual, including priestly robes, altars, ark of the covenant, relics, incense, and so on, originated from the Old Testament.
145 Chapman, Pope St. Clement I 1908.
146 Baring-Gould M.A. 1874, 34-35.
147 Baring-Gould M.A. 1874, 10-14.
148 Editors, Ebionite 2007.
149 Not to be confused with Paul's epistle to the Hebrews. The Gospel of the Hebrews was similar to Matthew, but without the Nativity.
150 Chapman, Clementines 1908.
151 Editors, Ebionite 2007.
152 Fox n.d.
153 Isaiah 28:13.

The Age of Heresy

The simplified map of our journey that is presented in figure 1 in chapter 1 shows a main "trunk" of "early Christianity." A simple image of a single trunk is appealing because it implies unspoiled Christian unity. But as we learned in the previous chapter, unity was fleeting, and by the close of the apostolic period divisions already existed. In addition to the gentile-Jew schism covered in the previous chapter, splinter groups emerged immediately in the gentile branch of the church. Very few, if any, of these exist today as denominations; however, they are worth studying because in them we can see the theological forces that shaped all of mainstream Christianity.

We will not make an exhaustive study of the splinter groups that existed during the first three centuries. Our goal is to review several offshoots and make observations about the general factors that led to splintering and the residual impact of this splintering on mainstream Christian doctrine. The fact that we are covering just a few early offshoots should not give us the impression that it was rare for splinter groups to form or that these were all of the sects that divided early Christianity. To give us a sense of just how diverse the Christian landscape became in the first three hundred years of its existence, let's fast-forward to the emergence of the Catholic Church under the authority of the Roman Empire. Constantine and subsequent emperors outlawed numerous sects that were considered heretical. Imperial edicts reveal just how widespread Christian sects had become. The edicts attempted to eliminate Donatists, Manicheans, Eunomians, Phontinians, Montanists, Priscillianists, Encratitans, Saccoforians,

Hydroparastantans, Macedonians, Pneumatomachi, Apotactites, Saccophori, Encratites, Apollinarians, Luciferians, Phrygians, Pelagians, Novatians, Sabbatians, Valentinians, Marcionites, Borborians, Messalians, Euchitans or Enthusiasts, Audians, Tascodrogitans, Paulianists, and Marcellians.[1] Another glimpse into the considerable number of Christian offshoots comes from a book written about fifty years after the momentous Council of Nicaea. In *Panarion*, which means "medicine chest"—an allusion to the book's purpose of being the antidote for poisons inflicted by heretics—a prominent bishop named Epiphanius described sixty Christian heretical groups![2]

From the earliest days of the church, there was every bit the propensity to splinter according to every imaginable doctrinal manipulation and interpretation. Had these "heretical" groups not been outlawed with severe punishments attached for practicing them, we can only suppose that early Christianity would have sprouted many thousands of denominations centuries before the explosion of denominations after the Protestant Reformation. In short, the appealing ideal of a singular trunk of early Christianity is a gross simplification.

Sexual Heresy

The story of the Israelites after they left Egypt illustrates the allure of pagan fertility deities. In the first months after leaving Egypt, the Israelites were repeatedly rescued from peril by miracles performed by Moses. The Israelites may have had a conceptual understanding of Jehovah, but they had a very real trust in their protector, Moses. Thus, when Moses left for an extended period, leaving the Israelites to languish in the desolate Sanai while he ventured into the mountains, they wavered. They hedged their bets and turned to the fertility god of their former Egyptian taskmasters. They insisted that Aaron make the symbol of that god, a golden calf, as a prerequisite to performing fertility rituals. It made sense in their twisted logic to practice fertility worship in the face of the imposing desert surrounding them. Moses returned to find the people naked and engaged in unrestrained reveling and dancing.[3] We can only suppose that their ritual included associated sexual acts.

This appeal to a fertility deity did not end on the plains of Sanai. The Israelites repeatedly introduced Baal, the Canaanite fertility god, into their worship.[4] Doing so didn't necessarily signal abandonment of their liberator, Jehovah. Like the people of so many other religions, the Israelites syncretized their worship of Jehovah with the worship of the god of the peoples they had partially displaced; this included Baal, the god that brought lifesaving rain to the arid lands they had conquered.[5] As in other fertility cults, Baal worship involved sexual ritual that included sacred prostitution.[6] The prophet Hosea gives us a sense of the nature of Baal worship: "they went to Baal-peor, and separated themselves unto that shame; and their abominations were according as they loved."[7]

The Greeks, and then the Romans by adoption, had their own variations of fertility deities. Among them was Dionysus, the Greek god of fertility.[8] The Greeks believed that

> under the influence of wine, one could feel possessed by a greater power. Unlike other gods, Dionysus was not merely a god to be worshipped, but he was also present within his followers; at those times, a man would possess supernatural powers and was able [to do] things he would not be able to do otherwise.[9]

The voluntary abandonment of personal will to the "possession" of Dionysus was central to the cult of Greek Dionysus and later to the cult of Roman Bacchus. These cults worshipped in the secrecy of the forests, where their members engaged in ritual orgies.[10]

Aphrodite was worshiped in her temples in part through sacral prostitutes called hierodule.[11] Lesser gods connected to fertility were worshipped as well, including Chloris, whom the Romans worshipped as Flora in an annual springtime festival called Floralia. This and other annual festivals were license for unrestrained promiscuity:

> The people themselves, whether forming part of the procession or acting in the role of onlookers, seem to have found these festivals occasions for the throwing to the winds of every shred of decorum and modesty. They joined in the singing, and indulged in promiscuity of the most flagrant description. The prostitutes of the town, in

particular, mixed with the crowds in a state of complete nudity.[12]

Given this context, into which gentile Christianity emerged, it is not surprising that sects developed within Christianity that, like the Israelites before them, syncretized sexual aspects of fertility worship with Christian worship. One example of this was in the Greek city of Pergamum—a city that rivaled any other Greek city in terms of sophistication, culture, and size. It was a center of learning with a library that rivaled Alexandria's. It had the full complement of Greek culture, with a gymnasium and multiple temples.[13] The gospel had taken root there even though, as recorded in Revelations, it was the "seat of Satan."[14] The Lord cautioned or, perhaps more appropriately, rebuked the members of the church in Pergamum for tolerating sects that were corrupting them.

One sect in Pergamum held the doctrine of Balaam, the worship of Baal described earlier, and another sect, called the Nicolaitans, was so corrupt that the Lord "hated" it.[15] It is rare indeed that God uses such strong language to describe divine displeasure. We get a glimpse into the extremely serious nature of the Nicolaitans from Irenaeus, an early church apologist who refuted the leading heresies of the second century in *Against Heresies*. He wrote that the Nicolaitans "lead lives of unrestrained indulgence. The character of these men is very plainly pointed out in the Apocalypse of John, [when they are represented] as teaching that it is a matter of indifference to practice adultery, and to eat things sacrificed to idols."[16] The Nicolaitan sect had infected Ephesus as well,[17] and its members were perhaps those Christians who Jude described as twisting the concept of grace into a license for sexual pleasure and perversion:

> For there are certain men crept in unawares, who were before of old ordained to this condemnation, ungodly men, turning the grace of our God into lasciviousness[18], and denying the only Lord God, and our Lord Jesus Christ. . . . Even as Sodom and Gomorrha, and the cities about them in like manner, giving themselves over to fornication, and going after strange flesh, are set forth for an example, suffering the vengeance of eternal fire. Likewise also these

filthy dreamers defile the flesh, . . . what they know naturally, as brute beasts, in those things they corrupt themselves. Woe unto them! for they have gone in the way of Cain, and ran greedily after the error of Balaam for reward. . . . These are spots in your feasts of charity, when they feast with you. . . . [They] walk after their own ungodly lusts. These be they who separate themselves, sensual, having not the Spirit.[19]

Whether the Nicolaitan sect specifically spread into Corinth is not clear; however, the church there had members engaging in the same behavior. Paul's teaching against the Law and his proclaiming of the efficacy of grace had evidently been twisted to an antinomian[20] extreme—some believed that Christians were free from all law:

St. Paul had proclaimed the emancipation of the Christian from the Law. They, having been Gentiles, had never been under the ceremonial Law of Moses. How then could they be set at liberty from it? The only freedom they could understand was freedom from the natural law written on the fleshy tables of their hearts by the same finger that had inscribed the Decalogue on the stones in Sinai.[21]

Paul's first epistle to the Corinthians was a direct response to reports he had received about them. Thus, he started a section of his epistle with, "It is reported commonly that there is fornication[22] among you."[23] Using the most egregious example of one "having" his father's wife, Paul reprimands the saints for not only allowing fornicators to continue in full fellowship in their midst but also glorying in their collective tolerance of it. He compares the fornicators to leaven—just a small amount affects the whole church: "Your glorying is not good. . . . Purge out therefore the old leaven. . . . Now I have written unto you not to keep company, if any man that is called a brother be a fornicator . . . with such an one no not to eat."[24] We don't know what Paul taught the Corinthians during his initial one and a half years with them. But he took pains in his first epistle to put boundaries around notions that they had latched onto, namely that "all things are lawful"[25] and that if a bodily function exists, it exists for a purpose, as in "meats are for the belly, and the belly for the meats"[26] and, by extension, sexual organs exist for sexual pleasure. Paul emphatically denounces the latter idea. The body is "not for fornication, but for the Lord; and the Lord for the body."[27] The body is a "temple of the Holy Ghost"; therefore, "Flee fornication."[28]

We see in Paul's epistle to the Romans the same attempt to clarify doctrines that were being twisted to justify sexual behavior. Paul wanted to emphasize the vastness and overwhelming impact of the grace afforded by Christ's suffering when he wrote, "The law entered, that the offence might abound. But where sin abounded, grace did much more abound."[29] Paul must have recognized how his words could be used to justify sin—the argument could be made that abundant sinning was a good thing because it called forth even greater grace. Thus, he immediately wrote, "Shall we continue in sin, that grace may abound? God forbid."[30]

The Nicolaitans and related sects are perhaps extreme examples of how libertine Greek and Roman cults and customs infected vulnerable members of the church. Nevertheless, they show us the pattern of syncretizing two different belief systems into one, and they illustrate the tendency for believers to twist guidance from leaders into the "truth" they want it to be.

Gnosticism

In chapter 2, we learned that Pythagoras, an early Greek philosopher, taught mystical ideas that harmonized spiritual beliefs related to the destiny of the soul with numbers and mathematics.[31] Pythagoras was viewed as a mortal imbued with the divine. Aristotle suggested that Pythagoras was superhuman—a wonder-worker with a golden thigh.[32] The combination of his mystical teachings and persona inspired many to join him in an exclusive community. Pythagoreanism proliferated with a strict code and defined ritual. While the Pythagorean way of life was known in general terms by successive philosophers including Plato and Aristotle, the details of its beliefs were secret, its many truths passed along verbally through "sayings" called *acusmata*.[33] Pythagoreanism is but one example of a pattern that has been repeated throughout ages—a wise or supernatural figure imparts secret knowledge to a committed group of initiates who use that knowledge to achieve fulfillment. Undoubtedly, examples can be found in most cultures and religions. Egyptians had the cult of Osiris and the Greeks the cult of Dionysus, and so on.

The concept of acquiring knowledge through perception and personal experience was given a name by the Greeks—*gnosis*, meaning "having knowledge." In a religious context, the term means to have mystical knowledge directly from the divine.[34] Jesus's teachings of receiving truth from the Holy Ghost was a type of gnosis.[35] Indeed, one of the early bishops of the church, Clement of Alexandria, spoke favorably of the "learned" or "gnostic" Christian.[36] However, by the second century, innovative intellectual Christians comingled the Christian doctrines of Christ and the Christian ideals of divine knowledge through the Holy Ghost with existing Greco-Roman mystery cults to form new Gnostic sects. By 180, writing in *Against Heresies,* Irenaeus lumped a number of Christian splinter groups together into one heretical bucket that he pejoratively called Gnostics. Gnosticism by its nature is mysterious and ill-defined;[37] however, scholars agree that the various Gnostic sects shared the following common notions that are based largely on Greek philosophy:[38]

1. All matter is evil, and the nonmaterial spirit realm is good.
2. There is an unknowable God, who gave rise to many lesser spirit beings called Aeons.
3. The creator of the (material) universe is not the supreme god but an inferior spirit.
4. Gnosticism does not deal with sin, only ignorance.
5. To achieve salvation, one needs to get in touch with secret knowledge.

In the following paragraphs we will explore in detail three Gnostic sects: Valentinianism, Marcionism, and Manichaeism.

Valentinianism

The most widespread Gnostic group was started in the early second century by a man named Valentinus (c. 100–c. 160). Much of what is known about him and his motives is gleaned from his opponents—not always the most reliable source for accurate history. Nevertheless, Valentinus was apparently a man of immense intellectual and oratorial talents. He became a Christian in Egypt and studied in Alexandria, one of the most advanced centers of Greek learning.[39] He undoubtedly studied Greek philosophy, especially Platonism, and was exposed to the example of Philo of Alexandria, who had proposed the doctrine of Logos by arguing that Jewish truth and Greek truth were merely two strands of the same universal fabric of truth.[40]

Evidently, Valentinus went to Rome in about 136, hoping to become bishop there. According to his opponents, when he failed to attain the bishopric, Valentinus started a new sect with heretical doctrine so well disguised that it drew large numbers in Rome and throughout all Christendom.[41] The heart of the doctrine echoed Paul's teaching of the war between the material sinful flesh and the immaterial good spirit:[42]

> He [Valentinus] taught that there were three kinds of people, the spiritual, psychical, and material; and that only those of a spiritual nature received the gnosis (knowledge) that allowed them to return to the divine Pleroma, while those of a psychic nature (ordinary Christians) would attain a lesser or uncertain form of salvation, and that those of a material nature were doomed to perish.[43]

To attain the spiritual ideal required special knowledge—knowledge that Valentinus asserted he had received from a man named Theudas, a member of Paul's inner circle.[44] Valentinus's followers believed that they had received from him secret wisdom that Paul had received during his visionary encounter with Jesus.[45] Irenaeus in *Against Heresies* described Valentinian Gnosticism as a complex cosmology in which the Aeons, emanations from the unknowable God Bythos, formed new Aeons including Christ and the Holy Ghost:

> When this world has been born from Sophia in consequence of her passion, two Aeons, Nous (mind) and Aletheia (truth), by command of the Father [Bythos], produce two new Aeons, Christ and the Holy Ghost; these restore order in the Pleroma, and in consequence all Aeons combine their best and most wonderful qualities to produce a new Aeon (Jesus, Logos, Soter, or Christ), the "First Fruits" whom they offer to the Father. And this celestial redeemer-Aeon now enters into a marriage with the fallen Aeon [Sophia]; they are the "bride and bridegroom."[46]

Whether Irenaeus accurately described Valentinianism is largely irrelevant because it is unlikely that the majority of people that flocked to Valentinianism were motivated by its complex cosmology. Rather, they were attracted to the piety of the movement and the egalitarian nature of its worship. Everyone was equal. There were no superior clergy. Members administered the sacraments. Women were seen as equal and participated in teaching and administering sacraments.[47] Later in this book, we will see how these characteristics attracted many to the congregational denominations of Protestantism.

Undoubtedly, some members progressed in learning to gain the special knowledge, or gnosis, imparted by the complex cosmology. But this was not what Valentinus taught the masses. His teaching used the scriptures of the time, including the Old Testament and circulating gospels. Valentinians considered themselves Christian, and although the intellectual elite of Rome, including Irenaeus and Tertullian, could see the destructive implications of the Valentinian heresy, the lay members of the church could hardly distinguish Valentinian believers from proto-Orthodox believers.[48]

Marcionism

Marcion of Sinope (85–160) was a contemporary of Valentinus. He was the son of the bishop of Sinope and according to Epiphanius's *Panarion* was excommunicated by his father for sexual misconduct—an accusation that has to be taken with some doubt given the span of hundreds of years between Marcion's life and the writing of *Panarion*. Whatever the cause of his excommunication in about 144, Marcion found himself outside the bishop-led church.

He believed that Paul was the true apostle and thus based his teachings solely on Paul. He found in Paul's writings the dualism of Gnosticism—the evil of material things and the perfect nature of spiritual things. Consequently, many of Marcion's beliefs mirrored those of the Gnostics.[49] He taught that there are two gods, the supreme perfect god and a lesser god called the Demiurge, the creator of the material world. Marcion concluded that Yahweh (Jehovah), as the creator of the material world and as the god of the warlike and destructive Israelites, was the Demiurge, also known as Lucifer. By extension, the Law of the Old Testament was the law of the Demiurge and was not to be followed by Christians, who were to follow the higher immaterial god whose teachings were revealed by Jesus.

Marcion's reasoning led him to denigrate Judaism and reject the Old Testament. Marcion believed that Jesus had been on earth as an apparition—an immaterial form of a mortal. He developed for his followers one of the first canons of scripture that was limited to selected writings of Paul and an edited version of the Gospel of Luke that excluded the story of a mortal birth. Like Valentinus, Marcion attracted a significant following that expanded greatly and represented a serious challenge for hundreds of years to what became the Orthodox Church.[50]

Marcion's teachings relative to Jesus's illusory mortality reveal the general conundrum Jesus posed to those holding Greek-centered beliefs. Jesus claimed to emanate from God and to be equal to the perfect God. Yet He was mortal and as such was material. In Greek philosophy, Jesus's materiality was incompatible with His claim of being a perfect God. Some Gnostic Christians like Marcion resolved the paradox by adopting a doctrine called Docetism, which viewed Jesus's mortality as an illusion.[51] Docetic teachings began to be circulated very early in the Christian church, as evidenced by John's counter-teachings:

> For many deceivers are entered into the world, who confess not that Jesus Christ is *come in the flesh*. This is a deceiver and an antichrist.[52]

Manichaeism and Augustine

We will explore one more Gnostic sect that gained significant presence in the western church and arguably had the most profound influence on both Catholic and Protestant doctrine—Manichaeism. The founder, Mani, was born in Iran in 216 to parents who belonged to a Jewish-Christian Gnostic sect called Elcesaites.[53] In addition to the religion of his parents, Mani's eastern birthplace exposed him to Eastern religions including Zoroastrianism and Buddhism. He claimed to have received revelations starting at age twelve that imparted to him new truths that filled in the gaps left by the previous prophets of the major religions, including Jesus.[54] The religion he started was a mix of Gnosticism, Christianity, and Eastern religions, and the ultimate goal of its followers was to become "an Elect" through the acquisition of light or knowledge. Although Manicheanism came from a very different part of the civilized world than the Gnostic sects we've already covered, its beliefs were Gnostic in nature. These beliefs included dualism of good and evil, with an immaterial perfect God and an opposing evil demigod who was the author of evil and the creator of all material things; freedom from accountability for sin because evil originated outside the sinner; rejection of the Old Testament; and acceptance of Paul's preeminence. Like other Gnostic sects, it taught "salvation" through the acquisition of knowledge and the possibility of becoming "the elect" of God.[55]

Mani was an effective missionary, and Manichaeism grew quickly in both the East and the West. Having been created from many world religions, it readily morphed in different places as it syncretized with local religious beliefs. Thus, as Manichaeism took root in the West at the close of the third century, it appeared to be a Christian religion, and adherents considered themselves Christian. It grew in size to compete directly with the proto-Orthodox church.[56]

In northern Africa, a young man and hopeful philosopher named Augustine (354–430) had lived a riotous life until he discovered Manicheism. In the sect he found piety, purpose, and direction. Unlike the simplistic Christianity of his mother, Manicheism was a religion that championed the attainment of knowledge. He converted and became an auditor, or "hearer," for almost a decade. The Roman emperor Theodosius I deemed the sect heretical and outlawed it in 382. Five years later, in 387, Augustine left the sect. He took great pains to separate himself from the Manicheans and became a vocal critic of them. In 392, he debated a Manichaean elder named Fortunatus in Augustine's home city of Hippo. Augustine recorded the two-day debate in a tract called *Disputation.* At the heart of the debate was the problem of evil and sin. If God is perfect and incorruptible and only creates that which is good, from where did evil and sin come? Fortunatus quoted Paul and argued according to the Gnostic doctrine of Manichaeism that evil substance existed independent of God and independent of man's soul. It was this substance that affected men's flesh and caused men to sin. Christ liberated men from the bondage of the evil substance.[57]

Augustine had been part of the Manichaean religion and knew that such a belief gave men license to sin in a resigned "devil made me do it" acceptance of sinful flesh. Also, Augustine knew Gnostic doctrine and pressed Fortunatus to admit that in Manichaean doctrine God was responsible for creating evil, for in the cosmology of the Gnostic the Demiurge was an Aeon emanating from the perfect God.

Augustine argued the orthodox position that men have free will to choose between moral options and that it is men's free will alone that results in sin. Evil does not exist outside of men's choices. Thus, men are culpable and need to repent to earn back the reward of God's pleasure. We can see Augustine's position in the following excerpt from the debate:

> He [God] did not make sin, and our voluntary sin is the only thing that is called evil . . . but that evils have their being by the voluntary sin of the soul, to which God gave free will. Which free will if God had not given, there could be no just penal judgment, nor merit of righteous conduct, nor divine instruction to repent of sins, nor the forgiveness of sins itself which God has bestowed upon us through our Lord Jesus Christ. . . . Hence also there is reward, because of our own will we do right. . . . Who doubts that reward is only bestowed upon him who does something of good will?[58]

Augustine's position at this point of his doctrinal journey was centered on free will—there is no sin other than the choice of man to act contrary to God's will, and the exercise of free will merits reward or punishment. If we fast-forward another decade, it is startling to see how far his philosophy evolved from the doctrinal positions he took against Fortunatus.

Augustine turned his philosophical interest to Platonism and attempted to formulate a doctrine of salvation compatible with both a philosophical framework and an orthodox framework.[59] He wrote prolifically, including authoring a series of thirteen books between 397 and 400 that he collectively called *Confessions*.[60] In them and in other works, we see Augustine come full circle, evolving from the firm anti-

Gnostic position he took in the debate with Fortunatus back to the essence of the Manichaeism he had studied during his formative years.[61]

His attempts to rationalize Paul's words in Romans[62] took him back toward Manichaeism's dualism and human incapability.[63] In Augustine's new thinking, Adam's sin—passed to all his offspring in the form of depraved sexual instinct—became the analog to Manichaeism's "evil substance." The conclusion was the same: mankind was incapable of doing good. Augustine's notion of free will evolved. Gone was his position that free will is the ability for man to choose between morally opposed choices. It was replaced with a belief that free will is "only he who accomplishes with delight the will of his master."[64]

Man's incapability to do good without divine intervention was reflected in a prayer Augustine included in the *Confessions*, "Grant what Thou commandest, and command what Thou dost desire."[65] Said another way, God would command according to His sovereign desire, but obedience to such a command was possible only if God granted or enabled a person to obey.

Confessions circulated throughout Christian cities, including Rome. There, an intellectually gifted British monk named Pelagius read it and was dismayed. He had arrived in Rome in about 380 and soon correlated the moral depravity he observed in Christian Rome with the residents' pervasive Gnostic beliefs, including those he found in Augustine's influential writings.[66] Therefore, he publicly criticized Augustine. Pelagius argued that man is capable of and accountable for acts of righteousness and therefore in a sense has "earned" God's reward. Ironically, in these arguments, Pelagius was taking essentially the same position that Augustine had taken in his debate decades earlier with Fortunatus.

With his criticisms, Pelagius had taken on the articulate and influential Augustine, and a contest of words ensued. The battle intensified when Pelagius, fleeing an invasion of Rome in 410, settled in Carthage in North Africa, close to Augustine's home in Hippo.[67] Pelagius's disciple Caelestius took the doctrine of free will to extremes that Pelagius most likely never taught or intended. Nevertheless, the movement grew under Pelagius's name, and Augustine wrote prolifically against "Pelagianism." In so doing, Augustine sharpened his own positions on original sin[68] and human depravity. He formulated other key doctrines that were logical extensions of these first doctrines and were like two sides of the same coin—the doctrines of the free gift of grace and of predestination. Augustine reasoned: If man is incapable of doing good, then God has to impart grace first to enable sinful man to even have faith or to do good, and nothing man does warrants God's gift of grace. What then prompts God to impart grace? God imparts the gift of grace to the elect that He has predestined to be saved according to His sovereign will. All that happens does so according to God's sovereign will; therefore, no willful act of man can initiate or deny God's ultimate gift of grace to that person.

Pelagianism was deemed heretical in the Council of Carthage in 418, but it did not die or even fade. Rather, the questions of grace, free will, and so on, reflected in the very public debates between the contemporaries Pelagius and Augustine have persisted to this day. Other capable theologians like Julian of Eclanum took up the cause of Pelagianism and moderated its doctrine.[69] In a formula called semi-Pelagianism, man and God interact synergistically, man through exercise of free will and God through grace to achieve salvation. Augustine continued to condemn even the moderate formula of semi-Pelagianism, writing late in his life in the year 428 his most definitive position on original sin, grace, and predestination in two works, *On the Predestination of the Saints* and *On the Gift of Perseverance*.[70]

The importance of Augustine's doctrines cannot be overstated. Original sin and the doctrines that flow from it, such as human depravity, predestination, irresistible grace, and infant baptism, found their way into Christian orthodoxy. Augustine's theology became the foundation of Protestantism. Given Augustine's immense influence on Christian doctrine, even suggesting that Manichaeism played a role in Augustine's theology is controversial. Clearly, it would be an uncomfortable notion to the majority of Christians if the foundational doctrines of salvation believed by Orthodox branches and Protestants alike derive from the Gnosticism of Manichaeism. Thus, Christian historians assert that Augustine's motive for leaving Manichaeism was due to doctrinal dissatisfaction, that his conversion to Orthodoxy was a clean and definitive break with Manichaeism, and that his doctrines reflected Augustine's own tortured journey through sin and subsequent redemption.[71] Nevertheless, Pelagius and Julian accused Augustine of Manichaeism during their respective battles, and scholars have agreed that Augustine was undoubtedly influenced by his former religion.[72]

Although today no denominations are ostensibly Gnostic, Augustine's doctrines are the foundation of Protestant Christianity, and the questions of evil, free will, sin, grace, and so on, are every bit as relevant today as they were in the time that Augustine engaged in protracted debates with Manichaeans and Pelagians. Later in this book, Augustine will factor into the narrative as we learn about the Protestant Reformation.

The Gift of Prophecy and the Montanists

In chapter 1, we read Paul's words, "And he gave some, apostles; and some, prophets; and some, evangelists; and some, pastors and teachers . . . for the edifying of the body of Christ: Till we all come in the unity of the faith."[73] The twelve apostles were specifically commissioned by Jesus and had clear authority from Him. What about the next group Paul listed—the prophets? Clearly, they were important or Paul wouldn't have mentioned them. Paul's inclusion of prophets echoes the sentiment from the Old Testament, "Surely the Lord GOD will do nothing, but he revealeth his secret unto his servants the prophets."[74] The gospels affirmed the validity of prophets, repeatedly pointing out the fulfillment of prophecy in Jesus's life.[75] However, the church also recognized the reality of false prophets. Jesus warned, "Beware of false prophets, which come to you in sheep's clothing, but inwardly they are ravening wolves,"[76] and He prophesied that "many false prophets shall rise, and shall deceive many."[77] John warned the early church that false prophets were already among them: "Beloved, believe not every spirit, but try the spirits whether they are of God: because many false prophets are gone out into the world."[78]

Belief in prophets and prophecy has always had an inherent dilemma—prophecy is a legitimate channel through which God communicates, but prophecy can be easily counterfeited. Thus, the belief in prophecy leads to challenging questions: Were prophets set apart and commissioned like the twelve apostles? Were prophets always ecclesiastical leaders, and were all clergy also prophets? What was the ecclesiastical role of a prophet? How were saints to recognize true prophets? Did new prophecy supersede former canon? Were prophecies of doctrine applicable to the whole church? Questions like these were not new with Christianity. They were just as relevant to the Jews and ancient Israel.

Our de facto acceptance of a fixed set of books known as "the prophets" in our Old Testament obscures the reality that the people of the Old Testament had little to no evidence that a person claiming to be a prophet was indeed a true prophet. With few exceptions, prophets appeared on the scene, from Moses onward, with no particular credentials, no graduation certificate, and no particular clerical authorization.[79] They were their own witness to their calling. Moses, of course, was very convincing with his staff and his demonstration of divine power, starting with the plagues in Egypt, but what about the prophets that appeared on the scene with just words and no miracles? How were the Israelites supposed to know whether they were true prophets or self-promoting imposters?

Through Moses, Jehovah established the expectation that Israel would listen to and follow the prophet:

> I will raise them up a Prophet from among their brethren, like unto thee, and will put my words in his mouth; and he shall speak unto them all that I shall command him. And it shall come to pass, that whosoever will not hearken unto my words which he shall speak in my name, I will require it of him.[80]

But then Jehovah dealt with the practical problem. How were the people supposed to know who was a true prophet? He provided a litmus test of sorts:

> But the prophet, which shall presume to speak a word in my name, which I have not commanded him to speak, or that shall speak in the name of other gods, even that prophet shall die. And if thou say in thine heart, How shall we know the word which the LORD hath not spoken? When a prophet speaketh in the name of the LORD, if the thing follow not, nor come to pass, that is the thing which the LORD hath not spoken, but the prophet hath spoken it presumptuously: thou shalt not be afraid of him.[81]

The litmus test was simple. If the prophesied event happened, the prophet was not a fake. Such a test was inherently retrospective—based on evidence that perhaps may not be clear for decades or even centuries. Thus, believers in prophets have always faced the problem of deciphering the true from the false prophet in *real time.*

Consider the prophet Jeremiah. He was a Levite from a relatively small town outside of Jerusalem—in other words, he was not from a distinguished background. The Lord directly called and commissioned him with no witnesses except himself. Jeremiah's prophecies were dire and unwelcome by the princes and kings of his time. Undoubtedly, he seemed crazy as he traveled from city to city wearing a yoke on his shoulders as a symbol of the impending bondage to the Babylonians. Importantly, Jeremiah was just one of many purported prophets circulating in the area. "Prophets" were already allied with the princes as advisers.[82] Jeremiah's encounter with a self-professing prophet named Hananiah illustrates the dilemma faced by Israelites:

> Hananiah the son of Azur the prophet, which was of Gibeon, spake unto me in the house of the Lord, in the presence of the priests and of all the people, saying, Thus speaketh the Lord of hosts, the God of Israel, saying, I have broken the yoke of the king of Babylon. Within two full years will I bring again into this place all the vessels of the Lord's house, that Nebuchadnezzar king of Babylon took away from this place, and carried them to Babylon: And I will bring again to this place Jeconiah the son of Jehoiakim king of Judah, with all the captives of Judah, that went into Babylon, saith the Lord: for I will break the yoke of the king of Babylon. . . . Then Hananiah the prophet took the yoke from off the prophet Jeremiah's neck, and brake it. And Hananiah spake in the presence of all the people, saying, Thus saith the Lord; Even so will I break the yoke of Nebuchadnezzar king of Babylon from the neck of all nations within the space of two full years. *And the prophet Jeremiah went his way.*[83]

Even Jeremiah took Hananiah's prophecy at face value and "went his way." Hananiah's prophecy was great news compared to the dismal prophesies that Jeremiah had been sharing. It's understandable that Jeremiah himself wanted to believe they were true. The scriptures record Jeremiah saying, "Amen: the Lord do so,"[84] and then walking away from the encounter. But Hananiah was a false prophet. That is clear to us because we can judge him with the benefit of history. He was wrong. But it became clear only at the time because the Lord revealed it to Jeremiah and sent him back for another round with Hananiah.

> Go and tell Hananiah, saying, Thus saith the Lord; Thou hast broken the yokes of wood; but thou shalt make for them yokes of iron. . . . Then said the prophet Jeremiah unto Hananiah the prophet, Hear now, Hananiah; The Lord hath not sent thee; but thou makest this people to trust in a lie.[85]

How were the Jews of Jeremiah's time to know that Jeremiah and not Hananiah was the true prophet? Surely, it was nearly impossible for them to distinguish in real time. Similarly, when false prophets appeared in the early Christian church, they found a ready and gullible audience.

The early church accepted prophets[86] and recognized prophecy as a legitimate gift of the Spirit,[87] or *charism*,[88] leaving Christians vulnerable to false prophets. Sometime in the middle of the second century, a new convert named Montanus and two of his female colleagues, Priscilla and Maximillia, began prophesying.[89] Their movement became known as the New Prophecy and ultimately led to deep divisions within the church. At times, these three prophets from the rural region of Phrygia in Asia Minor spoke as if possessed by the Lord, saying things such as "I am God" to precede their declarations. Some of their predictions and sayings were in intelligible language; however, they commonly prophesied in a frenzied state, uttering incomprehensible things.[90] Eusebius, an early church historian, describes Montanus's prophesying:

> And he [Montanus] became beside himself, and being suddenly in a sort of frenzy and ecstasy, he raved, and began to babble and utter strange things, prophesying in a manner contrary to the constant custom of the Church handed down by tradition from the beginning.[91]

The Montanists were perhaps even more pious than average Christians. They observed a strict moral code and practiced regular fasts. They believed the second coming was imminent and prophesied that the location of the New Jerusalem was in Phrygia. However, many who joined the sect were arguably not motivated by a unique doctrine of the millennium but by the sense that Montanism had recaptured the Pentecostal vitality of the early church with its manifestations of the Holy Spirit. Even Tertullian, a leading theologian and staunch critic of heretics, joined the Montanists for a time.[92] The new movement met with rigorous opposition from the proto-Orthodox branch of the church. Perhaps some of this was less about doctrine and more about the new clergy that Montanus appointed as salaried preachers.[93] In spite of intense opposition, Montanism persisted for centuries and remained an identifiable sect until at least 428 when emperor Theodosius II included Montanists, Priscillians, and Phrygians in the list of banned heretical sects.[94]

We will see in this book that the Montanists' rise and fall was not the last time that prophets and prophecy were central to the formation of a new Christian group. The fundamental question that Israelites and then the early Christians faced of how to distinguish a true prophet would be central to the rise of existing denominations, including The Church of Jesus Christ of Latter-day Saints, Christian Scientists, and Iglesia Ni Cristo, among others. The role of prophecy as an ongoing gift of the Spirit is a defining characteristic of the growing Pentecostal movement covered in a later chapter.

The Donatists and Meletians

For the first three hundred years of its existence, Christianity was illegal according to Roman law. Christians did not honor the Roman gods by participating in feasts or making obligatory sacrifices. Christians were held in suspicion and were accused of secrecy and black magic. However, what persecution existed was locally perpetrated.[95] For the most part, Christians were left to worship as they pleased until the reign of Emperor Decian, who rose to power in 249. The empire was in the midst of crisis. Emperor Alexander Severus had been murdered by his own troops in 235, and the fighting between generals threatened to tear the empire apart.[96] The general Decius seized power in 249 just as a pandemic swept through the empire.[97] By some accounts, five thousand people a day were dying with hemorrhagic symptoms.[98]

Many, including the new emperor Decius, believed that the gods were punishing Rome for tolerating the evil Christian religion growing within it. Decius launched a program to restore the state by restoring the rightful place of the pagan state religion. Consequently, in early 250, he issued an edict requiring all the inhabitants of the empire to sacrifice to the pagan gods of Rome before the local magistrate and to receive a certificate of compliance.[99] Those who refused to sacrifice were imprisoned, tortured, or executed. Christians across the empire responded with varying degrees of resistance. Some refused to sacrifice, including the leading theologian Origen, who suffered torture. The bishops of Rome and Antioch also refused and were imprisoned and died as martyrs.[100] Other Christians rationalized the pagan sacrifice, concluding that it was a necessary evil to continue practicing their faith. The bishop of Smyrna sacrificed and encouraged others to do to the same. Still others left the church and renounced their Christian faith.

This "apostacy" was particularly acute in Carthage in northern Africa.[101] The varying response to the persecutions sowed discord. How were Christians to view each other as they dealt with the persecutions with different degrees of valor? Martyrs were worthy of reverence but were dead. Others had compromised and were still alive. Others had abandoned the faith altogether.

The intense persecutions lasted until 260, when the new emperor, Gallienus, ended the persecution and ushered in forty years of relative religious tolerance and peace for the Christians. During this time, Christianity flourished, and Christians rose to positions of prominence in Rome's government and military. When Diocletian became emperor in 284, he did not immediately resume persecutions; however, he was deeply committed to Rome's traditional religion and was an activist leader, looking to reform all aspects of Roman life. He surrounded himself with elite who vilified Christians, such as the Roman philosopher Porphyry, who wrote a fifteen-volume work entitled *Against the Christians* in about 290.[102] With such criticism of Christianity by trusted advisors, Diocletian became increasingly suspicious of the Christians.

Diocletian established the tetrarchy, a governing model with two senior co-emperors with the title of Augustus and two junior emperors with the title of Caesar, one Caesar serving each Augustus.[103] Diocletian was the first Augustus and appointed a fellow general named Maximian as the second Augustus. Constantius and Galerius were named as Caesars to each Augustus, respectively.[104] In 299, the junior emperor Galerius crushed the Persian armies in one of the most decisive victories in a centuries-old conflict with the Persians.[105] Diocletian joined Galerius in Antioch to congratulate him and to consider the affairs of the eastern empire. As was the custom in the ancient Roman religion, the two men along with their senior military leaders consulted with a haruspex, a person trained to divine the future from the entrails of sacrificed animals. Evidently, among the military leaders were Christians who were undoubtedly very uncomfortable participating in the pagan ritual. The Christians repeatedly made the sign of the cross during the ritual, and the haruspex blamed his failure to divine the future on the Christians who were present. Diocletian was enraged and commanded that all members of the military perform sacrifices or face discharge.[106] Thus began a new wave of persecution. It started with the eviction of Christians from the army but soon extended to Christians in government.

The junior emperor Galerius urged Diocletian to be even more hard on the Christians and advocated their extermination. Diocletian resisted for a time, but in late 302 he and Galerius again argued about the treatment of Christians. This time, he was willing to supplicate the God Apollo to settle their disagreement. When the messenger returned with the news that Apollo was unable to speak due to the Christians in the empire, Diocletian relented to Galerius. He issued an edict in early 303 to extinguish Christianity and to exterminate unyielding believers if necessary. The edict ordered the destruction of sanctuaries, scriptures, and liturgical books and prohibited Christian assembly to worship.[107] However, there was uneven enforcement of the edict. Constantius, the junior tetrarch under Diocletian in the west, generally did not enforce the edict, while Galerius enforced it throughout the east with zeal, including burning Christians alive.[108] In northern Africa, the Roman governor was satisfied when Christians handed over their scriptures,[109] a seemingly modest gesture that many Christians performed as a practical compromise to avoid extermination. As in the Decian persecutions forty years earlier, there were also those who refused to comply with the edict, considering any compromise to be a sin. These devout were ready to be martyred for the cause, and they scornfully labeled those who "handed over" the holy things as *traditors*—the Latin origin of our modern word *traitor*.[110] The sentiment of the purists was that bishops who succumbed to pressure from the empire had lost the grace of the Holy Spirit and were no longer in a position to consecrate new clergy or administer the sacraments.[111]

In 305, Diocletian and his fellow Augustus, Maximian, "retired," or abdicated. Constantius and Galerius were both promoted to Augustus, but soon thereafter Constantius died, ushering in a violent jostling for the positions of the tetrarchy. Constantius's son Constantine (280–337) was initially not a tetrarch, but his father's loyal troops declared him Augustus, a senior emperor, in 306.[112] Constantine, the son of the more tolerant Constantius, had a favorable view of Christians. Perhaps it was his father's example or his own revulsion at seeing the barbaric treatment of Christians while serving under Diocletian.[113] Upon gaining power, he immediately eased the persecutions of Christians. However, outside his western realm the opposite occurred. Persecution intensified in 308.[114] The years that followed were bloody as Constantine consolidated power through a series of civil wars. He forced the suicide of one claimant to the tetrarchy in 310. As he approached Rome with his armies in 312 to overthrow the self-proclaimed emperor in the heart of Rome, he had a vision in which he saw a cross with a legend that read "by this sign conquer." He had his army place the symbol of the cross on their shields prior to commencing a battle on Milvian Bridge. Constantine's armies defeated the "usurper" emperor Maxentius, a victory that Constantine attributed to the Christian god represented in the symbol.[115] From that point forward, he demonstrated a deep conviction that it was his duty to protect Christianity from enemies without and within the church.[116]

Constantine and Licinius, the remaining co-emperor, issued the Edict of Milan in 313, ensuring tolerance for Christians and restoring their previously confiscated property and titles.[117] Clergy could resume their positions, conduct worship services, and administer sacraments. However, instead of ushering in a period of peace within the church, the new toleration exposed the bitter division that had grown between those who had succumbed to persecution (the traditors) and those who had not (the purists). In northern Africa, the dispute between the traditors and the purists had led to two different splinter groups, one in the east and one in the west.

Meletians

In the eastern diocese and province of Aegyptus of northern Africa, a sharp dispute arose between the bishop of the city Lycopolis of the province of Thebais and the bishop of the capital city of the diocese and province in Alexandria.[118] Peter, the bishop of Alexandria, had fled during the Diocletian persecutions, which rendered him a traditor. In contrast, Meletius, the bishop of Lycopolis, courageously did not flee, which made him a hero of the purists. Meletius saw it as his duty and right to fill the clerical vacancies created by fleeing clergy. He ordained clergy, including bishops, throughout the area.[119] In 306, during a respite from persecution, Peter of Alexandria returned and after seeing what Meletius had done deposed him as bishop. However, the Roman persecution soon resumed, leaving the matter unresolved. In the renewed persecution, the Romans sent Meletius to do forced labor in Palestine—a sentence that only increased his prestige among the purists. The persecutions ceased in 311, and Meletius returned to his city. He ignored Peter of Alexandria's ruling given years before and refused to abdicate his office. His refusal openly challenged the authority of Peter. Meletius argued that Peter, the bishop of a distant city within a different Roman province, had no authority over him as bishop of Lycopolis. The conflict escalated and Peter excommunicated Meletius in 308.[120] Again, Meletius ignored Peter.

The Meletian conflict revealed that church hierarchy, that is, some bishops exercising authority over others, was not universally acknowledged at the time. The Meletian controversy divided the church in the eastern side of northern Africa for nearly two decades. It would not be resolved until its disruption ballooned to the point that Constantine mandated its resolution in the First Council of Nicaea in 325.

Donatists

A similar saga played out on the western side of northern Africa. In the capital city Carthage of the western diocese of Africae, a new bishop named Caecilian was consecrated by a traditor bishop in 311.[121] Some seventy nontraditor bishops under the leadership of the bishop of Numidia came to Carthage to consecrate an untainted bishop. They rejected Caecilian because of his consecration by a traditor and appointed Majorinus.[122] Unlike the Meletian disagreement that festered for decades, Constantine engaged very early to settle this dispute. Constantine's response to the unrest in Carthage suggests that he had only one purpose—to unify his new faith:

> Constantine's chief concern was that a divided church would offend the Christian God and so bring divine vengeance upon the Roman Empire and Constantine himself. Schism, in Constantine's view, was inspired by Satan.[123]

He gave no indication at that time that he had picked sides, but he did insist that the division be resolved. He first tasked the bishop of Rome to attempt a resolution. In response, the bishop held a commission that came to nothing.[124] The purists challenged the validity of the Roman bishop's authority over affairs in Carthage.[125] The failure prompted Constantine to call his first council as emperor. The council, held in Arles in 314, ruled in favor of Caecilian and against the purists. However, the purists had become even more organized. They called themselves Donatists, after the name of their new leader, Donatus, and they refused to accept the ruling.[126] When the council failed to quell the division, Constantine became personally involved and also ruled in favor of Caecilian. As before, the Donatists refused to accept his ruling, leading Constantine to issue a harsh edict in 316 or 317 threatening death to Donatists.[127] He later softened his position, issuing an edict of toleration in 321.[128] But the sect increasingly proved divisive to the church and disruptive to the stability of the empire.

The Donatists considered Rome to be the scriptural mammon and therefore opposed its interference with the church.[129] They also revered martyrdom to a point of obsession. In time, the line between Donatism and another sect that had developed in Carthage called the

Circumcellions blurred.[130] The Circumcellions came from roving bands of Berber Christians in northern Africa. Arguably, they were the hippies of their time. They practiced free love and were concerned with social issues—property rights, debt, slavery, and so on. But they also regarded martyrdom as the ultimate Christian virtue and thus sought to bring about their own martyrdom by civil disobedience and acts of violence against the military or other armed travelers.[131] In their reverence of martyrdom, they aligned with the Donatists, and although the two groups were truly different sects with different origins and doctrine, in the eyes of the state they were often conflated as a common nuisance. In 347, the Donatists were exiled to Gaul, but the sect survived into the seventh century.[132] The Donatists considered themselves the preservers of purity and unlike their proto-Orthodox fellow Christians rejected the companionship of the state.

As we close this chapter, it should be abundantly clear that there wasn't a homogeneous trunk of "early Christianity." By the time Constantine adopted Christianity, there were many significant divisions within it, including all those that we've covered in this chapter. Perhaps it's a new perspective for us to see that in order to pursue his passionate belief in Christian unity, Constantine had to effectively pick a winner from among options. We don't know why he decided to sanction the bishop-led proto-Orthodox branch of the church. Perhaps it was numerically larger. Perhaps the bishop of Rome was close by and persuasive. Perhaps it was pragmatism or even divine inspiration. Regardless, we should not overlook the fact that Constantine's adoption of the bishop-led branch and his rejection of Valentinianism, Marcionism, Manichaeism, Montanism, Donatism, and others legitimized what we know today as the Orthodox trunk of early Christianity.

Notes

---

[1] West, Imperial Laws and Edicts 2008.

[2] Wikipedia, Epiphanius of Salamis 2018.

[3] See Exodus 32:19–25.

[4] Examples are plentiful. A partial list includes Numbers 25:3; Judges 2:13; 1 Kings 16:31; 1 Kings 22:53.

[5] Bratcher 2016.

[6] Bratcher 2016.

[7] Hosea 9:10.

[8] Adopted by the Romans as Bacchus.

[9] Dionysus 2018.

[10] Editors, Dionysus 2018.

[11] Wikipedia, Nicolaism 2018.

[12] G. R. Scott 1941, 166.

[13] Editors, Pergamum 2013.

[14] Revelations 2:13. It is called Pergamos in Revelations.

[15] Revelations 2:14.

[16] Wikipedia, Nicolaism 2018.

[17] See Revelations 2:6.

[18] Lustful, sexual, and lewd.

[19] Jude 4, 7–8, 10, 11–12, 18–19.

[20] The doctrine that moral law is of no use or obligation because faith alone is necessary to salvation.

[21] Baring-Gould M.A. 1874, 303.

[22] Sexual relations between unmarried persons.

[23] 1 Corinthians 5:1.

[24] 1 Corinthians 5:6–7, 11.

[25] 1 Corinthians 6:12.

[26] 1 Corinthians 6:13.

[27] 1 Corinthians 6:13.

[28] 1 Corinthians 6:18–19.

[29] Romans 5:20.

[30] Romans 6:1.

[31] Thesleff 2013.

[32] Huffman 2014.

[33] Huffman 2014.

[34] Wikipedia, Gnosticism 2018.

[35] See John 14:26.

[36] Wikipedia, Gnosticism 2018.

[37] In 1945, a collection of Gnostic texts was found in the Egyptian town of Nag Hammadi. These documents have shed invaluable light on the doctrines of Gnosticism.

[38] Wikipedia, Gnosticism 2018.

[39] Wikipedia, Valentinus (Gnostic) 2018.

[40] Editors, Philo Judaeus 2017.

[41] Wikipedia, Valentinus (Gnostic) 2018.

[42] See Galatians 5:16–25.

[43] Wikipedia, Valentinus (Gnostic) 2018.

[44] Wikipedia, Valentinus (Gnostic) 2018.

[45] Wikipedia, Valentinus (Gnostic) 2018.

[46] Wikipedia, Valentinianism 2018.

[47] Wikipedia, Valentinianism 2018.

[48] Wikipedia, Valentinianism 2018.

[49] Scholars debate whether Marcionism was Gnostic because, unlike Valentinianism, Marcion did not profess secret knowledge; however, the sect he founded indisputably included many Gnostic concepts Wikipedia, Marcionism 2018.

[50] Wikipedia, Marcion of Sinope 2018.

[51] Editors, Docetism 2014.

[52] 2 John 4:7.

[53] Wikipedia, Manichaeism 2018.

[54] Wikipedia, Manichaeism 2018.

[55] Augustinians Australia n.d.

[56] Wikipedia, Manichaeism 2018.

[57] Wikisource Contributors 2010.

[58] Wikisource Contributors 2010.

[59] BeDuhn 2013.

[60] Augustinians Australia n.d.

[61] BeDuhn 2013.

[62] Including Romans 5:13–19 and 7:14.

[63] Bonaiuti and La Piana 1917.

[64] Bonaiuti and La Piana 1917.

[65] Augustinians Australia n.d.

[66] Wikipedia, Pelagius 2018.

[67] Wikipedia, Pelagius 2018.

[68] "Original sin is then described as an infection which propagates itself from father to son through the act of generation, which being an act of organic trouble caused by the sin, is a sin itself and determines the transmission ipso facto of the sin to the new creature." Bonaiuti and La Piana 1917.

[69] Wikipedia, Julian of Eclanum 2018.

[70] Augustinians Australia n.d.

[71] See for example Schaff's *History of the Church* P. Schaff 1997.

[72] As examples, see the following references: Ort 2006., BeDuhn 2013., Bonaiuti and La Piana 1917.

[73] Ephesians 4:3, 11–14.

[74] Amos 3:7.

[75] For examples, see Matt 3:3; 4:14; 8:17; 12:17.

[76] Matthew 7:15.

[77] Matthew 24:11.

[78] 1 John 4:1.

[79] In some cases, prophet leaders received authority from another recognized leader. Joshua was Moses's protégé. Elijah passed his mantle to Elisha. Samuel was raised in the temple by Eli the priest.

[80] Deuteronomy 18:18–19.

[81] Deuteronomy 18:20–22.

[82] See Jeremiah 26:11.

[83] Jeremiah 28:1–4, 10–11 (emphasis added).

[84] Jeremiah 28:6.

[85] Jeremiah 28:13, 15.

[86] A notable example is Agabus. Acts records that prophets came up to Antioch from Jerusalem; among them was Agabus, who prophesied that "there should be a great dearth throughout all the world" (Acts 11:27–28). Agabus and his prophetic daughters later visited Paul and prophesied about his impending bondage at the hands of the Jews (Acts 21:9–10).

[87] See 1 Corinthians 12:10.

[88] The Greek word *charisma* means "favor" or "gift." Thus, in a Christian context, it refers to a gift of the Holy Spirit for the good of the church.

[89] Wikipedia, Montanism 2018.

[90] Stewart-Sykes 1999.

[91] Wikipedia, Montanism 2018.

[92] Wikipedia, Montanism 2018.

[93] Stewart-Sykes 1999.

[94] West, Imperial Laws and Letters Involving Religion, AD 395-431 2008.

[95] For example, Nero executed Christians for their alleged involvement in the fire of Rome in 64 AD. But the executions were limited to Rome Wikipedia, Diocletianic Persecution 2018.

[96] Lumen Learning n.d.

[97] The pandemic is called the Plague of Cyprian because it was particularly bad in northern Africa where bishop Cyprian ministered in Carthage.

[98] Wikipedia, Plague of Cyprian 2018.

[99] Wikipedia, Decius 2018.

[100] Wikipedia, Diocletianic Persecution 2018.

[101] Wikipedia, Diocletianic Persecution 2018.

[102] Wikipedia, Diocletianic Persecution 2018.

[103] Lumen Learning n.d.

[104] Lumen Learning n.d.

[105] Wikipedia, Roman-Persian Wars 2018.

[106] Wikipedia, Diocletianic Persecution 2018.

[107] Wikipedia, Diocletianic Persecution 2018.

[108] Wikipedia, Diocletianic Persecution 2018.

[109] Wikipedia, Donatism 2018.

[110] *Traditor* in Latin derives from *trader*, meaning "to hand over."

[111] Wikipedia, Donatism 2018.

[112] Lumen Learning n.d.

[113] Matthews and Nicol 2018.

[114] Meletius of Lycopolis 2006.

[115] Roman Emperor Constantine's conversion to Christianity 2018.

[116] Scholars debate whether Constantine's conversion to Christianity was for political purposes; however, there is evidence of a sincere conversion. Perhaps, the best understanding of how he felt about his own calling was manifest in his final resting place. He built and was entombed in a church dedicated to the apostles, the Church

of the Apostles in Constantinople (modern-day Istanbul). Constantine considered himself one of them Matthews and Nicol 2018.

[117] West, Imperial Laws and Edicts 2008.

[118] The Roman Empire was divided into dioceses, and these were subdivided into provinces.

[119] Meletius of Lycopolis 2006.

[120] Meletius of Lycopolis 2006.

[121] Editors, Donatist 1998.

[122] Editors, Donatist 1998.

[123] Matthews and Nicol 2018.

[124] Wikipedia, Donatism 2018.

[125] The entire incident illustrates the reality that the bishops of northern Africa did not recognize that the bishop of Rome had authority over them.

[126] Editors, Donatist 1998.

[127] This edict is referenced by other edicts, but is lost. West, Imperial Laws and Edicts 2008.

[128] West, Imperial Laws and Edicts 2008.

[129] Editors, Donatist 1998.

[130] Editors, Donatist 1998.

[131] Wikipedia, Circumcellions 2018.

[132] Editors, Donatist 1998.

Chapter 6

Orthodox Schisms

The two prior chapters made it abundantly clear that there were many splinter groups in the three centuries between Jesus's death and the rise of Constantine. We now know that figure 1, first presented in chapter 1 is a gross simplification of reality. Nevertheless, it helps us focus in on the bishop-led faction of Christianity, what is often called the proto-Orthodox church. After Constantine's endorsement, the proto-Orthodox church became the Orthodox Church and became so dominant that it is useful to equate it to *the* trunk of early Christianity.

However, we should state up front that there are divergent opinions, disagreements really, about whether the proto-Orthodox church was itself a homogenous church. The differing views are consequential. Did orthodoxy always exist as the Catholics believe? Do the characteristics of orthodoxy, including hierarchy, doctrine, and forms of worship, date back to the apostolic period or, better yet, back to Jesus? Our answers to these questions inform our understanding of the three Orthodox schisms we will cover in this chapter. Therefore, even though this book is intended to be denominationally neutral, it must take a position on these questions.

Catholics believe that the Catholic Church existed from the very beginning of Christianity. The church was "universal" or, in Greek, *katholikos* from the beginning. In Catholics' view, Peter established the bishopric of Rome to be the "first among equals" and to be the "father" of all bishops, or in Greek, the *papa*.[1] Catholics believe that the episcopal[2] hierarchy within the church, with some bishops having authority over others, was established and preserved by the authority granted by Peter to the bishop of Rome. The church was homogenous and "catholic," preserved from dissent and heresy by the recognized authority of the pope—the vicar of Christ and supreme pontiff. According to the Catholic view, the schismatic groups we've covered thus far had once accepted papal authority but then rebelled against it as heretics.

Secular and Protestant historians disagree with the Catholic view and generally describe the postapostolic church as a dispersed collection of independent bishop-led churches with a hierarchy that *evolved* over time. This book adopts this perspective because it is most consistent with known characteristics of the early church and with the events associated with Constantine and the ecumenical councils that followed the adoption of Christianity as the state religion. Constantine's authoritative engagement to resolve divisions would make little sense in the context of a preexisting universal church with an established centralized authority and hierarchy. Conversely, his actions do make sense if we recognize that when Constantine adopted Christianity, authority was decentralized and dispersed and the proto-Orthodox church was far from homogenous. One implication of this perspective is that schismatics did not leave anything and did not rebel against anyone. Rather, schismatics could assert the validity of their own church, or group of churches in a shared communion, as the preservation of original Christianity.

The New Testament has scant details relative to Jesus's intent for governing the faith he started. Paul placed Timothy and Titus in the office of bishop.[3] The apocrypha suggest that Peter and other apostles also appointed bishops.[4] Indeed, by the second century, bishops presided over dozens of Christian congregations throughout the Roman Empire.[5]

When the apostles died, authority was spread to the many hands of the apostles' appointees, the bishops. Importantly, the bishops and their congregations were loyal to and appealed to the authority of the evangelist who converted them. We'll see an example of this later in the chapter relative to the church in Smyrna continuing to practice Jewish customs according to the teaching of the apostle John. Other evidence of such loyalty can be found in Paul's epistle to the Corinthians, which admonished the saints for their split loyalty to their respective evangelists.[6] An excerpt quoted previously in chapter 4 points out the likelihood that the evangelizing apostles Paul and Peter established separate congregations in Rome:

> St. Peter's successors in the see of Rome have been a matter of perplexity. It has impressed itself on ecclesiastical students that Linus and Cletus ruled simultaneously. I have little doubt it was so. The Judaizing Church was strong in Rome. Probably each of the two communities had its bishop set over it, one by Paul, the other by Peter.[7]

Like any movement or organization, Christianity was not launched with a fully matured organizational hierarchy and bylaws. It was forced to mature as it faced challenges: the apostles died, first-generation bishops passed away, doctrinal deviations and disagreements emerged, people of different cultures syncretized their native rituals with their new faith, and so on. As a pragmatic matter, there arose the administrative need for a higher authority to appoint and censure bishops and to resolve disputes among equal bishops.

By the second century, the custom developed to yield authority to peer bishops generally in accordance to the Roman administrative map. Rome divided its empire into dioceses, and these in turn were subdivided into about 120 provinces.[8] Each province had a metropolis or capital (one province's metropolis in each diocese doubled as the capital of the diocese). It was thus natural that the bishop located in the province's metropolis emerged as the senior bishop to whom the other bishops in the province looked for senior authority.[9] These senior bishops came to be called metropolitans and in later times came to be known as archbishops; however, prior to Constantine's rule, they were simply known as "first bishops," "heads of provinces," or "chief bishops."[10] We'll use the term *metropolitan* in this chapter for convenience to describe the pre-Constantine church, even though the term was applied later. The bishop of Rome was a metropolitan over his own province, as were the bishops of Alexandria, Antioch, Caesarea, Ephesus, Corinth, Lyon, and so on.[11]

Each metropolitan was equal in authority to and independent from other metropolitans. In other words, each province was its own church, also called a *see*.[12] However, metropolitans communicated with and generally supported each other's decisions in a relationship that can be described as a "mutual consociation."[13] For example, if a province held a synod to consider a doctrinal question, the conclusions were published to the other provinces although the decisions were not binding upon them. The decision within one province to excommunicate a member or depose clergy was generally honored by metropolitans in other provinces.

Doctrines and practices differed between metropolitan churches. Consider the following examples: Many eastern provinces continued to observe the seventh-day Sabbath. Scriptures differed between provinces—churches in the east rejected the *Apocalypse* of John (Revelations) and its doctrine of a one-thousand-year millennium, churches in the west rejected Paul's epistle to the *Hebrews*, and many churches used books later deemed noncanonical, such as the *Shepherd of Hermas*.[14] In Rome, members fasted on Saturdays in remembrance of the Sabbath, while in Milan they did not.[15] In many western churches, Christians fasted on Wednesdays and Fridays and partook of the sacrament of the Lord's Supper during each fast as well as on Sunday, the Lord's day. The Alexandrian church, in contrast, took the sacrament of the Lord's Supper only on the Lord's day.[16] Worship services differed significantly between provinces prior to Constantine—and these differences were later formalized in widely different liturgical rites.[17] In short, it was entirely acceptable for there to be differences between provinces for nonessential elements of the church. But, of course, the judgment of what was nonessential and what was an inviolable truth was determined by the opinion of the beholder.

An example of these differences in the second century is illustrative. We learned in chapter 4 that the early apostolic church was effectively split between Jewish Christians and gentile Christians. Those with strong ties to Judaism, mainly in Jerusalem and Asia Minor, continued many practices dear to Judaism, including the seventh-day Sabbath and the celebration of Easter as part of the Jewish Passover, according to the Jewish calendar. These churches celebrated Easter on the fourteenth day of the Jewish month of Nisan.[18] Thus, Easter fell on a different day of the week each year. Other senior bishops, including the metropolitan of Rome, strongly condemned this practice, believing that the purpose of Easter as the celebration of the resurrection required that it be celebrated on Lord's day, or Sunday.

The notable metropolitan bishop Polycarp of Smyrna, who by tradition was appointed by John the Apostle, visited Rome sometime before 153 and discussed the issue of Easter with the metropolitan bishop of Rome.[19] Neither was able to convince the other, a clear indication of their independence. Each church continued to celebrate Easter in very different ways. Fast-forward to the close of the second century. Bishop Victor of Rome took up the issue, believing that it was a matter of orthodoxy. In about 193, he asked his metropolitan counterparts to hold local synods within their respective provinces to rule on the matter.[20] Polycrates, the metropolitan of Ephesus,[21] presided over the province's local synod, which decided to continue the tradition of celebrating Easter according to the Jewish calendar and the tradition established by John the Apostle. He communicated the decision to Bishop Victor with the boldness that comes from independence.[22] For a time, Victor cut off Polycrates and the churches in Asia Minor from communion with the Roman see.

The disagreement over Easter persisted until the Nicaean Council, which ruled in favor of the practice in Rome and in the western churches.[23] The incident illustrates that, prior to Constantine, as long as the metropolitan bishop sanctioned a doctrine or practice it was not heretical within his jurisdiction. Metropolitan bishops could essentially agree to disagree with each other and thus preserve a form of Christian-wide unity by tolerating independence.

Over time, there emerged the same pragmatic need for superior authority over metropolitans as there had been over provincial bishops. Again, a natural solution was to align authority with the Roman administrative map, in this case with the dioceses.[24] As before with provincial bishops, metropolitans within a diocese gradually yielded authority to their peer metropolitan located in the capital city of the diocese. In time, these diocese-level metropolitan bishops were given the deferential title of primate or patriarch to distinguish them from their metropolitan peers.[25] The timing for this evolution is unclear, but this change was at the heart of the Meletian conflict we learned about in the last chapter. Alexandria was the capital city of the diocese in which Lycopolis was located. Peter, the bishop of Alexandria, attempted to assert authority over Meletius, the bishop of Lycopolis. Recall that Peter deposed Meletius and rejected all the clergy Meletius had ordained. Meletius objected and challenged Peter to prove the presumption that bishops in the capital city of a diocese wielded superior authority. It became a matter dealt with in the First Council of Nicaea, as we will explore later in this chapter.

Decentralized authority exercised primarily at the level of the province was incompatible with Constantine's ambition for unity and with his quest for personal consolidated power. As organized, the church had no mechanism other than consultation, persuasion, and voluntary agreement to resolve differences between metropolitans. Thus, it was a sea change in the operation of the church when Constantine imposed his imperial authority on the church to resolve the dispute between purists and Donatists in the Council of Arles in 314. The Donatist controversy was minor compared to the substance of later councils, but the precedent set in the Council of Arles was profound. No longer could disagreeing metropolitans or patriarchs agree to disagree. No longer could they stick to their positions as a matter of principle. The Council of Arles established that an ecumenical[26] council had not only the right but also the obligation to make a binding decision applicable to all bishops. Soft power, politicking, and compromise were instantly required of the assembled bishops.

The Council of Arles started Constantine down the path of personal engagement in church affairs and set the precedent for state influence over the church. A decade later, Constantine again turned to the ecumenical council as a means for resolving disputes roiling the eastern churches.

Nicaea

From the earliest days of the apostolic church, the doctrine of the Godhead—the doctrines related to Jesus's divinity and His relationship to the Father and the Holy Ghost—confounded the church. Jesus had said things that on the surface were difficult to reconcile.

Early in His ministry He taught and demonstrated His separateness from the Father. Many had been eyewitnesses to Jesus's baptism and had heard the voice of the Father proclaim, "This is my beloved son, in whom I am well pleased."[27] They had seen Jesus pray to the Father on multiple occasions.[28] They had heard Jesus speak of His complete submission to the guidance of the Father.[29] But to the consternation of all, He proclaimed late in His ministry that "I and my Father are one."[30] In the intimate setting of the Last Supper, He acknowledged that throughout His ministry He had taught the doctrine of the Father obscurely: "These things have I spoken unto you in proverbs: but the time cometh, when I shall no more speak unto you in proverbs, but I shall shew you plainly of the Father."[31] But what followed continued to reflect the hard-to-reconcile doctrine of the Godhead. He taught, "He that hath seen me hath seen the Father . . . I am in the Father, and the Father in me . . . the words that I speak unto you I speak not of myself: but the Father that dwelleth in me, he doeth the works. Believe me that I am in the Father, and the Father in me."[32] These words expressing total unity with the Father were followed by an apparent contradiction: "my Father is greater than I."[33] Naturally, early Christians sought to reconcile apparently confusing or contradictory truths relative to Jesus and the Father through various formulas shaped by their respective preexisting beliefs.

Jewish Christians were devout monotheists who had been instructed that beside Jehovah, there was no other God. The message was clear in scriptures such as "Hear, O Israel: The LORD our God is one LORD"[34] and "I am the first, and I am the last; and beside me there is no God."[35] Jewish Christians could readily accept Jesus as the Messiah—or in Greek, as the Christ. It had always been their belief that the Messiah would be sent by God. But to equate Jesus to God created all sorts of challenges requiring creative formulas.

Converted gentile Christians believed firmly that Christian truth and Greek philosophy were two manifestations of the same truth. Philosophy was not a corrupting influence to be shunned but rather another lens through which to see the same eternal truths found in Hebrew scripture. Truth could not contradict truth, and so with optimism borne of a deep commitment to Greek philosophy, Christian theologians committed themselves to integrate the two worlds of belief in pursuit of a more complete understanding of God. Consequently, Christian theologians framed the doctrines of the Godhead and of Jesus in Greek terms and concepts.[36] Admittedly, to most of us, these concepts are hair-splitting minutiae—suitable only for philosophers—and they may seem generally irrelevant to us. However, subtle differences in the finest points of these concepts led to major schisms in the church.

Theologians wrestled to define the doctrine of the Godhead and of Christ that met many preestablished "givens": from the Jews—there is one and only one God; from the Greeks—God is immaterial, uncreated, and incomprehensible. The constraints had obvious conflicts if Jesus were to be taken as divine and equal to the Father: If two beings were divine and equal, then Christians faced the abhorrent prospect of polytheism. The mortality of Jesus suggested that He could not be of the same substance as that of the Father and thus could not be equal to the Father. An immaterial and perfect God could not as a matter of principle suffer, but Jesus suffered. The substance of God could not be created, yet Jesus was begotten. And so it went with theologians facing truly challenging conundrums.

And yet, in spite of the paradoxes and conundrums arising from the application of Greek philosophy to the Godhead, the Greek philosophical framework was never challenged. It's as if the theologians accepted that the Greeks had established the puzzle pieces of truth and it was a matter of arranging them in the correct way. Theologians were truly creative as they assembled the puzzle pieces into doctrinal formulas. One example of this was highlighted in chapter 5. Marcion and other Gnostics skirted the problem of Jesus's mortality by teaching the doctrine of Docetism—that Jesus was not mortal at all but instead was a mirage.[37] Others proposed that Jesus was a man infused by God or , in other words, a dualistic being.[38] In another formula called modalism or Monarchianism, the same God manifested Himself in three different forms or modes.[39] Jewish Christians in particular believed in adoptionism—Jesus was a mortal but was "adopted" by God at some momentous event such as at His baptism and ultimately received of God's glory after fulfilling the necessary elements of His mission on earth.[40] In a somewhat similar formula known as subordinationism, Jesus was begotten before the earth was created and was God's agent in the creation.

Subordinationism spread widely in the fourth century due to the teaching of a priest named Arius (c. 256–c. 336). So effective was

Arius's promotion of subordinationism that *Arianism* became synonymous with *subordinationism*. Arius, although just a priest, began accusing his superior, the bishop of Alexandria, of teaching a form of modalism. Arius insisted that because Jesus was begotten by the Father He was not of the same substance as the Father:

> If the Father begat the Son, he that was begotten had a beginning of existence: and from this it is evident, that there was a time when the Son was not. It therefore necessarily follows, that he [the Son] had his substance from nothing.[41]

Importantly, Arius continued to frame his doctrine in Greek philosophy. In doing so, he reached patently heretical conclusions, such as "the Son can have no direct knowledge of the Father."[42]

Alexander, one of the most influential and important bishops of the time as the metropolitan of Alexandria, took a hard position against Arius. In 321, he organized a synod that excommunicated Arius.[43] Later events suggest that a talented young deacon serving under Alexander named Athanasius[44] was one of the primary intellectual and motivating forces against Arius.[45]

Arius sought refuge in the eastern churches of Palestine near Antioch, where he had studied under Lucian. Many other prominent church leaders in the east and Asia Minor had also studied under Lucian and were sympathetic to or outright supportive of Arius. One such bishop was Eusebius, the metropolitan bishop of Nicomedia. Given Nicomedia's importance as the then-capital of the eastern empire, Eusebius was one of the most powerful bishops.[46] He called a council within his own province to consider the matter, with the result that Arius was accepted into communion with the Syriac church.[47] This was a momentous departure from the long-held precedent that metropolitans respected the judgments made by other metropolitans. Nicomedia essentially snubbed Alexandria.

With the support of his proponents, in 323 Arius published a poem in Greek that cleverly encapsulated his doctrine of the Godhead. The poem, called the Thalia, was an innovation in the theological war of words.[48] Like wind dispersing the seeds of a dandelion, the poem carried Arius's ideas quickly and widely as laborers and travelers repeated the poem among all classes of people.[49] To counteract the Thalia, Alexander published an anti-Arian confession of faith and sent it throughout Christendom, asking fellow bishops to sign it.[50] Alexander's request effectively forced bishops to pick sides in a doctrinal battle.

Unlike the other doctrinal differences in the formative centuries of the church in which metropolitans had the leeway to agree to disagree, this division blossomed just as Constantine consolidated power. A year after the Thalia first emerged, Constantine executed his co-emperor of the east, Licinius, in 324.[51] It is not entirely clear how Constantine became aware of the doctrinal dispute in the church. Perhaps, as he settled into Licinius's former palace in Nicomedia, Eusebius, the bishop there and a distant family relative of Constantine, brought the issue to Constantine's attention. What is clear is that Constantine did not initially understand the fundamental importance of the controversy. He simply wished it to be resolved for the purpose of unity. He sent Bishop Ossius of Cordova, Spain, to resolve what he considered to be "petty arguments over unintelligible minutiae."[52] When Ossius's efforts at reconciliation failed, Constantine opted for the tactic he had used with the Donatists a decade earlier. He called a churchwide council to be held in Nicaea, a community close to Nicomedia, in 325. Although eighteen hundred bishops were invited, about three hundred attended.[53] This relatively small group of bishops held the fate of orthodoxy in their hands.

Constantine may not have fully appreciated the magnitude of his mandate. He was effectively requiring the assembled bishops to determine by debate, persuasion, and compromise the very nature of the Godhead. The majority of the assembled bishops in the council ultimately agreed upon a Trinitarian[54] formula for God and issued the Nicene Creed, which became the bedrock doctrine for more than 90 percent of Christians to this day:[55]

> We believe in *one* God, the Father Almighty, Maker of all things visible and invisible. And in one Lord Jesus Christ, the Son of God, begotten of the Father (the only-begotten; that is, *of the essence of the Father*, God of God), Light of Light, very God of very God, begotten, *not made, being of one substance* with the Father; . . . Who for us men and for our

salvation came down [from heaven] and was incarnate and was made man. He suffered and the third day he rose again, and ascended into heaven(. . . (*But those who say: "There was a time when he was not;" and "He was not before he was made;" and* "He was made out of nothing," or *"He is of another substance" or "essence,"* or *"The Son of God is created,"* or *"changeable,"* or "alterable"— *they are condemned* by the holy catholic and apostolic Church.)[56]

In a creed issued years later and attributed to Athanasius, the doctrine was further clarified:

we worship *one* God in Trinity and Trinity in Unity. Neither confounding the *Persons*, nor dividing the *Substance*. For there is one *Person* of the Father, another of the Son, and another of the Holy Ghost. But the Godhead of the Father, of the Son and of the Holy Ghost is all One, the Glory Equal, the Majesty Co-Eternal. Such as the Father is, such is the Son, and such is the Holy Ghost. The Father Uncreate, the Son Uncreate, and the Holy Ghost Uncreate. The Father Incomprehensible, the Son Incomprehensible, and the Holy Ghost Incomprehensible. The Father Eternal, the Son Eternal, and the Holy Ghost Eternal and yet they are not Three Eternals but One Eternal. As also there are not Three Uncreated, nor Three Incomprehensibles, but One Uncreated, and One Incomprehensible. So likewise the Father is Almighty, the Son Almighty, and the Holy Ghost Almighty. And yet they are not Three Almighties but One Almighty. So the Father is God, the Son is God, and the Holy Ghost is God. And yet they are not Three Gods, but One God.[57]

In the words of these creeds, we can see a rebuttal of the various formulas that were circulating, including Arianism, as well as the intent to satisfy the requirement of monotheism. Jesus was not made. There was never a time when He did not exist. He is of the same *ousía*, or substance, as the Father—they are *homoousion*. They are incomprehensible to mortals by the very definition of their *ousía*.[58] The three of the Trinity are distinct persons, or *hypostases*.[59]

The Christian historian Phillip Schaff summarizes the influences and lead-up to the creeds issued from Nicaea and other councils:

> The church was now in possession of the ancient philosophy and learning of the Roman empire, and applied them to the unfolding and vindication of the Christian truth. . . . The ecumenical councils were the open battlefields, upon which the victory of orthodoxy was decided. The doctrinal decrees of these councils contain the results of the most profound discussions respecting the Trinity and the person of Christ; and the Church to this day has not gone essentially beyond those decisions. . . . The truth is, Christianity itself is the highest philosophy, as faith is the highest reason; and she makes successive philosophies, as well as the arts and the sciences, tributary to herself, on the Pauline principle that "all things are hers."[60]

It is impossible to overstate the importance of Nicaea. The collective weight of the bishops, along with an imperial mandate, cemented the creed and set the expectation that with the authority and mandate of the state, the church was to be unified and universal, or to use Greek terminology, to be *katholikos.*

Arguably, the Catholic Church originated at Nicaea. After additional schisms occurred (covered later in this chapter), the term *Roman* had to be added to distinguish the Roman Catholic Church from the other Orthodox branches that stemmed from the same Catholic trunk. Today, the Roman Catholic Church is by far the largest Christian denomination. It has roughly 1.3 billion members.[61] Nearly 50 percent of Christians in the world are Roman Catholic.

The Assyrian Church of the East

While the Nicene Creed established a foundation for defining the Godhead, there was still much that it left undefined. The ambiguity left by Nicaea was filled with new formulas requiring yet more councils. In the century after Nicaea, debates continued to rage about the nature of Christ. The figurative tide of support flowed between doctrinal positions based in part on the talent and hierarchical position of those proposing the doctrine.

The Nicene Creed settled the matter of whether Jesus is a separate person from the Father and whether He is of the same substance as the Father, but Greek-inspired concepts still left a conundrum. The mortal Jesus could not be a perfect God; conversely, the godly Jesus could not suffer and die like a mortal. After a devout monk named Nestorius (c. 386–c. 451) was appointed bishop, metropolitan, and patriarch of Constantinople[62] in 428, he used his new position of influence to promote a doctrine called *dyophysitism*, meaning that Jesus was of two natures.[63] Nestorius objected to common references that suggested that God suffered, that God died on the cross, or even that Mary was *Theotokos*, meaning "god-bearer." He believed that all these phrases were inconsistent with an omnipotent God. Nestorius argued that Jesus must have had two natures, one entirely divine and one distinctly human. It was Jesus's human nature that allowed Him to undergo intense mortal suffering.[64] The doctrine didn't explain the mystery of how two natures coexisted in a single person, but it addressed the philosophical riddle of Jesus's concurrent godliness and humanity. Nestorius's doctrine reignited the simmering Christological debate. Additionally, Nestorius's resulting prominence provoked the rivalry between two of the leading Christian patriarchates—Constantinople and Alexandria.

Cyril was the metropolitan and patriarch of Alexandria. He was particularly attuned to the rivalry between the ascendant Constantinople and Alexandria. His uncle had preceded him as patriarch of Alexandria, and Cyril had accompanied his uncle to a synod with the intent to depose John Chrysostom, the patriarch of Constantinople.[65] Cyril challenged Nestorius with as much energy as his uncle had exerted against John Chrysostom. He opposed Nestorius through a series of letters and published tracts.[66] In response, Nestorius appealed to the emperor Theodosius, who called a council. In the ecumenical Council of Ephesus in 431, Cyril outmaneuvered Nestorius by starting the council before any of the pro-Nestorian bishops arrived.[67] Not surprisingly, the council rejected Nestorianism and banished Nestorius.[68]

The council's decision led many eastern churches in today's Iraq and Iran, where Nestorianism had taken hold, to form their own communion of churches called the Assyrian Church of the East.[69] It should be noted that the Assyrian split was arguably also motivated in part by geopolitics. The Persians had successfully broken away from the Roman Empire and had reached a tenuous peace in 387.[70] Consequently, the Christians in Persian territory were suspected of disloyalty. As long as they belonged to the Catholic Church, which was subject to the Roman state, Christians in Persia were suspected of allegiance to Rome. Therefore, there was a growing necessity for these churches to demonstrate their independence from the Roman *Empire* by breaking away from the Roman *pope*. The doctrinal ruling from Ephesus, including the underhanded maneuvering used by Cyril to obtain it, proved to be the catalyst for the first major schism of the Catholic Church.

The Assyrian Church of the East had many zealous missionaries and spread eastward through Central and East Asia, including China. For a time, it flourished.[71] Today, the Assyrian Church still exists but has less than one million members.[72]

The Oriental Orthodox Church

The Council of Ephesus was a victory for Cyril. The bishop of the rival patriarchate of Constantinople had been humiliated and banished. The doctrine of dyophysitism, the dual nature of Christ, had been rejected. However, while the council had decided what Christ was not, it had not established an alternative. It was perhaps natural that Cyril would consider himself the "champion of truth" after his successful personal role in the council; likewise, he considered the council's ruling as vindication of his anti-dyophysitism position.

Cyril wrote prolifically, teaching that "although Jesus is fully God and fully man—'There is only one physis (nature) in Christ.'"[73] This may seem to us nontheologians as splitting hairs. If Cyril did not reject the idea that Jesus was fully God and fully man, how is that different from Nestorius's dyophysitism with dual natures? Again, the nuances of Greek concepts governed the debate. The Greek concept of *physis*, translated as "nature," had a distinct meaning apart from the synonyms we might commonly use for the word *nature*, such as "characteristics" or "personality." By arguing for one physis in Jesus, Cyril proposed a doctrine that within the Greek-philosophical context was distinctly opposed to dyophysitism.

After Cyril's death in 444, a priest named Eutyches (c. 380–c. 456) advanced Cyril's doctrine to an extreme—he argued that Jesus's single nature was divine and not human. Eutyches's position was truly monophysitism. Eutyches's extreme position led to accusations of heresy, soon followed by a local synod in Constantinople that excommunicated him in 447. In an echo of the rivalry between patriarchates, the Alexandrian patriarch, Bishop Dioscursus, successfully petitioned the emperor to call a council, over which he presided. The Second Council of Ephesus was held in 449, and Dioscursus ensured a favorable selection of bishops that reinstated Eutyches and excommunicated his accusers from Constantinople.[74] Thus began another tug-of-war within the church involving councils, counter-councils, excommunications, and counter-excommunications. Bishop Leo of Rome called the council the "robber council" and refused to accept its findings.[75] Competing emperors even leveraged the enmity between opposing doctrinal camps for political purposes.

The newly ascended emperor Marcian convened another council in 451 in Chalcedon, within greater Constantinople. This council rejected Eutyches and monophysitism and issued the following canon:

> We confess that one and the same Christ, Lord, and only-begotten Son, is to be acknowledged in *two natures* without confusion, change, division, or separation. The distinction between natures was never abolished by their union, but rather the character proper to each of the two natures was preserved as they came together.[76]

Additionally, the council deposed Bishop Dioscursus of Alexandria, the senior bishop of all the eastern churches, ostensibly for his role in the "robber council" of Ephesus.[77]

The ruling of the Council of Chalcedon attempted to tread a fine line. It clearly rejected monophysitism, but it attempted to do so without reaffirming the dyophysitism that had been rejected two decades earlier. Nevertheless, many metropolitan churches in northern Africa, Syria, and Turkey that had fully accepted Cyril's teachings viewed the Chalcedonian canon as a swing back to dyophysitism and Nestorianism. Undoubtedly, the heavy-handed treatment of the bishop of Alexandria also was a factor in their discontent with the outcome of the council. Rather than accept the council's rulings, six like-minded patriarchates split to form an independent communion called the Oriental Orthodox Church.[78] In forming a communion without a central leader, the six churches retained the historical pattern of independent churches at the level of the diocese—an arrangement called *autocephalous*, meaning "led by independent patriarchs."

There were important but subtle differences between Cyril's and Eutyches's respective teaching of "one" nature. Eutyches's "one" was emphatic. Jesus's single nature was divine. Cyril's "one" was nuanced. Jesus's single nature had both divine and human characteristics. The Greeks had the vocabulary to distinguish between these two subtle variations of "oneness." The Greek masculine prefix *mono*, meaning "one," was definitive and unambiguous. The feminine prefix *mia*, also meaning "one," was less emphatic and more nuanced.[79] The Oriental Orthodox Church considers itself miaphysite, as opposed to monophysite, which it considers to be a heresy. [80]

Today, approximately eighty-six million people belong to the communion of the Oriental Orthodox Church, which includes the autocephalous churches: the Coptic Orthodox Church of Alexandria, the Syriac Orthodox Church of Antioch, the Armenian Apostolic Church, the Ethiopian Orthodox Tewahedo Church, the Eritrean Orthodox Tewahedo Church, and the Malankara Orthodox Syrian Church in India.[81] The largest of these is the Ethiopian Orthodox Tewahedo Church, with close to fifty million members, followed by the Coptic Orthodox Church, with just over fifteen million.[82]

As we conclude this section, consider just how divisive the doctrine of the Godhead was. We've seen that after the establishment of the Catholic "trunk" of Christianity, it was the single most divisive factor for the first several centuries, resulting in two major schisms.

The Eastern Orthodox Church

While the Council of Nicaea is best known for settling the question of the Godhead, two of its canons addressed issues of episcopal authority and planted the seeds for what would ultimately be the largest schism prior to the Protestant Reformation of the sixteenth century.

In the previous chapter, we learned about the dispute between Meletius of Lycopolis and Bishop Peter of Alexandria—a consequence of the Diocletian persecutions in the eastern diocese of northern Africa. When Constantine addressed the divisiveness of the Donatists in the western diocese of northern Africa by calling the Council of Arles in 314, he evidently did not know about the similar Meletian dispute or did not consider it of sufficient gravity to warrant his attention. But the Arian controversy that blossomed in Alexandria exposed a companion dispute in the same diocese—the Meletian controversy. The spread of Arianism forced the obvious question, Could bishops adopt Arianism without regard to the patriarch of Alexandria? We recall that Meletius refused to abdicate his office as bishop after being deposed and excommunicated by Peter of Alexandria. Meletius's key question was, By what precedent did the metropolitan bishop in Alexandria claim superior authority as a patriarch over metropolitan bishops of neighboring provinces in which Meletius was bishop? Thus, the Arian controversy and the Meletian dispute became intertwined and viewed together as a threat to the unity of the empire and of the faith. Constantine mandated that both be resolved in the Council of Nicaea.

Canon 6 issued by the council has been one of the most debated canons of the Orthodox Church. Its interpreted meaning depends entirely upon which of the two views presented at the beginning of this chapter one holds. It reads:

> Let the ancient customs in Egypt, Libya and Pentapolis[83] prevail, that the Bishop of Alexandria have jurisdiction in all these, since the like is customary for the Bishop of Rome also. Likewise in Antioch and the other provinces, let the Churches retain their privileges. And this is to be universally understood, that if any one be made bishop without the consent of the Metropolitan, the great Synod has declared that such a man ought not to be a bishop.[84]

In a short time after Nicaea, the bishop of Rome asserted, as Catholics do now, that this canon established the bishoprics of Rome, Antioch, and Alexandria as the only patriarchates in the church and that the authority of the Alexandrian bishop existed because of the consent and authority of the bishop of Rome. Or said another way, the Roman bishop is the supreme pontiff, or father of all.[85] The patriarchs of Antioch and Alexandria understood that they were second only to Rome in importance and authority. The *Catholic Encyclopedia* states:

> The oldest canon law [Nicaea] admitted only three bishops as having what later ages called patriarchal rights—the Bishops of Rome, Alexandria, and Antioch. The successor of St. Peter as a matter of course held the highest place and combined in his own person all dignities. He was not only bishop, but metropolitan, primate, and patriarch; Metropolitan of the Roman Province, Primate of Italy, and first of the patriarchs.[86]

However, the matter was far from settled. Other metropolitans understood the canon differently. To them, including the patriarchs that left to form the Assyrian Orthodox Church and the Oriental Orthodox Church, the canon did not establish just three patriarchates and did not establish Rome as superior over others. Rather, the canon addressed the specific challenge in Alexandria. Meletius had questioned the precedent that gave Alexandria authority over his bishopric. In response, the council had no scriptural justification. What it could offer was "ancient custom," established over time, and it used the examples of the dioceses centered in Rome and Antioch in which metropolitans had ceded authority to their respective patriarchs without controversy. Far from establishing centralized authority, the canon enshrined the "ancient custom" of the metropolitans at the provincial level governing independent churches.[87] Note again the wording in light of this opposing view: "Let the ancient customs . . . prevail . . . since the like is *customary* for the Bishop of Rome, Antioch, *and the other provinces* . . . let the *Churches retain their privileges* . . . if any one be made bishop without the consent of the *Metropolitan.*"[88] Importantly, the Nicaean canon documents that the organizational hierarchy by which some bishops govern others is a matter of "custom."

John Calvin accepted that the canon established the pattern of superior authority of patriarchs, but he rejected the supremacy of Rome. He wrote,

> In regard to the antiquity of the primacy of the Roman See, there is nothing in favor of its establishment more ancient than the decree of the Council of Nice, by which the first

place among the Patriarchs is assigned to the Bishop of Rome, and he is enjoined to take care of the suburban churches. While the Council, in dividing between him and the other Patriarchs, assigns the proper limits of each, it certainly does not appoint him head of all, but only one of the chief.[89]

Canon 7 from the council also illustrates the evolving nature of episcopal hierarchy. Jerusalem, which was the birthplace of Christianity and the headquarters of the primitive church during apostolic times, was not the capital of a Roman province or of a diocese, leaving this important place without honor. Canon 7 gave Jerusalem an honorary position:

> Since custom and ancient tradition have prevailed that the Bishop of Ælia [i.e., Jerusalem] should be honoured, let him, saving its due dignity to the Metropolis, have the next place of honour.[90]

Here again, leaders of the church interpreted the canon in multiple ways. Some saw it as limited in scope to the local province, establishing the bishop of Jerusalem as the second in authority behind the metropolitan located in the metropolis city Caesarea. Others, particularly later bishops of Jerusalem, interpreted the canon to mean that the bishop of Jerusalem was a patriarchate with authority over provincial bishops.[91]

Just a few years after the Council of Nicaea, Constantine added an additional complication to the already disputed church hierarchy when he founded Constantinople[92] in 330 as the "new Rome"—a Christian city free from Roman paganism. Constantinople was to be the capital of the entire empire and capital of its diocese. It was natural that the city's clergy would expect to have the authority of a metropolitan and of a patriarch. The Council of Constantinople, called in 381 by Theodosius I, the emperor of the east, first established Constantinople as a patriarchate second only to Rome. The third canon of the council reads,

> The Bishop of Constantinople, however, shall have the prerogative of honour after the Bishop of Rome because Constantinople is New Rome.[93]

This council was arguably not an ecumenical council. Indeed, two of the most powerful figures in the church, the bishops of Alexandria and Rome, did not attend. These bishops rejected the council's canon relative to Constantinople, arguing that it violated the Nicene canon. Constantinople's relative place of authority remained controversial for decades and was an undertone to the doctrinal controversies of the time. You may recall the rivalry between Nestorius of Constantinople and Cyril of Alexandria—it occurred during this period of controversy.

The weight of the emperor's authority prevailed over the bishop of Rome's objections such that the Council of Chalcedon held in 451 ratified the decision issued seventy years earlier by the Council of Constantinople, making Constantinople a patriarchate second only to Rome.[94] As the centuries passed, the other principle patriarchates of the east, including Alexandria, Antioch, and Jerusalem, faded as the Muslims conquered those lands. This left the patriarchate of Constantinople as the supreme authority in the eastern churches.[95]

Rome and Constantinople became rivals. Tensions flared between them many times over the centuries, reflecting the many political, theological, and cultural struggles between east and west. The fight for authority erupted in 1054. Leo IX, the bishop of Rome, who by then was broadly considered "papa," or pope, had taken several provocative actions in the preceding years to assert Roman supremacy over Constantinople by unilaterally changing the wording of the Nicene Creed[96] and enforcing Latin customs on Greeks living in Southern Italy. These customs included clerical celibacy, limited performance of ordinances, and the forced use of unleavened bread in the Eucharist.[97] In response, the patriarch of Constantinople, Michael Cerularius, insisted that Latin churches in Constantinople use Greek language and eastern liturgical rites. When they refused, he closed the churches.[98] Rome dispatched emissaries to resolve the controversy, but the negotiations failed. As a parting "last word," the pope's representative "left a bull of excommunication (July 16, 1054) on the altar of the great church of Hagia Sophia. The bull anathematized (condemned) Michael Cerularius, the Greek doctrine of the Holy Spirit, the marriage of Greek priests, and the Greek use of leavened bread for the Eucharist."[99] Michael Cerularius retaliated by excommunicating the Roman pope.

The Great Schism,[100] as it came to be known, was like the proverbial humpty-dumpty perched precariously on the wall. Once the fragile unity was shattered, attempts to reconcile the two branches of Christianity "couldn't put it together again." The branches remain apart today.

The eastern split has about two hundred million members and is known as the Eastern Orthodox Church. It is a communion of thirteen autocephalous churches, each with its own patriarch, including the well-known Greek Orthodox and Russian Orthodox churches.[101] Eastern Orthodox churches have deep cultural ties to their respective countries:

> Each national church is autonomous. . . . Because of this polity Eastern Orthodoxy has identified itself more intimately with national cultures and with national regimes than has Roman Catholicism. Therefore the history of church–state relations in the East has been very different from the Western development, because the church in the East has sometimes tended toward the extreme of becoming a mere instrument of national policy while the church in the West has sometimes tended toward the extreme of attempting to dominate the state.[102]

We've seen in this chapter that prior to Constantine, Christianity was a community of independent churches with a common belief in Jesus but with different rites and even different doctrines. Metropolitan bishops could agree to disagree and thus the proto-Orthodox church had a form of unity by tolerating diversity. Of course, this loose unity was not necessarily unity in truth, and it arguably wasn't the kind of unity that Constantine sought when he adopted Christianity as a unifying force for the empire.

We might reasonably wonder if any of these schisms would have happened if the decentralized and dispersed authority of the early postapostolic church had persisted. Were the nuances of dyophysitism versus miaphysitism of such critical importance to justify the formation of Assyrian Church of the East and Oriental Orthodox Church? Why did Rome object so vehemently to the Greek rites in use in

Constantinople, such as the use of leavened bread for the Eucharist? Were the differences in rites of sufficient gravity to drive a wedge between the east and west? The questions go on. In the end, all of the three Orthodox schisms we covered in this chapter had some element of doctrinal disagreement, but all also occurred in part due to questions of authority.

We should note that the schisms had little effect on observable worship practices. As we learned in our figurative travel through the world in chapter 1, observable worship, including administration of the sacraments, is formulated in rites such as the Syriac Rite or Armenian Rite. Rites tend to be associated with the geography in which they developed. Thus, within a geographic area in which the Orthodox branches overlap, the Oriental Orthodox Church, the Assyrian Church of the East, the Eastern Orthodox Church, and even the Roman Catholic Church continue to practice a common rite resulting in similarity in terms of worship.[103]

Notes

1 Translated as "pope" in English.

2 The Latin word *episcopal* means "bishop," which stems from the Greek *episkopos,* meaning "overseer."

3 See 1 Timothy 3:1–3; Titus 1:7.

4 In the *Clementine Homilies*, for example, Peter addresses James as bishop. Clement of Rome is a bishop appointed by Peter The Clementine Homilies 1870.

5 See https://www.vox.com/world/2018/6/19/17469176/roman-empire-maps-history-explained.

6 1 Corinthians 1:10–13; 2:4–5.

7 Baring-Gould M.A. 1874, 34-35.

8 Rome's political divisions are well illustrated in the map of Rome in 400 AD. Cplakidas 2007. Within each diocese, the capital of one province was also the capital of the diocese. Antiochia (Antioch), for example, was the capital of the province of Syria and the capital of the diocese of Oriens. Other capitals of dioceses included Roma, Alexandria, Ephesus, Thessalonica, Mediolanum (Milan), Carthago (Carthage), and others.

9 Cave 1840, 380.

10 Cave 1840, 392.

11 Cave 1840, 391.

12 A *see* is the jurisdiction of a bishop.

13 Cave 1840, 375.

14 Bruce, Davis and Others 2018.

15 Cave 1840, 84-86.

16 Cave 1840, 87.

17 Liturgical Rites n.d.

18 Wikipedia, Pope Victor I 2018.

19 Wikipedia, Quartodecimanism 2018.

20 Cave 1840, 391.

21 Another of the seven churches in John's ministry located in Asia Minor.

22 Wikipedia, Quartodecimanism 2018.

23 Wikipedia, First Council of Nicaea 2019.

24 The Roman administrative lines changed over time such that there is an imperfect alignment between the dioceses of Constantine's time and the senior bishops. Diocletian did a major restructuring during his reign.

25 Cave 1840, 110.

26 An ecumenical council was a "worldwide" council with universal authority, as opposed to synods that were held within the jurisdiction of a particular metropolitan church.

27 Matthew 3:17.

28 For example, see John 11:41; Luke 6:12; Luke 10:21–22.

29 See John 5:19, 30, 36, and John 6:38.

30 John 10:30.

31 John 16:25.

32 John 14:9–11.

33 John 14:28.

34 Deuteronomy 6:4.

35 Isaiah 44:6.

36 The most fundamental of these was the Greek concept of *ousía*, a word often translated as "essence" or "substance." But to the Greeks, *ousía*—derived from the Greek verb "to be"—expressed closely connected concepts related to existence: (1) what something is in itself, its being or essence; (2) an entity which is what it is with respect to essential attributes, on its own and without dependence on any more fundamental entity of another type outside itself, as in Plato's perfect forms; (3) being, as opposed to becoming; and (4) existence, as opposed to nonexistence. A second related concept was *hypostasis*, a Greek word also used to describe an underlying substance. *Hypostasis* and *ousía* both referred to the underlying substance or essence; however, *hypostasis* was to *ousía* what an individual human is to humankind. One is particular and the other is general. The Greek concept of *prosopon*—derived from the Greek word for *mask*—meant the form in which hypostasis appears. Both *hypostasis* and *prosopon* referred to an individual and thus have both been translated as "person," but it is important to note that the latter referred to manifestation to the senses of an individual. Thus, the term *prosopon* could only apply to the mortal Jesus, but not to the immaterial and unknowable Father. Spanning these concepts was the concept of *physis*—usually translated as "nature." *Ousía* by definition had its own independent physis—its own attribute or nature. Hypostases—individuals of the same ousía—must be of the same physis. Importantly, in this construct, the physis of material things such as mortals was far inferior to the physis of the perfect Good.

37 A necessary corollary to the doctrine of Docetism was the Gnostic doctrine of the Demiurge. Jesus, the mirage of the perfect God, could not have been the creator of the material world. The creation had to be done by a lesser God whom the Gnostics called the Demiurge. Marcion, indoctrinated in Gnosticism by his mentor Cerdo, equated the Demiurge to the Old Testament's Yahweh (Jehovah), whom he also considered to be Satan.

38 This was championed by Paul of Samosata, a bishop in Antioch in the mid-third century Chapman, Paul of Samosata 1911.

39 The priest Sabellius was the leading advocate for this formula, and it was at times called Sabellianism Wikipedia, Monarchianism 2019.

40 Chapman, Monarchians 1911.

41 Wikipedia, Arius 2018.

42 Editors 2015.

43 Wikipedia, Pope Alexander I of Alexandria 2018.

44 Athanasius would become the prominent figure of the anti-Arians. He ascended to the bishop's office after Alexander and was extremely influential in the ongoing fight against Arianism and in the establishment of the canon of scripture.

45 Wikipedia, Pope Alexander I of Alexandria 2018.

46 Wikipedia, Eusebius of Nicomedia 2018. Nicomedia was then the capital of the eastern empire, and Eusebius, the bishop of Nicomedia, was already one of the most influential metropolitans. When Constantine executed Licinius, the eastern emperor, Eusebius gained a position in Constantine's court. Undoubtedly, it helped that he was a distant relative of Constantine. One evidence of his influence is that he baptized Constantine Wikipedia, Eusebius of Nicomedia 2018.

47 Wikipedia, Pope Alexander I of Alexandria 2018.

[48] After Arius's teachings were rejected, Constantine ordered his works to be burned. It is through his opponents that we have portions of the Thalia:

God Himself then, in His own nature, is ineffable by all men.
Equal or like Himself He alone has none, or one in glory.
And Ingenerate we call Him, because of Him who is generate by nature.
We praise Him as without beginning because of Him who has a beginning.
And adore Him as everlasting, because of Him who in time has come to be.
The Unbegun made the Son a beginning of things originated;
and advanced Him as a Son to Himself by adoption.
He has nothing proper to God in proper subsistence.
For He is not equal, no, nor one in essence with Him.
Wise is God, for He is the teacher of Wisdom.
There is full proof that God is invisible to all beings;
both to things which are through the Son, and to the Son He is invisible.
I will say it expressly, how by the Son is seen the Invisible;
by that power by which God sees, and in His own measure,
the Son endures to see the Father, as is lawful.
Thus there is a Triad, not in equal glories.
Not intermingling with each other are their subsistences.
One more glorious than the other in their glories unto immensity.
Foreign from the Son in essence is the Father, for He is without beginning.
Understand that the Monad was; but the Dyad was not, before it was in existence.
It follows at once that, though the Son was not, the Father was God.
Hence the Son, not being (for He existed at the will of the Father),
is God Only-begotten, and He is alien from either.
Wisdom existed as Wisdom by the will of the Wise God.
Hence He is conceived in numberless conceptions:
Spirit, Power, Wisdom,
God's glory, Truth, Image, and Word.
Understand that He is conceived to be Radiance and Light.
One equal to the Son, the Superior is able to beget;
but one more excellent, or superior, or greater, He is not able.
At God's will the Son is what and whatsoever He is.
And when and since He was, from that time He has subsisted from God.
He, being a strong God, praises in His degree the Superior.
To speak in brief, God is ineffable to His Son.
For He is to Himself what He is, that is, unspeakable.
So that nothing which is called comprehensible does the Son
know to speak about; for it is impossible for Him
to investigate the Father, who is by Himself.
For the Son does not know His own essence,
For, being Son, He really existed, at the will of the Father.
What argument then allows, that He who is from the Father
should know His own parent by comprehension?
For it is plain that for that which hath a beginning to conceive how the Unbegun is,
or to grasp the idea, is not possible.

The Thalia of Arius n.d.

[49] Editors 2014.

[50] Wikipedia, Pope Alexander I of Alexandria 2018.

[51] Matthews and Nicol 2018.

[52] Wikipedia, Pope Alexander I of Alexandria 2018.

[53] The majority of the bishops were from the eastern church and thus tended to be allies of the bishop of Alexandria Wikipedia, First Council of Nicaea 2019.

[54] The term *Trinity* is not used in the New Testament; however, the triad of the Father, Son, and Holy Ghost are referenced multiple times (see references such as Matthew 28:19; 2 Corinthians 13:13; 1 Corinthians 21:4–5, etc.). The first use of *Trinity* in Christian writings was by Theophilus of Antioch in about 170 Wikipedia, Trinity 2019. However, it was the Latin theologian Tertullian (c. 155–c. 240) who used the doctrine of the Trinity to counter what he considered to be the heretical doctrines of his day: Docetism, Monarchianism, and Modalism. The essence of the Trinitarian doctrine is that the Father, the Son Jesus, and the Holy Ghost are three separate persons (*hypostases*) but of the same substance of God (*ousía*). Ironically, Tertullian's Trinity violated the philosophical definition of ousía. Tertullian taught that God the Father shared His substance with His created and subordinate Son, as if ousía was a material substance that could be apportioned and shared. But according to the implicit rules of the Greeks, a created Son could not be homoousion—of the same ousía—as the uncreated and perfect Father. In effect, Tertullian's Trinity was akin to Arius's subordinationism and would have been considered heretical had the creeds of later councils been applied to it. Nevertheless, Tertullian succeeded in establishing the basic elements—different persons (hypostases) of the same substance (ousía) such that the doctrine took hold among influential theologians Wikipedia, Tertullian 2017.

[55] All Orthodox branches and the vast majority of Protestant denominations accept the Nicene Creed. Non-Trinitarian denominations are all relatively small, such as The Church of Jesus Christ of Latter-day Saints, Jehovah's Witnesses, Unitarians, and Iglesia Ni Cristo.

[56] P. Schaff, Creeds of Christendom 1877. (emphasis added).

[57] Sullivan 1910. The full text of the Athanasian Creed reads:

Catholic Faith is this, that we worship one God in Trinity and Trinity in Unity. Neither confounding the Persons, nor dividing the Substance. For there is one Person of the Father, another of the Son, and another of the Holy Ghost. But the Godhead of the Father, of the Son and of the Holy Ghost is all One, the Glory Equal, the Majesty Whosoever will be saved, before all things it is necessary that he hold the Catholic Faith. Which Faith except everyone do keep whole and undefiled, without doubt he shall perish everlastingly. And the Catholic Faith is this, that we worship one God in Trinity and Trinity in Unity. Neither confounding the Persons, nor dividing the Substance. For there is one Person of the Father, another of the Son, and another of the Holy Ghost. But the Godhead of the Father, of the Son and of the Holy Ghost is all One, the Glory Equal, the Majesty Co-Eternal. Such as the Father is, such is the Son, and such is the Holy Ghost. The Father Uncreate, the Son Uncreate, and the Holy Ghost Uncreate. The Father Incomprehensible, the Son Incomprehensible, and the Holy Ghost Incomprehensible. The Father Eternal, the Son Eternal, and the Holy Ghost Eternal and yet they are not Three Eternals but One Eternal. As also there are not Three Uncreated, nor Three Incomprehensibles, but One Uncreated, and One Incomprehensible. So likewise the Father is Almighty, the Son Almighty, and the Holy Ghost Almighty. And yet they are not Three Almighties but One Almighty. So the Father is God, the Son is God, and the Holy Ghost is God. And yet they are not Three Gods, but One God. So likewise the Father is Lord, the Son Lord, and the Holy Ghost Lord. And yet not Three Lords but One Lord. For, like as we are compelled by the Christian verity to acknowledge every Person by Himself to be God and Lord, so are we forbidden by the Catholic Religion to say, there be Three Gods or Three Lords. The Father is made of none, neither created, nor begotten. The Son is of the Father alone; not made, nor created, but begotten. The Holy Ghost is of the Father, and of the Son neither made, nor created, nor begotten, but proceeding. So there is One Father, not Three Fathers; one Son, not Three Sons; One Holy Ghost, not Three Holy Ghosts. And in this Trinity none is afore or after Other, None is greater or less than Another, but the whole Three Persons are Co-eternal together, and Co-equal. So that in all things, as is aforesaid, the Unity in Trinity, and the Trinity in Unity, is to be worshipped. He therefore that will be saved, must thus think of the Trinity. Furthermore, it is necessary to everlasting Salvation, that he also believe rightly the Incarnation of our Lord Jesus Christ. For the right Faith is, that we believe and confess, that our Lord Jesus Christ, the Son of God, is God and Man. God, of the substance of the Father, begotten before the worlds; and Man, of the substance of His mother, born into the world. Perfect God and Perfect Man, of a reasonable Soul and human Flesh subsisting. Equal to the Father as touching His Godhead, and inferior to the Father as touching His Manhood. Who, although He be God and Man, yet He is not two, but One Christ. One, not by conversion of the Godhead into Flesh, but by taking of the Manhood into God. One altogether, not by confusion of substance, but by Unity of Person. For as the reasonable soul and flesh is one Man, so God and Man is one Christ. Who suffered for our salvation, descended into Hell, rose again the third day from the dead. He ascended into Heaven, He sitteth on the right hand of the Father, God Almighty, from whence he shall come to judge the quick and the dead. At whose coming all men shall rise again with their bodies, and shall give account for their own works. And they that have done good shall go into life everlasting, and they that have done evil into everlasting fire. This is the Catholic Faith, which except a man believe faithfully and firmly, he cannot be saved.

[58] Recall that in Greek philosophy the perfect form of the Good was incomprehensible to mortal minds.

[59] Catholic doctrine accepts that the theology of how three are one is essentially a mystery; however, the "economy" of God, that is the actions of God, are not clear evidence of singularity. The three persons of the Godhead act with such unanimity of purpose and will as to be inseparable Wikipedia, Trinity 2019.

[60] P. Schaff 1997.

[61] Wikipedia, List of Christian denominations by number of members 2018.

62 See the section on The Eastern Orthodox Church later in this chapter for the background on the rivalry between Constantinople and Alexandria.

63 Kelly, Nestorius 2014.

64 Tanabe, Nestorianism 2014.

65 Wikipedia, Cyril of Alexandria 2018.

66 Wikipedia, Cyril of Alexandria 2018.

67 Wikipedia, Cyril of Alexandria 2018.

68 Kelly, Nestorius 2014.

69 Tanabe, Nestorianism 2014.

70 Wikipedia, Roman-Persian Wars 2018.

71 Tanabe, Nestorianism 2014.

72 Wikipedia, List of Christian denominations by number of members 2018.

73 Tanabe, Monophysitism 2014.

74 Schaefer 1908.

75 Wikipedia, Second Council of Ephesus 2018.

76 Tanabe, Monophysitism 2014.

77 Wikipedia, Pope Dioscorus I of Alexandria 2018.

78 It should be noted that although the word *oriental* means "eastern," the Oriental Orthodox Church is not to be confused with the Eastern Orthodox Church, which is covered later.

79 Wikipedia, Miaphysitism 2017.

80 Wikipedia, Miaphysitism 2017. Cyril is considered a saint by both Catholics and Oriental Orthodox Churches. Accordingly, he could not be the originator of a doctrine later considered heretical. The exoneration of Cyril is reflected in the official *Catholic Encyclopedia*, which states, "The principal representatives of this teaching [monophysitism] were Dioscurus, Patriarch of Alexandria, and Eutyches, an archimandrite or president of a monastery outside Constantinople. The Monophysitic error, as the new error was called (Gr. *mone physis*, one nature), claimed the authority of St. Cyril, but only through a misinterpretation of some expressions of the great Alexandrine teacher" Schaefer 1908. Nevertheless, Cyril's doctrine was undoubtedly inconsistent with the Council of Chalcedon's canon. This incident illustrates the evolution of canon and the tightrope bishops walked when defining canon that would render as heretics formerly revered Christians.

81 World Council of Churches n.d.

82 Wikipedia, List of Christian denominations by number of members 2018.

83 Pentapolis referred to five major cities of the province of Libya Superior.

84 First Council of Nicaea (A.D. 325) 1900.

85 See the argument for this position in Loughlin 1880.

86 Fortescue, Patriarch and Patriarchate 1911.

87 Cave 1840, 378-382.

88 First Council of Nicaea (A.D. 325) 1900. (emphasis added).

89 Loughlin 1880.

90 First Council of Nicaea (A.D. 325) 1900.

91 The patriarchate of Jerusalem was granted authority over the three provinces of the diocese of Palestine in the Council of Chalcedon in 451 Schaefer 1908.

92 Modern-day Istanbul in Turkey.

93 Wikipedia, First Council of Constantinople 2017.

[94] Schaefer 1908.

[95] Stefon, Benz and Others, Christianity 2017.

[96] The Roman churches, without consulting the east, added "and from the Son" (Latin: Filioque) to the Nicene Creed Editors, Schism of 1054 2017.

[97] Editors, Schism of 1054 2017.

[98] Editors, Michael Cerularius 2007.

[99] Stefon, Benz and Others, Christianity 2017.

[100] The term *Great Schism* is also applied confusingly to the Western Schism of the Roman Catholic Church that occurred in 1378, in which there were two popes Martin, Jaroslav and Others 2018.

[101] Fairchild 2017.

[102] Stefon, Benz and Others, Christianity 2017.

[103] The use of common rites was illustrated in Table 1. Recognized Churches in Israel in chapter 1.

The Reformation

In the centuries following the Great Schism of 1054, the western church restrained divisions to remain by most measures a unified Catholic Church.[1] But protestors became increasingly vocal until in the early years of the sixteenth century, when the conditions were ripe for a radical upheaval in the western church. The upheaval known as the Reformation is an essential part of the story of Christian splintering.

At the close of Chapter 3: Headwinds, three "ingredients," or themes, were introduced: doctrine, governance, and practice. We've seen how the Orthodox schisms in the last chapter were driven by doctrine and by issues of governance but had little effect on practice. As we embark on a journey to explore the Reformation, it's useful to remind ourselves of these themes. Together, they are particularly useful as a lens through which to understand and contrast the many denominations that emerged from the Reformation. For example, we'll learn that King Henry VIII split from the Catholic Church almost entirely over authority—an element of governance—while John Calvin's reforms addressed all three. Let's consider the lead-up to the Reformation through the lens of these three themes.

Doctrine

We've learned that in the first centuries of the church, Christian theologians attempted to make sense of doctrine using the tools of Greek philosophy.[2] Theologians explored the mysteries of the divine and planted "seeds" that, as in the parable of the sower,[3] at times lay dormant and at times blossomed into full-blown doctrines. Some of the most important seeds that were planted long before the Reformation were planted by Augustine, the theologian-bishop of Hippo in northern Africa.[4] Augustine influenced the Catholic Church even prior to the Reformation. His doctrine of original sin, albeit in a softened form, was adopted as Orthodox by the Catholic Church in the Council of Orange in 539.[5] Also, his writings governing monastic life, called the "Rule of St. Augustine," became widely adopted by monastic orders.[6] However, it was in the lead-up to the Reformation and then during the Reformation that Augustine's seeds sprouted and fully blossomed. We learned in Chapter 5: The Age of Heresy that Augustine spent nearly a decade in the Gnostic sect Manichaeism, then for a time defended Orthodox positions of sin and salvation, only to evolve back to doctrines similar to those of his former faith. He solidified his enduring doctrines late in life as he battled Pelagianism.[7] In four works, *On the Spirit and the Letter* (412), *On the Grace of Christ and on Original Sin* (418), *On the Predestination of the Saints* (429) and *On the Gift of Perseverance* (429) Augustine articulated the interrelated doctrines of original sin, depravity of man, predestination of the elect, and irresistible grace.[8]

After Augustine's time, Greek philosophers were silenced in Christendom for centuries, a result of a decree of the Christian emperor Justinian closing the Platonic Academy in Athens in 529.[9] It was not until the twelfth century that the philosophical tradition that had so deeply influenced early Christian theologians including Augustine reemerged in a renaissance of sorts—the age of scholasticism.[10] Peter Lombard, a French theologian and bishop, compiled the works of early church fathers, including Augustine, into the volumes *Four Books of Sentences* between 1148 and 1151. The *Sentences* became the textbooks of universities and the starting point for a new generation of theologian-philosophers.[11] Late in the twelfth century, the works of Aristotle, accompanied by insightful Arabic and Hebrew commentaries, found their way into Western lands.[12] Inspired by this renaissance that pursued both faith and reason, Thomas Aquinas (1225–1274) emerged as one of the most important Christian theologians of all time. His crowning work, *Summa Theologica*, dealt with the entire body of Christian theology, citing frequently from the apostle Paul, the philosopher Aristotle, the theologian Augustine, the master Peter Lombard, and other Arab and Hebrew commentators.[13] He tackled the issues of justification, free will, and grace and, in doing so, reformulated Augustine's doctrines to ascribe some free will to man. He proposed three steps to salvation from man's fallen state:

1. Infusion of grace (*infusio gratiae*)—God infuses grace into the human soul—the Christian now has faith and, with it, the ability to do good—this step is entirely God's work and is not done by man, and once a man has faith, he can never entirely lose it—however, faith alone is not enough for salvation;

2. Faith formed by charity (*fides caritate formata*)—with man's free will restored, man must now do his best to do good works in order to have a faith formed by charity; and then

3. Condign merit (*meritum de condigno*)—God then judges and awards eternal life on the basis of these good works which Aquinas called man's condign merit.[14]

Note the use of the word *infusion*. Although Aquinas still held that only God could initiate the change in men—as opposed to a willful act—it suggested that once "infused" man was changed, endowed with capacity to act with free will to perform good works. Later disputes during the Reformation centered around whether grace was infused, as Aquinas suggested, or *imputed*, meaning that the righteousness of Christ was accredited to man, leaving man himself in the same incapable state of dependence.

The scholasticism of the thirteenth century refocused Christian theologians on the deep and difficult doctrines of salvation, including the tension between free will and grace epitomized in the Augustinian-Pelagian debates centuries earlier. It set the stage for renewed debate and for new examination of Augustine.

Another aspect of doctrine that should be mentioned before diving into the Reformation is that of canonicity. As we learned in the previous chapter, the First Council of Nicaea called by Constantine I in 325 set the pattern for settling disputes and codifying doctrine. Nicaea and subsequent councils issued canons considered to be on par with canonical scripture. Additionally, the bishop of Rome achieved preeminence over other bishops as the pope and thereby had the authority to issue papal decrees, called *bulls* or *encyclicals*. The accumulated council-issued canons and papal decrees, collectively the "tradition" of the church, expanded until it played a greater role than canonical scriptures in guiding the church. This became a major point of contention for Reformers. Ultimately, the Reformers affirmed the sole authority of the Bible.[15]

Governance, or Polity

By the late Middle Ages, the organization of the western church was established. In varying degrees, Reformers challenged two key aspects of that governance or polity[16]: the hierarchical authority within the church itself and the alliance between church and state.

Hierarchical Authority within the Church

The previous chapter went into detail about the evolution of the episcopal[17] hierarchy within the proto-Orthodox "trunk" of Christianity. The tiers of the hierarchy developed over time from decentralized bishop-led churches to metropolitan-centric dispersed churches, then to a patriarch-led collection of independent churches, and finally to a centralized church with a supreme pontiff in Rome. As church authority became increasingly centralized, it became increasingly compatible with and complementary to the secular hierarchy of the emperor or king. The resulting governance was characteristically top-down, with a means to foster and maintain "unity" by authoritatively defining doctrine and practice. Monarchies naturally favored episcopal governance and frequently aligned their secular power with episcopal authority in the form of state-sanctioned magisterial churches—more on that in the next section. Such a marriage of church and state inevitably fostered the criticism penned by one Englishman to a cleric, "Power tends to corrupt, and absolute power corrupts absolutely. Great men are almost always bad men."[18] Corruption of power became a major theme of the Reformation. Consequently, many Reformers sought to scripturally justify different forms of governance that would be less susceptible to the abuses of authority evident under multitiered episcopal governance.

Some Reformers insisted that the church be separate from the state. Such Reformers found themselves friendless, the enemy of both the secular government and fellow Reformers—and persecuted by both. Persecution and repression led some, such as the Swiss brethren, John Smyth, and Robert Browne, to organize—often covertly—their own congregations beholden to no higher authority. Congregational polity sits at the opposite extreme to episcopal polity. Independent congregations were threats to magisterial churches and therefore generally existed in secret until blossoming in the increasingly liberated religious climate of North America, particularly after religious freedom was guaranteed in the United States Constitution.

Moderate Reformers, Calvin being the notable example, rejected the episcopal model but also anticipated the ecclesiastical anarchy of the congregational model. Calvin sought a middle way. He instituted a church government in which elders, an order of priests, were to be elected locally, with a single representative elder from each congregation joining a governing council of elders. The council, called a presbytery, was to have authority over the congregations. The middle way was called Presbyterian in reference to the authority given to the presbytery, the council of elder-priests—the word *priest* deriving from the Greek word for priest, *presbyteros*.

Church and State

Constantine I started the church down the path of becoming a *magisterial* church, meaning the official church of the state. Secular and religious power became commingled and codependent. Some Reformers protested any "unholy alliance" between church and state, but they were the exception. Most major Reformers embraced the notion of becoming a new and holy magisterial church. Why? Surely, there were pragmatic reasons relative to survival; however, we can be confident that the Reformers justified the new magisterial churches in the same way that the Orthodox and Catholic churches had done centuries earlier.[19]

In the east, the autocephalous patriarchates of the Eastern Orthodox Church formed in the Great Schism of 1054 became the magisterial churches of their respective states. In the west, the fall of the Roman Empire in 476 left the Roman Catholic Church straddling two worlds—a no-man's land of sorts. The church in Rome and the bishop of Rome remained subject to the eastern Byzantine Empire centered in Constantinople, but its members were increasingly in the western and northern lands of Europe—territory no longer governed by a central government in Rome. At the beginning of the ninth century, the church in Rome turned to the west, to a new "Constantine."

The devout Christian Frankish[20] king Charlemagne conquered the heart of western Europe, including what is today Germany in the north to Italy in the south, all in the name of Christ and the Catholic faith. The pope at the time, in an act of treason to the Byzantine emperor in Constantinople, coronated Charlemagne as emperor. This was an act that ultimately resulted in a new empire—in time called the Holy Roman Empire.[21]

It is not our purpose here to dive deeply into European history. For purposes of understanding splintering in the Christian faith, we can suffice it to say that there was constant jostling for supremacy between local sovereigns, the Holy Roman Empire, and the Roman Catholic Church. Some elements of their alliance united them: Christian kings saw themselves as divinely ordained of God and thus required the blessing of the church for divine legitimacy of official acts such as coronation and marriage; all three groups accepted the duty to purge dissenters and heretics; the emperor enforced the ecclesiastical rulings of the church; and the church furthered the interests of the empire by unifying diverse kingdoms under a common faith. Other realities pushed them apart: sovereigns lost autonomy; magisterial treasuries were depleted by required support of holy wars, clergy, and church property; and the limits of ecclesiastical authority became ever murkier as clergy sought and obtained lordships and positions in government.

The struggle for supremacy between church and state became acute in 1302 when Pope Boniface VIII issued a bull, known as Unam Sanctam,[22] that asserted that the church carried both spiritual and secular swords and its spiritual authority superseded secular authority. The bull decreed that "it is necessary to salvation that *every human creature be subject to the Roman pontiff.*"[23] The French King Phillip IV responded defiantly, "we are nobody's vassal in temporal matters." The pope in turn excommunicated the king of France and threatened to depose the entire French clergy, an act that would have resulted in the complete loss of sacraments for the French people.[24] Allies of the French king broke into the papal residence, beat the pope, and held him prisoner for three days. Although soon released, the pope developed a fever and died within weeks of the incident.[25] The next pope died just nine months after election. The next papal election or conclave exposed the fractured loyalties among the cardinals as it remained deadlocked for eleven months.[26] Although the details are disputed as to how influence was exerted on the conclave, the French king was successful in getting a Frenchman and friend selected as pope.

The new French pope, Clement V, refused to move to Rome, moved the papal court to Arles in Southern France, and established the Avignon papacy.[27] Rather than fight secular authority for supremacy, the papacy supported the monarchy and reaped protection and rewards in return. For the next sixty years, a period known in Christian history as the Babylonian Captivity, the papacy resided in a palace in Avignon. Senior clergy of the church adopted many of the features of the royal court, living like princes with immense wealth and property[28]—all this excess was funded by controversial practices including onerous taxes, simony (the sale of clerical positions), and the sale of indulgences and absolutions as part of the sacrament of penance. The excesses and the means of funding them were critical catalysts for the Reformation.

Practices, or Liturgy

Rituals that represent the intersection of humanity's actions and the divine are called liturgy, which is derived from the Greek *leitourgia*, which literally means "work of the people."[29] Thus, a church's patterns of worship constitute liturgy.

Similar to its Jewish origins, Christianity has always included rituals in its worship. Even beyond the continuation of rituals from the Law of Moses that were practiced by Jewish converts, the New Testament records other rituals within the early church, including baptism,[30] ordination to positions of authority,[31] the laying on of hands associated with the receipt of the Holy Ghost,[32] and the Last Supper performed by Jesus in the upper room.[33] Collectively, these are called *sacraments* in many denominations and *ordinances* in others. The Catholic view of sacraments is useful:

> The *liturgical* life of the Catholic Church revolves around the Eucharistic sacrifice and the sacraments.... The purpose of the sacraments is to make people holy, to build up the body of Christ, and finally, to give worship to God; but being signs, they also have a teaching function. They not only presuppose faith, but by words and object, they also nourish, strengthen, and express it; that is why they are called "sacraments of faith." The sacraments impart grace, but, in addition, the very act of celebrating them disposes the faithful most effectively to receive this grace in a fruitful manner, to worship God rightly, and to practice charity.[34]

Practices are often the outward reflection of doctrinal beliefs. For example, the related doctrines of original sin and spiritual rebirth, sometimes called regeneration, correspond to the physical ritual of baptism. Thus, the line between doctrine and practice can be blurry; however, to the extent that doctrine motivates ritual, we'll consider doctrine through the lens of practices.

It was not until Peter Lombard's work *Sentences* and his enumeration of seven sacraments that the Roman Catholic Church settled on the seven sacraments that it practices today.[35] Reformers challenged many of them, often adopting only one or two. Two of the Catholic sacraments were flash points for Reformers, specifically, the sacrament of the Last Supper, known as the Eucharist from the Greek *eucharistia*, meaning "thanksgiving," and the sacrament of Penance.

The Catholic Church accepts the literal words of the Savior when He said, "take eat, this is my body," as well as the comparable phrase relative to His blood.[36] Therefore, the emblems of the Eucharist in Roman Catholic liturgy are believed to be literally changed, or transubstantiated, to become the actual body and blood of Christ. Protestants almost universally rejected the doctrine of transubstantiation; however, they could not agree among themselves what the doctrine should be. For example, attempts to unite the two contemporary Reformers Luther and Zwingli failed due to deeply held differences in their views of the Eucharist. Furthermore, Reformers could not agree about who should participate in the sacrament. Up through the twelfth century, the laity (members of the congregation) received both emblems of the Eucharist; however, by the thirteenth century, the chalice of consecrated wine was restricted to ordained priests.[37] Some Reformers were principally motivated by this issue and sought to extend to the laity the "blood of Christ."[38]

The sacrament of Penance along with its associated "payment" in the form of indulgences or absolutions was perhaps the most egregious practice railed against by protestors. As background, the following from the *Catholic Encyclopedia* explains the doctrinal rationale for indulgences:

> In the Sacrament of Penance the guilt of sin is removed, and with it the eternal punishment due to mortal sin; but there still remains the temporal punishment required by Divine justice, and this requirement must be fulfilled either in the present life or in the world to come, i.e., in Purgatory. An indulgence offers the penitent sinner the means of discharging this debt during his life on earth.[39]

Indulgences were seen by Reformers as pernicious for doctrinal reasons—the notion that sin and righteousness were akin to an accounting ledger that could be reconciled with money—and for its sheer corruption as a funding source for the church's many building projects and crusades as well as a means for funding the treasuries of sovereigns, who took a cut.

With the three useful lenses of doctrine, governance, and practices in hand, let's explore the Reformation. Often, the history of the Reformation begins with Martin Luther's famous nailing of his theses to the church door in Wittenberg. But starting there would miss important forerunners who set the stage through their arguments, criticisms, and personal courage. The leading Reformers built upon these forerunners and learned from them how to survive the perils of criticizing the church, in part by more expertly navigating the power dynamics between local sovereigns, the Holy Roman Empire, and the church.

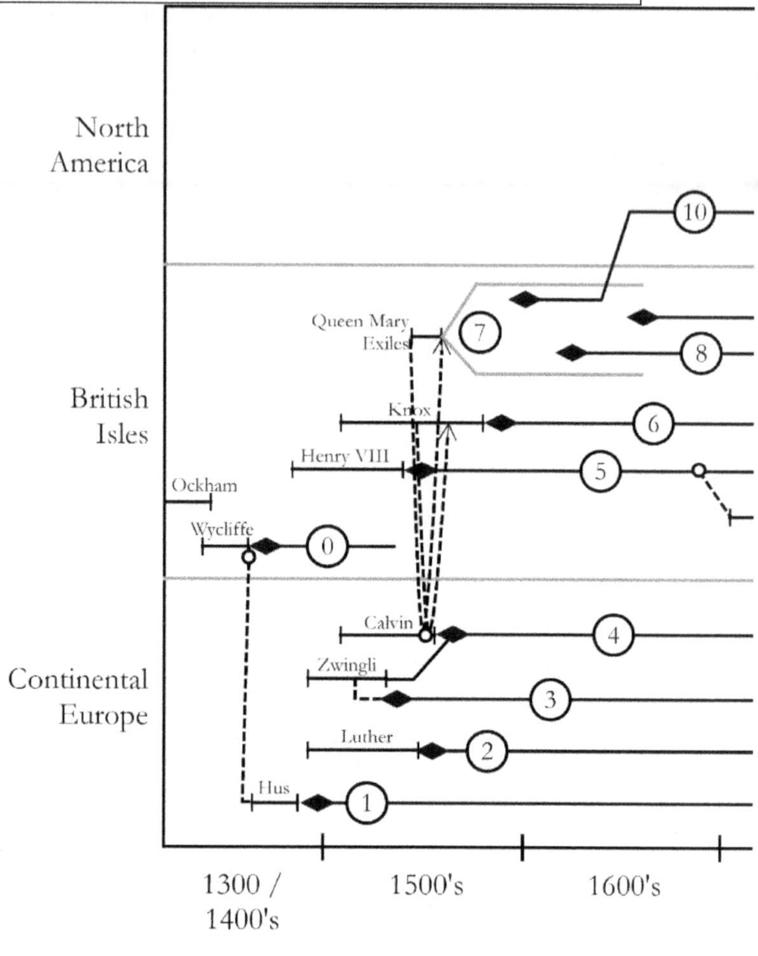

0. Lollards
1. Unitas Fratrum / Moravians (<1m today)
2. Lutheran churches (~80m)
3. Swiss Brethren (Anabaptists) Menonites, Amish (~4m)
4. Reformed churches (~35m*)
5. Church of England, Anglicans, Episcopalians (~85m)
6. Presbyterian (~45m)
7. Puritans & Congregationalism
8. Baptists (~105m)
9. Quakers (<1m)

* Excluding Presbyterianism

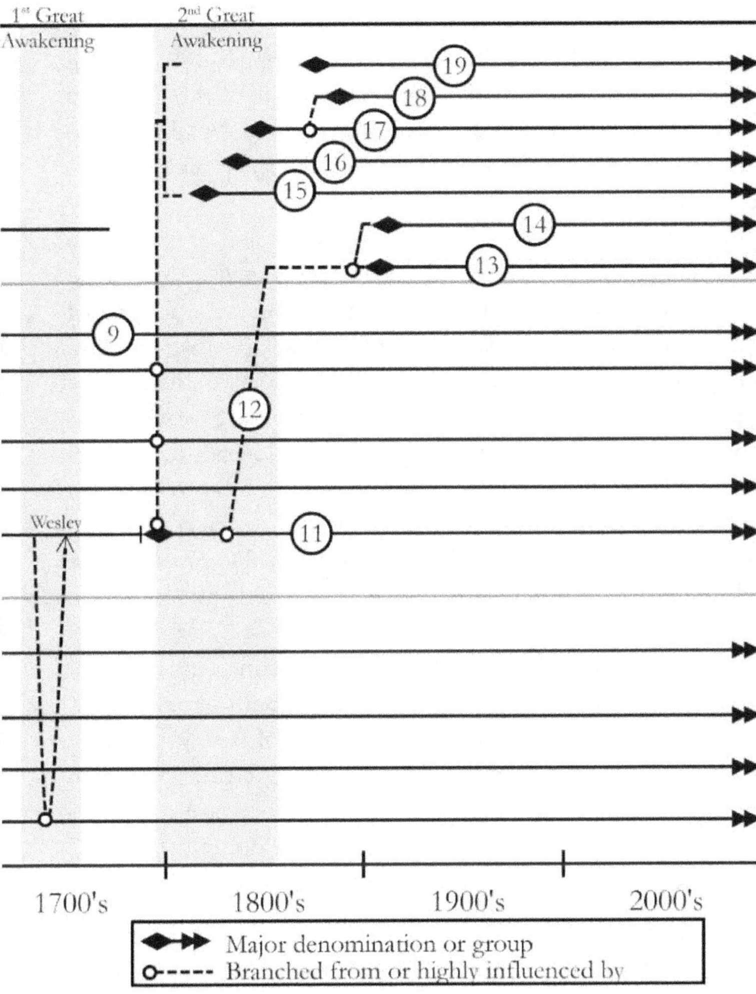

10. Pilgrims & Massachusetts Bay Colony
11. Methodists (~80m)
12. Holiness movement
13. Church of Nazarene, Wesleyan Church, others (~2m)
14. Pentecostal / Assemblies of God & Others (~280m)
15. Barton / Stone: Church of Christ & Others (~7m)
16. Church of Jesus Christ of Latter-day Saints (~16m)
17. Seventh-day Adventists (~20m)
18. Jehovah's Witnesses (~8m)
19. Christian Scientist (<1m)

The Avant-Garde Reformers

William Ockham (c. 1287–1347) is rarely listed among Reformers, but he was a notable forerunner in that he contributed to the doctrinal development of later Reformers, demonstrated complete willingness to oppose the papacy, and set a pattern for leveraging the power struggle between church and state.

Ockham was a Franciscan[40] born in England and trained as a philosopher-theologian at Oxford, where he developed an empirical natural philosophy that abandoned the Aristotelian metaphysics of unseen "substance" and Platonist "perfect forms" that had been in vogue among the scholastic theologians preceding him. Instead, he proposed a "nominalist" approach—that the simplest explanation is most likely the correct one.[41] He applied new logical techniques requiring demonstration and evidence. Thus, although he followed in the footsteps of his fellow Franciscan, the recently deceased Thomas Aquinas,[42] and rigorously studied Peter Lombard's *Sentences*, he interpreted its content in new ways and published a commentary on *Sentences* in the early 1320s.

As noted earlier, Aquinas had softened Augustine's doctrine of grace and free will but remained safely within the bounds of orthodoxy. Ockham, in turn, took an even more extreme view of free will, further separating himself from Augustine's original doctrine. Ockham ascribed more capability and more of the impetus for grace to man— believing that God rewards a person with grace for doing the best he or she is able to do:

> The Ockhamists argued that if a man loved God simply because of "infused grace," then man did not love God freely. They argued that before a man received an infusion of grace, man must do his best in a state of nature (i.e., based on man's reason and inborn moral sense). They argued that just as God awards eternal life on the basis of man's condign merit [merit that is fitting or deserved] for doing his best to do good works after receiving faith as a gift from God, so too, the original infusion of grace was given to man on the basis of "congruent merit," a reward for man's doing his best in a state of nature. Unlike condign

merit, which is fully deserved by man, congruent merit is not fully deserved, and includes a measure of grace on God's part. . . . According to the Ockhamists, a gracious God awards an individual with congruent merit when he or she does the best that he or she is able to do.[43]

Ockham's formulation in his commentary on the *Sentences* tended toward Pelagianism, with its core belief of man's ability to act independent of God's initial grace. In 1324, a local synod condemned his commentary. He was called or sent to the papal headquarters in Avignon to respond to charges of unorthodoxy.[44] Ockham's commentary rekindled the doctrinal debate started so long before between Augustine and Pelagius, and his reputation as a philosopher inspired Luther and others to study him centuries later. Thus, his writings were a catalyst for later Reformers' own formulation of the grace-free-will doctrine—although they almost universally embraced the Augustinian view.

Now in Avignon to defend himself, Ockham became embroiled in another controversy. In stark contrast to the opulence of the papacy and episcopal clergy, most of the Franciscans lived in poverty according to the example and rule of their founder, Francis of Assisi. They believed that the apostles did not own property, a doctrine called Apostolic Poverty.[45] Vocal Franciscans pressured the pope to accept the doctrine and to live by it. In 1322, the pope commissioned experts to examine the doctrine of Apostolic Poverty, recognizing that if affirmed, it would have profound implications far beyond the Franciscan order.[46] Ockham contributed to the review on the side critical of wealth and in favor of poverty.[47] When the commission ruled against the doctrine of poverty followed by a papal bull also rejecting it, the Franciscans were expected to accept the papal bull as binding canon, but they didn't. Vocal Franciscans including Ockham protested and in so doing ventured into heresy. They fled Avignon and found refuge in the court of the Holy Roman emperor, Louis IV of Bavaria. Under his protection, Ockham became a formidable critic of the papacy and went on to make virtually every argument against it— arguments that later Reformers would echo.[48] In a tit-for-tat battle, the pope excommunicated Ockham in 1328. In response, Ockham accused the pope of being a heretic, charging him with seventy errors and seven heresies.[49] Ockham's experiences and philosophy led him to become an advocate for the supremacy of the state over the church.[50]

Ockham's philosophy had a lasting impact on philosophy and theology, particularly in the leading universities of Oxford and Paris.[51] He was not a preacher and thus had many more intellectual protégés than religious disciples. He did not start a new church, but in virtually all other respects his life foreshadowed those of future protestors. His earnest pursuit of truth put him outside the bounds of Orthodox doctrine. His contempt of the financial corruption of the church catalyzed his bitter protest against it. Like the Reformers that followed, Ockham paid the spiritual price of excommunication from the church he had committed himself to and that he undoubtedly loved.

His legacy was a growing tendency toward Pelagianism in intellectual circles. This led the senior ecclesiastic in England, the Archbishop of Canterbury Thomas Bradwardine (c. 1290–1349), to publish a book in the early 1340s called *On the Cause of God against the Pelagians*.[52] Bradwardine believed, in the extreme opposite of Ockham, that God was in absolute control:

> Bradwardine taught that God was in absolute control over all that happened in time. He left no room for man's will to be free in any sense. . . . God is in absolute and determinate control of all. His eternal will . . . determined all that would happen in time. That will, he believed from Scripture, was free from any influence other than His own holy character. Out of this, Bradwardine concludes that nothing can move without God, and that only God can be the direct mover upon any creature. God is the cause, the preserver, and even the chief co-actor in every movement of His creation.[53]

Bradwardine breathed new life into pure Augustinian doctrine and spread it to a new generation of intellectuals, including a young Oxford student named John Wycliffe. Bradwardine's defense against renewed Pelagianism was more than intellectual repartee. It was the paradigm through which to see the horrors that enveloped Europe as that decade closed. Black Death spread through England on its way to decimating roughly 50 percent of the European population.[54] Some scholars have suggested that the young Wycliff saw the plague as evidence of the absolute sovereignty of God at the heart of Augustinian doctrine that was taught so passionately by Bradwardine. It was God's just retribution for the corruption of the church and the depravity of all mankind.[55]

John Wycliffe (c. 1320–1384) remained in the relatively free-thinking world of academia, attaining professorship at Oxford. He began publishing criticisms of the Catholic Church in 1374, particularly against the wealth of the clergy and the financial practices of indulgences and simony.[56] Like Ockham, he argued that clergy should make a vow of poverty and that the gospel could be preached by unconsecrated teachers such as himself.[57]

In 1377, the papacy entered a forty-year period of confusion that only further darkened Wycliffe's opinion of it. The Avignon Pope Gregory XI moved the papal residence back to Rome. Instead of restoring confidence in the papacy by bringing it out from under French control, it ushered in a period of intrigue, political maneuvering, and schism in the papacy itself.[58] Gregory soon died, and the College of Cardinals, meeting in Rome for the first time in a century, faced an angry mob that demanded a Roman pope. The cardinals, split nearly evenly between Italian and French nationals, reached a compromise by electing a non-Roman Italian who had been trained in Avignon, Pope Urban VI.[59] The new pope had not been a cardinal and therefore had little loyalty to them. He began insisting that the business of the church be carried out without the financial windfall of gifts, bribes, annuities, and so on, that had become the source of great wealth to the cardinals.[60] Additionally, he decided to remain in Rome rather than return to Avignon as had been hoped by the French cardinals. Five months after Urban's election, the French cardinals unilaterally deemed his election invalid and elected a Frenchman as pope to be seated in Avignon, ushering in the Western Schism. During the forty years that followed, two popes, and for a time three popes, claimed authority, creating a crisis in the church.[61] It had long been held, since the Donatist controversy, that sacraments performed by illegitimate clergy were themselves invalid; therefore, the crisis put in question the sacraments performed within the church. Staying neutral was not an option; the schism forced archbishops and monarchs to take sides.

Against this backdrop, Wycliffe intensified his criticism of the papacy and the church. Perhaps he recognized that the senior leadership of the church was weakened by the competing claims or was too mired in bigger issues to pay attention to him. Perhaps, he counted on the protection of Oxford.[62] Or perhaps he came to expect the ongoing support of nobles after publishing in 1379 *On the Church*, in which he argued, like Ockham before him, for the supremacy of the state over the clergy within it.[63]

His criticism was broad, and his proposed path forward was far-reaching: He objected to celibacy and monasticism, calling monks "pests of society" in his work *Objection to Friars*.[64] He claimed authority derived solely from the Bible. Accordingly, he, along with some colleagues, sought to make the Bible accessible to the English people by translating it into English from the Latin Vulgate. He embraced undiluted Augustinian doctrines of salvation.[65] In all these criticisms and doctrinal positions, he retained the support of Oxford and friendly nobility. But when he formerly rejected the doctrine of transubstantiation of the bread and wine in the sacrament of the Lord's Supper, he went too far. He lost the support of Oxford, which declared him heretical. Even sympathetic nobles like John of Gaunt could no longer support him.[66]

Wycliffe's vocal criticism and radical opposition to the church created a band of followers at Oxford. One of his colleagues, Nicholas of Hereford, started a new sect based on Wycliffe's doctrines. Like so many other denominations, the group was known by a pejorative nickname given to it by critics—the Lollards.[67] It was perhaps inevitable that Wycliffe's critical rhetoric against the authority of the church would light the flame of revolt against all authority, both secular and religious. In 1381, English peasants revolted and beheaded the archbishop of Canterbury. Wycliffe opposed the uprising; nevertheless, Wycliffe and the Lollards were accused as coconspirators of the revolt.[68] In 1382, a synod (local council of church leaders) condemned Wycliffe but stopped short of excommunicating him.

Wycliffe died two years later in 1384. By this time, the Lollards had multiplied among townspeople, merchants, gentry, and even some clergy.[69] In 1401, England passed a statute that prohibited the use of the Wycliffe Bible and prescribed the burning of the Lollard heretics—

a sentence fulfilled in many instances.[70] In the Council of Constance in 1415, the Catholic Church officially deemed Wycliffe a heretic. He was posthumously excommunicated, and his writings were banned throughout the Christian world. His remains were exhumed and given a heretic's punishment—that of being burned at the stake.[71] The Lollards were harshly persecuted, which sent them into hiding.[72] If the Lollards survived as a sect, as some suggest,[73] they merged into the Protestant mainstream centuries later, leaving no trace of them today as a distinct denomination.

Wycliff blazed the trail of the Reformation, challenging the Catholic Church on all three themes: doctrine, governance, and practices. His criticisms and doctrines foreshadowed those of the Reformers who followed two centuries later, earning him a place as the "morning star" of the Reformation.[74]

Wycliffe's writings spread into Bohemia, modern-day Czechoslovakia, and lit a similar flame of opposition there. Resentment for the senior clergy of the church was high—the church and its clerics owned about one-half of all the land in Bohemia, and simony was rampant.[75] Just when Wycliffe's works were banned in England, a young, recently graduated philosopher and consecrated priest named Jan Hus began using them as the basis of his preaching in the Bethlehem Chapel in Prague.[76] In a short time, Hus emerged as the leader of the Reform movement in Bohemia.[77]

Jan Hus (c. 1369–1415) initially had support, or at least cordial relations with, the archbishop of Prague and King Wenceslaus of Bohemia (1361–1419). However, allegiances were fragile against the backdrop of the turmoil in the papacy. Hus soon lost support from both powerful men.

The Council of Pisa held in 1409 attempted to resolve the Western Schism by deposing the two existing popes and electing a new one; however, the two existing popes refused to resign, leaving the church with three popes claiming equal authority and scope. The newly elected third pope sought supporters and thus responded to a request from the archbishop of Prague to eradicate Reformers, including Wycliffe and anyone who taught from Wycliff's works. The new pope issued bulls that empowered the archbishop to collect and burn Wycliff's works.[78]

The purge exposed Hus as an ardent supporter of Wycliffe, leading to Hus's excommunication in 1410.

King Wenceslaus became the emperor-elect of the Holy Roman Empire in 1376, just as the Western Schism paralyzed the papacy. Consequently, he was not coronated, leaving his status as emperor in question. Within a short time, German princes challenged his authority.[79] Thus, when Hus took up the cause in 1412 against an aggressive effort to raise funds for a new crusade by selling indulgences in Prague, he indirectly further threatened to weaken Wenceslaus because the king stood to take a cut of the funds raised through the sale of indulgences. Consequently, Hus also lost Wenceslaus's support.[80]

The fight over indulgences escalated to the point that some of Hus's followers publicly burned papal bulls, and others who openly railed against the indulgences were beheaded.[81] The pope prohibited the administration of the sacraments in Prague as a form of punishment.[82] As a result, Hus voluntarily left Prague in 1412 to defuse the conflict and lift the punishment. However, Hus's retreat to the countryside served only to increase his influence among the wider population such that Hussites became the majority of the Bohemian population.[83] Additionally, it gave him enough relief from persecution to write many treatises and sermons. The most important of these was entitled *De ecclesia* (*The Church*) and was largely based on Wycliffe's writings.[84] Late in his life, Hus adopted the doctrine of *utraquism*, meaning the giving of both the bread and wine to the laity.[85] So important and controversial was this doctrine that after Hus's death a major division of his followers distinguished themselves by it—calling themselves Utraquists.[86]

The Council of Constance, held in 1415, was organized by emperor-elect King Sigismund of Hungary[87] with the primary objective of reinstating unity within the church by resolving the multiple claims to the papacy. In the same vein of achieving unity, the council sought to eradicate the disruptive teachings of Wycliffe that had continued to grow through the likes of Jan Hus and others. The council demanded that Hus present himself, which he agreed to do only after receiving a guarantee of safe passage from Sigismund. The council found him guilty of heresy and, ignoring the guarantee of safe passage, turned him over to the secular court, which executed him as a heretic by burning at the stake.[88]

His followers were incensed and soon began disturbances against the church in Bohemia. These escalated into a series of conflicts that lasted for fifteen years and included a civil war and four church crusades against the Bohemian Hussites.[89]

The Hussite movement split into factions and ultimately fought against each other. One, called the Unitas Fratrum (United Brethren), spread throughout Bohemia, Moravia, and Poland, eventually going underground due to severe persecution. They emerged in Germany as Moravian exiles under the protection of Count Nicolaus Ludwig von Zinzendorf.[90] Hussite beliefs held by the Moravian exiles, German pietism, and Zinzendorf's unique religious passion converged to become the Moravian Church. Although small in numbers—today the Moravian denomination has less than one million members[91]—its traditions of worldwide missionary work, seeking personal experiences with Christ, prayer meetings, and personal piety have profoundly influenced many other denominations.[92]

Within a few decades of Jan Hus's death, Johannes Guttenberg (c. 1400–1468) invented the printing press with movable type.[93] Few inventions have had such a profound impact on human history. With the press, future protestors' grievances and ideas could spread quickly—far beyond national boundaries and to all classes of society.

Martin Luther and the Lutherans

Tradition has it that Martin Luther nailed his Ninety-Five Theses to the door of the Wittenberg Chapel in Germany on October 31, 1517, ushering in the Reformation; however, we've seen that the forces inspiring the Reformation were at work before this momentous event. The Ninety-Five Theses may have indeed been the start of the visible and enduring protest from which Protestantism takes its name, but it was hardly the beginning of the Reformation or even the beginning of Luther's own journey away from orthodoxy.

Martin Luther was a brilliant student of law and philosophy, earning his baccalaureate and master's degrees in the shortest possible time. But at age twenty-one in 1505, Luther experienced a life-threatening thunderstorm during which he promised that if he survived he would become a monk.[94] He was true to his promise and sought to earn God's love through monastic self-deprivation and punishment. But he felt nothing of God's love and instead became consumed with thoughts of God's eternal punishment.[95]

Luther studied the *Sentences* and other works, including those by Aquinas and Ockham, en route to becoming a teacher of theology. As he lectured on Psalms and the epistles of Paul in 1513–1514, he became convinced of Augustinian doctrine such that his understanding shifted from punishment to mercy. At some point during this personal journey, he had a conversion experience that he recorded:

> At last meditating day and night, by the mercy of God, I began to understand that the righteousness of God is that through which the righteous live by a gift of God, namely by faith. Here I felt as if I were entirely born again and had entered paradise itself through the gates that had been flung open.[96]

Luther concluded that Augustine was right. After the fall, man became depraved and unable to exercise will to do good. He rejected Ockham's optimistic view of free will and even rejected Aquinas's notion of infusion of grace. Rather, he came to believe that faith is an unmerited gift of grace, and that justification, the removal of sin, is by that faith alone, or in Latin, *sola fide*.[97] Man is justified, not because he is a new man infused with grace as Aquinas taught but because Christ's goodness is imputed to him, leaving him justified but still the depraved recipient of that grace. Luther crystallized his emerging understanding in *Disputation Against Scholastic Theology*, which he published in 1517.[98]

It was in this context of personal, intellectual, and spiritual transformation that Luther transitioned from an academic commentator to a public protestor. One month after publishing *Disputation Against Scholastic Theology* he took up a fight against indulgences. This was not a new dispute. Indeed, Wycliffe, Hus, and others had confronted the church over indulgences, but in Luther's time and place, indulgences took on an even more sinister aspect. In a ploy to raise desperately needed money, the German archbishop obtained approval from the pope to sell a new type of indulgence, called a plenary indulgence, that would allow the living to compensate the debt for sin of those already in purgatory. The terms of the pope's approval required that revenue from the indulgences be split fifty-fifty between the local archdiocese and Rome. Highly incented to have the indulgences raise funds, the church sent a specialist in the sale of indulgences named Johann Tetzel into Germany in 1516 to drum up demand. One of Tetzel's reported aphorisms was, "As soon as the coin in the coffer rings, the soul from purgatory ('into heaven') springs."[99] Luther was appalled to the point of publicly posting his Ninety-Five Theses in 1517. In them, he took a stand against Tetzel in particular and against the practice of indulgences in general.[100]

Luther did not initially intend to break from the Catholic Church; however, the pope and the emperor of the Holy Roman Empire were both inflexible on the matter, and after a series of warnings and very public debates Luther was excommunicated in 1521 and declared a heretic by the church and an outlaw by the Holy Roman Empire. The combination of these decrees was effectively a sentence of death.[101] Luther found protection in the form of a sympathetic noble, Frederick III, who sequestered him in the Wartburg Castle. From there, he wrote profusely, and through the marvels of the printing press his tracts spread widely through Europe.

Luther's protests were triggered by indulgences; however, he took exception to many other Catholic doctrines and practices. Like Wycliffe, he believed that the scriptures alone were the authoritative source of God's word and authority, a doctrine he called *sola scriptura*. Consequently, he rejected papal decrees and canonical tradition. Relative to the sacrament of the Eucharist, Luther rejected the doctrine of transubstantiation; however, he did not stray far from it. Luther continued to believe in the *real* presence of the body and blood of Christ in the consecrated bread and wine of the Eucharist in what he called *sacramental union*.[102] For Luther, the bread was still bread and the wine still wine; however, through sacramental union, the actual body and blood of Christ were offered to the partaker.[103]

His unyielding criticism of church authority, like Wycliffe's and Hus's criticisms before him, inspired a revolt against both clerical *and* secular authority. Contemporary radical reformers such as Thomas Müntzer tapped into the resentment of the peasant class,[104] which led to an uprising of peasants in 1524. The Peasants' War, as it was called, became brutal on both sides.[105] The peasants burned monasteries and convents, and the mercenary Swabian army slaughtered up to one hundred thousand of the poorly armed and ill-trained peasants.[106] Many expected Luther to side with the peasants, but instead he took a hard stand in favor of the princes, writing a tract *Against the Murderous, Thieving Hordes of Peasants*.[107] We can only speculate about Luther's motives. Surely, he had self-interest in siding with the source of his protection; furthermore, as an educated man, he knew the fate of the Lollards and the Hussites who had sponsored rebellion against their respective secular authorities. However, Luther's defense of secular authority may truly have been a philosophically principled position similar to Ockham's or Wycliffe's. Regardless of motive, his decision had profound consequences. Instead of banishing Lutheran protestants, German nobility sheltered and protected them and ultimately adopted their faith.

The doctrine of the Eucharist had been reformulated by both Wycliffe and Hus and similarly was important to Reformers of the sixteenth century. In nearby Switzerland, Ulrich Zwingli was teaching many of the same things about salvation as Luther was. Thus, in 1529, Philip I, a German prince, attempted to unite the various Protestant-leaning kingdoms under one religion. At the behest of Philip, nearly a dozen Reformers met at the Marburg Castle to consider uniting Protestantism into one body. Luther and Zwingli agreed on many points of doctrine, but in spite of the compelling political expediency and the strong urging from Philip to reconcile differences, the two could not agree on the doctrine of the Eucharist. Zwingli believed that the emblems of the Eucharist were *symbolic* representations of the body and blood of Jesus and not the *real* presence of the body and blood of Jesus, as Luther believed. The two Reformers were so committed to their positions that the attempt at unification failed.[108]

As Luther organized a new church in 1526, he purposefully tried to minimize radical change in liturgy.[109] Consequently, Lutherans preserved many features of Catholicism, such as observing festivals and worshiping with altars, crosses, candles, vestments, catechisms, and sacraments.[110] Luther interpreted the words of Peter the apostle to mean that all baptized members were part of the "priesthood of all believers."[111] Priesthood is authority that is an essential part of governance; however, governance was not a defining theme for Luther. Lutherans retained episcopal hierarchy with bishops and archbishops over diocese and archdiocese respectively.[112]

Luther had no objection to secular authority, as evidenced by his defense of the princes in the Peasants' War. Thus, Lutheranism was viewed favorably by sovereigns. The new religion spread throughout Germany with many German princes adopting the faith. It also spread into many Scandinavian countries beyond the borders of the Holy Roman Empire.[113] Each sovereign could form an independent magisterial Lutheran church offering the sacraments of salvation free from the requisite allegiance to the papacy as demanded by the Catholic Church.

The German princes that adopted Lutheranism directly violated the law of the Holy Roman Empire, of which they were a part. As a proactive measure, they formed an alliance in 1531 to defend against the empire should it retaliate against them. The alliance, called the Schmalkaldic League, became a meaningful political concern to Emperor Charles V such that after settling other wars Charles went to battle against the league, defeating it in 1547.[114] However, the emperor wisely recognized that Lutheranism had become too entrenched to eradicate it by edict. Thus, in 1555, he and the princes agreed to the Augsburg Peace that established the doctrine of *cuius regio, eius religio* (whose realm, his religion). Each prince would decide the religion of his followers! Notably, the only two allowed religions were Catholicism and Lutheranism.[115]

Today, there are about eighty million Lutherans worldwide with the highest concentration in Northern Europe.[116] In the United States, the two bodies are the Lutheran Church Missouri Synod (~2.3 million members) and the Evangelical Lutheran Church in America (~4.0 million members).

John Calvin and the Reformed Churches

As noted earlier, Luther was not alone in seeking reforms to the church. Reformers were active in all parts of Europe. However, the success of Reformation was directly proportional to political support. Where there was no political support, Reformation was met with repression, and Reformers were forced to flee to safe havens. Such was the case when John Calvin, a young lawyer in France, had an experience that convinced him of the Reform movement growing around him. He recorded,

> God by a sudden conversion subdued and brought my mind to a teachable frame, which was more hardened in such matters than might have been expected from one at my early period of life. Having thus received some taste and knowledge of true godliness, I was immediately inflamed with so intense a desire to make progress therein, that although I did not altogether leave of other studies, yet I pursued them with less ardour.[117]

Calvin deepened his association with Nicolas Cop, an outspoken mentor, academic, and Reformer. In 1535, Calvin followed Cop to Basel, Switzerland, fleeing a charge of heresy in France.[118]

Switzerland shared a border with France, and by the beginning of the sixteenth century, the confederacy of thirteen Swiss cantons had achieved de facto independence from the Holy Roman Empire—the prize for victory in the Swabian War of 1499. Driven by religious, sovereign, and economic interests, city councils within several of the cantons secularized the churches within their borders by appropriating church lands, tax revenue, schools, and even ecclesiastical administration. City-controlled churches created the intellectual freedom to preach non-Orthodox doctrines. Ulrich Zwingli, a pastor in Zurich, tested the ability to preach Reformation-minded doctrine using the event of Lent in 1522. Fasting was required by church tradition on Lent. To test the ability to rely solely on scripture and reject church tradition, Zwingli encouraged the citizens of Zurich to eat sausages during Lent. We may snicker at the idea of a serious protest in the form of eating sausage; however, the real issue at stake was whether church tradition could be trumped by scripture. Zwingli proclaimed, "Christians are free to fast or not to fast because the Bible does not prohibit the eating of meat during Lent."[119] The timing was right. Zwingli had the support of Zurich's magistrate, and Zwingli soon became a proponent of Zurich's secular appropriation of the church.[120] Other cantons followed suit. Geneva's city council lagged behind but ultimately decided to join Reform-minded cantons around 1536.

Calvin had been in exile in Reform-tolerant Basel, Switzerland, for several months, but in 1536 he returned to France during a six-month period of clemency offered to heretics. From France, Calvin intended to go to Strasbourg, an imperial city in which Reformers were protected. But military maneuvers blocked the direct route, causing him to divert through Geneva. There, he found fellow Frenchman William Farel, who had been the first into Geneva after its decision to join Reform-minded cantons. Farel urged Calvin to stay and assist in the formative Reformation of the church in Geneva—an invitation Calvin accepted.[121]

Calvin and Farel's work in Geneva was both religious and civic. They were empowered by the city council to develop a new code for the city, including religious catechisms and civil behavior. In mixing secular governance and theology in his work, Calvin's legacy is somewhat paradoxical. Like Luther, Calvin adopted the doctrine of justification by grace and not by works, a doctrine which led some to reject all law. A sense of liberation from laws and authority translated, as it had with the Lollards in England, the Hussites in Bohemia, and the peasants in Germany, into a rising tide of civil unrest. However, Calvin had no intention of equating salvation by grace to lawlessness. He proposed, and the council instituted, strict laws governing the behavior of Geneva citizens. So strict were these laws that entertainment was forbidden.[122]

Like the forerunners of the Reformation and Luther, Calvin adopted Augustinian doctrines of salvation. Although Calvinism and Lutheranism share Augustinian notions of justification by faith and not by works, original sin, depravity of man, and so on, Calvinism fully adopted the Augustinian doctrines of God's complete sovereignty and the predestination of the "elect." Just as the "elect of God" are predestined for eternal life, the damned must also be predestined. Bradwardine's teaching found a champion in Calvin—men's will is merely a reflection of God's sovereignty. Thus, the grace extended to the elect can't be earned and is "irresistible" by them.[123]

Importantly, neither Calvin nor Luther challenged the Trinitarian doctrine of the Godhead. Calvin, however, rejected the papacy and the top-down episcopal authority practiced by the Orthodox churches. In his seminal work, *Institutes of the Christian Religion,* he concluded that the central office of church authority is the priest, or, in Greek, the *presbyter*. Other offices and titles mentioned in the Bible are but priests fulfilling different roles. Calvin asserted that the title of bishop used by Paul relative to Timothy and Titus indicated a priest selected from among priests to preside. He equated the title of elder to that of priest. He taught that priests acted within one of three orders: "For from the order of presbyters [priests] (1) part were chosen pastors and teachers [pastors]; (2) the remaining part were charged with the censure and correction of morals [elders]; (3) the care of the poor and the distribution of alms were committed to the deacons [deacons]."[124]

With the sanction of Geneva's city council, Calvin organized a new church according to the Presbyterian model—a church that he called the Reformed Church. The respected periodical Christianity Today describes the Presbyterian model as follows:

> Pastors conducted the services, preached, administered the Sacraments, and cared for the spiritual welfare of parishioners. . . . In every district, elders kept an eye on spiritual affairs. If they saw that so-and-so was frequently the worse for drink, or that Mr. X beat his wife, or that Mr. Y and Mrs. Z were seeing too much of each other, they admonished them in a brotherly manner. If the behavior didn't cease, they reported the matter to the Consistory, the church's governing body, which would summon the offender. Excommunication was a last resort and would remain in force until the offender repented. Finally, social welfare was the charge of the deacons. They were the hospital management board, social security executives, and alms-house supervisors. The deacons were so effective, Geneva had no beggars.[125]

In this polity, there was no intrinsic priesthood superiority. All roles were filled by priests and were based on the doctrine of "priesthood of all believers"—any person could be chosen (or elected) from among the congregation to be an elder-priest. Pastors were trained and specifically ordained and were thus called traveling elders or ministers. The elders within each local congregation were to govern the congregation as a council, called a consistory, session, or kirk.[126]

Importantly, Calvin saw the need for governance above the local congregation. Congregations selected an elder to join a governing body, called the presbytery, made up of similarly selected elders from other congregations. The presbytery had governing authority over congregations. Similarly, presbyteries joined into governing councils called synods, and synods into general assemblies.[127] In this way, Calvin navigated a middle ground between the top-town authoritarian episcopal model of the Catholic and Orthodox churches and the potential anarchy of independent congregations. Calvin's innovation in polity fit hand in glove with the Swiss confederacy, in which each canton was relatively independent. Geneva's presbytery could govern Geneva's congregations, as could Zurich's presbytery govern Zurich's congregations, and so on for any other canton. Only in the matters of greatest common interest would synods overrule and exert authority over presbyteries.

Calvin's ideas spread throughout Europe. This was in part because Geneva and other Swiss cantons were safe havens for Reformers from all over Europe, including English protestors fleeing persecution at the hand of Mary, daughter of Henry VIII. Calvinism was taken back to England and was a major influence on the development of Protestantism in England, as we'll explore later in this chapter. However, only the Church of Scotland and its broader communion of Presbyterians consistently mirrored the Reformed Church set up by Calvin in continental Europe. Thus, Presbyterianism is included with the Reformed Church in sizing up present-day Calvinism. Nevertheless, by the end of this chapter, it will be clear that Calvinism had a much broader impact on many denominations emerging from England.

Today, roughly seventy to eighty million Christians belong to churches that directly descend from the Calvinist tradition. The Presbyterian Church is the largest with about forty-five million members.[128] Various Reformed churches exist around the globe with another twenty-five million members.[129] Although Calvin specifically established Presbyterian polity, today, there is a wide range of polity within Calvinism, from episcopal to congregational. Just as with Lutheranism, in most cases outside of the Swiss cantons where Calvinism became the state religion, episcopal governance prevailed due to its more centralized authority.[130] The Church of Scotland, with Presbyterian polity, is the major exception. Separatists in the fledgling American colonies resisted any external influence, including Presbyterian governance, and thus established Calvinistic congregational churches in the new colonies.[131] The United Church of Christ is the largest of the Calvinistic congregational churches today, with just over one million members.[132]

We shouldn't leave the story of Calvin without considering the theological backlash that his emphasis on predestination created. As the Reformed Church spread, theologians renewed the debate that Augustine and Pelagius had played out centuries before. A newly appointed professor in Leiden in 1603 became the figurehead for a formal confrontation. Jacobus Arminius had spent time studying theology in Geneva under Calvin's protégé. He concluded that Calvinism was wrong relative to its extreme position on predestination, and he emphasized that if predestination and unconditional election were true doctrines, then God was the author of evil. He argued that salvation had to be *conditional.* God's foreknowledge did not predestine man's actions. Indeed, man had free will and was thus accountable for his actions.[133]

Arminius's influential position as a professor of theology meant that his doctrinal rebuttal of predestination could not be ignored. He and like-minded theologians, collectively known as the Remonstrants, sought an official Reformed Church council to rule on the matter. Although Arminius died before a synod could be held—he died in 1609—his followers authored five articles of remonstrance (protest) in 1610.[134] In the Synod of Dort, held in 1618, the Reformed Church of the Netherlands formally rejected the Five Articles of Remonstrance and adopted five opposing articles called the Five Points of Calvinism.[135]

The Remonstrants were officially condemned as heretics.[136] Nevertheless, they survived and still exist today in small numbers throughout the Netherlands.[137] Still, their importance is not measured by their present-day numbers. Arminian Remonstrants championed the doctrine of free will at a time when the conditions were right, particularly in England, for the formation of many new denominations, including one started by John Wesley, as we will explore in a later chapter. Whether it is called the Augustinian-Pelagian or Arminian-Calvinism debate, the essence of the contested doctrine lives on. Many denominations today believe in free will and thus the accountability of humankind. Many more Christians, even many that belong to Protestant denominations descending from Luther and Calvin, accept that each person is accountable for exercising moral agency. After all, the very foundation of Western justice is based on this principle. Still, denominations that officially believe that the free-will choices and corresponding works of a person factor into their personal standing before God are often criticized as Pelagian—teaching that Christians "earn" salvation by receiving merit for good works. Indeed, the debate lives on.

Radical Reformation and the Anabaptists

We've learned that Reformation in the form of courageous, harsh, and often zealous criticism of the church often translated into civil uprising against all authority, spiritual and secular. We've seen contrasting examples of Reformers gaining and preserving the protection of monarchs or princes. Ockham survived to do most of his writing protected by the king of Bavaria. The followers of Wycliffe and Hus both enjoyed protection from sovereigns for a time, only to lose it and be driven underground. Luther, Zwingli, and Calvin succeeded in large measure because they remained in the good graces of their respective civil authorities. Other contemporary Reformers purposefully did not cozy up to sovereigns. Quite the opposite, they openly opposed all unholy alliances between church and state. This class of "radical Reformers" found themselves friendless—despised by Reformers and by civil governments.

We learned earlier about Thomas Müntzer, who played a role in the German Peasants' War of 1524. Other radical Reformers were not revolutionaries like Müntzer but still criticized the leading Reformers, predominantly Luther and Zwingli, for being too limited in their scope of reform and for being too cozy with secular authority. Early in the sixteenth century, Reformers flocked to Zürich, where Zwingli had the full protection and support of the city council. A group of Reformers began to publicly criticize Zwingli's close association with the state and his endorsement of infant baptism.[138] Of these, infant baptism became the most divisive. Zwingli had adopted Augustinian doctrines, which included the doctrines of original sin and the depravity of man. The need to baptize infants was a logical outcome of these doctrines. Thus, Zwingli supported infant baptism, but he also advocated the preeminence of scripture. Herein was a conflict. Infant baptism was not scriptural. Rather, the New Testament included only examples of baptism of converted believers.[139] Thus, some of Zwingli's followers split from him and began preaching that baptism was for "believing" adults only.

The contention between the doctrinal camps in Zürich became sharp, leading the city council to get involved. In January of 1525, the city council sided with Zwingli and ordered the dissenters to desist their public opposition to him. In defiance, the group gathered and rebaptized themselves, thereby becoming civil dissidents and sealing their split from the Zwingli-led Zürich church and its doctrine of infant baptism. The Swiss Brethren, as they came to be known, had started the Anabaptist movement.[140] Two years later in 1527, they formalized a confession of faith.[141] The Anabaptists were severely persecuted throughout Europe by both Protestants and Catholics.[142] Many of their leaders were executed for heresy.[143] With few exceptions, their pacifist beliefs caused them to flee to neighboring countries rather than fight.[144] Large Anabaptist communities grew in Moravia (Hutterites), northern Netherlands, and Germany. Even if given asylum within a country, they faced difficult odds, having access only to poor lands, paying heavy taxes, and living in the shadows. Their circumstances required a strong reliance on communal support, hard work, and simple living.[145]

Mennonites, Amish, and Hutterites are the present-day direct descendants of the Anabaptists. These denominations can be found around the world; however, they are still ethnically aligned with their roots in northern Europe.[146] In their self-imposed segregation, unique culture, and simple lifestyle we can see the evidence of their confession of faith and their history of persecution. Worldwide, there are about 2.1 million members of these descendant denominations.[147]

Other denominations reached doctrinal conclusions similar to those of the Anabaptists and rejected infant baptism. This is a distinguishing characteristic of Baptists; however, Anabaptists and Baptists should not be confused. They do not share a common heritage and have very different beliefs outside of baptism. We will cover the origin of Baptists later in this chapter.

The Church of England

Henry VIII assumed the throne at age seventeen in 1509. Like kings before him, he was coronated at the hand of the ranking local authority of the church, the archbishop. Henry's rise to the throne was complicated by his decision to proceed with a marriage to Catherine of Aragon. The marriage had been brokered between his parents and King Ferdinand of Spain after Henry's older brother, to whom Catherine had been married without consummation for five months, died at age fifteen. To preserve the alliance, Henry's father and Ferdinand betrothed the widowed Catherine to the younger preteen Henry VIII.[148]

Like all royal weddings, the future marriage of Henry VIII and Catherine required the pope's blessing, which in this case also required the pope to annul Catherine's previous marriage to Henry's brother. Although the pope had plenty of time to annul Catherine's previous marriage, he delayed. At age seventeen and soon to be coronated, Henry VIII fulfilled the agreement of his father and married Catherine of Aragon without the annulment and the pope's blessing. It is likely that the educated and astute Henry realized the value of the Spanish alliance as much as his father had.

Catherine did not bear a son. Consequently, Henry became increasingly desperate for an heir. At age thirty-two, Henry pursued a solution to the question of succession by seeking to have his marriage to Catherine annulled by the pope. The pope refused. It has been speculated that the pope's refusal was in retribution for Henry marrying Catherine without a papal blessing in the first place, or perhaps it was because the pope could not risk alienating Catherine's nephew, Charles V, who had subsequently been coronated as emperor of the Holy Roman Empire.[149]

In a series of defiant steps, Henry VIII broke with the pope. With the blessing of the newly instated archbishop of Canterbury, Thomas Cranmer, Henry married Anne Boleyn in 1533. Parliament supported Henry's marriage by naming Henry and Anne's daughter Elizabeth heir to the throne in the Succession Act of 1533. Parliament further snubbed the authority of the church at Rome by passing the Supremacy Act of 1534, in which the king of England was named the supreme head of the church in England. This act of defiance stood in stark contrast to Henry's actions just a decade earlier, when, in 1521, he had defended the supreme role of the papacy against Martin Luther in Germany in a work called *Defence of the Seven Sacraments*. Now, just twelve years later, he officially broke with Rome.[150] Henry VIII formed the Church of England, sometimes called the Anglican[151] Church, strictly due to issues of sovereignty and authority. Consequently, the Church of England initially retained essentially all of the beliefs and practices of the Roman Catholic Church. The archbishop of Canterbury took the role of the pope as the senior ecclesiastic and was second only to the king in the church.

Henry VIII understood that his new church needed to distinguish its body of doctrine from its Catholic origins, but it lacked the Reform-motivated purpose and the articulate guidance of a Luther, Zwingli, or Calvin. Henry turned to a council to define the nascent church's beliefs and practices. The council's efforts stretched beyond Henry's reign and was not completed until 1549, during the reign of his young son, Edward. The council's product was the *Book of Common Prayer.* Although it has been revised many times through the ensuing centuries, it remains the central confession for Anglican churches.[152]

As the British Empire spread, the Anglican Church spread with it. However, where it became the magisterial church of other countries, it is often known by the name of the state that adopted it; for example, the Anglican Church in Nigeria is simply known as the Church of Nigeria. Other Anglican denominations include the term *Anglican* in their title, and still others refer to themselves as Episcopal or Episcopalian—a clear reference to the episcopal polity retained by the Church of England. Even though many non-Anglican churches have an episcopal polity, including the Catholic Church, the Greek Orthodox Church, and others, the capitalized term *Episcopal* is associated with Anglican denominations throughout the world, including the Episcopal Church of the United States. Together, all the denominations of Anglican descent are part of the Anglican Communion and revere the archbishop of Canterbury as the spokesman for Christ on the earth, just as Roman Catholics look to the pope. Today, there are some eighty-five million Christians in the Anglican communion.[153]

What we've learned so far about the Protestant Reformation in England is like a set of bookends. We learned about its origin and the dominant Anglican branch that emerged from it. But this story is woefully incomplete. Between the bookends was a momentous period of sowing the seeds of future Christin splintering.

Religious Turbulence in England

During the brief reign of Henry VIII's successor, Edward VI, the young Church of England began to incorporate Protestant ideals from continental Europe.[154] Reformers such as John Hooper, who had personal experience with Reformers in continental Europe, pushed for Protestant ideals within the Church of England. But the *Book of Common Prayer*, completed in 1549, fell well short of the Protestant reforms that had taken root in Europe, leading John Hooper to demonstrate his opposition in 1550 by refusing to be ordained a bishop in the priestly clothing, or vestments, prescribed in the *Book of Common Prayer*. To him, the vestments were remnants of the church's Catholic past and were a symbol of the division between the church's "priesthood class" and its laity. The resulting dispute became quite sharp and was settled only when Calvin himself advised Hooper to drop the issue in 1551.[155] To Hooper and others that would follow, vestments were a highly visible measure of reform, or lack of it, within the Church of England.

Edward's reign was short-lived. He died at age fifteen in 1553. His older half sister, Mary I, daughter of Henry's first wife, Catherine of Aragon, ascended to the throne.[156] Mary and her mother had been exiled by Henry VIII and had remained faithful Catholics. Consequently, upon assuming the throne, Mary determined to return England to Catholicism with allegiance to Rome. Within months, she imprisoned leading Protestants. She restored heresy acts and in 1555 began executing leading Protestants, including the archbishop of Canterbury, Thomas Cranmer. In all, she executed more than 280 Protestants, mostly by burning. Her actions earned her the notorious epithet Bloody Mary.[157]

Hundreds of influential Protestants, including Protestant clergy, fled England, taking refuge in Protestant strongholds including

Geneva. As a group, these "Marian" exiles were deeply influenced by mainstream Protestantism, particularly Calvinism. When Mary I died after a short reign of five years, her half sister, the Protestant Elizabeth, ascended to the throne. The Protestant clergy returned to England expecting that they could shape the Church of England in the image of Calvin's Geneva with its characteristic Presbyterian form of governance, strict piety, equality of clergy and laity, and simplified liturgy and vestments.

However, many clerics and much of the citizenry in England were still essentially Catholic in practice and doctrine. Elizabeth sided with the proponents of limited change and thus decided to reinstate the *Book of Common Prayer* as completed under Edward VI. Parliament passed the Act of Uniformity of 1559, which required the use of formal vestments for clergy, igniting another vestments controversy similar to Hooper's rebellion eight years earlier. Dissenting clergy sought constitutional means to reform the Church of England through a convocation called in 1563. However, the Calvin-inspired Reformers failed to gain sufficient support and the traditionalists prevailed.[158] The clerics who refused to conform with the vestments ruling were called nonconformists. The crisis came to a head in 1566 when the archbishop assembled the clergy in the London diocese, placed a fully dressed priest wearing the required vestments in front of them, and then required a vote of commitment from each cleric. Of those present, sixty-one conformed and thirty-seven declined to conform. Those who declined were immediately suspended from their clerical duties and stripped of their living.[159]

The term *puritan* emerged as a nickname for nonconformists. Puritanism was not a new denomination but a movement to reform English Christianity. Given that the movement's principal leaders were Marian exiles who had been heavily influenced by Calvinism, the Puritans reflected many of Calvinism's beliefs and practices, including simple dress, strict moral behavior, belief in the depravity of man, and notions of the covenant elect of God.[160]

Robert Crowley, a former Marian exile and vestments nonconformist, ignored his suspension from his post as vicar of St. Giles. A month after his suspension, he stopped some choir members attending a funeral from entering "his" church because they were wearing formal vestments. The incident escalated, and the archbishop formally stripped Crowley of all clerical benefits. His punishment failed to dampen the Puritan groundswell, however, as Crowley returned to his trade as a printer and began a literary war that energized the Puritan movement. Crowley's first work, *A Briefe Discourse Against the Outwarde Apparel of the Popishe Church,* has been called the "the earliest puritan manifesto."[161] In a tit-for-tat, tracts for and against vestments were published. Inevitably, the right of secular authority to dictate religious practice came to dominate the debate. The conflict started over the visible aspects of liturgy (i.e., vestments) but quickly evolved to be about governance of the church itself. Nonconformists railed against the authoritarian rule of the episcopal system manipulated by secular power. In 1572, Puritans published an *Admonition to Parliament*, urging Parliament to reject the episcopal system of church governance and adopt a presbyterian system; however, Parliament rejected the proposal and the Church of England remained episcopal.[162]

When the war of words failed to change the Church of England, the most radical nonconformist Puritans went underground and established independent congregations. By their very nature, these were separatist congregations from the Church of England. Given that religious obedience was enforced by state law, these underground congregations were inherently also politically separatist. The first official discovery of a separatist congregation was in 1567 in Plumbers Hall in London.[163] As a natural byproduct of their formation, these congregations were autonomous, answering to no other higher authority, thereby creating a self-governing form of church governance at the opposite extreme from the episcopal polity of much of the Christian world. Naturally, it came to be called "congregational" polity.

Other Puritans struck a moderate tone, believing they could reform the church from within. Nonseparatist Puritanism grew within the ranks of nobility and Parliament and flourished in intellectual circles at Oxford and Cambridge.[164] Robert Browne began his journey in this camp; however, he came to believe that the only way to establish a church according to the New Testament model was outside the Church of England. In 1581, he set up a separatist congregational church. Browne was arrested but released due to the influence of his kinsman William Cecil, one of the most powerful advisors to Queen Elizabeth.

Browne and his followers sought refuge in Middelburg, Netherlands, in the same year.[165] However, Browne had a change of heart and decided to rejoin the Church of England and return to England just a few years later in 1585. Nevertheless, he left two important legacies. First, the congregation he led to the Netherlands persisted, and a portion of it known as the "pilgrims" emigrated from the Netherlands to the new colonies in America in 1620 aboard the *Mayflower*. Second, Browne was influential in formalizing congregational polity through his tract called *A Booke which sheweth the life and manners of all True Christians*.[166] Through the pilgrims and other separatist groups like them, Puritan ideals and congregational polity became firmly entrenched in North America.

The Rise of Presbyterianism

John Knox of Scotland joined other Protestants in Geneva during Queen Mary I's reign. He was deeply impressed with both the doctrines and the "fruits" of Calvinism. He observed in a letter to a friend that Geneva "is the most perfect school of Christ that ever was in the earth since the days of the apostles."[167] In 1559, Knox returned to Scotland and gained the agreement of the Scottish Parliament to reform the Church of Scotland. With Parliament's commission, in 1560 he, along with five collaborators, published the Scots Confession—statements of faith reflecting Knox's understanding of Calvinism. Later that same year, the Scottish Parliament adopted the *Book of Discipline*, which outlined a Presbyterian church polity.

In the ensuing decades, the British Isles seesawed between strains of Protestantism with Calvin-inspired offshoots at one end and the Anglicans of the Church of England at the other. The tension between these camps was violent at times and changed the course of British history. Charles I, following the lead of his father, James I, attempted to impose the Anglican model on the Church of Scotland, which had previously adopted Calvinism. A series of deadly skirmishes in Scotland resulted, called the Bishops' Wars of 1639-1640.[168] When the English Parliament, which was increasingly dominated by Calvinistic Puritans, refused to fund these wars, Charles bypassed Parliament to fund his military campaigns. The wars and other actions by Charles led Parliament to narrowly pass the Grand Remonstrance in 1641, which contained a list of royal grievances.[169] The king ignored them, which resulted in the English Civil War that erupted in 1642. Parliament and the king were now combatants. In 1646, the pro-Puritan Parliament swung the pendulum by abolishing episcopal governance in favor of presbyterian polity. Presbyterianism was ascendant throughout the combined kingdoms of England and Scotland, giving rise to a consolidated confession of faith in 1649 to be known as the Westminster Confession. So important was this new confession that it replaced the Scots Confession and is used to this day as the Presbyterian confession of faith.

In the same year, 1649, the monarchy fell. King Charles I was beheaded, and his heir, Charles II, fled into exile, ushering in the English interregnum, a period during which no king or queen ruled the British Isles. Oliver Cromwell, a key military figure on the side of Parliament during the English Civil War and a Puritan, emerged as the dominant leader from 1653 until his death in 1658.[170] With Parliament's support and Cromwell's leadership, Calvinistic Puritanism came to dominate English life.[171] However, after Cromwell's death, the pendulum swung to the opposite extreme. Cromwell's son lost the support of a faction of the military. The military removed the younger Cromwell and seated a new parliament that favored the monarchy and reinstated Charles II as monarch in 1660.

Charles II promptly reinstated the *Book of Common Prayer* as the confession of faith for the Church of England, along with its episcopal polity. In 1662, like déjà vu from the earlier reign of Queen Elizabeth, Parliament passed an Act of Uniformity requiring compliance with the *Book of Common Prayer*. Puritans, who had enjoyed a period of state-sanctioned prosperity, were instantly disenfranchised. About two thousand Puritan clergy were now on the wrong side of the law. They resigned from their ministries and joined the groundswell of Congregationalists, Baptists, and English Presbyterians.[172]

When Charles II died in 1685, England again experienced an about-face in religious dominance. James II, Charles's brother, was heir to the throne and had reportedly converted to Catholicism, perhaps in response to the influence of his Italian wife.[173] Protestant nobles, fearing that James II would reintroduce a Catholic monarchy, encouraged William of Orange, husband to James's daughter Mary, to invade England with an army—an invitation that William acted on in late 1688 in the Glorious Revolution.[174]

The extreme religious swings moderated under William. He encouraged greater religious tolerance, reflected in the passage of the Toleration Act of 1689, which guaranteed religious toleration of non-Anglican Protestants such as Presbyterians and Baptists. While this was a welcome step toward tolerance, the act fell far short of religious freedom. It did not extend tolerance to Catholics or to non-Trinitarians such as Unitarians, Anabaptists, and non-Christians.[175] The Toleration Act was an important precursor to the Act of Union in 1707 that joined Scotland and England to form the United Kingdom and formally recognized Presbyterianism as the official church of Scotland.[176]

Presbyterianism spread throughout the American colonies and then throughout the world largely through Scottish immigrants. Today, there are some forty to fifty million Presbyterians that, along with another twenty to thirty million members of Reformed churches throughout the world, preserve Calvinism's theology, polity, and liturgy.

The Formation of the Baptists

Like Robert Browne, John Smyth, a Cambridge graduate and Puritan, led a separatist congregation from Lincolnshire to seek asylum in Amsterdam, Netherlands, in 1608. Smyth concluded through his study that if "the churches of the apostolic constitution consisted of saints only . . . then baptism should be restricted to believers only."[177] He expounded his views in a book published in 1609, *The Character of the Beast*, and then proceeded to baptize himself and thirty-six other believing adults. Only later did Smyth learn of an Anabaptist community in Amsterdam that was also practicing "baptism of believers." Smyth proposed joining with them; however, outside of their shared belief in baptism of believers and a shared distant heritage of Swiss-based Protestantism, the two groups were culturally and theologically very different. Thomas Helwys led a group to resist Smyth's efforts at unification with the Anabaptists and split with the Amsterdam group, returning to London to establish a *general* Baptist Church there in about 1612.[178]

Another variant of Baptists led by John Spilsbury, a Calvinistic minister, emerged from nonseparatist Puritans in 1638.[179] This group placed far more emphasis on Calvin's teaching of the predestined elect and reflected this belief in the title of their new church, the Particular Baptist Church—the word *particular* indicating that only the elect are saved. These two very different strains of Baptists were indicative of the future family of Baptist denominations. Its congregational origins meant that there was no single leader or universally accepted set of beliefs. The core of its doctrine was Protestant-Calvinism, and Baptists share a few common "distinctives," including the doctrine of the baptism of believers, but otherwise there is wide diversity across individual churches. Nevertheless, in a very organic way the faith resonated with millions of spiritually minded adults for whom the baptism of their infancy was little more than a religious check mark.

In 1677, Particular Baptist churches created the first confession of faith based on the Calvinist-inspired Presbyterian's *Westminster Confession*, modifying it to reflect their distinct beliefs of baptism of believers and congregational polity. The confession was not officially accepted until after the Act of Toleration in England in 1689 and is therefore known as the *1689 Baptist Confession of Faith*.[180] Particular Baptists in the colonies adopted the confession as *The Philadelphia Confession of Faith* in 1742.[181]

During the English Civil War described in the previous section, the Baptist faith spread around the campfires of Cromwell's armies.[182] It took root in the colonies when Roger Williams, banished from the Massachusetts Bay Colony, founded a Baptist church in 1638 in the future Rhode Island.[183] It spread quickly in England and America during the Great Awakenings that will be discussed in future chapters. Estimates suggest that the Baptists grew from nearly five hundred congregations just before the American Revolution to nearly twelve hundred twenty years later.[184] Within a few decades, congregations of American Baptists joined together to form missionary societies that evangelized foreign lands.

The American Civil War drove a wedge between Baptists who opposed slavery and restricted slaveholders from missions and those who supported slavery. The proslavery Southern Baptist Convention, made up of nine Southern state Baptist conventions, split from the

Northern Baptist societies in 1845.[185] After the Civil War and emancipation, Baptist congregations proliferated among the newly freed African Americans. Black congregations formed their own National Baptist Convention in 1895.[186]

The Baptists were again divided in the early 1900s when confronted with modernism, including new scientific theories and biblical reinterpretation. Baptists were not alone. A conflict between modernism and fundamentalism rocked many denominations, as described in more detail in in chapter 10. The Northern Baptist Convention tended toward modernism, leading some congregations to split to form fundamentalist associations.[187] Conversely, the Southern Baptist Convention adopted fundamentalism, leading some Southern congregations to split to form more moderate conventions.

Because southerners in the United States are most commonly Baptists[188] and are often religiously and politically conservative, it is all too easy to conflate Baptists with fundamentalists, but that view misrepresents progressive Baptists around the world. Furthermore, many Baptists are evangelical "born-again" Christians, and so it is common to conflate evangelicalism with the Baptists, but doing so would misrepresent traditional Baptists. In short, Baptists defy generalizations and stereotypes. With the Baptists' congregational polity, diverse doctrines, and fractured heritage, there are arguably many denominations. In cities with many congregations, there is an element of "shopping" for a compatible church and pastor.[189] Nevertheless, using the denominational term, albeit loosely, is still appropriate because there are common Baptist "distinctives."[190] In the words of one Baptist,

> Baptists come in a variety of "flavors." They hold different interpretations and views on certain issues, such as the Second Coming of Christ, worship styles and denominational organization. But all Baptists have the same basic ingredients. There are certain ingredients that must be included, or the recipe does not produce a Baptist.[191]

Arguably, more than any other denomination, Baptists are woven into the fabric of America and reflect America's story, diversity, and contradictions. The faith grew out of English Puritanism, but it flourished in America. Its history includes the stain of slavery and the attempt to heal from it.[192] Millions within it share a common bond yet remain segregated in different congregations that are fiercely independent. From it have arisen some of the most outwardly influential leaders, including Martin Luther King Jr. and Billy Graham, and within it are some of the most inwardly focused conservative fundamentalists. Baptists demonstrate expansive charity through their missions while at the same time use the pulpit to spread prejudice against Christians who, in their view, fail litmus tests for being true Christians.

Baptist congregations span the globe, with an estimated 75 million to 105 million Baptists worldwide.[193] The Southern Baptist Convention in the United States is the largest association, with about 15 million members, followed by the African American counterpart, the National Baptist Convention, with 7.5 million members. The Baptists are a key part of the broader treatment of evangelicalism in chapter 10.

The Quakers

Many other separatist groups emerged in England during the unsettled period of the English Civil War, including the Seekers and the Ranters. One group is particularly noteworthy, not for its ultimate size, but for its disproportionate impact on history and its distinct emphasis on personal revelation. A devout young Englishman named George Fox struggled for years to find inner peace through the help of clergy. Ultimately, he had a personal revelation from God. He related the following:

> As I had forsaken the [Anglican] priests, so I left the separate [separatist] preachers also, and those esteemed the most experienced people; for I saw there was none among them all that could speak to my condition. And when all my hopes in them and in all men were gone, so that I had nothing outwardly to help me, nor could tell what to do, then, oh, then, I heard a voice which said, "There is one, even Christ Jesus, that can speak to thy condition"; and when I heard it my heart did leap for joy. Then the Lord let

> me see why there was none upon the earth that could speak to my condition, namely, that I might give Him all the glory; for all are concluded under sin, and shut up in unbelief as I had been, that Jesus Christ might have the pre-eminence who enlightens, and gives grace, and faith, and power. Thus when God doth work, who shall let [i.e., prevent] it? And this I knew experimentally.[194]

In 1647, Fox began traveling around England teaching the new doctrine of personal revelation through the Holy Spirit, piety, and simplicity. He was a persuasive preacher, attracting thousands to a "religious society of friends," a term that was later adopted as an official name, during the confusing time of religious turmoil and civil war. The Friends Church considered themselves to be the restoration of the church of Christ after centuries of apostacy.[195] They deemphasized scholastic doctrinal questions arising from biblical interpretation, confessional creeds, and the role of clergy in approaching God. Each person was encouraged to follow an inner light bestowed by the Holy Spirit.[196] As with many denominations, critics of this church pejoratively applied a nickname that stuck. The Religious Society of Friends came to be known as Quakers, a reference to the prophecy that hearers would "tremble" at the word.[197] The Quakers, like the Anabaptists and others without magisterial sponsorship, were persecuted in both England and the new colonies, particularly the Massachusetts Bay Colony, leading an eminent Quaker, William Penn, to establish the Commonwealth of Pennsylvania as a safe haven for Quakers and other dissenting groups. Arguably, the democratic ideals of Quakerism profoundly shaped the Bill of Rights, trial by jury, equal rights for men and women, and public education.[198] Today, there are fewer than one million Quakers.

The purpose of this chapter has been to explore the origins of the major Protestant branches of Christianity that arose during the Protestant Reformation. Of necessity, we have waded into European history. However, we have barely scratched the surface of the complex history of this period in Christian Europe. It would be simplistic to assert that religion was the singular motivating force in the tumultuous centuries surrounding the Reformation. Europe was undergoing many changes, including the explosion of knowledge, advancement of science, mercantilism, colonialism, and so on. However, religion and sovereignty were inexorably linked, like two sides of the same coin, such that religion was always a principle factor in the wars that gripped Europe for decades.[199]

Much good came from the Reformation: The dark age of religious ignorance lessened as the Bible and other religious tracts were published in many different languages and thus became available to all classes of society. Canonized scripture regained its place of superior moral authority over tradition due to the Protestant doctrine of *sola scriptura*. Reformers had the courage to challenge corruption in pursuit of New Testament ideals. The emphasis on faith and grace surely had a personal spiritual impact on many millions as they sought a relationship with God. The Catholic Church arguably emerged as a holier church as it responded with a counter-Reformation canonized in the Council of Trent in 1563—a council that directly addressed the many issues that had catalyzed the Protestants.[200]

However, not all of the fruits of the Reformation were sweet. Christianity became even more splintered than before such that Jesus's aspiration "that they may be one" was even further out of reach. Intolerance and persecution persisted with new and more varied actors.[201] Wars motivated by a confusing mix of religious conviction and political aspiration were fought across Europe. The climax of this convulsion in Europe was the religiously motivated Thirty Years' War from 1618 to 1648, in which the Catholic alliance of the Hapsburgs and the Holy Roman Empire fought against Protestant Dutch and Swedish powers allied with the anti-Hapsburg Catholic French. This war eventually engulfed nearly every European state[202] and became one of the most deadly and destructive conflicts in history with an estimated eight million causalities.[203]

The Thirty Years' War ended with a series of peace treaties signed in 1648, known collectively as the Peace of Westphalia. The treaties addressed issues of national sovereignty and the balance of power in Europe and, given the interconnected nature of religion and the state, also addressed religion. The Peace of Westphalia expanded the principle of *cuius regio, eius religio* (whose realm, his religion) to include Calvinism. Each sovereign had the right to determine the magisterial religion of his own state.[204] Significantly, for the first time, most Christians living in principalities where their denomination was not the established church were guaranteed the right to practice their faith in public during allotted hours and allowed to worship at will in their private quarters.[205]

As continental Europe exited the Reformation and its associated period of religious wars, Lutheranism dominated northern Europe in today's Scandinavian countries, the northern and central lands of Germany, and the countries bordering the Baltic Sea. Calvinism dominated Switzerland, Southern France (Huguenots), Hungary, Scotland, and the Netherlands. Much of the corridor of the Rhine along Germany's western border was a mix of Lutheranism and Calvinism. Catholicism and other Orthodox religions dominated southern and eastern Europe, including what is today Spain, much of France, Italy, the Balkans, Greece, Austria, Poland, the Czech Republic, Slovakia, Ukraine, and lands to the east and south. England was a mix of Anglicanism and Calvin-inspired offshoots.[206]

This chapter briefly touched on the fledgling call to piety and the search for the spiritual gifts described in the primitive Christian church.[207] This will be the focus of the next chapter, which covers the major branches of Christianity that arose from a spiritual Great Awakening first stirring with the likes of George Fox and the Quakers.

Notes

---

1 See Chapter 11: Counterfeit Unity—Coerced Belief for a more complete perspective.

2 Many of the early church fathers were philosophers/theologians, including Justin Martyr, Origen, Irenaeus of Lyons, Clement of Alexandria, Athanasius of Alexandria, John Chrysostom, Cyril of Alexandria, the Cappadocian Fathers (Basil of Caesarea, Gregory Nazianzus, Gregory of Nyssa), Tertullian, Augustine, and later theologians like Thomas Aquinas.

3 See Matthew 13.

4 See the section "Manichaeism and Augustine" in Chapter 5: The Age of Heresy for background on Augustine.

5 Wikipedia, Original Sin 2019. The Augustinian doctrine of original sin and human depravity led to fierce debates in the western church. John Cassian (c. 360–435) softened the doctrine by teaching that man was not totally depraved and retained moral freedom to choose to follow God. Catholics adopted the softened doctrine and believe that original sin changes human nature, wounding it, weakening it, and inclining it to the influence of the flesh, but that mankind remains capable of moral choice Wikipedia, Original Sin 2019.

6 Wikipedia, Rule of St. Augustine 2018.

7 See the section "Manichaeism and Augustine" in chapter 4 for background on Pelagianism.

8 O'Donnell, St. Augustine 2017. also see Augustinians Australia n.d.

9 Pieper 2015.

10 Martin, Jaroslav and Others 2018.

11 Editors, Peter Lombard 2017.

12 Martin, Jaroslav and Others 2018.

13 Wikipedia, Summa Theologica 2019.

14 Wikipedia, History of the Calvinist–Arminian debate 2018.

15 Protestant doctrine called *sola scriptura*, or "only scripture," captured the rejection of issued council and encyclical canons; however, the Reformers did not reject the canons of the first three ecumenical councils that defined the Godhead. Furthermore, Protestant denominations codified their doctrine and worship in books that were treated for all intents as canon.

16 The word *polity* is derived from the Greek *politeia*, meaning "citizenship" or "government."

17 The Latin stems from the Greek *episkopos*, meaning "overseer."

18 The Phrase Finder n.d.

19 See a treatment of this subject in Chapter 11: Counterfeit Unity—Coerced Belief.

20 The Franks were a Germanic-speaking people from what is present-day northern France, Belgium, and western Germany.

21 Barraclough 2017.

22 A Latin term taken from the first sentence of the bull, meaning "one holy" church.

23 Kirsch, Unam Sanctam 1912.

24 Wikipedia, Avignon Papacy 2019.

25 Wikipedia, Unam Sanctam 2018.

26 Wikipedia, Unam Sanctam 2018.

27 Wikipedia, Avignon Papacy 2019.

28 Wikipedia, Avignon Papacy 2019.

29 Wikipedia, Liturgy 2018.

30 See Matthew 3:13–17 and John 3:5.

31 See Mark 3:14, Acts 6:6, and Acts 13:3.

32 See Acts 8:16–17.

33 See Matthew 26:26–28.

34 Roman Catholic Church n.d. (emphasis added).

35 Editors, Peter Lombard 2017. "There are seven sacraments in the Church: Baptism, Confirmation, Eucharist, Penance, Anointing of the Sick, Matrimony, and Holy Orders" Roman Catholic Church n.d.

36 Matthew 26:26.

37 Toner 1908.

38 Wikipedia, Utraquists 2018.

39 Kent 1908.

40 The Franciscans, along with their fellow mendicants the Dominicans, were the defenders of orthodoxy and the leading theologians of the day. For a good treatment of these two orders, see P. Schaff, History of the Christian Church, Volume V: The Middle Ages. A.D. 1049-1294 1910, 290-294.; see also Martin, Jaroslav and Others 2018. Members of these orders vowed poverty. Unlike other monastic orders, they were activists for change with the people. Their sworn devotion to the papacy translated into leading roles in the Inquisition and the persecution of the late Middle Ages. They became professors and the scholarly elite of their time.

41 Ockhamism 2006. His logical method is known as Occam's Razor Wikipedia, Occam's Razor 2018.

42 P. Schaff, History of the Christian Church, Volume V: The Middle Ages. A.D. 1049-1294 1910, 293.

43 Wikipedia, History of the Calvinist–Arminian debate 2018.

44 Wikipedia, William of Ockham 2018.

45 Wikipedia, Apostolic Poverty 2018.

46 Wikipedia, Apostolic Poverty 2018.

47 Wikipedia, William of Ockham 2018.

48 Martin, Jaroslav and Others 2018.

49 Wikipedia, Avignon Papacy 2019.

50 Wikipedia, William of Ockham 2018.

51 Ockhamism 2006.

52 Wikipedia, John Wycliffe 2018.

53 Cory 2015.

54 Wikipedia, Black Death 2019.

55 Wikipedia, John Wycliffe 2018.

56 Wikipedia, John Wycliffe 2018.

57 Wikipedia, John Wycliffe 2018.

58 Martin, Jaroslav and Others 2018.

59 Wikipedia, Pope Urban VI 2018.

60 Wikipedia, Pope Urban VI 2018.

61 Wikipedia, Western Schism 2019.

62 Wikipedia, Lollardy 2018. For perspective on the intolerance for criticism during this time period, see the section "The Inquisition to Stamp Out Heresy" in Chapter 11: Counterfeit Unity—Coerced Belief.

63 Wikipedia, John Wycliffe 2018.

64 Wikipedia, John Wycliffe 2018.

65 Wikipedia, John Wycliffe 2018.

66 Wikipedia, John Wycliffe 2018.

67 The term derived from the Middle Dutch word *lollaert*, meaning "mumbler." It was applied to the uneducated English-speaking laymen who joined the movement Editors, Lollard 2016.

68 Editors, Lollard 2016.

69 Editors, Lollard 2016.

70 Editors, Lollard 2016.

71 Wikipedia, John Wycliffe 2018.

72 Wikipedia, Lollardy 2018.

73 See Editors, Lollard 2016.

74 Wikipedia, John Wycliffe 2018.

75 Bartosi and Spinka 2019.

76 Hus connected with the people. Like Wycliffe, he believed that the people should hear the gospel in their own language, so he preached in Czech rather than in Latin.

77 Bartosi and Spinka 2019.

78 Wikipedia, Jan Hus 2018.

79 Bartosi and Spinka 2019.

80 Bartosi and Spinka 2019.

81 Wikipedia, Jan Hus 2018.

82 Bartosi and Spinka 2019.

83 Wikipedia, Reformation 2018.

84 Wikipedia, Jan Hus 2018.

85 Wikipedia, Hussite Wars 2019.

86 Wikipedia, Utraquists 2018.

87 Sigismund was the half brother of Wenceslaus and had successfully usurped the title of emperor-elect from him.

88 Wikipedia, Council of Constance 2019.

89 Wikipedia, Hussite Wars 2019.

90 Moravian Church n.d.

91 Wikipedia, List of Christian denominations by number of members 2018.

92 Burns 2015.

93 Wikipedia, Johannes Gutenberg 2018.

94 Martin Luther Passionate Reformer n.d.

95 Martin Luther Passionate Reformer n.d.

96 Martin Luther Passionate Reformer n.d.

97 The early Reformers used terms such as *sola fide* (by faith alone), *sola scriptura* (by scripture alone), and *sola gratia* (by grace alone). By the twentieth century, two more *solae* were added to characterize Protestantism: *solus Christus* (through Christ alone) and *soli Deo gloria* (Glory to God alone) Wikipedia, Five solae 2018.

98 Wikipedia, History of the Calvinist–Arminian debate 2018.

99 Wikipedia, Martin Luther 2018.

[100] Wikipedia, Martin Luther 2018.
[101] Wikipedia, Martin Luther 2018.
[102] Wikipedia, Martin Luther 2018.
[103] Wikipedia, Sacramental Union 2017.
[104] Wikipedia, Thomas Müntzer 2018.
[105] Wikipedia, Martin Luther 2018.
[106] Wikipedia, German Peasants War 2018.
[107] Wikipedia, Martin Luther 2018.
[108] Wikipedia, Marburg Colloquy 2017.
[109] Wikipedia, Martin Luther 2018.
[110] Rosten 1975.
[111] See 1 Peter 2:9.
[112] Some Lutherans in the United States, such as the Lutheran Church–Missouri Synod, the second largest body of Lutherans in the United States, adopted a congregational polity with democratic midlevel districts and a national council called a synod.
[113] Wikipedia, Lutheranism 2018.
[114] Wikipedia, Schmalkaldic League 2017.
[115] Wikipedia, Cuius regio, eius religio 2017.
[116] Wikipedia, Lutheranism 2018. See also Wikipedia, List of Christian denominations by number of members 2018.
[117] Wikipedia, John Calvin 2018.
[118] Wikipedia, John Calvin 2018.
[119] Wikipedia, Affair of Sausages 2017.
[120] Wikipedia, Reformation in Switzerland 2018.
[121] Wikipedia, John Calvin 2018.
[122] Wikipedia, John Calvin 2018.
[123] Wikipedia, Irresitable Grace 2017.
[124] Huff 2009.
[125] John Calvin Father of the Reformed Faith 2018.
[126] Wikipedia, Presbyterian Polity 2018.
[127] Wikipedia, Presbyterian Polity 2018.
[128] Wikipedia, List of Christian denominations by number of members 2018.
[129] Wikipedia, List of Christian denominations by number of members 2018.
[130] Wikipedia, Congregatonal Church 2017.
[131] Wikipedia, Congregatonal Church 2017.
[132] Wikipedia, List of Christian denominations by number of members 2018.
[133] Wikipedia, History of the Calvinist–Arminian debate 2018.
[134] Wikipedia, Five Articles of Remonstrance 2018.
[135] Some Reformed churches use the term *five-point* in their title. In contrast, churches that have rejected the point of atonement applying only to the elect call themselves "four-point" Calvinists.
[136] Wikipedia, History of the Calvinist–Arminian debate 2018.
[137] Wikipedia, Remonstrants 2018.
[138] Wikipedia, Swiss Brethren 2018.
[139] For example, see Acts 8:35–39.

140 Editors, Anabaptist 2016. In Greek, the prefix ana means "again." Anabaptist means "baptized again."

141 The Swiss Brethren gathered in Schleitheim and adopted seven statements Wikipedia, Schleitheim Confession 2018.:
1. Only adult believers should be baptized.
2. A Christian should be admonished in private, then in public.
3. Only those who are baptized take of the bread.
4. Believers should be segregated from all outside evil influences, political and religious.
5. Pastors should be men of good repute.
6. Violence must not be used in any circumstance.
7. No (oaths) including giving testimony should be taken.

142 This is explored in more detail in Chapter 11: Counterfeit Unity—Coerced Belief.

143 See chapter 11

144 In one notable exception, Anabaptists settled in Münster, Westphalia, in sufficient numbers to elect an Anabaptist majority to the city council in 1533. The Anabaptists persecuted and expelled all non-Anabaptists from the city, creating a messianic kingdom under John of Leiden. However, their supremacy was short-lived. The city was surrounded in 1534 by an army of Catholics and Protestants. The city was captured in 1535, and the Anabaptist leaders were tortured and killed and their bodies hung in steel cages from the steeple of St. Lambert's Church Editors, Anabaptist 2016.

145 Wikipedia, Mennonite 2018.

146 Wikipedia, Mennonite 2018.

147 Wikipedia, Mennonite 2018.

148 Wikipedia, Henry VIII 2018.

149 Wikipedia, Henry VIII 2018.

150 Wikipedia, Henry VIII 2018.

151 The prefix *anglo* comes from *Anglia*, the Latin word for "England."

152 Wikipedia, Book of Common Prayer 2018.

153 Wikipedia, List of Christian denominations by number of members 2018.

154 Edward VI was only nine years old when he assumed the throne in 1547; therefore, England was governed by executors that allowed a drift toward the reforms taking place in continental Protestantism Wikipedia, Reformation 2018.

155 Wikipedia, Vestments Controversy 2018.

156 By the time of Edward's death, Parliament had reinstated Mary as heir to the throne.

157 Wikipedia, Mary I of England 2018.

158 Wikipedia, Convocation of 1563 2018.

159 Wikipedia, Vestments Controversy 2018.

160 Editors, Puritanism 2018.

161 Wikipedia, Vestments Controversy 2018.

162 Wikipedia, Vestments Controversy 2018.

163 Wikipedia, Vestments Controversy 2018.

164 Editors, Puritanism 2018.

165 Wikipedia, Brownist 2018.

166 Wikipedia, Brownist 2018.
167 John Calvin Father of the Reformed Faith 2018.
168 Wikipedia, Bishops Wars 2018.
169 Wikipedia, Grand Remonstrance 2018.
170 Wikipedia, Puritans 2018.
171 Wikipedia, Interregnum (England) 2017.
172 Wikipedia, Act of Uniformity 1662 2017.
173 Wikipedia, James II of England 2018.
174 Wikipedia, Glorious Revolution 2018.
175 Wikipedia, William III of England 2018.
176 Wikipedia, Acts of Union 1707 2018.
177 Hudson 2017.
178 Hudson 2017.
179 Wikipedia, Baptists 2017.
180 Wikipedia, 1689 Baptist Confession of Faith 2018.
181 Wikipedia, 1689 Baptist Confession of Faith 2018.
182 Hudson 2017.
183 Hudson 2017.
184 Hudson 2017.
185 Wikipedia, Baptists 2017.
186 Wikipedia, Baptists 2017.
187 Wikipedia, Baptists 2017.
188 According to the Pew Religious Landscape Study, about one-third of southern Christians are Baptist, which is by far the most dominant denomination in the southern states Pew n.d.
189 The example of Rick Warren's Saddleback Church is given in the section "Era of Televangelism, Celebrity Pastors, and Megachurches" in Chapter 10: Evangelicals and
Related Movements
190 From W. M. Pinson Jr. 2017., the Baptist "distinctives" are the following:
- the Lordship of Jesus Christ
- the Bible as the sole written authority for faith and practice
- soul competency (the God-given freedom and ability of persons to know and respond to God's will). Baptists believe that God gives people competency—that is ability—to make choices W. Pinson Jr., Is Soul Competency the Baptist Distinctive? 2017.
- salvation from sin and eternal death to forgiveness and eternal life only by faith in Jesus Christ as Lord and Savior, who is the grace gift of God
- the priesthood of each believer and of all believers in Christ
- believer's baptism
- baptism and the Lord's Supper as wonderfully symbolic *but not essential* for salvation
- church membership composed only of persons who have been born again
- religious freedom and its corollary, the separation of church and state
- congregational church governance under the Lordship of Christ

- the autonomy of churches
- voluntary cooperation for various causes

191 W. M. Pinson Jr. 2017.
192 The Southern Baptist Convention formally apologized for its role in slavery in a resolution adopted in 1995 Wikipedia, Baptists 2017.
193 Wikipedia, List of Christian denominations by number of members 2018.
194 Wikipedia, George Fox 2018.
195 Wikipedia, Quakers 2018.
196 Wikipedia, George Fox 2018.
197 See Isaiah 66:2.
198 Wikipedia, Quakers 2018.
199 Herlihy, Weinstein and Others 2016.
200 Wikipedia, Council of Trent 2018.
201 See Chapter 11: Counterfeit Unity—Coerced Belief
202 Notably, England did not officially participate in the war, although tens of thousands of Britons and Scots fought with Dutch and Swedish troops Wikipedia, Thirty Years War 2017.
203 Wikipedia, Thirty Years War 2017.
204 Three religions were allowed by the Peace of Westphalia: Catholicism, Lutheranism, and Calvinism. The Anabaptists, Hussites, and others, were excluded. England, which had not joined the Thirty Years' War, was not a signatory to the peace treaties. Thus, the Anglican Church of England and the various branches of Protestantism springing up in England were not covered by the treaty.
205 Wikipedia 2018.
206 Wikipedia, Protestantism 2018.
207 Charismata refers to the collective supernatural gifts of the Holy Ghost. The Greek word *charism* is the singular form. *Charismata* or *charisms* are both the plural form of *charism*.

Chapter 8

Great Awakenings and Gifts of the Spirit

The New Testament records the uniqueness of the primitive Christian experience, which included intensely pious living and the witnessing of supernatural manifestations. The following are examples of this experience: The early Christians abandoned material possessions and met together in prayer and daily worship.[1] The Jews that had gathered for the feast of Pentecost witnessed a spiritual outpouring, including the speaking of tongues, among the earliest Christians. Those who witnessed these events were "pricked in their hearts," leading to thousands of baptisms.[2] Peter and John healed a lame man.[3] The gentile Cornelius and Peter received interconnected personal revelations followed by a second Pentecostal-like experience.[4] In a visit to Ephesus, Paul encountered about a dozen devout brethren who had been baptized but had not learned of the Holy Ghost and its gifts. Paul conferred on them the Holy Ghost, and they had a Pentecostal-like experience.[5] Paul's epistle to the Corinthians establishes the legitimacy of spiritual gifts, or in Greek, *charismata.*[6]

A focus on piety had led Protestants as diverse as William Ockham, John Wycliffe, Jan Hus, John Calvin, the Swiss Brethren (Anabaptists), and Puritans to pursue a simpler holy life without materialism and sin. Indeed, the door to spiritual gifts was cracked open slightly during the early sixteenth-century Reformation, especially in the context of the Reformers' personal experiences of conversion. Doctrines related to "regeneration" or being "born again" by grace through the Holy Spirit were a key part of the theology adopted by the Reformers; however, the early Reformers' experiences were intimate and subdued.[7]

Charismata had always provoked suspicion and created tension within the organized church. After all, there had always been imitators of divine power.[8] How was one to discern the gifts of the Spirit from the possession of devils? How could decorum and reverence be maintained in public worship if worshippers had outbursts of spontaneous unbridled gifts? Paul himself cautioned against public charismata in the same epistle to the Corinthians in which he legitimized their existence.[9] While he recognized that the gifts should not be forbidden, "forbid not to speak in tongues,"[10] he did so with a warning and with constraints. Anticipating that public spiritual manifestations could lead the ungrounded believers to stray and cause confusion, he encouraged the limited use of speaking in tongues in public worship: "Yet in the church I had rather speak five words with my understanding, that by my voice I might teach others also, than ten thousand words in an unknown tongue."[11] And he cautioned about gullibility: "Be not children in understanding . . . in understanding be men."[12] He closed with a standard of church protocol: "God is not the author of confusion. . . . Let all things be done decently and in order."[13]

Perhaps the greatest obstacle to charismata arose from one of the very pillars of Protestantism—*sola scriptura*. Protestant Christians generally accept sola scriptura, meaning they believe that the Bible is the sole authority or, in others words, God's canon is closed. To these Protestants, the scriptures are infallible, inerrant, and sufficient.[14] Strict adherence to sola scriptura essentially closes the door to the dangerous possibility that the gift of prophecy could expand canonical scripture. A statement from a modern Protestant denomination articulates this point:

> We have seen that charismatic continuationism is not a viable position if it is committed to the principle of Sola Scriptura, where the Scripture is understood as a closed canon. . . . We are then confronted with the hermeneutic [referring to biblical interpretation] choice between open canonicity or sufficiency of the closed canon. . . . Charismatic continuationism would be attractive if there were still apostles who manifest the signs of apostleship. If

there were such apostles, the open canonicity of Scriptures together with the charismatic continuationist view would be more plausible. It is either all or nothing. Most charismatics are in-between, not totally consistent. Few would say that we have such apostles. Therefore, if the ministry of apostleship has ended, why then insist that we still have prophets in the Church?[15]

In spite of the prevailing antagonism to charismata within established churches, there were those who courageously spoke of spiritual experiences and incorporated the same into the doctrine of new denominations—one notable example from the previous chapter was that of George Fox and the Religious Society of Friends (Quakers) he founded. But these were isolated exceptions during the Reformation proper.

In this chapter, we will see that movements created to evangelize the non-Christian and awaken the sleeping Christian emphasized experiences of the Holy Spirit. These movements identified a pious life and the outpouring of the Holy Spirit as defining attributes of the converted Christian. After the Reformation, the swell of Christian fervor ebbed and flowed, but two waves were so intense as to be called Great Awakenings—the first awakening spanning the 1730s to the 1740s and the second from roughly 1795 to 1835.[16] The Great Awakenings would be yet another catalyst for new denominations within Christianity.

The First Great Awakening (1730–1750) and Pietism

As Lutheranism transitioned from a protest movement to an established denomination with magisterial sanction, it faced many of the same challenges of the proto-Orthodox "trunk" of Christianity that we learned about in Chapter 6: Orthodox Schisms. Theses challenges included doctrinal controversy, heresy, disagreement over liturgical practices, balance of power with the secular, and so on. Internal divisions threatened to tear Lutheranism apart or so obscure its identity as to see it absorbed into an all-Protestant union.[17] German princes appointed theologians to create a uniquely Lutheran confession of faith. From their efforts emerged the *Book of Concord* that was adopted by the majority of Lutheran churches in 1580.[18] Although Luther had himself taken a stand against the scholasticism of Aquinas's era in *Disputation Against Scholastic Theology*, the *Book of Concord* ushered in a new era of Aristotelian-inspired scholastic orthodoxy with an emphasis throughout the church on proper doctrine and pure teaching. Increasingly lost was Luther's emphasis on the individual experience of feeling God's mercy and receiving justification through grace.[19] Dogma and strict liturgical worship was not translating into Christian living. Lutheranism, born of Reform, was itself in need of reform.

A devout Lutheran named Philipp Spener (1635–1705) published a work urging reform called *Pia Desideria (Heartfelt Desire for God-pleasing Reform)* in 1675. He courageously criticized Lutheran sovereigns and clergy—asserting that their pursuit of worldly success, their mechanistic sacraments, and their endless nuanced doctrinal arguments were barren seeds not producing the fruits of the gospel.[20] He argued that Christians justified by God should be filled with such gratitude and love toward God that Christian fruits of piety would flow freely.[21] Spener offered a six-point proposal for reform with the objective of individuals becoming true Christians. To that end, many of his proposals were directed to the common membership: Every family should have a Bible and read from it every day. Small groups should gather to study and worship in a practice he called *collegia pietatis* (pious gatherings). Nonclerical laity should exercise their right of "priesthood of all believers" in the privacy of their own homes in these small gatherings. He stressed to both clergy and laity that "study without piety is worthless" and that, in relative terms of importance, it is far more important for clergy to inspire piety than to articulate doctrine.[22] Piety, in Spener's view, was not a threat to orthodoxy but a necessary counterweight—the two coexisting with healthy tension. However, if removed from the context of orthodox discipline, piety ran the risk of swinging too far in the other direction—from objective to subjective, from unity to doctrinal anarchy, from community to individuality.[23]

Pia Desideria became the manifesto of a new movement known by Spener's theme of piety:[24]

> Pietism emphasized experience in worship as opposed to mastering creeds and outer conformity—a reaction against the doctrinaire attitude of Scholastic theology. Three

general characteristics were common to pietism's manifestations: First, a mystical element that *emphasized emotional experience* and heartfelt expression existed especially in the context of personal Bible study. Second, the practice of holy living and active compassion developed out of this emphasis on experience. Third, emerging from this active compassion, Pietists concerned themselves with the unevangelized heathen.[25]

The epicenter of Pietism was the university in Halle, Germany, and it was at this university that a young nobleman named Count Nicolaus Ludwig von Zinzendorf (1700–1760) become deeply committed to the ideals of Pietism and joined prayer groups in Halle. Upon leaving Halle in 1727, Zinzendorf established a community house in Herrnhut[26] committed to Pietism regardless of denomination. Herrnhut saw rapid growth as Lutheran Pietists and persecuted Anabaptists and the Hussites's United Brethren flocked there. Gone was the context and counterweight of uniform orthodoxy. The diversity of beliefs in the community forced the group to focus on what joined them in devotional life, such as community prayer, and relegate to indifference their credal discrepancies. The Moravians emerged out of Herrnhut with a motto reflecting its origin: "In Essentials, Unity; In Nonessentials, Liberty; In All Things, Love."[27]

John Wesley and the Unexpected Methodists

John Wesley (1703–1791) studied theology at Oxford, preparing to be a priest in the Church of England. He immersed himself in the literature of Pietism, and while at Oxford he and his brother Charles started a group dedicated to pious living and strict religious observance, including daily prayer, weekly communion, and weekly fasting. The group's critics derisively called them the "Holy Club" and "Methodists," a reference to their well-defined religious methods. As is so often the case, what was intended to be a pejorative nickname stuck with Wesley and his associates in the Holy Club like a badge of honor.[28]

As meaningful as the Holy Club was to Wesley, he felt that something was missing in his faith. After finishing at Oxford, he was ordained a priest in the Church of England and took an assignment as parish priest in Savannah in the colony of Georgia. On the way there, a terrible storm engulfed the ship. Most passengers cowered with fear, but a group of Moravians were calm and composed, singing hymns and expressing joy during the trial. Wesley was deeply impressed and could not help but wonder if perhaps the Moravians had the component of inner conviction and faith that he lacked.[29]

Wesley's two-year term in Georgia was controversial, leaving him depressed upon his return to England in late 1737. His experience on the ship to Georgia inspired him to attend a Moravian meeting at Aldersgate Street in London in May 1738. It was there that he had a transformational, even a charismatic experience:[30]

> In the evening I went very unwillingly to a society in Aldersgate Street, where one was reading Luther's Preface to the Epistle to the Romans. About a quarter before nine, while he was describing the change which God works in the heart through faith in Christ, I felt my heart strangely warmed. I felt I did trust in Christ, Christ alone for salvation, and an assurance was given me that he had taken away my sins, even mine, and saved me from the law of sin and death.[31]

Soon after this experience, Wesley joined the Moravian Fetter Lane Society in London and journeyed in 1738 to Herrnhut to meet Zinzendorf and study. He started the year 1739 deeply engaged with the Moravians as part of the Fetter Lane Society. Wesley recorded in his journal on January 1, 1739, that

> Mr. Hall, Hinching, Ingham, Whitefield, Hutching, and my brother Charles were present at our love feast in Fetter Lane with about 60 of our brethren. About three in the morning, as we were continuing in prayer, the power of God came mightily upon us insomuch that many cried out for exceeding joy and many fell to the ground. As soon as we were recovered a little from that awe and amazement at the presence of His majesty, we broke out with one voice, "We praise Thee, O God, we acknowledge Thee to be the Lord."[32]

In May, his close friend George Whitefield invited Wesley to take over a ministry to miners in Bristol. Whitefield had been teaching the poor working-class that rarely went into the formal cathedrals of the Church of England. Rather, he taught them in their public places.[33] Wesley was reluctant to accept the invitation because of the stigma of open-air preaching. Yet, although a priest in the Church of England, he did not have an assigned parish. Thus, he accepted. Teaching in the open to the poor, indigent, and dispossessed was transformational for him. It became a pattern for his life and a cornerstone of Methodism.

Later in 1739, Wesley preached a sermon called "Freedom of Grace," promoting Arminian doctrines including unlimited atonement. By giving this speech, he publicly rejected Calvinism's key tenet that only the elect were predestined to be saved. As Wesley saw it, such a doctrine "represented God as worse than the devil."[34] In contrast to Calvinism, Wesley believed that "God willeth all men to be saved." From this core belief, he taught four key doctrines:

1. A person is free not only to reject salvation but also to accept it by an act of free will.
2. All people who are obedient to the gospel according to the measure of knowledge given them will be saved.
3. The Holy Spirit assures a Christian of their salvation directly, through an inner "experience" (assurance of salvation).
4. Christians in this life are capable of Christian perfection and are commanded by God to pursue it.[35]

Wesley's rejection of orthodox Calvinism became an irreconcilable wedge between himself and the Moravians. They firmly believed that conversion and the accompanying forgiveness of sins was by grace alone and that the assurance that flowed into one's soul during conversion had to be certain. If not, conversion had not really happened. This belief prompted a Moravian teacher from Fetter Lane to teach its members that unless they had received a *full* assurance of forgiveness, meaning a compelling conversion experience, the member was to abstain from all means of grace until they had a full assurance. That is, they were to wait upon God and abstain from doing good works, praying, worshiping, and partaking of communion.[36]

Wesley's sermon made it impossible for him to remain within the Moravian society, and he separated from them 1740.[37] His sermon also created a breach with George Whitefield, his longtime friend and fellow Holy Club Methodist, leading them to part ways in 1741.[38]

After breaking with the Moravians, Wesley tirelessly pursued the formation of new holy societies patterned after Fetter Lane. He was indefatigable, at times preaching two or three sermons a day. It has been estimated that he traveled on horseback 240,000 miles and preached more than 40,000 sermons.[39] These societies expected piety from members and fostered and celebrated charismatic conversion experiences. As the number of societies multiplied, preachers were needed. Wesley selected holy men from the societies to be itinerant preachers to travel in circuits serving one-to-two-year terms. Importantly, these men were not trained theologians or ordained clergy. The need for chapels required fiscal administration. The growth in membership necessitated standards for membership and protocols for discipline. Coordination between circuit preachers became necessary, and the first "Methodist" conference was held in 1744, opening the door to centralized authority over the societies.

Wesley would always claim that he did not intend to break from the Church of England and that he believed that he and his fellow "Methodists" in England were still a part of the Church of England. He accepted the *Book of Common Prayer*, and after the Revolutionary War of Independence he adapted it for American Methodists. However, by any reasonable measure, he had diverged significantly from the Church of England: Methodist societies ignored the boundaries of parishes and the authority of ordained Anglican parish priests and bishops. His use of itinerant preachers and unsanctioned leadership conferences challenged the polity of the Church of England. Methodists exercised their own discipline.

The split became particularly acute after the Revolutionary War. In the new nation, there were no Anglican bishops to offer sacraments to the members of the Methodist societies there. By 1784, Wesley felt he could no longer wait for the Church of England to find a solution, so he took it upon himself to ordain men that he sent to America using the authority he had as a priest in the Church of England. He called them "superintendents" of the Methodist Episcopal Church in the United States, being very careful not to call them by the formal titles of clergy such as "bishop"—a title used by Anglicans as inherited from the Catholic Church. However, in short order the superintendents encouraged the Methodist membership in America to drop the unbiblical term *superintendent* and use the title bishop instead. Wesley had effectively created a new ecclesiastical order, separate from the Anglican hierarchy to which he still proclaimed loyalty.[40]

After Wesley's death in 1791, leadership passed to the council of leaders gathered in annual conference. Within a short time, the Methodists formalized what was already a de facto reality. They formally separated from the Church of England and its Episcopalian cousin in the United States. Methodism grew rapidly in the coming decades, particularly among the poorer classes, criminals, and dispossessed. Today, there are some eighty million Methodists worldwide.[41]

We have covered the emergence of the Moravians and the Methodists from the First Great Awakening, but we should understand that the awakening was a broad surge of personal religiosity among many denominations. In some forms such as Pietism, the Moravians, and Methodism it was a hopeful message of improved Christian behavior in response to the goodness and mercy of God. In other forms, stern Puritanism prevailed, inspired by the rigorous application of Calvinism. Jonathan Edwards (1703–1758) sought to arouse righteous action through the fear of hellfire and damnation. One of Edwards's most famous speeches, entitled "Sinners in the Hands of Angry God," leaves little question of Edwards's staunch adherence to Calvin's notions of human depravity.[42]

The Second Great Awakening (1795–1835) and Revivalism

After the American Revolution, a new era of spiritual interest swelled in America spurred by large revivals. The belief, inspired by the Moravians and so notable in Methodism, that conversion equated to a definitive and certain experience became so prevalent that *revival* became synonymous with camp meetings that were orchestrated to provoke such experiences.[43]

Camp meetings started in 1791 in North Carolina and spread through the south and the frontier after the Revolutionary War.[44] On the final day of a camp meeting in 1800, the approximately five hundred attendees experienced "a mighty effusion of Spirit and the floor was soon covered with the slain; their screams for mercy pierced the heavens."[45] One of the most famous camp meetings took place in Cane Ridge, Kentucky, in 1801 and lasted seven days. It was organized by Barton Stone (1772–1844), the minister of the Cane Ridge Presbyterian Church. Some twenty thousand people attended the event to listen, along with dozens of ministers from Presbyterian, Methodist, and Baptist denominations. One minister present, Reverend Moses Hoge, described the Cane Ridge Revival:

> The careless fall down, cry out, tremble, and not infrequently are affected with convulsive twitchings. . . . Nothing that imagination can paint, can make a stronger impression upon the mind, than one of those scenes. Sinners dropping down on every hand, shrieking, groaning, crying, for mercy, convulsed; professors praying, agonizing, fainting, falling down in distress, for sinners or in raptures of joy! . . . there can be no question but it is of God. The subjects of it, for the most part are deeply wounded for their sins, and can give a clear and rational account of their conversion.[46]

As an important side note, the huge success of Cane Ridge led Barton Stone to leave Presbyterianism and begin a journey to find a pure form of Christianity. We will explore this more fully in the next chapter.

One scholar characterized camp meetings this way:

> There they engaged in an unrelenting series of intense spiritual exercises, punctuated with cries of religious agony and ecstasy, all designed to promote religious fervor and conversions. These exercises ranged from the singing of hymns addressed to each of the spiritual stages that marked the journey to conversion, public confessions and renunciations of sin and personal witness to the workings of the spirit, collective prayer, all of which were surrounded by sermons delivered by clergymen especially noted for their powerful "plain-speaking" preaching.[47]

In the north, Charles G. Finney (1792–1875) was arguably the most notable face of the Second Great Awakening. He had no qualms about carefully orchestrating his revivals to render the desired conversions. He deployed a variety of practices to provoke intense experiences. So impactful were Finney's revivals that one convert commented,

> The whole community was stirred. Religion was the topic of conversation in the house, in the shop, in the office and on the street. The only theater in the city was converted into a livery stable; the only circus into a soap and candle factory. Grog shops were closed; the Sabbath was honored; the sanctuaries were thronged with happy worshippers; a new impulse was given to every philanthropic enterprise; the fountains of benevolence were opened, and men lived to good.[48]

In western New York, Finney and others held so many revivals across the region that Finney dubbed it "the burned-over district."[49]

In a later chapter, we will explore how revivalism and the notion of conversion as an experience became deeply rooted in the evangelical movement.

Holiness Movement

One of John Wesley's core teachings was that Christian perfection or sanctification was possible in this life as a second act of grace (sometime after justification). Sanctification would be accompanied by a personal spiritual manifestation, some form of charismata, and would enable the person to live a holy life free from the desire to willfully sin.[50] A sanctified soul would be reflected in outward holiness. This "second act of grace" evidenced by a manifestation of the Spirit was a core part of Methodist doctrine and became a theme of camp meetings and evangelist preachers during the Second Great Awakening in America. It spawned new "Holiness" societies dedicated to the combined goals of Methodism with an emphasis on Christian perfection. The Salvation Army sprang from the movement in 1878.[51]

The pursuit of the sanctifying experience started within Methodism but spread to other Protestant denominations and thus became a movement broader than just the Methodists. The movement gained national attention after the Civil War when Holiness advocates started holding annual camp meetings in 1867. The meetings created an emotional climax in which participants demonstrated public displays of the Spirit. The annual camp meetings grew quickly and gained national attention such that by the third camp meeting, *Harper's Weekly* reported on the events.[52]

Many traditional Methodists were uncomfortable with the Holiness movement's emphasis on charismata as indication of Christian perfection. Methodism split over the issue in their 1898 conference, and rules were passed prohibiting the unauthorized holding of camp meetings—effectively prohibiting Holiness gatherings. As a result, various Holiness groups splintered from the Methodists, with the largest being the Church of the Nazarene, which split in 1908. Today, it has about 2.5 million members.[53] The Pilgrim Holiness Church split from the Methodist Episcopal Church in 1897 and later merged with another offshoot to form the Wesleyan Church in 1968.[54] Many of the congregations of these denominations refused to join the merger and remained independent Holiness denominations.

Holiness Leads to Pentecostalism

In 1900, a Holiness evangelist named Charles Fox Parham started a school near Topeka, Kansas. He extended Methodist and Holiness doctrine by teaching that baptism by the Holy Ghost was a third act of grace, distinct from the two recognized and taught by Wesley.[55] Additionally, he narrowed the charismatic evidence of baptism by the Holy Ghost to speaking in tongues. Parnham's students had a Pentecostal experience of speaking in tongues in early 1901, and he started teaching the doctrine of baptism by the Holy Ghost more broadly.[56] In 1905, he moved to Houston and again started a Bible school. One of his students, William J. Seymour, took the message to Los Angeles in 1906, where his preaching sparked a three-year-long revival, called the Azusa Street Revival.[57] Perhaps the revival would have gained momentum under any circumstances, but its notoriety was nearly immediate. On April 16, 1906, the first day of revival in the Azusa Street mission, one prophetically proclaimed that "God was going to do a great shaking." Two days later, the great San Francisco earthquake occurred.[58]

Notably, Seymour was black and the Azusa mission was integrated. The revival attracted people from all over the United States from many different denominations. The participants returned to their home congregations full of the "fire" of the experience and more often than not found their denominations uncomfortable with the charismatic display of the Spirit.

It can't be overstated how unique the Azusa Street Revival was within the traditions of both Protestant and Orthodox Christendom. Some in the Holiness movement quickly adopted Pentecostalism.[59] Others became vocal critics. Public speaking in tongues was radical compared to the subdued charismatic experiences of Wesley and the traditional Methodists or even compared to the more expressive charismatic experiences of the Holiness movement. Outsiders viewed the revival with derision. The *Los Angeles Daily Times* reported on April 18, 1906, in an article entitled "Weird Babble of Tongues," that

> breathing strange utterances and mouthing a creed which it would seem no sane mortal could understand, the newest religious sect has started in Los Angeles. Meetings are held in a tumble-down shack on Azusa Street near San Pedro, and devotees of the weird doctrine practice the most fanatical rites, preach the wildest theories, and work themselves into a state of mad excitement in their peculiar zeal. Colored people and a sprinkling of whites compose the congregation, and night is made hideous in the neighborhood by the howlings of the worshippers who spend hours swaying back and forth in nerve-racking attitude of prayer and supplication. They claim to have the gift of tongues and to be able to comprehend the babble. Such a startling claim has never yet been made by any company of fanatics even in Los Angeles, the home of almost numberless creeds.[60]

Pentecostalism spread quickly, especially in the south among black communities and the poor. Independent Pentecostal congregations proliferated.

Early Pentecostals believed that the tongues they spoke were actual languages and naturally assumed this gift would empower worldwide missionary work. However, as they landed on foreign shores, they were sorely disappointed to learn that these were not actual languages at all.[61] Nevertheless, missionaries made rapid inroads, particularly in sub-Saharan Africa and Brazil—the latter becoming the largest concentration of Pentecostals in the western hemisphere.[62]

Like the other Christian branches before it, Pentecostalism soon split into factions based on doctrinal disagreements. To the many non-Methodists joining the movement, the inherited Wesleyan doctrine of two distinct acts of grace, conversion and sanctification, was controversial. Baptists, Presbyterians, and other denominations with Calvinistic origins did not share this distinctly two-step Methodist doctrine. Consequently, in 1910, a Pentecostal named William Durham proposed an alternative that he called "Finished Work"—a doctrine that combined the events of conversion and sanctification into one act of grace. After conversion, a Christian could progressively grow in grace with the baptism of the Holy Ghost empowering such growth. This doctrine was controversial and separated Pentecostalism from its Methodist roots.[63] In another doctrinal deviation, a Pentecostal named Frank Ewart claimed to have received a divine prophecy revealing that Jesus alone was God, thereby rejecting the Trinitarian creeds. His opponents called him and his followers "Jesus Only" or "Oneness" Pentecostals.

The creation of the Oneness subgroup within Pentecostalism was emblematic of the doctrinal free-for-all that is possible when charismatic gifts, including prophecy, are exercised by all members. Thus, there is not one Pentecostal denomination. There are thousands. However, fellowships have been forged to create recognizable denominations. One such fellowship called the Assemblies of God was formed in 1914 based on a common rejection of the Finished Work doctrine and the Oneness Pentecostal views of the Trinity. Today, Assemblies of God is a fellowship of about 140 independent churches.[64]

Consider for a moment the unprecedented growth of Pentecostalism. A Pew Forum study in 2011 estimated that there about are 280 million Pentecostals worldwide.[65] In the span of time between 1906 (Azusa Street Revival) and 2011, Pentecostalism grew at a compound rate of about 20 percent per year! In spite of its size, it may not be perceived as the largest Protestant branch by Christians in the Western world. As Paul Freston, an expert on worldwide Pentecostalism explained,

> So the characteristics of global Pentecostalism that are important for its political impact include the fact that it's very institutionally divided; it's disproportionately amongst the poor in already poor countries; it's nontraditional; and it often lacks international contacts, which gives it a certain invisibility and is why it's often missed by Western academia and media. Pentecostalism, in short, is world Christianity distant from power and wealth, associated largely with poverty.[66]

Pentecostalism and the Charismatic Movement

During the 1800s and most of the 1900s, mainline Christian denominations generally disapproved of charismata. Members of such denominations who experienced charismatic outpouring of the Spirit often felt compelled to leave and join Holiness or Pentecostal denominations. That began to change in the 1960s. Clergy within major denominations became more courageous about sharing experiences with charismatic gifts and began preaching the virtue of charismata within mainline churches. It was rocky at first. An Episcopalian rector in Van Nuys, California, named Dennis Bennett shared his personal charismatic experience in an Easter sermon in 1960 and was summarily dismissed.[67] However, over time, denominations became more tolerant and then accepting of the groundswell of revivalism inspired by the Charismatic movement that grew within all the major traditional branches of Western Christianity.

The Charismatic movement embraces charismata as part of believers' personal Christian experience, just as Methodists, Holiness, and Pentecostals do; however, the Charismatic movement differs from the Holiness and Pentecostal movements in significant ways: Charismatic Christians see the gifts of the Spirit as enablers but not necessarily as dogmatic signposts of salvific events. Therefore, they can experience charismata without abandoning their denomination's doctrine of salvation. The Catholic Catechisms gives a sense for this view of charismata:

> (799) Whether extraordinary or simple and humble, charisms are graces of the Holy Spirit which directly or indirectly benefit the Church, ordered as they are to her building up, to the good of men, and to the needs of the world.

> (800) Charisms are to be accepted with gratitude by the person who receives them and by all members of the Church as well. They are a wonderfully rich grace for the apostolic vitality and for the holiness of the entire Body of Christ, provided they really are genuine gifts of the Holy Spirit and are used in full conformity with authentic promptings of this same Spirit, that is, in keeping with charity, the true measure of all charisms.

> (801) It is in this sense that discernment of charisms is always necessary. No charism is exempt from being referred and submitted to the Church's shepherds. "Their office [is] not indeed to extinguish the Spirit, but to test all things and hold fast to what is good," so that all the diverse and complementary charisms work together "for the common good."[68]

The Catholic Catechisms reveal another important difference. Pentecostalism is egalitarian such that each person's prophecy is as valid as the next. Its polity is largely congregational, so no governing body can enforce doctrinal discipline. In contrast, denominations with episcopal or presbyterian polity retain authority to discern the validity of charismata within their denominations. For example, the Catholic Catechisms recognize the possibility of false gifts in the words, "Charisms are to be accepted . . . provided they really are genuine gifts of the Holy Ghost and used in full conformity." The church retains authoritative oversight: "No charism is exempt from being referred and submitted to the Church's shepherds."

Charismatic Christians may speak in tongues, but they do not place the same emphasis on it as the Pentecostals do. Additionally, Charismatic Christians are not necessarily as evangelically minded, that is, inspired to do missionary work to non-Christians, as those in the other movements are. Charismatics will tend to look inward to revival within their denomination.[69]

———————————— ❧ ❧ ————————————

Christians who passionately believe in charismata are not fringe Christians! Pew Research estimated in their 2011 report on global Christianity that there are 305 million Charismatic Christians.[70] Pew Research estimates that, combined with Pentecostals, there are 584 million Christians, one out of every four total Christians, for whom charismata is an essential element of their faith and experience.[71]

In recent times, megachurches have emerged, attracting tens of thousands to weekly services and often broadcasting to many more thousands. For the most part, these churches are Pentecostal or nondenominational Charismatic churches. Services are filled with emotion, raised hands, healings, and so on. We'll cover this relatively new form of Christian splintering in more detail in a later chapter.

Notes

---

[1] See Acts 1:14; 2:44–47.

[2] See Acts 2:2–5, 37–38.

[3] See Acts 3:1–11.

[4] See Acts 10:22–48.

[5] See Acts 19:2–6.

[6] See 1 Corinthians 12.

[7] See the conversion experiences of Luther and Calvin in Chapter 7: George Fox, the founder of the Quakers, was a significant exception to this statement.

[8] Acts 8:9–11 tells of one named Simon who through sorcery had bewitched the locals such that they thought his powers were from God. Acts 13:7–10 speaks of a sorcerer who Paul confronted. Acts 19:13–19 speaks of exorcists that acted as if they had spiritual power.

[9] See the cautions expressed in 1 Corinthians 14.

[10] 1 Corinthians 14:39.

[11] 1 Corinthians 14:19.

[12] 1 Corinthians 14:20.

[13] 1 Corinthians 14:33, 40.

[14] Inerrancy suggests that everything in the Bible is accurate and contains no errors. Infallibility suggests that the Bible is completely trustworthy as a guide to faith and salvation. Sufficiency suggests that the Bible contains *all* that is needed for salvation. No additional guide, source of doctrine, or revelation is needed.

[15] The End of Charismatic Gifts n.d.

[16] Editors, The Return of the Spirit: The Second Great Awakening 1989.

[17] Editors, Book of Concord 2007.

[18] Editors, Book of Concord 2007.

[19] Maschke 1992.

[20] Maschke 1992.

[21] Maschke 1992.

[22] Maschke 1992.

[23] Maschke 1992.

[24] Wikipedia, Pietism 2018.

[25] Burns 2015.

[26] Herrnhut is on the eastern edge of Germany, which is notable due to its proximity to Czechoslovakia, the cradle of Protestantism started by Jan Hus. Herrnhut became a place of refuge for persecuted Hussite Protestants.

[27] Moravian Church n.d.

[28] Wikipedia, Methodism 2018.

[29] Wikipedia, John Wesley 2018.

[30] So important was Wesley's evangelical conversion at Aldersgate Street that to this day Methodists celebrate Aldersgate Day Wikipedia, John Wesley 2018.

[31] Wikipedia, John Wesley 2018.

[32] Wikipedia, Fetter Lane Society 2018.

[33] George Whitefield was one of the most persuasive and gifted preachers of the eighteenth century. His oratorial talent created intense emotions in his audiences. He made seven trips to the colonies and became a primary face of the First Great Awakening of 1740 in America. Tens of thousands gathered in revival meetings to

hear him speak. Arguably, he was one of the most influential evangelical preachers Wikipedia, George Whitefield 2018.

34 Wikipedia, John Wesley 2018. Later in his life, in 1778, Wesley began the publication of the *Arminian Magazine*, not, he said, to convince Calvinists, but to preserve Methodists.

35 Wikipedia, Methodism 2018.

36 Wikipedia, Fetter Lane Society 2018.

37 Wikipedia, Fetter Lane Society 2018.

38 Wikipedia, George Whitefield 2018. Wesley and Whitefield later reconciled as friends but never reconciled their differences relative to "limited" (Calvin's elect) versus "unlimited" atonement.

39 Wikipedia, John Wesley 2018.

40 Wikipedia, John Wesley 2018.

41 Wikipedia, Methodism 2018.

42 Wikipedia, Jonathan Edwards 2018.

43 D. Scott, Evangelicalism, Revivalism, and the Second Great Awakening n.d.

44 Editors, The Return of the Spirit: The Second Great Awakening 1989.

45 Editors, The Return of the Spirit: The Second Great Awakening 1989.

46 Editors, The Return of the Spirit: The Second Great Awakening 1989.

47 D. Scott, Evangelicalism, Revivalism, and the Second Great Awakening n.d.

48 Wikipedia, Charles Grandison Finney 2018.

49 Wikipedia, Second Great Awakening 2018.

50 Wikipedia, Holiness Movement 2018.

51 Wikipedia, Holiness Movement 2018.

52 Wikipedia, Holiness Movement 2018.

53 Church of the Nazarene n.d.

54 Wikipedia, Pilgrim Holiness Church 2018.

55 Wikipedia, Pentecostalism 2018.

56 Wikipedia, Pentecostalism 2018.

57 Wikipedia, Pentecostalism 2018.

58 Butler, Freston and Miller 2006.

59 A notable example is the Church of God in Christ, one of the largest denominations in the Unites States with over six million members. In the 1890s, black Baptist ministers taught their Baptist congregations the Wesleyan/Holiness doctrine of a second act of grace, namely sanctification. For this, they were rejected from the Baptists and formed a Holiness church in 1897. In 1906, one of their leaders attended the Asuza Street Revival and was baptized by the Holy Ghost. The leader pushed the new church to embrace Pentecostalism. In response, the church split in 1907 between more conservative Holiness and Pentecostalism, forming the Pentecostal Church of God in Christ. Although this was likely the first organized Pentecostal body, its black leadership was not invited to the all-white convention in 1914 from which Assemblies of God was formed Wikipedia, Church of God in Christ 2018.

60 Butler, Freston and Miller 2006.

61 Wikipedia, Pentecostalism 2018.

62 Wikipedia, Pentecostalism 2018.

63 Wikipedia, Pentecostalism 2018.

[64] Wikipedia, Pentecostalism 2018.
[65] Hackett and Grim 2011.
[66] Butler, Freston and Miller 2006.
[67] Wikipedia, Charismatic Movement 2018.
[68] Roman Catholic Church n.d.
[69] Wikipedia, Charismatic Movement 2018.
[70] Hackett and Grim 2011.
[71] Hackett and Grim 2011.

Chapter 9

Restoration Movements and the Millennium

The previous chapter started with the Great Awakenings and traced how the revivalism that animated Methodism resulted in successive generations of new offshoots with Holiness, Pentecostal, and Charismatic movements following. In this chapter, we will retrace our steps to the Second Great Awakening and look at a number of denominations that emerged not as offshoots of others but as independent, new denominations.

From the time Jesus promised to return, Christians have debated the meaning of the revelations pertaining to a millennial reign of Christ. Prophecies in the Old and New Testaments speak of the Son of Man returning to earth and receiving a kingdom with dominion over all of it.[1] The millennium is described in various scriptures: Christ reigns for a thousand years during which time the devil is bound.[2] Peace pervades the earth and war is no more.[3] The earth is renewed, and disasters, disease, and human despotism are gone. People grow old, plant, and reap without fear. Animals and people live together in peace without predation.[4]

The primitive church awaited eagerly the return of Jesus. The early Christians not only pooled their resources in communal support for each other but also sold all their possessions and goods and spent all their time in the temple.[5] Their actions are compelling evidence that they believed Jesus's return was imminent. However, Paul tried to reset expectations, warning the saints in Thessalonica that the coming of Christ would not come soon.[6]

After the apostolic period, early church leaders continued to believe in an earthly millennium, one that would liberate the Christians from the oppression of Rome. However, once the Roman Empire became the benefactor and protector of the church and became intertwined with it under Constantine, Rome could no longer be viewed as the evil Babylon that would be conquered by a victorious returning Christ. Rather, Rome itself came to be seen as the protector of God. Thus, the philosopher Origen (c. 184–c. 253) argued in favor of an allegorical millennium. Augustine adopted Origen's allegorical doctrine and taught that the millennium had already begun and was symbolical of Christ's reign with the saints in heaven.[7] By the Middle Ages, the Catholic Church had adopted the Augustinian doctrine and rejected the doctrine of a literal one-thousand-year reign on the earth. Luther, Zwingli, and Calvin retained the Catholic doctrine and criticized other Reform groups, including the Anabaptists, for adopting a literal view of the millennium.[8]

In contrast, the Puritans believed in a literal millennium due to the teaching of preachers such as Jonathan Edwards, one of the most influential theologians and preachers of the First Great Awakening. He taught of a literal earthly millennium, and as he observed the outpouring of religious fervor in the First Great Awakening, he speculated that the coming millennium would start in the colonies of America:

> Tis not unlikely that this work of God's Spirit, this is so extraordinary and wonderful, is the dawning, or at least a prelude, of that glorious work of God, so often foretold in Scripture. . . . And there are many things that make it probable that this work will begin in America.[9]

Edwards taught that Christ would come at the end of the millennium—a doctrine called postmillennialism. It would come about by degrees created by the progressive righteousness of Christians and victory of the church over the world.[10] The new colonies full of Christians with religious zeal could be such a place where righteousness blossomed.

Postmillennialists believed that through the progressive righteousness of the church that would be accomplished through the social policies it advocated, the entire world would evolve into its millennial condition of peace and righteousness. Theirs was an optimistic and outwardly focused view of the role and capacity of the church to change the world.[11] Premillennialists, on the other hand, concluded that evil will nearly conquer all and that if it were not for the advent of Jesus Christ, all would be lost. Premillennialism was inherently defensive and inwardly focused. It created an us-versus-them worldview in which the victory of a Christian was to persevere against the escalating forces of evil.

As the Revolutionary War closed and the Second Great Awakening blossomed, Edward's teachings were republished and widely circulated. Thus, it was not a coincidence that the Second Great Awakening, spanning roughly from 1795 to 1835, coincided with the end of the American Revolutionary War and the formation of the United States of America. The fact that this new nation was formed against tremendous odds was taken as evidence by many that it was created by God for the purpose of ushering in the prophesied millennial reign of the Lord.

No one taught of an imminent millennium more fervently than Charles Finney, one of the most prominent preachers of the Second Great Awakening. Allegedly, Finney asserted that "if the church will do her duty, the millennium may come in this country in three years."[12] The result was that the ushering in of the millennium was one of the central themes of the Second Great Awakening.

The revivalism of the Second Great Awakening inspired religious engagement, and countless people joined the Methodists, Baptists, and Presbyterians—the denominations at the heart of the Great Awakening. However, the increased religious study and diligent searching inspired by the Great Awakening also led some to doubt that existing denominations reflected the church that Christ had intended and that a restoration of the apostolic church was needed.

Such doubts and call for restoration—as opposed to reformation— were not unique to religious leaders of the Second Great Awakening. Roger Williams, the founder of Rhode Island, started his religious journey as an Anglican, then became a "separatist" Puritan, and then a

Baptist. But in time, he left formal denominations and became a "seeker," stating, "There is no regularly constituted church of Christ on earth, nor any person qualified to administer any church ordinances; nor can there be until new apostles are sent by the Great Head of the Church for whose coming I am seeking."[13]

The Stone-Campbell Restoration Movement

Two leading figures of the Second Great Awakening found themselves, like Roger Williams, seeking the restoration of primitive Christianity. Each journeyed alone for a time but joined together into a unified movement.

One of these figures was Barton Stone, a person we learned about in the previous chapter. In 1801, as a Presbyterian minister, he organized the Cane Ridge Revival in Kentucky. By almost any measure, the revival was a success, with an estimated twenty thousand people attending[14]. The revival was hosted by the Presbyterians but brought together ministers from the Baptists and the Methodists. At the revival, doctrines were taught that were contrary to the Presbyterian Westminster Confession. When the Presbyterian Kentucky Synod determined to censure the minister who taught the contrary doctrines, Barton Stone revealed his own doubts about doctrines in the Westminster Confession. More fundamentally, he had doubts about the validity of all denominations and their credal confessions.

As a result, Stone and four other ministers formed the Springfield Presbytery, a denominationally independent group. The new group grew quickly, attracting over a dozen congregations from Ohio and Kentucky. The leaders quickly recognized that they were soon becoming a new denomination and resolved to disband the group just a year after it was formed. In the document disbanding the group, they expressed a singular desire for Christian unity and acceptance of the simple truths of the Bible as the standard of Christian faith and practice.[15] They shunned the idea of a new denominational title and called themselves simply Christians. Of course, it is impossible to stand for something in the form of an organized group and not walk and talk like a denomination. By all measures, the group was a denomination, and in time the group, which measured in the low tens of thousands by 1830, became known as the Christian Church.

The other figure was Thomas Campbell (1763–1854), an Irishman who was raised an Anglican but was later ordained a Presbyterian minister. In his studies, Campbell was deeply influenced by the ideas of John Locke, one of the most important thinkers of the great Enlightenment. Locke had proposed a remedy for religious division that was similar to the Moravian motto. Campbell's remedy is as follows: "Reduce religion to a set of essentials upon which all reasonable persons might agree."[16] After coming to America in 1807, Campbell became vocal about his disagreements with Presbyterianism's underlying doctrines, leading the Presbyterian synod to suspend his ministerial rights. In 1809, Campbell launched a new group, later called Disciples of Christ, intent on restoring the apostolic church. The group adopted the practice of baptism by immersion and was therefore invited by the Baptists to join their association, which it did in 1815. Alexander Campbell, Thomas's son, joined the movement and became the most influential leader, publishing the journal *The Christian Baptist.*[17] However, the group distilled its beliefs and practices down to the "essentials" and in so doing did not adhere to the Philadelphia Confession of faith held by American Baptists. Consequently, in 1830, Campbell's group separated from the Baptists.[18]

In 1832, Barton Stone and delegates from the Campbell movement agreed to join ranks. There were differences of belief between them, but both groups agreed that Christian unity was possible if the creeds of denominations were rejected in favor of the essential elements of the apostolic church. The combined Stone-Campbell movement stressed unity in the essentials, restoration, and millennialism. Although joined, they couldn't agree on a common name, and so the churches emerging from the Stone-Campbell Restoration movement were known as Christian Churches, Disciples of Christ, and Churches of Christ. They had a congregational polity, which meant that there was no superior authority to resolve theological and liturgical differences. By the late 1800s, the group was effectively split between more progressive, educated, and wealthy Northerners who emphasized ecumenical unity and adopted musical instruments within their worship and the more conservative, rural, less-educated Southerners who rejected anything not explicitly described in the New Testament. The former called themselves Disciples of Christ and the latter Churches of

Christ.[19] Today, the combined movement has about seven million members.[20]

Joseph Smith and the Latter-day Saints

In 1820, a young man of fourteen named Joseph Smith was caught up in the fervor of the Second Great Awakening in his home of Palmyra, New York. He and his family attended revivals from different denominations, and although Smith's family split along denominational lines, he was reluctant to join a church until he was convinced which one was true. After reading the promise from God in James 1:5 to reveal wisdom to anyone that lacked it, Smith decided to pray to know which church to join. He found a secluded grove, and Smith testified that, upon praying, the heavens opened and two beings appeared, God the Father and His Son, Jesus Christ. They told him not to join any of the churches and that through him the church of Christ would be restored.[21]

As Smith shared his vision, it quickly earned him the scorn of the religious leaders in the community. Understandably, the vision's conclusion that the existing churches were all wrong was not easy for other denominations to accept. Additionally, the vision was considered heretical in that two figures in the form of men directly contradicted Trinitarian creeds.

Smith received other revelations preparing him to organize the restored church. One angelic visitor told him of a buried record, written by a branch of the house of Israel that had inhabited portions of the Americas. The record, Smith was told, would be a second witness of Jesus Christ, in addition to the Bible.[22] Smith obtained the ancient record as directed by the angel, translated it, and then published it in early 1830 as the Book of Mormon—the title being a reference to one of the principle authors of the book. Members of the denominations stemming from Joseph Smith consider the Book of Mormon to be scripture comparable in authority to the Bible.

Other angelic visitors restored the priesthood.[23] Thus empowered, in April 1830, Smith and a small band of believers formed the Church of Christ, later named The Church of Jesus Christ of Latter-day Saints.[24] However, as is so often the case, critics were quick to label members "Mormons"—a pejorative reference to the belief in the Book of Mormon. Smith received revelations guiding the organization of the church according to the pattern of the apostolic church with apostles, seventies, elders, bishops, and so on.[25] His revelations received during the early years of the church were compiled into a book considered canonical by Latter-day Saints called today the Doctrine and Covenants.[26]

From its inception, the church sent out missionaries, and it grew relatively quickly. Like others of the Second Great Awakening, Smith believed that the millennium was imminent. In 1831, he received a revelation that Jackson County, Missouri, a place on the ragged frontier of the new nation, was to be the center of the millennial Zion.[27] Converts were encouraged to emigrate to America and the future Zion. Tens of thousands of converts heeded the call.

From 1836[28] to 1846,[29] the Latter-day Saints experienced a period of intense persecution—including an official edict from the governor of Missouri to exterminate the Mormons.[30] As a result, the saints migrated from gathering place to gathering place: from Kirtland, Ohio, to Independence, Missouri; from Independence to Far West, Missouri; and then on to Nauvoo, Illinois. Certainly, the persecution stemmed in part from the unique scriptures and doctrines of the church; however, it would be too simplistic to suggest that this alone fueled the persecution. In fact, in each place, persecution was inspired by different combinations of religion, culture, economics, and politics. The rapid influx of gathering saints would strain any community, but against a backdrop of a monetary crisis in the mid 1830s, the burgeoning contest over slavery, and the political threat posed by a block of voters loyal to their prophet's direction, the gatherings in Kirtland, Missouri, and Nauvoo were inevitably a threat to those communities and states in which the saints settled.

Nauvoo, Illinois, was a brief respite from persecution, and the saints enjoyed a period of autonomy and prosperity. Nauvoo became the second largest city in Illinois after Chicago—a fact not lost on religious and political rivals throughout the state. Perhaps the most important development in Nauvoo was Smith's introduction of the practice of plural marriage, or polygamy, among a select group of church leaders in 1841.[31] The practice caused divisions and controversy within church leadership. Some senior leaders abandoned the church and became virulent anti-Mormons. Conflict ensued and culminated in the assassination of Joseph Smith in 1844 while he was awaiting trial in the county jail in Carthage, Illinois.[32]

The twelve apostles under the leadership of Brigham Young determined to seek refuge in the valleys of the Rocky Mountains outside the boundaries of the United States. In 1847, the Latter-day Saints established a foothold in the desert valley of the Great Salt Lake. Over the following decades, tens of thousands of converts, many of whom were immigrants from Europe, particularly Great Britain, trekked across the plains into the valley.[33] Many were then assigned by Brigham Young to colonize communities throughout the West.

The Church of Jesus Christ of Latter-day Saints is now an international church with over sixteen million members worldwide.[34] Today, the majority of the membership is outside the United States.

William Miller, Ellen White, and the Adventists

William Miller (1782–1849) was born and raised a Baptist, but he was pulled away from formal denominations through his exposure to the works of Voltaire, Hume, and other Deists.[35] After his service in the War of 1812, he had a spiritual experience that drew him back to Christianity, but he determined to return only if a detailed study of the Bible satisfactorily resolved the contradictions of denominational Christianity. If they did not, he would remain a Deist.[36] He undertook his study in the context of the Second Great Awakening with its dominant theme of the imminent second coming of Christ. His study led him to two important conclusions about the millennium.

First, he concluded that the postmillennialism that had been taught by Jonathan Edwards was unbiblical. His reading of the Bible convinced him that Christ would come at the beginning of the millennium to end a period of severe tribulation and thereby usher in the millennium.[37] The timing of Christ's appearance was not just a matter of semantics. It directly translated into a Christian's worldview and action. Miller adopted premillennialism, which was inherently defensive and inwardly focused. It created an us-versus-them worldview in which the victory of a Christian was to persevere against the escalating forces of evil.

Miller's second major conclusion, based on his interpretation of Daniel 8:14 in the Old Testament, was that Christ would return sometime between 1843 and March of 1844.[38] He reached this conclusion as early as 1818 but didn't publish it widely until 1831. In 1832, he published his calculations first in a series of articles in a Baptist magazine and then in a book. He became an overnight celebrity with numerous invitations to speak. A pastor named Joshua Himes became Miller's self-appointed publicist in 1840 and created an elaborate illustration of Miller's calculations, purchased a huge tent to hold lectures, and published a paper called *Signs of the Times*.[39] He turned Miller into a national figure. Believers in Miller's predictions grew rapidly, perhaps to as many as fifty thousand true disciples and as many as one million expectant onlookers.[40] As 1843 dawned, the Millerites waited in anticipation for the advent of Christ. But 1843 passed. Miller then recalculated and set a firm date of March 21, 1844. When that date also passed, Miller appeared discredited until a devout disciple pointed to other scriptures speaking to a seven month "tarry." A new date of October 22, 1844, was thus established.[41] Again, the new date passed with no advent of Christ—a "Great Disappointment" to Miller's disciples.[42] Most of the Millerites abandoned the cause and returned to their denominations; however, some did not and continued to meet as Adventists.

In December 1844, close on the heels of the Great Disappointment, the Adventist Ellen Harmon, later Ellen White, claimed to have had a vision in which she saw the heavens open and Adventists approach the throne of God. She would go on to receive somewhere between one hundred to two hundred revelations during the ensuing years. Importantly, Ellen White clarified Miller's doctrine—the *date* was right but the *place* was wrong. She taught that in 1844 Jesus had entered the *heavenly* "holy of holies" and had begun to judge the dead according to their works recorded in the book of life. This judgement, which she called the "investigative judgment," began in 1844 and would continue until the advent of Christ on the earth.

One of White's fellow Adventists, Joseph Bates, was exposed to the practice of the seventh-day Sabbath through a tract written by a fellow Millerite—the tract itself was inspired by a group of "seventh-day" Baptists.[43] Bates convinced his fellow Adventists that Sabbath worship should be done on the seventh day as prescribed in the original covenant God made with Israel. In 1863, the growing Adventist group formally organized a church calling themselves the Seventh-day Adventists.[44]

The Seventh-day Adventists established their doctrine, guided by Ellen White's prophetic leadership. Some of their doctrines initially diverged from core Protestant beliefs, particularly reliance on prophecy and the Trinitarian creeds.[45] However, the doctrines evolved to square with Protestantism such that today the church is considered a Protestant denomination—believing in the doctrines of scriptural infallibility, justification by faith alone, and the Trinitarian creeds while still maintaining its unique doctrines of investigative judgment and seventh-day worship, and so on.[46] The church spread its message through Ellen White's prolific writings, expansive publishing operations, and prolific missionary efforts throughout the world. Today, over twenty million people belong to the Seventh-day Adventist Church.[47]

Charles Taze Russell and the Jehovah's Witnesses

Charles Taze Russell (1852–1916) was born into a Scottish family and was raised Presbyterian.[48] He was deeply religious but increasingly uncertain of the Presbyterian view of eternal hell. As a young teen, he left the Presbyterians and joined the Congregationalists,[49] but there, too, Calvinism's unflinching view of predestined eternal hell left him searching and skeptical.[50] In 1870, at age eighteen, he attended a presentation by an Adventist preacher. The Adventist's approach of using the Bible to calculate critical dates pertaining to the end of times captured Russell's imagination, talents, and financial resources. Russell determined to undertake an analytical review of the Bible and organized a group, which called themselves simply Bible Students, to join him. The group was deeply influenced by the Adventists and agreed that the millennial return of Jesus was imminent; however, they did not limit their doctrinal focus to the millennium. Russell concluded through his studies that Trinitarianism was unfounded, as were common Christian doctrines related to hellfire, resurrection, and the immortality of the soul.[51]

In about 1876, Russell read *Herald of the Morning*, published by an influential Adventist. He was so motivated by the journal and the predictions within it that he contacted the publisher, Nelson Barbour, and within a year the two collaborated on additional millennial texts to be published in 1877 in the *Herald*.[52] They were committed to Barbour's prediction that the harvesting of the prophesied 144,000 Christians who would rule with God in heaven[53] would end in 1878.[54] Russell added his own chronological prediction—that Christ's "invisible return" and beginning of the harvest had actually started in 1874.[55] Bible Students believed that they would be "harvested," or translated— the implication being that they would *not* live long lives and would *not* face death.

Like the Great Disappointment of the Millerites, 1878 came and went with Bible Students still very much alive and untranslated. The failed prediction in 1878 was initially Barbour's, giving Russell some justification for criticizing it and offering a new prediction. Disagreement ensued and the two men split in 1879. Immediately, Russell started his own millennial journal called the *Zion's Watch Tower and Herald of Christ's Presence*.[56] He recalculated the end of the harvest as 1881. When that date passed, he offered no new date. Instead, he reset expectations that the Bible Students would be instantaneously translated after death.[57]

A few years after the missed prediction in 1881, Russell started the Zion's Watch Tower Tract Society, later shortened to the Watch Tower Bible and Tract Society—a publishing group that would become one of the most prolific publishers of religious tracts.[58] Through it, Russell published six volumes, spanning from 1886 to 1899, of a series on millennial themes that was initially entitled Millennial Dawn and later renamed Studies in the Scriptures.[59] In the series, Russell predicted that Christ's "visible presence" would usher in the "end of the Gentile times" and the beginning of the millennial kingdom in October, 1914. His belief that this would be the *end* of conflict and trouble was evident in a response he offered to readers' questions: "1914 is not the date for the *beginning*, but for the *end* of the trouble."[60]

Russell's fame spread such that in 1903 newspapers began publishing his sermons to millions. So prolific were Russell's writings and so widespread their distribution through the Watch Tower Society and through newspapers that the "journal *Overland Monthly* calculated that by 1909 his writings were the most widely distributed privately produced English-language works in the United States" and the "third most circulated on earth."[61]

The year 1914 indeed proved to be a seminal year, but, rather than usher in a golden age and the millennial kingdom following the advent of Christ, it ushered in the most devastating war in the history of humankind. Russell reevaluated his predictions to conclude that the Great War was the *beginning* of Armageddon and that the *end* of trouble would occur in 1918, rather than 1914 as previously predicted.[62] Russell died in 1916 before his followers endured yet another disappointment. Russell's replacement as president of the society, Joseph Rutherford (1869–1942), softened the disappointment by explaining that the millennium would come *within the lifetime* of those alive in 1914.[63] He reset 1914 as the *beginning* of the end-times and the year in which Satan and his demons were cast to earth.[64] As for the unfulfilled prophecy related to 1918, he adopted a similar doctrine to the Adventist's view of 1844 and investigative judgment, namely, that 1918 was the time Christ entered the heavenly temple for the purpose of judgment.

Rutherford's election was contested by four of the seven Society's directors leading to opposing camps and splinter groups; however, Rutherford remained the leader of the main group.[65] In 1931, he changed the name of the Bible Students to Jehovah's Witnesses.[66] He instituted strong centralized leadership that controlled doctrine and the selection of congregational leaders. The denomination adopted many of Russell's unorthodox doctrines, including the doctrine of God—that Jehovah alone is God and Christ is Jehovah's agent. The Holy Ghost is not a being, but the name of God's force.[67] The denomination rejects the doctrine of eternal hellfire and punishment—unrighteous souls that die cease to exist.[68] It still believes in the special role of 144,000 spiritual co-rulers with Christ in the Millennial Kingdom; however, the rest of the righteous will be resurrected and will live in a cleansed paradisiacal earth.[69]

Since its inception, the denomination has drawn criticism on several fronts. It has continued to make millennial predictions only to see the dates pass with prophecies unfulfilled.[70] It teaches that sectarian Christianity will collapse and fail.[71] Its doctrine of the Godhead is not consistent with Christian creeds. It teaches a strict separation from secular power, and therefore its members do not serve in the military and do not vote. They do not observe any holiday or practice that has pagan origins, including Christmas, Easter, and even birthdays. They refuse blood transfusions, based on the prohibition in Leviticus of consuming blood.[72]

In spite of criticism and controversy, the Jehovah's Witnesses have grown worldwide. Their prolific publishing is coupled with active evangelism from their members. "Active" members spend as much time as possible evangelizing and report monthly to the church on their activities. Members that do not submit reports for six consecutive months are considered "inactive."[73] The church uses this strict measure of activity to define its membership, which today is about 8.5 million active members. However, roughly twenty million participate in their annual memorial service—the difference in numbers resulting from unbaptized children and "inactive" members that worship but do not proselyte.[74]

Mary Baker Eddy and the Christian Scientists

Mary Baker Eddy (1821–1910) was raised a devout Congregationalist with Calvinist roots and was a devoted student of the Bible. Her formative years shaped her later life. She writes that as a child she suffered from chronic indigestion and resorted to a diet of water, bread, and vegetables—sometimes eaten just once a day.[75] She experienced bouts of hysteria, described as suddenly falling, writhing, and screaming until unconscious.[76] Her adulthood was no less fraught with suffering. Her first husband died after contracting yellow fever in 1844, after just six months of marriage. His death left her stranded in North Carolina, and she, now six months pregnant, had to travel to her parents' home in the north, a journey that left her physically and mentally exhausted. Then followed a series of personal traumas. She had long ago rejected Calvinism's notions of predestined suffering and the hellfire of the Congregational faith of her youth; however, her religious background still framed her worldview that disease and its ravages were the manifestation of evil, just as guilt resulted from sin. Thus, she sought to reconcile disease and suffering with belief in a loving and sovereign God.[77]

Her personal experiences focused her mind on disease, and she delved into the bewildering medical practices of her day. But she found there a "dim maze" with more "scientific guessing" than established fact.[78] Indeed, medicine was still largely the domain of the supernatural, and practitioners relied on wide-ranging methods including Samuel Hahnemann's (1755–1843) homeopathy;[79] hydrotherapy[80] clinics, hundreds of which could be found across the United States; and the use of allopathic[81] concoctions, to name a few. However, within this milieu, the seeds of Western medicine were sprouting. In nations far removed from Eddy, science-based empirical analysis was leading to groundbreaking medical discoveries. In France, Louis Pasteur discovered germs and developed vaccines.[82] Surgeons such as Joseph Lister, in Scotland, used empirical evidence to introduce sterilization.[83] The transmission of diseases through parasites was discovered in 1877, unlocking the cause of malaria in 1897.[84]

In hindsight, it is clear that empirical science would transform medicine and was thus an ally in the contest against disease. However, it was less clear in the infancy of modern medicine. At that time, "science" was a squishy concept related to general wisdom and knowledge. Furthermore, Christians had cause to distrust aspects of science because it threatened to rationalize away the divine and supernatural. There is no more poignant example of this than the challenge to Christian faith from Charles Darwin's seminal work, *On the Origin of Species,* published in 1859.[85]

In 1862, just a few years before Pasteur revealed the nature of infectious disease and developed vaccines,[86] Eddy became a patient of Phineas Quimby, a healer who fused religious doctrines of light and wisdom with the practical techniques of mesmerism or hypnotism. In a twist on the notion of science, Quimby equated illness to a darkness created by ignorance. He wrote, "Our misery lies in this darkness. This is the prison that holds the natural man, till the light of Wisdom bursts his bonds, and lets the captive free."[87] Eddy improved under Quimby's care and was deeply influenced by him, and she retained a copy of his manuscript, which contained the outline of a "moral science."[88]

A few years later, she once again faced a health crisis after falling. She experienced healing as a result of spiritual reflection.[89] These experiences convinced her that the "cause of disease was rooted in the human mind and that it was in no sense God's will,"[90] and that "sickness is an illusion that can be corrected by prayer alone."[91] She began her own healing practice using Quimby's manuscript and advertised for and taught students the principles of mental healing. Ultimately, in 1875 she published her beliefs in the book *Science and Health*:

> It is plain that God does not employ drugs or hygiene, nor provide them for human use; else Jesus would have recommended and employed them in his healing. . . . The tender word and Christian encouragement of an invalid, pitiful patience with his fears and the removal of them, are better than hecatombs of gushing theories, stereotyped borrowed speeches, and the doling of arguments, which are but so many parodies on legitimate Christian Science, aflame with divine Love.[92]

She organized the Church of Christ, Scientist in 1879, centered on the belief that medicine and Christian Science are incompatible: "Medicine asserts that something needs to be fixed, while Christian Science asserts that spiritual reality is perfect and beliefs to the contrary need to be corrected."[93] She organized a school to train additional healers, called practitioners. Aspiring healers undergo two weeks of training, after which they can earn a living charging for Christian Science healing prayers.

Eddy incorporated the core belief of the mind controlling the physical into the entire theology of the new faith, including the doctrine of God. She referred to God as the "divine Mind."[94] Her beliefs would have fit comfortably within the realm of Greek-inspired Gnosticism— which professed that material things are divorced from the infinite immaterial God. Consider the similarity between Gnostic ideas described in chapter 5 and the following excerpt from Eddy's work:

> That God is corporeal or material, no man should affirm. The human form, or physical finiteness, cannot be made the basis of any true idea of the infinite Godhead. . . . Mind, not matter, is the creator. Love, the divine Principle, is the Father and Mother of the universe, including man. The theory of three persons in one God (that is, a personal

Trinity or Tri-unity) suggests polytheism, rather than the one ever-present I AM. "Hear, O Israel: the Lord our God is one Lord." The everlasting I AM is not bounded nor compressed within the narrow limits of physical humanity, nor can He be understood aright through mortal concepts. The precise form of God must be of small importance in comparison with the sublime question, What is infinite Mind or divine Love? . . . No form nor physical combination is adequate to represent infinite Love. A finite and material sense of God leads to formalism and narrowness; it chills the spirit of Christianity. A limitless Mind cannot proceed from physical limitations. . . . If Mind is within and without all things, then all is Mind; and this definition is scientific. . . . The divine nature was best expressed in Christ Jesus, who threw upon mortals the truer reflection of God and lifted their lives higher than their poor thought-models would allow,—thoughts which presented man as fallen, sick, sinning, and dying. The Christlike understanding of scientific being and divine healing includes a perfect Principle and idea,—perfect God and perfect man,—as the basis of thought and demonstration.[95]

In the early decades of the twentieth century, Christian Science became one of the fastest growing religions in the United States, peaking in the 1930s at just over a quarter of a million members served by over eleven thousand practitioners.[96] In the early years, the compelling testimonies of the healed stood in favorable contrast to the victims of the still infant and crude medical profession. However, as modern medicine matured with the advent of Penicillin in 1928 and the rapid advances made during World War II, medical science demonstrated its validity, and the denomination entered a long decline. The church does not publish membership statistics, but today there are likely less than one hundred thousand members served by less than one thousand practitioners.[97] Nevertheless, Christian Science continues to shape modern thought through its Pulitzer Prize–winning publication, the *Christian Science Monitor*.

———————— ❧ ❦ ————————

The close of this chapter takes us past the Second Great Awakening. We can now look back and see its profound effect on Christianity. Most importantly, it rekindled Christian passion. The denominations that fostered it—the Baptists, Methodists, and Presbyterians—grew rapidly as a result, but so did the new denominations we've covered in the previous two chapters. As this chapter has shown, many American Christians believed that within their new nation the conditions were uniquely aligned to restore primitive Christianity and usher in the promised millennium.

The influence of the Second Great Awakening persists through the denominations that formed during it as well as through the resurgence of its themes in the twentieth century. Keep this in mind as we transition to "modern" times. The themes of the Second Great Awakening of evangelism, charismatic experiences, spiritual healing, restoration, and millennialism continue to profoundly shape and splinter modern Christianity, as we will soon learn as we journey into the next chapters.

Notes

---

1 See Daniel 7:13–14.
2 See Revelations 20:1–4.
3 See Isaiah 2:3–4.
4 See Isaiah 65:17–25.
5 See Acts 2:45–46.
6 2 Thessalonians 2:2–4.
7 Wikipedia, Premillennialism 2018.
8 Wikipedia, Premillennialism 2018.
9 Pointer 1999.
10 Pointer 1999.
11 Pointer 1999.
12 Pointer 1999.
13 Source: Statement of rejection of formal sectarian organizations and claims, as quoted in *Picturesque America* (1874) by William Cullen Bryant, p. 502.
14 Wikipedia, Cane Ridge Revival 2018.
15 Wikipedia, Barton W. Stone 2017.
16 Wikipedia, Disciples of Christ (Campbell Movement) 2017.
17 Wikipedia, Alexander Campbell (clergyman) 2018.
18 Wikipedia, Restoration Movement 2018.
19 Wikipedia, Restoration Movement 2018.
20 Wikipedia, List of Christian denominations by number of members 2018.
21 Smith, Joseph Smith - History 1981, 47-50.
22 Smith, Joseph Smith - History 1981, 51-57.
23 Smith, Joseph Smith - History 1981, 57-58.
24 Wikipedia, Latter Day Saint Movement 2018.
25 Smith, The Doctrine and Covenants 1981, 215-221.
26 Smith, The Doctrine and Covenants 1981.
27 Smith, The Doctrine and Covenants 1981, 95-96.
28 An apostasy precipitated by a financial crash started troubles in Kirtland, Ohio.
29 The saints abandoned Nauvoo.
30 Wikipedia, Missouri Executive Order 44 2019.
31 Church Educational System 1993, 256.
32 Church Educational System 1993, 280-283.
33 The Church of Jesus Christ of Latter-day Saints 2013.
34 Wikipedia, List of Christian denominations by number of members 2018.
35 Deism is a philosophical belief that posits that God exists and is ultimately responsible for the creation of the universe, but He does not interfere directly with the created world. Thus, Deists reject the supernatural, including divine revelation and miracles. Wikipedia, Deism 2018.
36 Wikipedia, William Miller (preacher) 2018.
37 Wikipedia, William Miller (preacher) 2018.
38 B. Shelley 1999.
39 B. Shelley 1999.
40 B. Shelley 1999.
41 B. Shelley 1999.
42 Wikipedia, William Miller (preacher) 2018.

43 Wikipedia, Seventh-day Adventist Church 2018.

44 Lechleitner 2013.

45 Lechleitner 2013.

46 Seventh-day Adventist Church n.d.

47 Wikipedia, List of Christian denominations by number of members 2018.

48 Wikipedia, Charles Taze Russell 2018.

49 The Congregational Church originated from the Reformed branch, or Calvinism; however, it adopted congregational, rather than presbyterian polity.

50 Editors, Charles Taze Russell 2019.

51 Wikipedia, Charles Taze Russell 2018.

52 Wikipedia, Charles Taze Russell 2018.

53 See Revelations 7:4.

54 Wikipedia, Watch Tower Society unfulfilled predictions 2018.

55 J. G. Melton, Jehovah's Witness 2018.

56 Wikipedia, Charles Taze Russell 2018.

57 Wikipedia, Watch Tower Society unfulfilled predictions 2018.

58 Wikipedia, Charles Taze Russell 2018.

59 Wikipedia, Charles Taze Russell 2018.

60 Wikipedia, Watch Tower Society unfulfilled predictions 2018.

61 Wikipedia, Charles Taze Russell 2018.

62 Wikipedia, Watch Tower Society unfulfilled predictions 2018.

63 Wikipedia, Watch Tower Society unfulfilled predictions 2018.

64 Wikipedia, Jehovah's Witnesses 2018.

65 Wikipedia, Watch Tower Society presidency dispute (1917) 2019.

66 J. G. Melton, Jehovah's Witness 2018.

67 J. G. Melton, Jehovah's Witness 2018.

68 Wikipedia, Jehovah's Witnesses 2018.

69 Wikipedia, Jehovah's Witnesses 2018.

70 Rutherford predicted the resurrection of the Patriarchs in 1925. The denomination widely taught that the millennium would begin in 1975 and then more broadly that it would definitely begin in the 20th century Wikipedia, Watch Tower Society unfulfilled predictions 2018.

71 Wikipedia, Jehovah's Witnesses 2018.

72 Wikipedia, Jehovah's Witnesses 2018. See Leviticus 3:17.

73 Wikipedia, Jehovah's Witnesses 2018.

74 Wikipedia, Jehovah's Witnesses 2018.

75 Wikipedia, Mary Baker Eddy 2018.

76 Wikipedia, Mary Baker Eddy 2018.

77 Wikipedia, Mary Baker Eddy 2018.

78 Wikipedia, Mary Baker Eddy 2018.

79 A treatment method based on the idea that "like cures like." A substance that causes a disease in a healthy person would heal the same disease in a sick person. In practice, the remedy was to be prepared by extensive and repeated dilution of substances prescribed according to holistic combination of symptoms, personal traits, and life history Wikipedia, Homeopathy 2019.

80 Treatment based on the belief that pure water entering the body through cracks and openings would displace disease, ultimately pushing it out as pus. At its peak in

the late 1800s there were an estimated two hundred hydrotherapy clinics in the United States Wikipedia, Hydrotherapy 2019.

[81] Treatment of symptoms with drugs that induced the opposite symptom Wikipedia, Allopathic medicine 2019.

[82] Ullmann 2019.

[83] Rhodes, Guthrie and Others 2017.

[84] Rhodes, Guthrie and Others 2017.

[85] Wikipedia, Charles Darwin 2018.

[86] His work to save the silkworm industry in the 1860s led to the understanding of infectious diseases. By chance, he discovered immunology and developed vaccines for animals and humans in the 1870s and 1880s Ullmann 2019.

[87] Wikipedia, Mary Baker Eddy 2018.

[88] Wikipedia, Christian Science 2018.

[89] Wikipedia, Mary Baker Eddy 2018.

[90] Gottschalk and Melton, Christian Science 2016.

[91] Wikipedia, Christian Science 2018.

[92] Wikipedia, Mary Baker Eddy 2018.

[93] Wikipedia, Christian Science 2018.

[94] Eddy 1875, 255:6.

[95] Eddy 1875, 255:6.

[96] Wikipedia, Christian Science 2018.

[97] Wikipedia, Christian Science 2018.

Chapter 10

Evangelicals and Related Movements

Few Christian terms are as ambiguous as the term *evangelical*. Nevertheless, it is worth the effort to sort through the ambiguity because evangelicalism is one of the most dynamic and influential movements within Christianity today. In this chapter, we will see that the grouping of evangelicals varies widely based on context. We will explore the following generally distinct uses of the term:

- confessional evangelicals within the Lutheran and Reformed traditions
- denominations and movements associated with the revivals of the Great Awakenings
- neo-evangelicals arising from a twentieth-century split from fundamentalism
- "born-again" Christians
- political evangelicals
- televangelism, including nondenominational ministries and megachurches

As we move through each "flavor" of evangelicals, we find a few common characteristics that together represent the most accepted definition of an evangelical. The common foundation of evangelicalism is contained in its name. The term *evangelical* is not used in the Bible, but the root of the term is. The Greek word *evangelion*, meaning "good news," was used to describe the overall message of Christ.[1] In Old English, *evangelion* was translated as "gospel." At its most basic level, *evangelical* refers to a person or movement committed to the good news of the gospel of Jesus Christ. Beyond this commonality, lines get blurred quickly.

One measure of the ambiguity is the widely disparate estimates made by different research groups of the number of evangelicals worldwide. Some surveys add up all denominations that belong to evangelical associations.[2] Others do statistical sampling asking survey respondents theological questions to identify evangelicals.[3] Yet others simply ask respondents to self-identify as an evangelical based on the single criteria of being "born again."[4]

The World Christian Database (WCD) estimated in 2010 that there were three hundred million Evangelicals worldwide. However, the group explicitly separated Evangelicals with a capital "E," of which they estimate three hundred million, from evangelicals with a lowercase "e," a group the WCD estimated to be seven hundred million worldwide. WCD recognized that millions of Christians from mainline protestant churches actively *evangelize* by sharing their faith in Jesus through organized missions to the world and are thus evangelical. But these are evangelicals with a lowercase "e," meaning that these are Christians fulfilling the great commission to share the gospel. WCD distinguishes capital "E" Evangelicals as those that have three distinct characteristics: a born-again conversion experience, the acceptance of the Bible as the sole word of God, and a commitment to actively evangelize nonbelievers throughout the world.[5]

Another report, Operation World, used a four-point theological standard[6] to count Evangelicals and estimated that there were 550 million worldwide in 2010.[7] The Operation World number is nearly twice the WCD estimate for capital "E" Evangelicals. Yet another study done by the Pew Research Center estimated in their 2011 report on global Christianity that there were 285 million Evangelicals. Pew used denominational membership to estimate the number.[8] Clearly, there is a wide range due to the imprecise definition of what it means to be evangelical and the imperfect overlap between self-identifying evangelicals and evangelical denominations.

Confessional Evangelicals

Martin Luther adopted the term *evangelical* to distinguish Protestant Christians from Catholics. The two concurrent Protestant movements of Luther and Zwingli were referred to respectively as Evangelical Lutherans and Evangelical Reformed.[9] Many Lutheran and Reformed churches still consider themselves "confessional evangelicals," believing that the core tenets of Protestant doctrine establish these branches as evangelical. Confessional evangelicals are generally firmly committed to their respective denominations and believe in their respective confessions of faith.

It is not uncommon for mainline Protestant churches to include the term *evangelical* in their name. This is particularly prevalent in continental Europe. The Evangelical Church in Germany, the largest organized Protestant body in Germany with twenty-two million members, is a federation of twenty regional churches from the Lutheran and Reformed traditions that also generally use the term *evangelical* in their titles.[10]

Confessional evangelicals generally believe in the Protestant doctrines of *sola fide* and *sola scriptura*.[11] *Sola fide* refers to the belief that it is by faith alone that we are justified and that such faith is given as a gift of grace from God. However, we will see later in this chapter that these core tenets of Protestantism are interpreted in widely varying ways across the evangelical spectrum. Confessional evangelicals align with the more subtle and private experiences of Luther, Calvin, Wesley, and others, in which they felt assured that they had received such grace and were thus justified, regenerated, or born-again. Indeed, belief in being converted, regenerated, or born-again is a defining characteristic of an evangelical; however, the experiences recorded by Luther, Calvin, Wesley, and other early Protestants are very different than the expectations of Pentecostals. We'll explore later in this chapter how being born-again has been interpreted in a variety of ways. Similarly, confessional evangelicals believe in *sola scriptura*—a belief that the Bible alone is canonical—but their belief is quite progressive and open-minded compared to fundamentalists. As we have with born-again doctrine, we will discover later in this chapter that *sola scriptura* doesn't mean the same thing to all evangelicals.

Evangelical Revivalism of the Great Awakenings

Evangelism, the spreading of the gospel of Jesus Christ, has been a part of the Christian mandate since Jesus first commanded His apostles to

"Go ye into all the world, and preach the gospel to every creature."[12] Paul spoke of evangelists, those who commit their life—their vocation if you will—to evangelism.[13] Jesus did not prescribe the method of evangelism, and, indeed, a wide variety of teaching methods are found in the book of Acts: large public gatherings as on the day of Pentecost, Philip's one-on-one teaching of the eunuch,[14] Peter's private teaching in a household,[15] or Paul's teaching in synagogues.[16] The only common feature was a commitment to spread the gospel to all. Thus, a defining characteristic of an evangelical is one who is committed to share the good news of the gospel with nonbelievers.

The Great Awakenings discussed in earlier chapters were fueled by evangelism. However, the evangelism of large revivals was unlike anything from the New Testament. Traveling preachers addressed crowds with the express purpose of inducing a conversion experience in those attending. The use of oratorial skills and presentation techniques to whip up religious enthusiasm were means to the desired goal of conversion:

> These movements emphasized conversion experiences, reliance on Scripture, and missionary work rather than the sacraments and traditions of the established churches. . . . The revivalism of the Great Awakenings is generally referred to as the "Evangelical revival."[17]

Denominations that promoted the Great Awakenings, including the Methodists and the Baptists, as well as denominations that sprang from the awakenings, including the Adventist, Holiness, and Pentecostal denominations, are often collectively considered evangelical given their association with the evangelism at the heart of revivalism.

The revivalism of the Great Awakenings continues today in the form of crusades and in the worship practices of Charismatic denominations. The very essence of revivalism has been to inspire spiritual awakening through an emotional crescendo in an ecstatic experience. Charismatic experiences are thus commonly associated with evangelicalism, leading to a common perception that Charismatic groups are all evangelical.[18] But the lines are blurry. No one disputes that there is significant overlap between Charismatic groups and evangelicalism, but the overlap can be large or small depending on definitions.

In those surveys based solely on self-identified born-again Christians, the overlap is undoubtedly very large because Charismatic groups believe in a born-again event evidenced by charismata. In contrast, consider the data from Pew Research. It reported in their study on Global Christianity that Pentecostals and Charismatic Christians combined totaled over 580 million worldwide; whereas, it counted only 285 million evangelicals, suggesting that the majority of Pentecostals and Charismatics are *not* evangelical.[19] Pew's limited overlap is reinforced in another survey in which Pew questioned leaders attending the major worldwide evangelical gathering, called the Lausanne Conference, about their denominational affiliation—25 percent identified as Pentecostal and 31 percent as Charismatic.[20] Keep in mind that Pew uses membership in denominations that belong to evangelical associations to categorize Christians as evangelical. Thus, a Charismatic Catholic may self-identify as a born-again evangelical but would not be counted as evangelical. Conversely, members of a non-Charismatic Baptist congregation might all be counted as evangelical because of their formal affiliation with the National Association of Evangelicals or the international Lausanne Movement.

Revivalism, with its emphasis on charismata, is stereotypically linked to evangelicalism, but it should be well understood that some evangelical denominations take a very cautious view of charismata. For example, the Southern Baptist Convention, one of the most prominent evangelical groups in the United States, forbids or discourages the Pentecostal practice of speaking in tongues.[21]

Arguably, the legacy of revivalism-centric evangelicalism is controversial. Dangers lurk when believers become vulnerable under the influence of a talented and persuasive preacher. In contrast to the good accomplished in the crusades of the likes of Billy Graham, countless Christians have willingly succumbed to swindlers and charlatans while in the frenzy of emotional ecstasy. This will become clearer as we explore televangelism later in the chapter.

The Rise of Fundamentalism and Neo-Evangelicalism

A logical extension of the principle of *sola scriptura* is the belief that God said all He needed to say relative to salvation in the pages of the Bible. Its completeness coupled with the fact that God cannot lie means that the Bible is, in a word, infallible. Protestants that accept *sola scriptura* have a wide range of views about whether the infallibility of the Bible applies to both matters of faith and history. The literalist end of the spectrum asserts that the Bible is inerrant in all its details—it is completely literal and accurate in every detail. At the other end of the spectrum are those, such as scholars, who see the Bible figuratively or allegorically.

The different views along this spectrum of biblical infallibility and inerrancy remained relatively noncontroversial until theories of modern science challenged the historicity of the Bible, and modern scholarship challenged its authorship.

Science and religion have had a rocky relationship. Take, for example, the emergence of our modern understanding of planetary motion. The heliocentric solar system described by Copernicus, Galileo, Kepler, and Newton was at that time heresy according to Catholic dogma. Eventually, Newton and his fellow scientists reassured the church that natural philosophy—the forerunner of natural science—was guided by a firm belief that scientific laws could be discovered precisely because they were governed by God. The "universe had been arranged by an all-knowing, all-powerful creator."[22] Thus, after the initial suspicion of science, religion and science made peace, and for a time science became the champion of God, not His rival. That changed when natural philosophers advanced concepts completely incompatible with a literal reading of the biblical story of creation and time.

In 1785, James Hutton introduced his work *Theory of the Earth; or an Investigation of the Laws observable in the Composition, Dissolution, and Restoration of Land upon the Globe* to the Royal Society of Edinburgh.[23] Prior to Hutton, scientists generally accepted the biblical account of the catastrophic flood described in Genesis. In contrast, Hutton theorized that the earth had been formed over millions of years through sedimentation, uplift, and erosion. At the heart of his theory was uniformitarianism—the idea that processes of the past have always been the same and continue today. Canyons were carved over "geologic time" measured in millions or perhaps billions of years. Geologic time opened new possibilities to explain the origin of life and was foundational to the theory of evolution proposed by Charles Darwin in 1859 in *On the Origin of Species.*[24] Darwin's proposed evolution required eons of time in which small mutations from generation to generation could transform species into others.

Science increasingly explained away the mysteries of the divine. Institutions of higher learning, many of them sponsored by Christian denominations, adopted the new science. Inevitably a crisis developed within the Christian ranks—a battle between the modernists, those who accommodated the new science by seeing the Bible as allegorical and figurative, and the fundamentalists, those who accepted the literal words of the Bible as history. It should be noted that geologic time and evolution were not the only battles between the modernists and the fundamentalists. Liberalizing social norms and scholarly biblical criticism, among other issues, were also keenly divisive. However, evolution was the tip of the spear of the escalating confrontation. In 1919, those who believed the Bible to be inerrant, true in every aspect, formed the World's Christian Fundamentals Association.

Fundamentalists turned away from modernism and against the universities that had succumbed to it. Bob Jones Sr., an eminently popular and gifted evangelist, founded Bob Jones College (later Bob Jones University) in 1927 as a defense against liberal education, including evolution.[25] Fundamentalists lobbied state legislatures to ban the teaching of evolution in the public schools and for a time had some success, as in the state of Tennessee, which barred the teaching of evolution in early 1925. The famous "Scopes monkey trial" a few months later was symbolically far more important than the narrow question on trial, which was whether John T. Scopes, a science teacher, had defied state law by teaching evolution. The trial did not address the larger issues of constitutionality such as, Did the state law violate the separation of church and state? In public curriculum, should secular theories be given precedent over religious ones? Rather, it narrowly addressed whether Scopes violated state law, which he undoubtedly had. Scopes was convicted and given a fine.[26] Yet the trial took on enormous significance and made national headlines because it was emblematic of the battle between biblicism and secularism. From its outset, the trial was intended to gain national attention by pitting two national figures against each other—William Jennings Bryan, a former candidate for president of the United States and a devout Christian, against Clarence Darrow, a leading member of the American Civil Liberties Union. The fundamentalists won the trial, but the victory was temporary. The ban on evolution could not withstand changing public opinion and acceptance of science in the classroom. The state reversed its ban on evolution in 1967.[27]

The most conservative fundamentalists separated from or were rejected by existing denominations. An important example was John Gresham Machen (1881–1937), an ordained Presbyterian and teacher of the New Testament at Princeton Theological Seminary. Machen resisted the liberalizing influences in the academic seminary and in his Presbyterian church. He and several others were tried in an ecclesiastical court and defrocked in 1937.[28] In response, Machen and a talented student named Carl McIntire founded the Westminster Theological Seminary and the Orthodox Presbyterian Church.[29] McIntire went on to help found new fundamentalist organizations including the American Council of Christian Churches and its counterpart, the International Council of Christian Churches. He created a defiant, separatist, and militant tone through his weekly newspaper, the *Christian Beacon*, and in a work, *Outside the Gates*, which he published in 1967. Fundamentalists became increasingly critical of any group or person who compromised or even associated with liberal modernists.[30]

By the 1930s, the antagonism of fundamentalists toward education and institutes of higher learning earned them the reputation of being anti-intellectual and religious and cultural separatists.[31] More moderate fundamentalists, many of whom had stayed in their respective denominations, believed that there was room for scholarship and social integration without sacrificing belief in biblical inerrancy and infallibility. This more progressive wing of fundamentalism called themselves "neo-evangelicals" and split into a new movement in the 1930s. In time, *neo-evangelical* was shortened to just *evangelical,* adding another flavor of evangelicalism to the mix.[32] Neo-evangelicals started a new periodical, *Christianity Today,* opened Fuller Theological

Seminary, and organized the National Association of Evangelicals in 1942.[33] Billy Graham (1918–2018) became the most recognizable and influential neo-evangelical. He preached to over two hundred million people and reportedly inspired 3.2 million people to "accept Jesus."[34] Unlike the fundamentalists who were ardent separatists, Billy Graham sought to expand the reach of his crusades by seeking broad ecumenical support.[35] Graham's ministry arose in a time of racial segregation, so it was controversial within fundamentalist and neo-evangelical circles when he invited Martin Luther King Jr. to speak at his 1957 New York crusade.[36] He lent his support to the moderate National Association of Evangelicals, which had been founded in 1942, and in 1966 co-founded an international evangelical organization known as the Lausanne Movement.[37]

Neo-evangelicals have come to dominate the evangelical movement worldwide. Through the National Association of Evangelicals (NAE) in the United States and the international Lausanne Movement, they seek to clarify for the world what it means to be an evangelical. The NAE advocates a four-point theological test similar to that first proposed by David Bebbington, a professor of history at Scotland's University of Stirling.[38] Articles posted on the NAE website provide evidence of the progressive shift of the official organization.[39] However, neo-evangelicalism's roots are in the fundamentalist movement, and the reality is that neo-evangelicals tend toward the literalist end of the biblical spectrum and thus continue to share many beliefs and values with fundamentalists. Thus, among the rank and file there is a blurry line between fundamentalists and evangelicals. It is not uncommon for the terms *evangelical* and *fundamentalist* to be used interchangeably or for the groups to be lumped into one bucket. As we will see later in this chapter, this conflation is particularly true in the context of politics. But this can be misleading, and the leadership of both groups strive to make a distinction between themselves. As noted, the NAE's guidance to evangelicals is far more progressive and moderate on issues of science, politics, the environment, and so on, than fundamentalists. For their part, fundamentalists unequivocally distinguish themselves from neo-evangelicals to the point of hostility toward them. The fundamentalists' response to Billy Graham's passing illustrates the divide. The fundamentalist American Council of Christian Churches wrote,

> Billy Graham was also a powerful threat to the historic orthodoxy and separatist practice of Biblical Christianity. . . . The legacy that the late Dr. Graham has left is an evangelical movement bereft of any unyielding theological moorings. By embracing the strategy of compromise with those who denied the faith of the Scriptures, he, like his new evangelical colleagues, did not influence the liberals to a more Biblical position.[40]

Graham's inclusiveness earned him the disdain of the fundamentalists and rejection by the likes of McIntire and Bob Jones Jr. (1911–1997),[41] who reportedly said,

> For a long time I believed that Billy was doing more harm than any other living man. What a tragedy to see him building the church of Antichrist, masking the wickedness of popery[42] and providing a sheep's cloak of Christian recognition for the wolves of apostasy.[43]

Consider how Jerry Falwell (1933–2007) was ostracized by fellow fundamentalists. Falwell was a bona fide fundamentalist. In the 1970s, he was the leading spokesperson for fundamentalism; led the Baptist Bible Fellowship, one of the largest fundamentalist denominations; and started what was to become a leading fundamentalist university, Liberty University, in 1971. However, when he founded the Moral Majority in 1979, he reached out to politically conservative like-minded Christians from many denominations, including Catholics, Jews, neo-evangelicals, Charismatics, Mormons, and others. In associating with these groups, he became the target of criticism by other fundamentalists. "Bob Jones University declared the Moral Majority organization 'Satanic,' holding that it was a step toward the apostate one-world church and government body."[44] Jerry Falwell was arguably a fundamentalist as measured by his unwavering belief in biblical inerrancy and his extreme social conservatism; however, he become known as an evangelical once he violated the separatist norms of fundamentalism and increasingly associated with neo-evangelicals.[45]

Strident separatism, hostility toward science, and uncompromising beliefs are characteristics of the fundamentalist movement, shared to some degree by a meaningful number of neo-evangelicals, as we will see later in this chapter.

Born-Again Christians

As noted previously in this chapter, one simplistic measure of evangelicals is to ask if one considers himself or herself a born-again Christian. In the United States, about 35 percent of the population answers yes to that question.[46] Considering that the overall percentage of Christians in the United States is somewhere between 70 and 75 percent, roughly 50 percent of all Christians in the United States are evangelical as measured by this simple standard. At first blush, this may seem high, but the surprising thing about the ratio is that it is as low as it is. After all, nearly all Christian denominations believe that being born again is an essential requirement of salvation. Jesus gave it as a requirement for entry into the Kingdom of God.[47] However, as we've already learned, there is a born-again stereotype—a perception that being born-again is a cathartic experience such as the ecstatic crescendo felt at crusades, revivals, Pentecostal services, or Charismatic megachurches. Perhaps Christians participating in these groups more reliably self-identify as born-again Christians. However, the prevalence of this stereotype makes other denominations' doctrines relative to being born-again no less biblically justified. Consider a sampling of the breadth of doctrines relative to being born-again.

Given that Lutheranism is the heart of confessional evangelicalism, it is interesting that Lutherans believe in a passive version of born-again. They believe that regeneration, or being born-again, coincides with receiving faith as a gift of grace. Because faith is a gift and not a choice, a person cannot make a cognitive decision to accept Jesus. Baptism is one means through which grace operates; thus, a person can be regenerated through the faith received at baptism. This doctrine is manifest in the Lutherans' practice of infant baptism. Being born-again may take place as an infant—a passive receipt of faith as a gift. Yes, adults can receive faith and be converted as well, but Lutherans "steadfastly repudiate any reliance on conversion experiences or 'charismatic gifts' for the certainty of salvation."[48]

In contrast, Pentecostals consider the born-again conversion a precursor and separate experience to the baptism of fire so notable among Pentecostals. Therefore, while being born-again does not require speaking in tongues, it is accompanied by an infilling of the Holy Spirit—a charismatic experience.

Methodists, like Lutherans, see the "new birth" as a gracious gift, a point at which the receiver can now see and understand God's word. Baptism is the usual channel through which the gift is received, but it can happen prior to baptism. Methodists, who adopted the Arminian belief in free will, emphasize that the new birth is the beginning of a journey that requires effort and striving toward sanctification. New birth is not a lifelong guarantee of salvation.[49]

Catholics believe they are "born again" at baptism, as do many other Christian denominations.[50]

Billy Graham frequently taught those attending his rallies that they must be born again by receiving a new heart with conviction to follow Christ. He invited all those willing to accept Christ to come to the front of the platform and confess that they are sinners and openly accept Jesus Christ—asserting that this act of confession and conviction constitutes being born again. Importantly, Billy Graham deemphasized baptism when he said, "I think we violate the Scriptures when we make baptism the prime requirement for salvation."[51]

Undoubtedly, surveys that use "born again" as the litmus test of an evangelical presume the recipient of the survey will respond according to the dominant stereotype of one who has had a charismatic experience or, at least, one who has committed to Christ in a revivalist setting. However, as we now know, the term *born again* varies widely based on denomination, rendering it a poor litmus test to distinguish evangelicals.

Evangelicals and the Religious Right in America

Social upheaval roiled the United States after World War II with the civil rights movement, the Vietnam War, the changing role of women, the elimination of prayer from schools, the fight against communism, and the sexual revolution. Christians fretted about whether America was becoming a modern Gomorrah.[52] But in the sixties and seventies fundamentalists and evangelicals alike did more hand-wringing in private than politicking in the public square—albeit with some exceptions, such as the vocal opposition by some neo-evangelicals like Billy Graham against communism. The separatist views of the fundamentalists deterred political action and engagement.[53] However, ongoing defeats in the culture wars of the 1970s catalyzed conservative Christians to coalesce into a political force. In 1971, the Equal Rights Amendment was reintroduced and quickly passed by Congress with a 1979 ratification deadline.[54] In 1973, the Supreme Court ruled in favor of a woman's right to choose abortion in *Roe v. Wade*. The United Nations declared 1975 International Women's Year. The United States helped fund a National Conference on Women in 1977—a conference in which feminists ratified an alliance with homosexual rights groups.[55] In 1976, the IRS revoked the tax-exempt status of fundamentalist Bob Jones University due to its racially discriminatory practices.[56]

Evangelicals and fundamentalists took hope in the election to the United States presidency of one of their own in 1976, a self-proclaimed born-again Sunday School teacher from Georgia named Jimmy Carter. So important were the evangelicals in the election of Jimmy Carter that Gallup declared 1976 the year of the evangelical;[57] however, evangelicals were soon disappointed in Carter when he opposed a constitutional amendment banning abortion, supported the Equal Rights Amendment, and helped fund the 1977 National Conference on Women.[58]

Jerry Falwell, then a fundamentalist Baptist minister, had by the late 70s become well known based on his televangelism and successful Thomas Roads Baptist Church. He, along with two political conservatives, Catholic Paul Weyrich and Jew Howard Phillips, organized the Moral Majority[59] in 1979 to mobilize conservative voters in support of candidates favorable to a morally acceptable agenda. As noted earlier, some fundamentalists such as Bob Jones Jr. criticized the Moral Majority for its inclusion of Catholics, Jews, and Mormons. In spite of the criticism, Falwell successfully enlisted social conservatives of many stripes, including fundamentalists, neo-evangelicals, Pentecostals, Charismatics, Catholics, Jews, and others, in a common cause. The Moral Majority helped elect Reagan in 1980 and enjoyed a period of unprecedented access to the White House.[60] But the organization was short-lived. The Moral Majority, fraught with internal issues and financial woes, disbanded in the late 1980s. Still, it had demonstrated the political power of an organized religious civic-minded movement. From it, the "religious right" made up of *political* evangelicals was born.

Although Reagan failed to pursue the religious right's agenda,[61] the religious right had flexed its political muscle with him and concluded it could accomplish even more. Pat Robertson, a well-known evangelist and founder of the Christian Broadcast Network, ran for president in 1988—surprising many with a strong showing in the white-evangelical Iowa. He dropped out soon after Iowa due to poor results in other primaries, but rather than leave the political field he organized the Christian Coalition with a self-described "guerrilla fighter," Ralph Reed, at its head. The Christian Coalition set about to influence national politics and to elect evangelicals around the country. Late in 1997 the Christian Coalition of America was ranked by *Fortune* magazine as the seventh most powerful political organization in America.[62] However, like the Moral Majority before them, they faded as financial woes and leadership struggles overtook them.

Each presidential election cycle in the United States brings the political importance of the religious right back to the center stage. The election in 2016 elevated the role of evangelicals. Donald Trump established an evangelical advisory board to advise his campaign and rally their millions.[63] Franklin Graham Jr.[64] and Jerry Falwell Jr., the sons of luminaries in the evangelical movement, used their enormous influence to strongly support Donald Trump by holding national prayer rallies and leveraging Liberty University for that purpose. Televangelists and megachurch pastors such as Paula White and Robert Jeffress shepherded their flocks to Trump. Conservative black evangelical pastors like Mark Burns and Harry Jackson were enlisted to urge African Americans to break away from their traditional support of the Democrats. Trump's advisory board was an impressive assemblage of who's who in evangelicalism.[65]

The 2016 election illustrated common perceptions and misperceptions about evangelicals and politics. On November 9, 2016, stories in the press abounded about the role of evangelicals in electing Trump. The story in *Time* magazine was titled "How Evangelicals Helped Donald Trump Win."[66] In it, members of Trump's evangelical council and other leading evangelicals offered sound bites relative to the role of evangelicals in Trump's win. Robert Jeffress, a member of Trump's evangelical advisory council, was highlighted:

> He reminded Trump that he thought evangelicals would respond to his performance in the third debate, especially his positions on the Supreme Court and on abortion. . . . "I told him I thought it [evangelical turn-out] would be very strong. . . . No Republican candidate has made greater effort to reach out to evangelicals than Trump. . . . There is a silent Trump vote that polls did not capture and many of those votes are evangelical."[67]

The article provided insight into the viewpoint of evangelical leaders and their paradoxical acceptance of a well-known philanderer:

> Falwell [Jerry Falwell Jr.] says many in the media and political class might have been less surprised at the election's outcome if they better understand the evangelical community. "Evangelical theology is all about forgiveness," he says. "When you look at the issues, he ended up being the dream candidate for conservatives and evangelicals. The evangelical community has not been divided on Trump, just the leadership—the people were smarter than their leaders."[68]

The article, especially its quotes from evangelical leaders, illustrates the generalization that is so commonly made both within and without the evangelical movement—evangelicals as a group are the conservative religious right. The reality is more nuanced.

Race and age are important factors in understanding *political* evangelicalism. About two out of every three evangelicals in the United States are white.[69] No doubt this is a dominant majority, but to generalize evangelicals without considering that 36 percent of evangelicals are nonwhite and do not tend to be conservative is misrepresenting evangelicals. Like most black Americans, black evangelicals vote reliably for the Democrats. Furthermore, younger evangelicals are increasingly racially diverse. Only 50 percent of evangelicals in the United States under thirty years of age are white,[70] in contrast to the 77 percent of evangelicals over sixty-five that are white.[71] Yet, older citizens vote more reliably than younger citizens do, and so characterizing evangelicals based on who votes misrepresents the evangelical community.

When the press talks about political evangelicals, they are usually referring to older white evangelicals who vote. Still, political evangelicals have an outsized presence. One press headline reported, "Trump Elected President, Thanks to 4 in 5 White Evangelicals."[72] The statistic was based on exit polls, which by definition count those who voted. White evangelicals, which represent about 17 percent of the total population,[73] accounted for 26 percent of voters![74] The overrepresentation of political evangelicals in 2016 reflected a simple truth—motivated voters show up!

When we contrast the reality of evangelical demographics—only 49 percent of white evangelicals belong to the Republican Party[75]—with the headlines relative to political evangelicals, there is a huge disconnect that can be resolved only if we recognize that the notion of political evangelicals is a catchall bucket of older, white, politically active, and conservative Christians drawn from neo-evangelicals, fundamentalists, Pentecostals, and even Catholics, Mormons, and others.[76]

The association of the religious right with evangelicalism, deserved or not, is so pervasive that the term *evangelical* has been stigmatized. Some evangelicals are beginning to shy away from the term because of how it has been coopted by the political religious right. In January 2018, the National Association of Evangelicals surveyed its leaders and concluded that "83 percent of evangelical leaders do not believe evangelicals in America should be identified with the person and policies of the current president."[77] In the view of many, the term *evangelical* has been tarnished. An article in the Atlantic magazine addressed this:

> As the prominent evangelical pastor Tim Keller—who is not a Trump loyalist—recently wrote in the *New Yorker*, "'Evangelical' used to denote people who claimed the high moral ground; now, in popular usage, the word is nearly synonymous with 'hypocrite.'" So it is little wonder that last year the Princeton Evangelical Fellowship, an 87-year-old ministry, dropped the "E word" from its name, becoming the Princeton Christian Fellowship: Too many students

had identified the term with conservative political ideology. Indeed, a number of serious evangelicals are distancing themselves from the word for similar reasons.[78]

Leith Anderson, the president of the National Association of Evangelicals, addressed the stigma in an open letter to neo-evangelicals:

> "Are you ready to abandon the term evangelical?" has become the most frequent question I'm asked as president of the National Association of Evangelicals. And, almost always, the question comes from fellow evangelicals and not from the mainstream press or non-evangelicals. When I ask why "evangelical" should be abandoned, the answer is almost always about politics. They tell me that our name has been co-opted by politicians and policies that are polarizing and painful. They say they are being identified with policies contrary to the Bible and blamed for practices they don't approve. They contend that self-described evangelicals claim to speak for them but don't speak for them. Most of all, they lament that every news story with politics and "evangelical" in the same sentence is a barrier to evangelism and ministry.[79]

It's tempting to equate the themes of the religious right to nationalism with its characteristic racism, xenophobia, intolerance, and hate. However, such a view will likely lead to mischaracterization of political evangelicals. Conservative themes of the religious right can be best understood through the worldview of fundamentalism—a worldview shaped by the Bible. The Bible is a book that if taken literally tells the story of a favored ethnic group blessed by divine providence, asserts absolute truth and rightness, contains a divine command to never compromise, prohibits cultural assimilation, prophesizes of apocalyptic evil in the last days, and shows both a God of mercy and a God of wrath and justice. We can see these themes reflected in the religious right: compromise is evil, modern secular institutions of government and science are suspect, multiculturalism is dangerous, and biblically deviant practices are a sign of the end-times and will incur God's wrath. Political evangelicals believe they are acting in accordance with biblical precedent. For the most part, they are faithful Christians.

Understanding their biblical worldview can help fellow Christians and fellow citizens focus the debate with political evangelicals on the core question—should the Bible be central to the culture and laws of what has become a multicultural and democratic nation? This is not an easy question with a simple answer. Perhaps the cautionary tales in the next chapter will influence the answer.

Era of Televangelism, Celebrity Pastors, and Megachurches

"I believe that if Jesus were alive today, he would be on TV," Jim Bakker, a prominent televangelist, purportedly said at the height of his days at the PTL Club in the 1980s.[80] The term *televangelism* has a strict meaning, of course; namely, the preaching of the gospel through television. However, television and broadcast media have been major enablers of several interrelated trends that are reshaping evangelical Christianity. Thus, the terms *televangelist* and *televangelism* are useful stand-ins for the entire bundle of related trends. In this section, the term *televangelism* is shorthand for media-enabled, consumer-oriented, and mass-appealing ministries and megachurches. *Televangelist* is shorthand for the celebrity pastors who start them.

The act of preaching the gospel through mass media is not in itself controversial. Virtually every major denomination produces media and either broadcasts, publishes through their website, or publishes through media providers such as YouTube. Preaching over the radio, which took off in the 1930s, and television, which surged in the 1950s, started as natural extensions of face-to-face evangelism. Televangelism was as likely to be from mainline denominations as from the neo-evangelical movement. In fact, the term *televangelist* was used as early as 1952 by *Time* magazine to describe the telegenic Roman Catholic bishop Fulton Sheen.[81] Billy Graham was known for in-person crusades, but he also became a leading televangelist, using radio and then television to broadcast his crusades and a weekly program, *Hour of Decision*, that ran for fifty years.

In spite of its innocent beginnings and ongoing legitimate use, televangelism has gained a reputation as the realm of swindlers and charlatans.[82] It did not earn its dubious reputation because of these early adopters of mass media or the media broadcasts of mainline denominations. Rather, the reputation emerged as money came to dominate Protestant charismatic televangelism. A money-centered interpretation of the gospel, called "word of faith" or "the prosperity gospel," emerged in the late 1940s just as television took hold.[83] The prosperity gospel fit seamlessly with the prosperity mindset and ascension of Western capitalism in the years after World War II. Its message in simple terms is that God will reward faith. Put crassly, God is the ultimate capitalist—invest seeds of faith and get returns of health, wealth, and happiness. Televangelists shamelessly ask believers to demonstrate the degree of their faith by the size of their seed donation. Christian television,[84] which ballooned with the expansion of cable in the late 1970s and 1980s, has been dominated by the charismatic prosperity gospel. Many of the new televangelists have adopted the lifestyle of the rich and famous, which is perhaps appropriate because they have become true celebrities. As living examples of the prosperity gospel, they have no need to hide their wealth from their congregations or from the world.

But are televangelists, their ministries, their megachurches, and their broadcast networks evangelical? Sort of. In popular perception, as reflected in press articles, websites, biographies, and ministry histories, these groups are usually considered evangelical. However, as with other ambiguous uses of the term covered in previous sections of this chapter, calling religious broadcast networks and their associated televangelists *evangelical* is controversial and potentially misleading. Many Christian networks, including Daystar, SonLife, TBN, and Hillsong, were founded by Pentecostals and liberally stream charismatic content with its vibrant music and abundant charismata, including speaking in tongues, prophesying, and being "slain in the Spirit." Much of the charismatic content is infused with the prosperity gospel. These attributes of televangelism lead mainstream evangelicals to classify televangelism outside of evangelicalism. One online evangelical forum asked readers, "What do evangelicals think of televangelists?" Multiple contributors emphasized that as evangelicals they do not want to be associated with televangelists. One evangelical participant pleaded, referring to televangelists, "We just hope that the general population doesn't have that same impression of Christian evangelicals in general, since we're not all like that."[85] In spite of public perception that conflates televangelism with evangelicalism, 90 percent of worldwide evangelical leaders reject the prosperity gospel![86]

Jim Bakker, a prominent televangelist of the 1980s, became the poster child for the greed and fraud of televangelism. His story is covered in more detail later in this chapter. Unfortunately, the patterns of Jim Bakker's ministry are not unique to him and did not end with him. U.S. Senator Chuck Grassley initiated a probe in 2007 into six prominent televangelist ministries. The unabashed wealth of the founding pastors seemed incongruous with the tax-exempt treatment afforded churches and their pastors under IRS code. The probe focused on the ministries led by Paula White, Joyce Meyer, Creflo Dollar, Eddie Long, Kenneth Copeland, and Benny Hinn.[87] Like Bakker, all of these ministries taught the prosperity gospel and raked in many tens of millions of tax-free dollars in the form of donations from and book sales to their millions of believers.

Grassley's probe intended to investigate IRS violations including *inurement*, meaning excessive compensation and benefits, and *conversion*, a term used when for-profit companies are created to benefit from nonprofits. Only two of the six ministries opened their financial books. The probe stalled in the face of a national recession in 2008 and political pushback from religions of all stripes. Ultimately, Grassley closed the probe when he relinquished his chairmanship of the Committee on Finance in 2011. The report issued by the committee was vague and toothless.[88]

There is a common pattern to today's celebrity televangelists, their ministries, and their megachurches. This pattern did not start with the six ministries investigated by Senator Grassley. Nor did it start with Jim Bakker, who used it to the point of demonstrable fraud. Oral Roberts was the great innovator who established the pattern of modern televangelism. We'll explore his story in a moment. First, let's examine the pattern itself.

The heart of evangelism is the gospel of Jesus Christ, but the heart of television is business. To best understand the pattern of televangelism, we need to look more to business than to Jesus. The pattern of business is growing from a start-up into a mature, robust, and sizable concern. This might seem like a negative metaphor because it insinuates baser motives; nevertheless, it is strikingly applicable. It is true that there is no way to know a televangelist's true motives. Many may indeed be motivated by heavenly goals, but all leverage the tools of contemporary business.

The pattern looks something like this: A telegenic and charismatic pastor[89] has a communication from God to start a ministry—usually a nondenominational or independent ministry. The pastor is a talented public speaker, salesperson, and entertainer. He or she offers a sufficiently differentiated blend of Charismatic Christianity and the prosperity gospel—healing and miracles, self-help/feel-good theology, and road-to-wealth theology. The target market is usually evangelicals, Pentecostals, and Charismatic Christians. He or she reaches the market through Christian broadcasting. The pastor and his or her spouse creates a loyal kernel of followers by starting a church or television club, or by holding revivals. He or she starts broadcasting, reaching the target market far outside the geography of the local church. The growing publicity of the pastor and the church attracts new members. The pastor expands the umbrella ministry[90] beyond the local church. The ministry requests donations, promising that the "seeds" planted by the donors will come back to them as prosperity. The ministry implies a direct connection between donations and its worthy causes.[91] The church grows into a megachurch[92] and needs a new, grander sanctuary and campus requiring yet more donations. The pastor writes books and produces media. The expanding number of congregants and the ballooning media audience buy the books, DVDs, and CDs. A virtuous cycle of growth ensues with its own ecosystem—megachurch attendance drives media penetration, which drives book sales, which drives attendance, and so on. The pastor becomes a celebrity within the evangelical community. Although the tens of thousands of weekly attendees at the megachurch and the audience over the air will rarely have personal contact with the pastor, believers call the pastor by his or her first name, suggesting an intimate relationship with the pastor. The pastor aspires to make a bigger impact through the ministry and pursues large projects such as universities, hospitals, world relief, and even theme parks. The projects justify and necessitate persistent requests for donations, often called "partnerships." As the scope of the ministry grows, the pastor needs efficient travel, and the ministry gets airplanes. The pastor becomes wealthy through tax-free income from the ministry and/or from book sales and lives large in tax-exempt "parsonages" sometimes provided by the ministry. The abundant lifestyle is as an example to all the believers of how God prospers the faithful.

The pattern just described is undeniably a generalization, and individual ministries can deviate from it, but let's look at several examples of past and present televangelists and we will clearly see the pattern. These examples scratch the surface of this burgeoning strain of Christianity.

Oral Roberts (1918–2009) started out in poverty and did not finish college. He struggled as a part-time preacher in Oklahoma until a turning point in 1947, when, during a period of personal depression, his Bible fell open to 3 John 1:2, which says, "I wish above all things that thou mayest prosper and be in health, even as thy soul prospereth."[93] The next day, he acted on faith and bought a Buick, and then God appeared and directed him to heal the sick.[94] The story of the Buick was emblematic of the prosperity gospel Roberts began to preach—blessings of happiness, health, and wealth could be obtained in this life from a loving God if we only exercise a seed of faith. His message of "positive faith" stood in contrast to the sin-and-salvation of classical Calvinism taught by Billy Graham.[95] Roberts traveled across the United States and then around the world, conducting over three hundred healing crusades with tens of thousands lining up in long lines to be prayed over by him. He created a televised program, *The Abundant Life*, and started publishing books with titles such as *If You Need Healing Do These Things* (1952), *The Miracle of Seed Faith* (1977), and *A Daily Guide to Miracles* (1980). Roberts preached prosperity and requested "seed" donations from followers, promising that God would multiply their offerings a hundredfold. "In 1954, he offered 'blessing packs'—packets including fabrics imprinted with his right hand, or anointing oils, in return for a harvest, meaning a windfall of cash."[96] The donations supported his comfortable lifestyle and his ministry's ambitious projects. In 1963, responding to a command from God, he founded Oral Roberts University in Tulsa, Oklahoma. In 1977, Roberts received a vision from Jesus telling him to build a magnificent hospital. The operational magnitude of his ministry required constant fundraising. In

1987, he told followers that he needed to raise $8 million within months or he would "be taken home."[97]

Jerry Falwell (1933–2007) emerged from fundamentalist ranks, as covered earlier in this chapter, and became one of the most recognizable evangelicals in the 1980s as founder of Moral Majority. Soon after graduating from Baptist Bible College in Springfield, Missouri, in 1956, he returned to his hometown of Lynchburg, Virginia, and founded the Thomas Road Baptist Church and concurrently started a radio ministry called the Old Time Gospel Hour. Within months, he added television broadcasts of the program that would eventually reach fifty million regular viewers.[98] Thomas Road Baptist Church grew rapidly from its original thirty-five members into a megachurch with over twenty thousand members by the time Falwell died. It moved several times into larger campuses with correspondingly larger sanctuaries. In 1971, Falwell founded Liberty University in Lynchburg. He began publishing books in the 1970s, including a "How-To" series and a few politically oriented books.

Robert Tilton (1946–) started a small church outside of Dallas in 1976 and soon thereafter started a local television show, but the growth of both was limited. He saw an opportunity in the form of the emerging late-night infomercial format. He relaunched his limited television program as a one-hour infomercial called *Success-N-Life*.[99] It was pure prosperity gospel, teaching that God will bless you with health and wealth as a spiritual harvest for planting "seeds of faith." He was an innovator for using informercials to hawk miracles in exchange for donations. In addition to television, Tilton used direct mail to persistently solicit money. He sent prayer cloths, oils, and so on, to believers and asked for prayer-request letters and cash in return. Tilton published books with titles such as *God's Laws of Success* (1986) and *The Power to Create Wealth* (1988).[100] The success of his television program fueled book sales and the growth of his church, which grew into a megachurch with eight thousand members at its height.[101] Tilton's "miracle business" came crashing down in 1991 when ABC's *Primetime* revealed just how commercialized the operation was and how prayer-request letters returned by the faithful were trashed after the cash was removed.[102] Tilton laid low for a brief time but relaunched *Success-N-Life* and continues today using media to promote the prosperity gospel.

He continues to publish prosperity books such as *How to Be Rich &* *Have Everything You Ever Wanted* (2004) and *Strike It Rich* (2006).[103]

Jimmy Swaggart (1935–) started poor and married young at just seventeen. He grew up in a small Pentecostal church and was a talented musician. He started preaching throughout the American south in 1955 and began recording gospel music in 1960. He was ordained a minister by the Assemblies of God (Pentecostal) in 1961 and soon thereafter started a radio ministry. In the late 1960s he founded a Pentecostal church, the Family Worship Center. Swaggart expanded to television in the late 1960s and early 1970s with the *Jimmy Swaggart Telecast*. By the 1980s, the telecast, which was notable for gospel music, was transmitted to over three thousand stations and cable networks. Swaggart opened Jimmy Swaggert Bible College in 1984. He transformed the Family Worship Center into a megachurch with a seventy-five-hundred-seat sanctuary. Swaggart's legacy was tarnished in 1988 when he confessed to serious sexual sin and was defrocked by the Assemblies of God. Scandal arose once more in 1991 when he was again caught with a prostitute. After his defrocking, Swaggart started the nondenominational Jimmy Swaggart Ministries, which continues today, headquartered out of the Family Worship Center.[104]

Pat Robertson (1930–) was mentioned earlier in this chapter under the section on the religious right. He was the son of a U.S. senator and expected to pursue a life in law; however, in 1955 after failing to pass the bar, he had a religious conversion and pursued a divinity degree, which he obtained in 1959.[105] Soon after, he founded the Christian Broadcast Network (CBN) and was ordained a minister of the Southern Baptist Convention. CBN had a rough start financially, and in a fundraiser in 1966, Robertson set a goal of getting seven hundred donors to support the station—this was the birth of the the *700 Club*, a gospel variety show that has broadcast continuously since 1966.[106] Robertson founded CBN University in 1977, which was renamed Regent University in 1989.[107] He became a prolific author, writing books about subjects ranging from conspiracy theories about the New World Order to wealth management.

Jim Bakker (1940–), along with his first wife, Tammy Faye, are perhaps the most notorious televangelists from the 1980s. They are the cautionary tale of the extremes to which the pattern can lead. The

Bakkers learned about the fruits of recurring donations from their days co-anchoring Robertson's *700 Club*. They set up their own club, the *PTL* (Praise the Lord) *Club* and distributed it through their own satellite system. The *PTL Club* plied the prosperity gospel. Viewer donations were estimated to exceed $1 million per week and were ostensibly used to fund the construction of Heritage USA, a Christian theme park in South Carolina.[108] Jim Bakker began publishing PTL devotional material and added books such as *God Answers Prayer* (1980) and *You Can Make It!* (1983). The Bakkers didn't hide their lavish lifestyle, which drew the attention of detractors and the press. The *Charlotte Observer* published more than six hundred stories about the PTL in 1987 alone. The paper would go on to win a Pulitzer in 1988 for its exposé on the Bakkers and the PTL.[109] Certainly, the revelation that Jim Bakker paid hush money to the church secretary to conceal his sexual relationship with her was fodder for the press, but it was financial corruption that landed the Bakkers in jail. An IRS report claimed that the Bakkers received $9.36 million in excessive compensation between 1981 and 1987 (recall Grassley's concern about inurement).[110] Additionally, the Bakkers sold "Lifetime Partnerships" at $1,000 apiece for rooms in Heritage USA. The problem was that they sold the partnerships twice, and, in spite of the money intake, the PTL was behind on construction payments.[111] Jim Bakker was convicted in 1988 and sentenced to forty-five years in prison. His sentence was later reduced to eight years, and he was paroled before serving even five years.[112] Bakker is back to televangelism, mixing product sales of emergency freeze-dried food with prophecy of the end-times on his *Jim Bakker Show*.[113]

Kenneth Copeland (1936–) was a performance and recording artist prior to his conversion experience in 1962. He loved to fly airplanes and earned his pilot's license. He enrolled in Oral Roberts University with little money but soon became Oral Robert's pilot and chauffeur.[114] His close association with Roberts deeply influenced him. He and his wife, Gloria, started the Kenneth Copeland Evangelistic Association in 1967, proclaiming the prosperity gospel. They began publishing the *Believer's Voice of Victory* in print form in 1973, which evolved into a radio broadcast in 1979 and then into a television broadcast in 1989.[115] The umbrella ministry was changed to Kenneth Copeland Ministries along the way, and they founded the Eagle Mountain International

Church. Copeland started publishing prosperity books in the 1990s with titles such as *Prosperity, the Choice Is Yours* (1992) and *The Laws of Prosperity* (1995). He and his wife continue to publish frequently with titles such as *The Blessing of the Lord: Makes Rich and He Adds No Sorrow With It* (2012). Today, Eagle Mountain International Church is a nondenominational megachurch[116] outside Dallas, and Kenneth Copeland Ministries has worldwide operations.[117] The Copelands live in a luxurious multimillion-dollar lakefront "parsonage" in Fort Worth with an onsite private air field. The ministry has bought multiple aircraft to facilitate the Copelands' extensive travel, the latest being the exclusive Gulfstream V.[118]

Creflo Dollar (1962–) began World Changers Christian Center, later named World Changers Church International, in 1986, a couple years after graduating from college with a degree in education. Dollar added a weekly radio broadcast, and church attendance swelled. In 1995, the church moved into the World Dome, becoming a megachurch with a sanctuary holding eighty-five hundred.[119] He became a prolific author with books including prosperity titles such as *No More Debt!: God's Strategy for Debt Cancellation* (2001); *The Holy Spirit, Your Financial Advisor: God's Plan for Debt-Free Money Management* (2013); and *You're Supposed to Be Wealthy: How to Make Money, Live Comfortably, and Build an Inheritance for Future Generations* (2014). The ministry purchased a Gulfstream III to facilitate Dollar's travel. When that plane was totaled in a November 2014 runway mishap, the ministry controversially asked international members in 2015 to donate $300 each to raise $65 million for an upgraded Gulfstream.[120] The Dollars live large with multiple million-dollar "parsonages" and Rolls Royce cars.[121]

Jesse Duplantis (1949–) began preaching the prosperity gospel at age twenty-seven on the Trinity Broadcast Network. He started the Jesse Duplantis Ministries and, with his wife, founded the Covenant Church in 1997 in St. Charles Parish, a suburb of New Orleans. In the same year, he published *God Is Not Enough, He's Too Much!* He continues to publish. Duplantis once boasted at a camp meeting held at Cornerstone Church, itself a megachurch founded by John Hagee, that "he [Duplantis] is not just a millionaire, but a multi-millionaire and then said 'The Lord, I give Him the glory, is my comforter. If He is my comforter, Dr. Hagee, I live in comfort. That's not only spiritually—that's physically too. Because when you've got some stuff it brings you comfort."[122] In May 2018, Duplantis controversially asked his followers to fund another jet worth $54 million to replace the three previous jets already purchased by the ministry.[123]

Benny Hinn (1952–) immigrated with his family from Israel to Toronto in the late 1960s. As a senior in high school, he converted from Greek Orthodox Christianity to Pentecostalism. He was deeply influenced by the miracle crusades of Kathryn Kuhlman.[124] In 1983 he founded his own church, the Orlando Christian Center, teaching the prosperity gospel. The church soon attracted members to the charismatic preacher who could speak in tongues and heal the sick. He branched out from his local church, undertaking healing crusades patterned after Kuhlman's crusades. In the early 1990s he launched a show on the Trinity Broadcast Network called *This Is Your Day*, which aired clips of his miracle crusades.[125] Hinn solicited seed donations at crusades and through his program. He started publishing books in the mid 1990s with titles centered on healing and the Holy Spirit, such as *The Biblical Road to Blessing* (1996), *The Anointing* (1997), and *Welcome, Holy Spirit: How You Can Experience the Dynamic Work of the Holy Spirit in Your Life* (1997). Hinn admitted to CNN that in 1997 he received an income of between $500 thousand and $1 million from the ministry and book royalties. He once revealed in 2003 that his ministry received $89 million.[126] In 1999, Hinn left the Orlando ministry to start another in the Dallas, Texas, area called World Healing Center Church. He continued doing miracle crusades, about twenty-four a year, traveling in leased Gulfstream jets. His nephew, who served with Hinn and then became disillusioned with the prosperity gospel, spoke publicly of Hinn's lavish lifestyle, which included staying in hotels costing $25,000 per night.[127] Hinn recognizes that "healing" is the differentiated "product" that attracts his followers. Hinn said in an interview, "People say, 'Look, I'm not going to watch you if you don't have healings.' Our supporters support us for one reason, people pray for us for one reason—because of the healing ministry."[128] Hinn's ministry differs from the common pattern in at least one respect: his churches did not grow into megachurches, although his crusades are some of the largest in history.

This brief review of several televangelists and their ministries just scratches the surface. The field of celebrity pastors continues to grow, along with their associated ministries, megachurches, and television broadcasts. You may know others:

- John Osteen and his son Joel Osteen, former and current pastors of the nondenominational Lakewood Church in Houston, Texas
- Paula White, pastor of the nondenominational New Destiny Christian Center in greater Orlando, Florida
- T. D. Jakes, pastor of the nondenominational The Potter's House in Dallas, Texas
- Joyce Meyer, president of Joyce Meyer Ministries in Fenton, Missouri
- Rick Warren, pastor of the Saddleback Church in Lake Forest, California[129]
- John Hagee, pastor of the nondenominational Cornerstone Church in San Antonio, Texas
- Chris Hodges, pastor of the nondenominational Church of the Highlands in Birmingham, Alabama
- Andy Stanley, pastor of the nondenominational North Point Community Church in greater Atlanta, Georgia

This section has focused on the United States, but the pattern is not unique to North America. Many of the largest evangelical churches and many of the wealthiest pastors are outside the United States. The details of their ministries are outside the scope of this book; however, collectively it is clear that televangelism is a worldwide burgeoning strain of Christianity. Arguably, televangelism, including worship services in today's megachurches, is attracting millions around the globe who have never been Christians or who had become disinterested in traditional denominations. As examples, the single largest evangelical megachurch is in the traditionally non-Christian country South Korea. Several of the largest megachurches are in India, also a generally non-Christian country.[130] Surely, these churches are fulfilling in part the great commission of Christ to evangelize all the world.

But there are controversies and dangers associated with televangelism. The fusion of media, celebrity, and prosperity readily distorts commonly accepted Christian ideals. Consider the following dangers:

Watered-Down Gospel. Not all celebrity pastors and their megachurches teach the prosperity gospel, but even those that don't tend to preach a watered-down feel-good gospel. Take, for example, Saddleback Church, founded by Rick Warren. It is associated with the Southern Baptist Convention and so is nominally Baptist, but it shies away from the Calvinist themes of its roots. The church's website gives the history of the church: "The young pastor and his bride dreamed of planting a church that would be a place where the hurting, the depressed, the confused can find love, acceptance, help, hope, forgiveness and encouragement. From the beginning, Pastor Rick wanted his church to be a place for people who didn't like church."[131] The mission statement suggests that the church was formed to appeal to those who abandoned mainstream denominations. In effect, the church would offer something more appealing than other denominations provided to the target demographic. This is not meant to condemn Rick Warren for starting a church addressing a particular demographic. The point is that in today's consumer-driven society, holding on to believers is tough for all denominations. There is a need to be consumer-driven to attract and hold on to members. Megachurches and televangelist ministries have stepped in and offered differentiated options. Undoubtedly, they attract many who would otherwise abandon formal religion; however, the reality is that nondenominational Christians "shop" for a church, and it's a hard sell in the "evangelical market" to offer anything but a feel-good gospel.

Decline of Denominations and Their Sacraments. Megachurches and their ministries tend to be nondenominational or independent.[132] Members of megachurches associate themselves more with evangelicalism than with a denomination. These churches publish a set of beliefs, but as a nondenominational church they operate independently with no constraints on doctrine or worship practices. The result is an explosion of pseudo-denominations with unique doctrines and practices. Some differences are significant, such as the prosperity gospel itself, and some are subtle. It is little wonder that people "shop" for a church, looking for a likable pastor, agreeable doctrine, and engaging worship. A softer, upbeat gospel dominates these churches with messages of hope, healing, and happiness. The Augustinian doctrines of original sin and man's depravity that undergird Protestantism are faint echoes. The essential sacraments common to Orthodox Christianity and traditional Protestant denominations have become discretionary and nonessential for salvation.[133] This results from both theological drift due to evangelical born-again teaching as explored earlier in this chapter and the practical consequence of the number of people in large sanctuaries and the growing block of "virtual attendees"—those who participate in church strictly through media.

Cult-Like Characteristics. Evangelicals tend to be the most vocal at "calling-out" other Christians for belonging to cults—something we will explore in the next chapter. They often define a cult by a set of characteristics that ironically apply to this group of televangelists and megachurch pastors: a cult follows a central, highly persuasive leader, and it uses nonbiblical canon. Many evangelical megachurches and their celebrity pastors meet these criteria. Relative to leadership, the pastor and pastor's spouse are the founders of the church or ministry, and they are answerable to no superior governing denominational body. The pastor is the interpreter and provider of dogma. They shape the nondenominational theology and liturgy and do most of the preaching. They engender immense loyalty. Their church or ministry becomes a family affair, and their children become their heir-apparent, furthering loyalty to the family. They yield incredible influence on the political and social beliefs of their followers. Relative to canonicity, many of these churches practice the gift of prophecy. It is not uncommon for their pastors to claim that God told them "such and such," as if they had been having a conversation with God. God may have told them to buy a bigger jet,[134] or God may have told them that the pastor's teaching would raise the dead,[135] or God may have given special insight related to the end-times.[136] All of this prophecy is nonbiblical.

Charismatic Deception. Most of the ministries covered in this section practice Pentecostalism, even if the ministry is nondenominational. Televangelism has undoubtedly played a major role in the unprecedented growth of Pentecostalism and Charismatic

Christianity. A viewer of Christian television can't help but draw the conclusion that charismata—the speaking of tongues, healings, prophecy, writhing on the ground from being "slain in the Spirit"—are the norm. If you are a firm believer in this form of Christianity, then you undoubtedly praise God at the proliferation of Charismatic ministries and the explosion of believers in them. But there are dangers in Charismatic-based faith: there is the danger of being duped by the performance art of charlatans.[137] When reason is set aside in favor of emotion, humans are susceptible. Human emotion is malleable and influenced by more than religious experience. Through personal experience, we all know that music, literature, and drama, whether divine or not, can affect emotions. There is danger that sacred gifts of the Spirit can be counterfeited. When public display of charismata is the ticket for entry into the "club" of divine approval, there is undoubtedly pressure for those present in a sermon or crusade to demonstrate that they are part of the "club" and that they are healed, have been "baptized by the Holy Ghost," have an infilling of the Holy Spirit, or are "slain in the Spirit." There is no way to distinguish sacred gifts from self-induced counterfeits. Belief in charismata is not benign when it prompts a believer to donate seed money he or she can hardly afford to give, encourages a believer to stop receiving professional help for ailments, or causes a believer to rearrange their life according to false prophecy of the end-times. The danger is evident in the many documented cases of unfilled prophecy and of followers getting caught up in the fervor of a crusade and believing God has healed them, when in fact the disease or infirmity persists.[138]

Potential for Financial Fraud. Jim Bakker went to jail for fraud, making him the poster child of sleaze in the name of Christ, but his singular conviction among the prominent televangelists is not a vindication of the others. The characteristics of his ministry are evident elsewhere. Pastors are accumulating astonishing wealth. In spite of this, these ministries have millions of donors, who are often the most vulnerable and poor. Why is this so? There is not a single or simple answer, but perhaps it is because the prosperity gospel gels perfectly with modern consumerism and capitalism—spend and invest to get returns. Additionally, in the prosperity gospel the accumulation of wealth is a sign of divine blessing, not a sign of greed. The lack of transparency afforded to religious nonprofits by the United States tax code and the money-centered prosperity gospel are a toxic combination. The fact that the Grassley investigation that started in 2007 led to no penalties was due to political expediency and was not a vindication of the six ministries involved or of similar ministries. The Committee on Finance chaired by Grassley had to deal with the 2008 recession, a focus that persisted until Grassley gave up his chairmanship in 2011. Furthermore, challenging religious nonprofit tax rules is treacherous political territory, particularly for a Republican reliant on the evangelical vote. Grassley's probe "punted" by encouraging the ministries to join the Evangelical Council for Financial Accountability (ECFA). The ECFA was founded in 1979 by ninety-one charter members, including the recognizable Billy Graham Evangelistic Association. The 700 Club mentioned earlier in this section joined in 1995. To become a member of the ECFA, a religious organization agrees to adopt Seven Standards of Stewardship, including transparent finances, and to subject itself to accreditation.[139] Joyce Meyer Ministries is the only one of the six ministries investigated by the 2007 senate probe to join ECFA. It is a credit to her ministry that it joined in 2009 before knowing that the probe would be dismissed. *None* of the megachurches listed earlier in this chapter are members. This does not mean they are committing fraud, but it does mean that the ingredients for it are present, and it is a matter of trust alone that the pastor, ministry, or church will not abuse that trust.

Unlike the previous chapters that told of the formation of new branches and denominations, this chapter has been about a movement. Yet, evangelicalism, considered broadly in all the variants covered by this chapter, including the often-conflated Charismatic movements, fundamentalism, televangelism, and nondenominational Christianity, is the motivating force behind thousands of new churches around the world. Although it may stretch the official definition of the term to consider these churches *denominations*, each new church has its own variation of doctrine, governance, and worship. They walk and talk like denominations; thus, we can at least consider them pseudo-denominations because they have the attributes of distinct denominations.

If this chapter has one clear message, it is that the term *evangelical* is ambiguous. The term's meaning depends on context! We've seen in this chapter the need to discern between a neo-evangelical and a fundamentalist, between a political evangelical and a born-again evangelical, between a Charismatic evangelical and a member of a non-Charismatic evangelical denomination, between a denominationally aligned neo-evangelical who broadcasts on television and a nondenominational televangelist plying the prosperity gospel, and so on.

Arguably, revivalist evangelicalism coupled with Charismatic Christianity aided by mass media has spread Christianity more widely and quickly than at any time in history. Hundreds of millions around the globe have turned to Christ because of it. In this, evangelicalism is a vibrant force in Christianity today. However, as this chapter has pointed out, not all outcomes are rosy. Evangelicalism will likely continue to spawn pseudo-denominations with their feel-good gospel, and the beliefs and practices of some flavors of evangelicalism will continue to deepen fault lines in Christianity.

Notes

---

[1] 2098. euaggelion n.d.

[2] This is the methodology of Pew Research, an approach that tends to understate the percentage of nonwhite evangelicals Cox and Jones 2017.

[3] Barna, a Christian research firm, uses a nine-point test The Barna Group, Ltd 2007. Operation World uses a four-point theological test devised by historian David Bebbington Lausanne Movement 2011.

[4] This is the approach used by Public Religious Research Institute Cox and Jones 2017.

[5] Lausanne Movement 2011.

[6] These were (1) a belief in the crucified Christ, (2) an experience of a personal conversion, (3) theological foundation in the Bible as the word of God, and (4) active missionary evangelism or preaching of the gospel. Three of these overlap with the three-point standard used by the WCD.

[7] Lausanne Movement 2011.

[8] Hackett and Grim 2011.

[9] Wikipedia, Lutheranism 2018.

[10] Wikipedia, Evangelical Church in Germany 2018.

[11] See Chapter 7: The Reformation.

[12] Mark 16:15.

[13] Phillip was called an evangelist by Luke in Acts 21:8. Paul recognized that evangelists are one of the offices of the organized church in Ephesians 4:11.

[14] See Acts 8:26–39.

[15] See Acts 10:27–36.

[16] See Acts 19:8.

[17] J. G. Melton 2016.

[18] Wikipedia, Evangelicanism 2018.

[19] Hackett and Grim 2011.

[20] Pew 2011.

[21] Pew 2011.

[22] Dolnick 2011, 34-41.

[23] Wikipedia, James Hutton 2018.

[24] Wikipedia, Charles Darwin 2018.

[25] Wikipedia, Bob Jones Sr. 2018.

[26] The fine of $100 was subsequently overturned by the state supreme court for being excessive.

[27] Wikipedia, Clarence Darrow 2018.

[28] Wikipedia, John Gresham Machen 2018.

[29] Wikipedia, John Gresham Machen 2018.

[30] Wikipedia, Carl McIntire 2017.

[31] Melton and Sandeen, Christian Fundamentalism 2016.

[32] J. G. Melton 2016.

[33] J. G. Melton 2016.

[34] Wikipedia, Billy Graham 2018.

[35] Wikipedia, Bob Jones Sr. 2018.

[36] Wikipedia, Billy Graham 2018.

[37] Wikipedia, Billy Graham 2018.

38 Bebbington proposed a four-fold test based on conversionism, activism, biblicism, and Crucicentrism. The NAE's four-point belief standard is similar:
• The Bible is the highest authority for what I believe.
• It is very important for me personally to encourage non-Christians to trust Jesus Christ as their Savior.
• Jesus Christ's death on the cross is the only sacrifice that could remove the penalty of my sin.
• Only those who trust in Jesus Christ alone as their Savior receive God's free gift of eternal salvation Stetzer 2017/2018.

39 One article advises that evangelicals can have a wide range of beliefs relative to how God created the universe. The only dogma is that He did NAE 2017. NAE published a group of essays in 2015 called "When God and Science Meet Surprising Discoveries of Agreement." The general conclusion of the essays was that evangelicals need not be hostile to science Hutchinson and Others 2015. Another article entitled "Evangelicals Leaders Don't Want Partisan Political Identity" contained the survey results of members of the NAE relative to the Trump White House. The quoted leaders expressed a strong desire to be nonpartisan NAE 2018.

40 American Council of Christian Churches 2018.

41 Bob Jones Jr. took over for his father at Bob Jones University.

42 Related to the Catholic pope.

43 Wikipedia, Bob Jones Jr. 2017.

44 Wikipedia, Jerry Falwell 2018.

45 Wikipedia, Jerry Falwell 2018.

46 Kurtzleben 2015.

47 See John 3:3.

48 Concordia Publishing House 2009, 9.

49 Burton-Edwards n.d.

50 Catholic Answers n.d.

51 Staff 2014.

52 Banwart 2013.

53 McVicar 2018.

54 Wikipedia, Equal Rights Amendment 2018.

55 Banwart 2013.

56 McVicar 2018.

57 McVicar 2018.

58 McVicar 2018.

59 The Moral Majority was actually five distinct entities: (1) Moral Majority, Inc., a tax-exempt, non-tax-deductible political lobbying organization; (2) Moral Majority Foundation, a tax-exempt, tax-deductible project designed to educate ministers and laypeople on the finer points of voter registration and mobilization; (3) Moral Majority Legal Defense Fund, part of a growing network of public law firms dedicated to reversing the legacy of liberal firms such as the American Civil Liberties Union (ACLU); and (4) Moral Majority Political Action Committee, a PAC designed to help fund the political campaigns of conservative candidates McVicar 2018.

60 Banwart 2013.

61 Banwart 2013.
62 Wikipedia, Christian Coalition 2018.
63 Members of the advisory group were the following:
  • Mark Burns — co-founder and CEO of the NOW Television Network in Easley, SC
  • Tim Clinton — president, American Association of Christian Counselors
  • James Dobson — author, psychologist and host, *Family Talk*
  • Jordan Easley — pastor of Englewood Baptist Church in Jackson, TN; chairman of Southern Baptists' Young Leaders Advisory Council
  • Jerry Falwell Jr. — president, Liberty University in Lynchburg, VA
  • Ronnie Floyd — author and senior pastor, Cross Church in northwest AK; former Southern Baptist Convention president
  • Jack Graham — author and pastor of Prestonwood Baptist Church in Plano, TX; former Southern Baptist Convention president
  • Rodney Howard-Browne — co-founder of the River at Tampa Bay Church and Revival Ministries International in Florida
  • Harry Jackson — senior pastor, Hope Christian Church in Beltsville, MD; co-founder of The Reconciled Church: Healing the Racial Divide
  • Robert Jeffress — senior pastor, First Baptist Church of Dallas; hosted Fourth of July event at Kennedy Center featuring Trump as a speaker
  • Richard Land — president, Southern Evangelical Seminary in Matthews, NC; former president, Southern Baptist Convention Ethics and Religious Liberty Commission
  • Greg Laurie — author and senior pastor of Harvest Christian Fellowship in Riverside, CA
  • Eric Metaxas — author and host, the *Eric Metaxas Show*; speaker, 2012 National Prayer Breakfast
  • Johnnie Moore — author, religious freedom advocate, and public relations executive; serves as unofficial spokesman for group of evangelicals advising Trump administration
  • Frank Page — president and CEO, Southern Baptist Convention Executive Committee; former Southern Bapti• st Convention president; former member of President Obama's Advisory Council on Faith-based and Neighborhood Partnerships
  • Tony Perkins — president, Family Research Council
  • Ralph Reed — founder, Faith and Freedom Coalition; former executive director, Christian Coalition
  • Tony Suarez — executive vice president, National Hispanic Christian Leadership Conference
  • Paula White — senior pastor, New Destiny Christian Center in Apopka, FL; first clergywoman to give an invocation at an inauguration A. Banks 2017.
64 Franklin Graham Jr. was not a member of the advisory board but is mentioned here due to his influence and ardent support for Donald Trump.
65 See note 63
66 Dias 2016.
67 Dias 2016.
68 Dias 2016.

69 Cox and Jones 2017.
70 Cox and Jones 2017.
71 Cox and Jones 2017.
72 Shellnutt 2016.
73 Cox and Jones 2017.
74 2016 Presidential Election Exit Polls 2016.
75 Cox and Jones 2017.
76 McVicar 2018.
77 NAE 2018.
78 Gerson 2018.
79 Anderson 2017/2018.
80 Wikipedia, Jim Bakker 2018.
81 Wikipedia, Televangelism 2018.
82 Balmer 2018.
83 Wikipedia, Word of Faith 2018.
84 A partial list of the major Christian broadcasting networks past and present include Pat Robertson's Christian Broadcast Network, Marcus and Joni Lamb's Daystar Network, Jimmy Swaggart's SonLife Broadcasting Network, Paul and Jan Crouch's Trinity Broadcast Network, and Brian and Bobbie Houston's Hillsong Channel Wikipedia, List of United States over-the-air television networks 2018.
85 What do Evangelical Christians think about televangelists? 2015-2016.
86 Pew 2011.
87 Keteyian 2007.
88 Zoll 2011.
89 Not all televangelists are trained or ordained.
90 There are usually many subministries set up under the umbrella ministry, such as a youth ministry, disaster relief ministry, school ministry, and so on.
91 In the United States, unlike nonreligious nonprofits, churches are not required to disclose financial details such as payroll expenses, administrative costs, and so on.
92 A Protestant church is considered a megachurch if it has more than two thousand people attend its services weekly Thumma PhD 1996.
93 Horowitz 2014.
94 Wikipedia, Oral Roberts 2018.
95 Horowitz 2014.
96 Rosin 2009.
97 Wikipedia, Oral Roberts 2018.
98 Editors, Jerry Falwell 2018.
99 Wikipedia, Robert Tilton 2018.
100 Wikipedia, Robert Tilton 2018.
101 Wikipedia, Robert Tilton 2018.
102 ABC News PrimeTime Live (November 21, 1991) 2016.
103 Rowe 1998.
104 Wikipedia, Jimmy Swaggert 2018.
105 Wikipedia, Pat Robertson 2018.
106 Wikipedia, The 700 Club 2018.
107 Wikipedia, Pat Robertson 2018.
108 Wikipedia, Jim Bakker 2018.

¹⁰⁹ Gareloch 2018.
¹¹⁰ Gareloch 2018.
¹¹¹ Gareloch 2018.
¹¹² Wikipedia, Jim Bakker 2018.
¹¹³ Wikipedia, Jim Bakker 2018.
¹¹⁴ Kenneth Copeland Ministries n.d.
¹¹⁵ Kenneth Copeland Ministries n.d.
¹¹⁶ It has a Pentecostal theology but is an independent church.
¹¹⁷ Kenneth Copeland Ministries n.d.
¹¹⁸ Gutierrez 2018.
¹¹⁹ Wikipedia, Creflo Dollar 2018.
¹²⁰ Blair 2015.
¹²¹ Wikipedia, Creflo Dollar 2018.
¹²² Hanegraaff 2012, 198.
¹²³ Wikipedia, Jesse Duplantis 2018.
¹²⁴ Charisma Magazine 2015.
¹²⁵ Lobdell, The Price of Healing 2003.
¹²⁶ Lobdell, The Price of Healing 2003.
¹²⁷ Kozar 2018.
¹²⁸ Lobdell, The Price of Healing 2003.
¹²⁹ Saddleback is associated with the Southern Baptist Convention, but this affiliation is not publicized. Its media presents the church as independent, just as other nondenominational megachurches do.
¹³⁰ Wikipedia, List of the largest evangelical churches 2018.
¹³¹ Saddleback Church n.d.
¹³² Thumma PhD 1996.
¹³³ See the quote from Billy Graham in the section "Era of Televangelism, Celebrity Pastors, and Megachurches" earlier in this chapter.
¹³⁴ Jesse Duplantis tells Kenneth Copeland of a conversation he had with God on his jet in which God tells him to get a bigger jet as a show of his faith in God News Division 2015.
¹³⁵ Benny Hinn prophesied, "You're going to have people raised from the dead watching [the Trinity Broadcasting Network]. I see rows of caskets lining up in front of this TV set and I see actual loved ones picking up the hands of the dead and letting them touch the screen and people are getting raised" Lobdell, The Price of Healing 2003.
¹³⁶ In December 1999, on the eve of the Y2K crisis, Jim Bakker proclaimed that God had shown him thirty-one prophecies, including a prophecy that the third world war would erupt in the Holy Land in the year 2000 McCumber 2012.
¹³⁷ A notorious case of fraudulent faith healing was that of Peter Popoff. In his crusades, he called forth people, miraculously knowing their name and ailment. Suspicious, an investigator used a radio receiver to intercept Popoff's wife feeding him personal details from the believers' prayer cards via radio and a hidden earpiece. The investigator revealed the scam on the *Tonight Show* in 1986 Openheimer 2017.
¹³⁸ Healing crusades are controversial. A *Los Angeles Times* article addressed Benny Hinn's miracle crusades Lobdell, The Price of Healing 2003. From that article, we

learn that those in the audience who believe they've been healed by being in attendance make their way to the front. Only a few make it past screeners. Once on the platform, they tell of their miraculous healing and are then usually "slain in the spirit" right there on stage. Clips of the healing are the content for future TV promotions. William Vandenkolk, a nearly blind eleven-year-old, made it into one of those clips. He believed he was healed at a Benny Hinn event and went to the front. "I liked it at first because I thought I was being healed. As soon as God healed me, I could see better." But he was not better. His eyesight never improved. "Brian Darby, who has worked for 21 years with severely handicapped people in Northern California, says he has witnessed firsthand the disappointment left in the wake of a Hinn Miracle Crusade. Over the years, he says, many of his clients have attended the events, where they were swept up in a wave of excitement, thinking they were about to walk for the first time or have their limbs straightened. 'You can't minimize the impact of not being healed on the person, the family, the extended family,' Darby says. 'They have a sense of euphoria at the crusade and then crash down. [Hinn is not] around to pick up the pieces'" Lobdell, The Price of Healing 2003. In 2001, HBO aired a documentary entitled *A Question of Miracles* A Question of Miracles 2014. The film's director revealed that in following up with seven "healed" cases over the next year they did not find any cases in which people were actually healed Wikipedia, Benny Hinn 2018.

[139] ECFA n.d.

Chapter 11

Counterfeit Unity—Coerced Belief

The preceding chapters, spanning from the Orthodox schisms to modern evangelicalism, revealed a common reality—that the "truth" of Christianity is elusive and that the constant attempt to define it, or to rediscover it as the case may be, has created a constant tendency toward division rather than unity. This tendency has been present from the beginning; however, we have seen two very different patterns relative to the rate of denominational splintering: the relative cohesion of the Orthodox and Reformation periods and the rapid explosion of denominations in modern times. This chapter is about the means by which the first pattern was achieved.

The rate at which new denominations formed over time has not been constant. It has increased sharply in the last two hundred years. The Orthodox schisms resulted in a few highly concentrated denominations, as we saw in the virtual tour of the world that we took in Chapter 1: From One to Many. Nearly 50 percent of all Christians are Catholic, and within many geographic areas such as Latin America and eastern Europe there are often high concentrations of Christians, usually 90 percent or more, belonging to the same denomination. Even during the Reformation the number of new denominations was modest. It was in the United States that a veritable explosion of denominations began, fostered by a culture of independence and protected by religious freedom. As religious liberty spread around the globe, so did denominational splintering.

We learned in Chapter 5: The Age of Heresy that there were numerous Christian sects at the time that Constantine made

Christianity into the religion of the empire. In fact, had it not been for imperial edicts and enforcement outlawing all but the proto-Orthodox church, prolific Christian splintering may have taken place in the early centuries. Similarly, we learned in Chapter 7: The Reformation that Lutheranism, Reformed (Calvinism), and Anglicanism were favored as magisterial churches during the Reformation. Indeed, the dominance of a denomination in a region is, in many cases, the legacy of the marriage of church and state. In other words, the resulting unity was at best a "counterfeit" unity achieved in part through coercion.

We will delve into counterfeit unity via a series of "snapshots"—historical examples that are broad enough to be representative but not so comprehensive as to attempt to cover all of Christian history. The chapter's purpose is to give us a sense of why and how unity was achieved through coercion, persecution, and intolerance. There is really no way to sugarcoat the disturbing history presented in this chapter. We are likely to feel uncomfortable about much of it. It might be tempting to attribute the brutal coercion described in this chapter to the unenlightened and uncivilized past. Unfortunately, the *beliefs* that motivated coercive force are not buried in the past. They are alive and well today, although manifested in a more muted form, as we will see at the conclusion of this chapter.

Justifying Coercion

The question of persuasion versus coercion was irrelevant in the early decades of the Christian church—a time when it survived in the shadows of the antagonistic Roman Empire. However, once the church was joined to secular power, the question was of paramount importance. Was the state endowed with power from God to preserve the faith? Should it enforce worship? The conjoined leaders of church and state looked to the scriptures and to theologians for answers.

The scriptures provide contrasting examples of God's approach to unity. Jesus offered *invitations* that suggest *voluntary* action—invitations whose words anticipate that not all hearers of the word would accept them: "*Come* unto me all ye that labor and are heavy laden,"[1] "*If* any man will come after me, let him deny himself, and take up his cross, and follow me,"[2] "*If* any man serve me, let him follow me."[3]

Similarly, Paul expressed the voluntary nature of unity to the Philippians, describing it as a personal journey based on *personal* attributes of striving—faith, love, and humility—and *not* on the exercise of power—strife, superiority, or force:

> that ye stand fast in one spirit, with one mind striving together for the faith of the gospel; . . . Fulfil ye my joy, that ye be likeminded, having the same love, being of one accord, of one mind. Let nothing be done through strife or vainglory; but in lowliness of mind let each esteem other better than themselves. . . . Wherefore, my beloved, as ye have always obeyed, not as in my presence only, but now much more in my absence, work out your own salvation with fear and trembling. For it is God which worketh in you both to will and to do of his good pleasure.[4]

However, the scriptures also have contrasting examples of coerced obedience. After Moses led the children of Israel out of Egypt, Jehovah established a theocracy through Moses in which moral sins were linked to civil penalties. The Law of Moses ostensibly prescribed the death penalty for a wide variety of offenses: cursing parents,[5] committing adultery,[6] engaging in homosexual acts,[7] and practicing bestiality.[8] Capital punishment was not an idle possibility.[9] In the early years after Moses left Egypt, Jehovah repeatedly enforced these principles. Consider the fate of the Israelites who built and worshiped a golden calf—God commanded the Levites to slay about three thousand idolaters.[10] Consider the immediate judgment of God upon three Levites who attempted to usurp power from Moses and Aaron—they and their families were swallowed up into the earth and their 250 followers were consumed by fire from heaven.[11] Consider the consequence of murmuring against God in the face of hardship—"Much people of Israel" died due to serpents.[12] Consider the swift judgment on Israelites who began worshipping the false gods of their neighbors—Moses had them slain and their heads displayed in public.[13]

These punishments may seem barbaric unless we also consider the context. Moses, like Enoch who had "walked with God,"[14] had been in God's presence.[15] He believed, and the Lord concurred, that the Israelites could qualify as a people to be in the presence of God:

Now therefore, if ye will obey my voice indeed, and keep my covenant, then ye shall be a peculiar treasure unto me above all people: for all the earth is mine: And ye shall be unto me a kingdom of priests, and an holy nation. . . . And all the people answered together, and said, All that the LORD hath spoken we will do. . . . And the LORD said unto Moses, Go unto the people, and sanctify them today and tomorrow, and let them wash their clothes, And be ready against the third day: for the third day the *LORD will come down in the sight of all the people* upon mount Sinai.[16]

For the LORD thy God walketh in the midst of thy camp, to deliver thee, and to give up thine enemies before thee; therefore shall thy camp be holy: that he see no unclean thing in thee, and turn away from thee.[17]

Everyone had to be pure and prepared! The holy Jehovah would not suffer the presence of *any* evil. The stakes were high and the situation unique. Essentially, the goal to be in God's presence as a people was jeopardized by the sins of just one person. In this unique context, banishment or capital punishment was not only a matter of punishment for the sinner but also a means of preserving the purity of the group.

Prophets prophesied that such circumstances will occur again when the Lord comes a second time. Isaiah prophesied the cleansing of Zion in the last days preparatory to the Lord's second coming:

And it shall come to pass, that he that is left in Zion, and he that remaineth in Jerusalem, shall be called holy, even every one that is written among the living in Jerusalem: When the Lord shall have *washed away the filth* of the daughters of Zion, and shall have *purged the blood* of Jerusalem from the midst thereof by the *spirit of judgment,* and by the *spirit of burning.*[18]

Awake, awake; put on thy strength, O Zion; put on thy beautiful garments, O Jerusalem, the holy city: for henceforth there shall *no more come into thee the uncircumcised and the unclean.*[19]

Many generations of Christians have believed that the second coming of the Lord was imminent in their respective time—and that it required a people prepared by the burning of the wicked.[20] Popes, clerics, Reformers, emperors, and kings have believed in their time that they, like Moses, were preparing their people for the imminent presence of the Lord; therefore, they considered Jehovah's instructions to Moses as applicable to themselves, including the use of corporal and capital punishment if necessary.

Additionally, church leaders relied on the reasoning of theologians such as Augustine of Hippo and Thomas Aquinas to justify their mandate to root out heresy and compel unity. We've learned much about Augustine in prior chapters. He was an incredibly influential bishop and theologian in the fifth century. He used the parable of the wheat and tares[21] as justification for civil authorities to root out and destroy heresy (tares) before it could overwhelm the truth (the wheat). He also saw in the parable of the householder's rejected feast[22] justification to compel heathens and heretics to be Catholic.[23] The extraordinarily respected theologian Thomas Aquinas added yet another angle on justified coercion—he taught that heresy is far more harmful than other capital crimes and should therefore be punished as a capital crime:

> There is the sin, whereby they deserve not only to be separated from the Church by excommunication, but also to be shut off from the world by death. For it is a much more serious matter to corrupt faith through which comes the soul's life, than to forge money, through which temporal life is supported. Hence if forgers of money or other malefactors are straightway justly put to death by secular princes, with much more justice can heretics, immediately upon conviction, be not only excommunicated but also put to death.[24]

We can see Aquinas's reasoning in the official position of the Catholic Church as explained in the *Catholic Encyclopedia*:

> The Church established by Christ, as a perfect society, is empowered to make laws and inflict penalties for their violation. Heresy not only violates her law but strikes at her

very life, unity of belief; and from the beginning the heretic had incurred all the penalties of the ecclesiastical courts. When Christianity became the religion of the Empire, and still more when the peoples of Northern Europe became Christian nations, the close alliance of Church and State *made unity of faith essential not only to the ecclesiastical organization, but also to civil society.* Heresy, in consequence, was a crime which secular rulers were bound in duty to punish. It was regarded as worse than any other crime, even that of high treason; it was for society in those times what we call anarchy.[25]

The Marriage of the Church and the Roman Empire

In the 140 years between the rise of Constantine and the fall of the western Roman Empire in 453, dozens of edicts were issued by Roman emperors relative to the Christian faith.[26] Some established preferences for Catholic clergy, including subsidies, tax forgiveness, and release from public service. Many others dealt with the numerable "heresies" that were sprouting within the church.[27] The punishments were severe and included prohibitions against free assembly, ordination of clergy, or the building of churches; banishment and exile; confiscation of property; loss of civic rank and exclusion from government positions; fines; and torture. Starting with Constantine, emperors issued increasingly harsh edicts against public pagan worship and then against pagans themselves. Initially, capital punishment was sparingly included as the ultimate punishment for heretics and pagans.[28]

Capital punishment for the crime of heresy against Christian orthodoxy was first practiced in the Roman Empire in 385. In 380 or so, a nobleman in Spain named Priscillian began teaching unorthodox doctrines, including asceticism based on apocryphal writings.[29] In spite of his doctrine, he was controversially elected bishop of Avila.[30] Ultimately, Priscillian and five of his followers were condemned as magicians in a synod in 384.[31] Because practicing magic was a capital offense under Roman law, the new emperor of the west, Maximus, carried out their execution in 385. It should be noted that this foray into the use of capital punishment was not sanctioned by the bishops of the time and that the bishop of Rome rebuked Maximus for usurping ecclesiastical power. Nevertheless, the execution of Priscillian and his followers foreshadowed the future harsh treatment of heretics.[32]

The Roman emperor Theodosius I (347–395) is considered a saint by the Catholic Church for his staunch support of the faith. He was not unique in issuing edicts, but he was known for the zeal with which he carried them out.[33] In 380, as emperor of the east, he issued the Edict of Thessalonica, which established the Nicene Creed as the litmus test of a true Catholic. All other beliefs were subject to punishment:

> According to the apostolic teaching and the doctrine of the Gospel, let us believe in the one deity of the Father, the Son and the Holy Spirit, in equal majesty and in a holy Trinity. We authorize the followers of this law to assume the title of Catholic Christians; but as for the others, since, in our judgment they are foolish madmen, we decree that they shall be *branded with the ignominious name of heretics*, and shall not presume to give to their conventicles the name of churches. They will suffer in the first place the chastisement of the divine condemnation and in the second *the punishment of our authority which in accordance with the will of Heaven we shall decide to inflict.*[34]

Theodosius consolidated power and later formalized Christianity as the official state religion across the empire. His edict in 391 banning paganism was later followed by military action in 394 against resistant pagan worshippers in Rome.[35]

The number of "heretical" sects sprouting within Christianity during the early Roman patronage of the Catholic Church as covered in Chapter 5: The Age of Heresy is a testament to the constant tendency of believers to innovate and follow their own path. The fact that these sects did *not* survive is in large part a testament to the effectiveness of imperial edicts and subsequent repression.

The Byzantine Empire

After the western half of the Roman Empire fell in the middle of the fifth century, around 453, the codex of the empire continued in effect within the eastern Byzantine Empire for another thousand years. As we learned in Chapter 6: Orthodox Schisms, the three major branches that split from the Roman Catholic Church dominated the eastern empire—the Assyrian Church after the Council of Ephesus in 431, the Oriental Orthodox Church after the Council of Chalcedon in 451, and the Eastern Orthodox after the East-West Schism of 1054. These branches continued to exercise the legal framework established by Constantine and his successors. Church and state remained conjoined. Heresy and paganism were not tolerated. Punishment was severe, but capital punishment was rare. Nevertheless, some eastern rulers resorted to capital punishment to eradicate heretics and pagans as recorded in the Catholic Encyclopedia by the church historian Joseph Blötzer, "As early as the tenth century Empress Theodora had put to death a multitude of Paulicians, and in 1118 Emperor Alexius Comnenus treated the Bogomili with equal severity."[36] North of the eastern empire, Vladimir the Great, leader of the Rus, married a Byzantine Christian princess and was baptized.[37] History is unclear whether he persuasively or forcefully Christianized his Rus people after his own baptism. What is clear is that mass baptisms of the Rus people occurred.[38]

Charlemagne and the Saxons

The Roman Catholic Church took a more extreme course than the three Eastern Orthodox branches did—a direct result of the political partnership it formed with Charlemagne (742–814).

After the fall of the western Roman Empire in the middle of the fifth century, the Roman Catholic Church found itself at the crossroads of competing empires. It was still officially under the imperial rule of the Byzantine Empire; however, the Lombards, a Scandinavian tribe that had emigrated through Germanic lands, invaded Italy from the north in 568 and conquered portions of northern and southern Italy.[39] In the meantime, the Franks, starting from their home in Germany, had successfully conquered much of western Europe.[40] When the Lombardy king, Desiderius, marched on Rome in 774, Pope Adrian I recognized that the Byzantine Empire, occupied as it was with wars against invading Muslims, could not protect Rome from the Lombards. Adrian appealed to the Catholic Charlemagne, king of the Franks. The pope's plea prompted Charlemagne to conquer the Lombards in northern Italy.[41]

The church in Rome passed into a period of uncertain allegiance. It was still formally subject to the Byzantine emperor, but it had been saved from the Lombards by a new champion and protector. Allegiance remained unsettled until Adrian's successor, Pope Leo III, faced a coup in 799. He fled across the Alps to Charlemagne for protection. Persuaded by the pope's case, Charlemagne returned with the pope to Rome to calm the church and ensure the pope's place. Charlemagne's reward came on December 25, 800, when Pope Leo III coronated Charlemagne as Augustus and emperor.[42] The act gave birth to a new Christian empire, later to be known as the Holy Roman Empire. Its vast and growing territories ultimately occupied most of western Europe.

It is important to recognize that Charlemagne's coronation as emperor came late in his military career. His exploits and tactics were widely known, including his practice of imposing Christianity on the heathen by force. Starting in 772, he repeatedly campaigned and then conquered the pagan Saxon tribes. As a condition of surrender, upon the threat of death, he required that each conquered leader and his people be baptized as Christians.[43] In 785, he issued the *Capitulatio de Partibus Saxoniae*, "If any one of the race of the Saxons hereafter concealed among them shall have wished to hide himself unbaptized, and shall have scorned to come to baptism and shall have wished to remain a pagan, let him be *punished by death*."[44] By coronating Charlemagne, the pope effectively sanctioned Charlemagne's methods—the use of force, including the threat of death, on behalf of the church.

The Crusades to Convert, Conquer, and Correct

The coronation of Charlemagne presaged the ultimate political and religious break from the eastern empire and its patriarch. As described in Chapter 6: Orthodox Schisms, the pope in Rome and the patriarch in Constantinople excommunicated each other in 1054, leading to the East-West Schism. Still, there remained a common Christian enemy— the encroaching armies of the Muslims. In 1095, Pope Urban II demonstrated the power of the papacy by calling an ecumenical council, the Council of Clermont, that proclaimed the first holy war, or crusade, to retake Christian lands in Palestine from the Muslims.[45] The Christian Crusades lasted for centuries and are the stuff of lore and legend. In general, the chivalry of the Crusades included tolerance for the temporarily conquered Muslims in Antioch, Jerusalem, and other conquered cities.[46] However, three events spawned by the Crusades are important counterexamples to the tolerance exercised in Palestine.

The call for a crusade was directed to nobility, but the initial call in 1095 was quickly heeded by commoners, such as in the People's Crusade led by Peter the Hermit—a crusade not against the Muslims in foreign lands but against Jews within the lands of the Holy Roman Empire. Count Emicho of Germany took up the cause of the People's Crusade against the Jews in cities along the Rhine, including Speyer, Worms, Mainz, and Cologne. Jews were forced by the crusaders to convert or die. Many died. By some accounts, some Jews killed their own children and committed suicide to spare their family from coerced baptism.[47]

Over the ensuing centuries, the nearly perpetual call for crusades led to the organization of monastic orders of knights. The Teutonic Knights were a German military order founded during the Third Crusade in 1190. As the crusade in the Middle East floundered, the order turned its attention to Christian enemies closer to home, including the pagan territories lying to the east of Germany. Initially supported by the papacy, the knights Christianized by force Transylvania, Prussia, and Lithuania.[48] The knights' reward was sovereignty over the lands they conquered—a reward so compelling that it ultimately put them in conflict with the territorial interests of the Holy Roman Empire. With lands and wealth as rewards, we can only wonder about the knights' true motives in Christianizing pagan peoples.

The Crusades were largely focused on the Muslim-conquered territories in the east that were formerly part of the Byzantine Empire; however, in 1208, Pope Innocent III called a crusade to eradicate a heretical sect within the heart of the Holy Roman Empire. The Cathars, or "pure ones," believed in Gnostic doctrines that had surfaced soon after the birth of the church.[49] They believed a person's spirit was good and was created by the God of the New Testament but that all material things, including the body, were evil and created by the God of the Old Testament, namely, by Satan. Cathars sought to conquer the material through ascetic, disciplined living and a sacrament of baptism administered twice in one's lifetime.[50] Pope Innocent III initially tried to correct the heresy by sending missionaries and emissaries. He sent a legate (authorized representative) to excommunicate a sympathetic local nobleman. When the papal legate was murdered while carrying out his duty, Innocent III abandoned persuasion. He called for a crusade, known as the Albigensian Crusade, to crush the heresy. The nobles who responded to the call of crusade had questionable motives. As compensation, the conquering crusaders were promised the Cathars' forfeited property. The Catholic crusaders lay siege to the town of Béziers in 1209, but many of the Catholic inhabitants refused to leave, apparently aware that this was not just a battle for religion but also a quest for land and wealth. Upon entering the city, a commander of the crusading army purportedly asked his superior how to tell the Cathars from the Catholics and was told, "Kill them all, the Lord will recognise His own."[51] Catholics and Cathars alike took refuge in the Church of St Mary Magdalene. The crusaders broke down the doors, dragged out the refugees, and slaughtered an estimated seven thousand men, women, and children. Thousands of others outside the church were mutilated and killed. The crusaders' leader, Arnaud-Amaury, wrote to Pope Innocent III, "Today your Holiness, twenty thousand heretics were put to the sword, regardless of rank, age, or sex."[52] The persecution of the Cathars did not end in Béziers. The Inquisition was established in large measure to root out remaining Cathars, and over the ensuing years hundreds of Cathars were burned to death as a result.[53]

The Inquisition to Stamp Out Heresy

By the end of the twelfth century, splinter groups considered by the church to be heretical, such as the Cathars, were widespread. In 1184, Pope Lucius III required bishops to make judicial inquiry, or *Inquisition*, into the state of heresy in their respective diocese. Bishop-led Inquisitions were initially ineffective and inconsistent. Consequently, in 1227, the pope appointed special investigator-judges—largely from the ranks of the Dominican monks—to perform Inquisitions throughout the church.[54] The power of the inquisitors grew immensely as they received the full support of the Holy Roman Emperor Frederic II.[55]

By imperial edict in 1224, unrepentant heretics were to receive the harshest of punishments, including death by fire.[56] It was nearly impossible to prove innocence, and failure to appear was considered evidence of guilt. The accused never saw their accusers and were tortured until they condemned themselves.[57] If the accused appeared but refused to confess, papal bulls issued in 1252 granted authority to use torture as a means to solicit confessions.[58] The accused who admitted and recanted their heresy faced penalties including prison, flogging, wearing a yellow cross on their clothing, or undertaking a holy pilgrimage. The accused who admitted to heretical beliefs but refused to recant them were turned over to civil authorities to be burned at the stake.[59]

It is a matter of historical debate how many heretics were condemned by the Inquisitions of the Middle Ages. The lines are blurry between church-led Inquisitions and civil criminal courts, which also controversially judged heretics.[60] Regardless of the court, the message was clear: heresy was tantamount to treason. As poignant examples of the coercion exercised by conjoined church and state: hundreds of Cathars were burned to death in multiple incidents;[61] eighty members of a group known as the Waldensians were burned, causing the remnant to go into hiding in the secluded valleys of the Italian Alps;[62] and one zealous inquisitor condemned 180 heretics to the flames in a single trial in 1239 in Champagne, France.[63]

The Inquisition as established by Innocent III was to root out heresy. However, soon other evils were subject to the Inquisition. As early as 1233, pope Gregory IX identified witchcraft as an evil to be rooted out.[64] The mythology of witchcraft came from pagan traditions, but since witchcraft shared many of the characteristics of the Christian devil and his demons, belief in witches was readily accepted within Christianity. Inquisitorial procedures against sorcery were formalized as early as 1270.[65] By the end of the fourteenth century, theologians cemented the linkage between sorcery and heresy, setting the stage for a mania that swept northern Europe in the fifteenth century. In 1484, Innocent VIII issued a papal bull acknowledging in the clearest terms the linkage between sorcery and demons. Maladies such as infertility, bad harvests, sick cattle, and others were deemed to be evidence of witchcraft. The historian Peter Scaff explained:

> It had come to his knowledge, so the pontiff wrote, that the dioceses of Mainz, Cologne, Treves, Salzburg and Bremen teemed with persons who, forsaking the Catholic faith, were consorting with demons. By incantations, conjurations and other iniquities they were thwarting the parturition of women and destroying the seed of animals, the fruits of the earth, the grapes of the vine and the fruit of the orchard. Men and women, flocks and herds, trees and all herbs were being afflicted with pains and torments. Men could no longer beget, women no longer conceive, and wives and husbands were prevented from performing the marital act. In view of these calamities, the pope authorized the Dominicans, Heinrich Institoris and Jacob Sprenger, professors of theology, to continue their activity against these malefics in bringing them to trial and punishment. He called upon the bishop of Salzburg to see to it that they were not impeded in their work and, a few months later, he admonished the archbishop of Mainz to give them active support. In other documents, Innocent commended Sigismund, archbishop of Austria, the count of the Tyrol and other persons for the aid they had rendered to these inquisitors in their effort to crush out witchcraft. The burning of witches was thus declared the definite policy of the papal see and the inquisitors proceeded to carry out its instructions with untiring and merciless severity.[66]

The burning of witches in Rome began immediately after the pope's bull in 1484. Some forty-one were burned in the diocese of Como in northern Italy in the year following the bull. In 1486, the two inquisitors in Germany who had been commissioned by the pope published the *The Witches Hammer* as a guide to recognizing and prosecuting witches. The book prescribed unspeakable torture to solicit confessions in spite of the predictable outcome that the accused were willing to confess to anything no matter how sordid the accusation. It is estimated that somewhere between forty thousand to sixty thousand were executed in Europe for witchcraft.[67] The belief in witches and the attempt to eradicate them lasted for centuries—the last execution occurred in Switzerland in 1782.[68] Witch hunts infected Protestantism and spread to the New World.

The nature of the Inquisition took an even more sinister turn in 1478 when the Spanish monarchs Ferdinand and Isabella obtained the pope's approval for a national Inquisition.[69] Spanish Christians had reconquered all of Spain from the Islamic Moors and near the end of the previous century had conducted pogroms of Jews, giving Jews a choice of death or baptism. Many Jews converted in name only and continued to practice their old religion. Consequently, Ferdinand and Isabella ruled a people of questionable loyalty and Christian fealty. The Inquisitions, first in Spain and then in Portugal, were established as *government* institutions with an administrative organization.[70] The first Spanish grand inquisitor, a Dominican by the name of Tomás de Torquemada, quickly grew the Inquisition from a single tribunal to a network of more than two dozen "Holy Offices."[71] Naturally, the permanent and sprawling organization required funds, but rather than receive monies from the church, the Inquisition funded itself through the confiscation of property from the "guilty." Much of the confiscated property went into the treasury of Ferdinand and Isabella, while some flowed to the treasury of the emperor of the Holy Roman Empire. With so much wealth for the taking, the Spanish and Portuguese Inquisitions were motivated by more than the maintenance of religious purity.[72]

After a brutal trial in which the accused was tortured to solicit a confession, the accused was brought before the public in a spectacle known as *auto-de-fé*, meaning an act of faith. The event was described by one historian:

> When the person impeached is condemned, he is either severely whipped, violently tortured, sent to the galleys, or sentenced to death; and in either case the effects are confiscated. After judgment, a procession is performed to the place of execution, which ceremony is called an auto de fe, or act of faith. . . . The chief inquisitor then descended from the amphitheatre, dressed in his cope, and having a mitre on his head. After having bowed to the altar, he

advanced towards the king's balcony, and went up to it, attended by some of his officers, carrying a cross and the gospels, with a book containing the oath by which the kings of Spain oblige themselves to protect the catholic faith, to extirpate heretics, and to support with all their power and force the prosecutions and decrees of the inquisition: a like oath was administered to the counsellors and whole assembly.[73]

Torquemada became synonymous with fanaticism and brutality. It is estimated that during his tenure tens of thousands were tried and some two thousand souls were burned at the stake.[74] At his urging, Ferdinand and Isabella issued the Alhambra Decree in 1492, the same year Columbus set sail for America, giving Spanish Jews the choice of exile or baptism. As in the pogroms of 1391, many tens of thousands of Jews chose to be baptized—perhaps as many as 200,000.[75] However, a large portion of the Jews refused. Estimates vary, but some 40,000 to 160,000 Jews were exiled from Spain.[76] The Muslims received similar treatment and, like the Jews, left Spain in the hundreds of thousands.[77]

Induced Conversion in the New World

Spain spread the Inquisition as it spread its empire throughout the world. After Columbus discovered the New World in 1492, Spanish monarchs sought assurances from the pope that the new lands they discovered would belong to their realm. In a series of papal bulls, Pope Alexander VI, a native of Spain,[78] granted to Spain and Portugal all discovered lands one hundred leagues west of the Azores.[79] The Catholic kings believed that the papal bulls gave them authority over both civil and ecclesiastical affairs—an authority that came with the duty to Christianize the native people.[80] Unlike the recently issued Alhambra Decree of 1492 in Spain, with its "convert or die" policy, Spanish conquistadores and missionaries "induced" the indigenous people of Central and South America to be baptized with less immediately threatening but still oppressive methods. Slavery was banned by the pope and the Spanish crown;[81] however, when conquistadores invaded Central America in 1519 and Peru in 1531, the crown gave the conquerors "grants" of forced labor in a system called *encomienda*—a feudal system of indentured labor.[82] In principle, the natives were entrusted, like children to parents, as "wards" to the *encomenderos* for physical protection, economic security, and spiritual nurturing.[83] In reality, encomienda was slavery, albeit with a twist. The encomendero, in addition to exploiting the enslaved labor, had the duty to instill the Spanish language and spread the Catholic faith. Economienda was enabled by gathering indigenous people into concentrated enclaves called "Indian reductions."[84] Missions stood at the center of reductions, where Franciscans, Dominicans, and later Jesuits evangelized and baptized the native inhabitants.

Options were grim for indigenous peoples—live peaceably as indentured labor in reductions or, if possible, remain outside. Those who remained outside reductions faced the risk of capture and enslavement by less scrupulous Spanish and Brazilian slave traders.[85] For the indigenous, the chances of survival improved by belonging to the missions and becoming Catholic.

Objections to conversion among the indigenous people softened as the local church appropriated indigenous sacred practices and sites, an example of syncretism.[86] Juan Diego Cuauhtlatoatzin, a native Mexican, claimed in 1531 to see the Virgin Mary at the base of the hill regarded as the sacred place of worship for Tonantzin, the Aztec mother goddess. A wave of as many as eight million indigenous people converted in the seven years following the vision of the Virgin of Guadalupe. Similar sightings were reported throughout the conquered territories, such as in Bolivia where the Virgin of Copacabana was sighted near the Isla Del Sol on Lake Titicaca, a sacred pagan worship site.[87]

The "conversion" of the indigenous people was so effective that today, even after centuries, 90 percent of Central and South Americans are Catholic. A similar pattern of conversion occurred in many of the European colonized countries of Africa and the Philippines.

Intolerance of the Reformation

The leading Reformers of the sixteenth century, including Zwingli, Martin Luther, and John Calvin were well aware of the fate of earlier Reformers and their followers. The likes of Peter Waldo and the Waldensians in Italy, John Wycliffe and the Lollards in England, and

Jan Hus and the Hussites in Czechoslovakia had all suffered the harsh persecution and suppression described in Chapter 7: The Reformation. Punishment and even death were not abstract risks facing the Reformers. Calvin fled France to Basel, Switzerland, in 1535 to escape the death that other French Reformers experienced. After posting his controversial Ninety-Five Theses in 1517, Luther was deemed a heretic, excommunicated, and sentenced in absentia by the Holy Roman emperor to an unspecified punishment—the likely nature of which was demonstrated by the burning at the stake of two of Luther's followers in Antwerp in 1523.[88] The prominent Reformers of the sixteenth century would surely have met the same fate as their predecessors had it not been for benevolent sovereigns who had gained a degree of political independence from the pope and the Holy Roman emperor.

In light of this persecution, we might assume that the protestors of Catholicism would have translated their own precarious position into an ardent advocacy for freedom of conscience and religion. This was not so. The Reformers aligned themselves with state powers as readily as Catholics had done before them and generally proved to be equally as intolerant to religious freedom. They challenged and reformed many doctrines, but the belief that it was the duty of divinely appointed nobility to protect and propagate the kingdom of God by coercive force was not one of them.

Zwingli and the Persecution of the Anabaptists

Zwingli's first challenge to the liturgy of the Catholic Church was in 1522, when he encouraged believers to eat sausage on Lent, an act prohibited by Catholic practice, but one that was not expressly prohibited in the Bible.[89] Zürich found itself arbitrating between the Catholic Church and Zwingli and sided with Zwingli, creating an alliance that was mutually beneficial. The city provided protection to the "heretical" Zwingli, and in turn Zwingli gave Zürich the theological justification to distance itself from the authority and taxation of the Catholic Church.[90] Religious reform catalyzed the alliance, but there was a delicate balance to maintain, and not all reforms were welcome. There was no place in this alliance for radical views that challenged Zürich's civic leaders or Zwingli. We learned in the section "Radical Reformation and the Anabaptists," part of Chapter 7: The Reformation, about the group called the Swiss Brethren that publicly challenged Zwingli's alliance with the state. The disagreement quickly became a civil affair.[91] In January of 1525, the city council sided with Zwingli against the dissenting Swiss Brethren and ordered them to desist their public opposition to Zwingli. In defiance, the group, which came to be known as the Anabaptists,[92] gathered and rebaptized themselves as adults. In response, the city council passed an edict in 1526 specifically prohibiting rebaptism with the punishment of death by drowning.

Felix Manz, a former close collaborator of Zwingli's and one of the original Swiss Brethren, defied the edict and continued to preach adult baptism. He was arrested, tried, and executed by drowning in 1527.[93] Given Zwingli's influence on Zürich's council, Zwingli was undoubtedly complicit in the execution of Manz and the subsequent expulsion of the Anabaptists from Zürich. The Anabaptists were successively expelled from city after city.[94] Many were arrested and executed. Michael Sattler, along with his wife and several other Anabaptists, was arrested in Germany in 1527. He was tried and sentenced to death for heresy, but before execution by fire, his tongue was cut out and red-hot tongs were used to tear pieces of flesh from his body. His wife was then drowned.[95] Balthasar Hubmaier and his wife were seized in Moravia and tried and convicted in Vienna in 1528. He was executed by burning, and then three days later, with a stone tied around her neck, his wife was thrown into the River Danube.[96] George Blaurock had been beaten and expelled from Zürich on the day Felix Manz was burned. He was later arrested in Innsbruck and burned at the stake in 1529.[97] Anabaptists, who viewed any alliance with secular power as unholy, were friendless. Consequently, over the ensuing centuries Anabaptists were persecuted by all, Protestants and Catholics alike.

Calvin's Persecution of Servetus

John Calvin was born in France and during his studies in law and philosophy found himself convinced by Reformation-minded thinkers such as the influential Nicolas Cop, rector of the university that Calvin attended. Calvin saw firsthand the consequences of religious protest. In 1534, many protesting Reformers around him were jailed, and twenty-four were executed. To escape the same fate, he fled to

Switzerland in early 1535.[98] A short time later, in 1536, he published the first edition of his treatise on faith, called *Institutio Christianae Religionis* (*Institutes of the Christian Religion*). It covered many things, including his opposition to the tyrannical oppression of conscience by the church, and extolled kindness and persuasion against the excommunicated. During this time, he wrote to the king of Denmark, "Wisdom is driven from among us, and the holy harmony of Christ's kingdom is compromised, *when violence is pressed into the service of religion.*"[99] These tolerant sentiments faded as he gained authority in a close relationship with Geneva's civil authorities.

Calvin ended up in Geneva and was commissioned by the Geneva city council to organize and govern a Reformed church. The confession of faith that he co-authored with William Farel (1489–1565) included rules that were comprehensive, strict, and pious to the extreme: entertainment was forbidden, church attendance was required, the nature of clothing was specified, and so on.[100] To many, it appeared as if Calvin had succeeded in creating the prophesied holy city, the New Jerusalem.[101] However, strict piety came at the cost of personal liberty. As time progressed, Calvin consolidated power as president of the Consistory of Pastors and dominated Geneva. Although an ecclesiastic and not a civil ruler, he bent unyielding secular rulers to his will by withholding the Lord's Supper from them, an act equal to excommunication.[102] His attitudes about tolerance evolved, and the punishments he promoted became increasingly severe.

Perhaps no example demonstrates this better than that of Michael Servetus. Servetus, a native Spaniard, was Calvin's fellow student at the university in Paris. Both had bright minds and passionate theological curiosity, and they freely exchanged theological speculation with the trusting confidence of schoolmates.[103] After the persecutions in Paris that led to Calvin's exile, Servetus stayed in France, taking the pseudonym Villaneuve or Villanovanus—the name of his birthplace. He became a scholar and doctor in Vienne, France.

Servetus, now settled with a promising profession underway, reengaged Calvin in 1546 through a mutual friend, a closet Protestant and bookseller in Lyon named Jean Frellon. Servetus approached Calvin with the same trust and expectation for open theological debate as they had shared as schoolmates. In letters to Calvin, he floated ideas in the form of questions and included excerpts from a book he was working on as answers. Initially, Calvin responded in good faith, but he quickly grew exasperated at Servetus's theology. To cut short the exchange, Calvin sent Servetus a copy of his own work, *Institutes of the Christian Religion*. Apparently, Servetus did not understand that this was Calvin's final word. Rather, in the spirit of theological debate, Servetus marked it up with critical commentary and sent it back. Calvin was so offended that he angrily terminated the correspondence. He revealed the depth of his animosity toward Servetus to his longtime mentor and collaborator William Farel:

> Servetus lately wrote to me and coupled with his letter a long volume of his delirious fancies, with the Thrasonic[104] boast, that I should see something astonishing and unheard of. He proposes to come hither, if it be agreeable to me. But I am unwilling to pledge my word for his safety, for if he shall come, *I shall never permit him to depart alive, provided my authority be of any avail.*[105]

Calvin didn't stop there. He exposed Servetus as a heretic in a 1550 tract called *De Scandalis*, in which he referred to the heretic Villanovanus.[106] The tract did not immediately trigger an Inquisition of Servetus in France where Servetus was living. It was a warning shot, but it did not dissuade Servetus from publishing his work. In 1553, he proceeded to publish under the name Villanovanus his book, *Christianismi Restitutio (The Restoration of Christianity)*. In the book, Servetus argued for the rejection of the Nicaean doctrine of the Trinity, the concept of predestination, and the practice of infant baptism. His book put him at odds with both Catholic and prevailing Protestant doctrine, including Calvinism.

Frellon the bookseller sent a complimentary predistribution copy to Calvin. This gave Calvin time to exert his influence to block the distribution of the one thousand copies that had been produced. More insidiously, Calvin arranged to have the first eight pages of the book sent to the Inquisition in France along with the true identity of the author.[107] As intended, the Inquisition put Servetus on trial. The evidence against Servetus was supplied by Calvin and included Servetus's own letters to Calvin and Servetus's published but undistributed book received from Frellon.[108] This was the epitome of hypocrisy. Calvin, the "heretical" Protestant, protected by Geneva from the authority of the Catholic Church, used the Catholic Church's Inquisition to condemn Servetus. Calvin was so certain of his own doctrine in *Institutio* that he considered Servetus's ideas heretical.

Servetus determined to escape the Inquisition and go to the kingdom of Naples. Although his destination was to the south, he undoubtedly believed that traveling through Catholic France was not wise and thus opted for the closest safe exit from France—a route largely through Switzerland. He stopped in Geneva, intending to travel by boat to Zürich. There, he made the mistake of attending a church service where he was recognized and, under Calvin's orders, was arrested and tried. By some indications, Geneva did not relish its role as prosecutor of Servetus, as evidenced by its appeal for consensus from the other Swiss cantons. Calvin wrote to his counterparts in the other Swiss cantons to enlist their support for a conviction of heresy. In the end, Servetus was judged guilty of heresy, condemned to die, and burned alive in late 1553.[109] Fellow Reformers, including Bullinger in Zürich and Luther's protégé Melanchthon, wrote to Calvin after the event affirming their support for the use of capital punishment to quell Servetus's heresy.[110] Calvin later justified his actions in his work *Defensio orthodoxae fidei* (*Defense of Orthodox Faith*), in which he justified the use of capital punishment for heretics:

> Thus, there is no doubt that by the mandate of God, it is the duty of the pious and holy magistrates to defend the kingdom of Christ. . . . Therefore [Paul] teaches that they are appointed not only for the duty of protecting piety by law, but also to promote it. Hence the sword is placed in their hands in order that they can defend the true doctrine. And by performing their duties they should not allow under threat of punishment the existence of impiety and corruption of the doctrine. May the ignorant and thoughtless men cease to negate that punishment should be exacted on the corruptors of the true doctrine if they do not want openly to oppose the will of God.[111]

Calvin's arguments mirror those of the Catholics in their brutal persecution of heretics. In a cruel twist, soon after Calvin wrote his defense, Calvinists in France, known as Huguenots, came under intense persecution. Between 1562 and 1598, millions in France died in a religious war between Catholics and Huguenots.[112] In one massacre alone in 1572, known as the St. Bartholomew's Day Massacre, an estimated ten thousand Huguenots were slaughtered. Protestantism was proclaimed illegal in France in 1685, and most of the remaining Huguenots dispersed to Protestant-friendly countries, leaving France a predominantly Catholic country.[113]

Luther and the Peasants' War

Late in 1523, Luther was a fugitive in hiding. He had been pronounced a heretic in 1521 and was to face punishment if captured. He had seen his likely fate when, in 1523, two of his followers were burned at the stake in Antwerp.[114] During this tenuous time, Luther argued for tolerance in his work *On Secular Authority*:

> Each must decide at his own peril what he is to believe, and must see to it that he believes rightly. Other people cannot go to heaven or hell on my behalf, or open or close the gates to either for me. And just as little can they believe or not believe on my behalf, or force my faith or unbelief. How he believes is a matter for each individual's conscience, and this does not diminish (the authority of) secular governments. They ought to content themselves with attending to their own business, and allow people to believe what they can, and what they want, and they must use no coercion in this matter against anyone.[115]

However, Luther's position on tolerance was soon challenged in the face of civil disobedience. Luther's position hardened in a dispute that, like Calvin's with Servetus, became surprisingly personal. A young Reformer named Thomas Müntzer engaged in far-reaching theological discussions with Luther in Wittenberg in 1517 and earned Luther's trust and affection to the point that Luther recommended him for a post. The affection was mutual, and during this early time Müntzer expressed his affection to Luther by closing a letter, "Thomas Müntzer, whom you brought to birth by the gospel."[116] However, their paths diverged. Unlike the highly public Luther, who drew the attention of the pope and the Holy Roman emperor and found refuge in the protection of German princes, Müntzer roamed among many different Reform communities. Over time, he developed a more apocalyptic, mystic, and radical view than Luther held. By 1522, he wrote to Luther's protégé Melanchthon criticizing Luther for "flattering" the princes and cozying up to them.[117]

Müntzer's ministry became increasingly threatening to the princes, forcing Luther to take sides. Luther and Müntzer began attacking each other via the pen. Luther condemned Müntzer in a letter to the princes of Saxony in a work entitled *Letter to the Princes of Saxony about the Rebellious Spirit*—the rebel referred to was Müntzer, who was teaching at Allstedt. Müntzer responded with harsh criticism of Luther in *A Highly Provoked Vindication and Refutation of the unspiritual soft-living flesh [Luther] in Wittenberg* and in another tract, *A Manifest Exposé of False Faith*.[118] Müntzer gravitated toward the rebellious actions of Reformers in southwest Germany who mixed doctrines of apocalyptic theology with political revolution. He soon found himself leading a faction of a peasant uprising that swept Germany in 1524. He met his death in a rout of his peasant "army."[119]

Luther took a stand against Müntzer and radical Reformers by writing a tract, *Against the Murderous, Thieving Hordes of Peasants*.[120] It is not clear whether Luther's tract changed the outcome of the German Peasants' War; however, it was symbolically profound. Luther placed himself on the side of the state, whose armies decimated peasants with a death toll estimated at over one hundred thousand.[121] To be clear, Luther was in a difficult position, and there is a conceptual difference between heresy that affects only conscience and heresy that affects political stability. After the ugly German Peasants' War, Luther's position was confusing and contradictory. In a tone favoring restraint, he wrote that excommunication was the only remedy of the church in cases of heresy and that "ministers ought not to mingle secular punishments with this ecclesiastical punishment, or excommunication."[122] But, confusingly, he wrote of the need for compulsion: "Although we neither can nor should force anyone into the faith, yet the masses must be held and driven to it in order that they may know what is right or wrong."[123]

Over the ensuing decades, Lutheran princes battled the Holy Roman emperor over religion and power. They reached a tenuous peace through the Peace of Augsburg in 1555. The compromise was a principle called *cuius regio, eius religio*, which in Latin means "whose realm, his religion."[124] The prince or king could decide the religion of his people and enforce adherence to it. Importantly, the agreement sanctioned only Catholicism and Lutheranism. It would take another hundred years and one of the most devastating religious wars in history, the Thirty Years' War, for Calvinism to be officially sanctioned in the Peace of Westphalia, signed in 1648.[125] This treaty preserved *cuius regio, eius religio* but also provided for limited religious pluralism. Those not belonging to the ruler's religion could practice one of the two other approved religions during limited times of the day. Other denominations, such as Anabaptism, were still considered heretical and the adherents were subject to death.[126] As transformative as it was, the Peace of Westphalia was not the separation of church and state and not the birth of religious toleration.

The Church of England and the Puritans

Coerced unity was not unique to continental Reformers. Intolerance and coercion were present in the development of Protestantism in England, as evidenced in the section "Religious Turbulence in England," in Chapter 7: The Reformation. In England's turbulent religious history, the oppressed become the oppressor, and vice versa. Following are a few additional poignant examples.

After Henry VIII broke ties with the papacy and the Catholic Church, John Fisher, a prominent Catholic bishop in England, and Thomas More, a senior government official holding the office of lord chancellor, refused to recognize Henry as the head of the church in England. Nor would they recognize his marriage to Anne Boleyn. Consequently, Henry had John Fisher and Thomas More beheaded in June 1535. Thomas More's execution for religion was an echo of the persecution he had dealt out as chancellor. He had been like Saul of Tarsus, zealously persecuting those who even studied Lutheran literature or who bought or distributed the recently translated Tyndale Bible. With his blessing, six people had been burned at the stake for heresy,[127] and he was known to personally participate in the punishment of heretics.[128]

After Henry VIII's death in 1547, England swung between Protestantism and Catholicism and then between different forms of Protestantism, like a weather vane rotating in the changing wind. The common characteristic of each transition was intolerance, persecution, and repression of the denominations not in power. We learned about Mary's execution of 280 leading Protestants in 1555 and the exile of many more. We learned how her successors forced compliance with the Anglican *Book of Common Prayer* using civil law in the Act of Uniformity of 1559 and later the Act of Uniformity of 1662.

The Puritans emerged as dissenters. For the most part, they were oppressed and had to practice religion covertly to avoid the severe persecution from the Church of England and the state.[129] When a profit-making venture named the New England Company for a Plantation in Massachusetts established the Massachusetts Bay Colony in 1627, tens of thousands of Puritans sought refuge by emigrating to the new colony.[130] In the Massachusetts colony, Puritans dominated every aspect of religion and government, effectively creating a theocracy. Sadly, the Puritans were every bit as intolerant of other denominations as the Church of England had been toward them. Consider three examples:

- Roger Williams came to Boston in 1631 to escape the intense persecution in England directed at the "separatist" Puritans.[131] He considered himself a Puritan, but he also firmly believed in and advocated for religious tolerance and the separation of church and state. He soon found that these positions put him at odds with the colony, and he was banished because of them.[132]

- Anne Hutchinson of the Massachusetts Colony believed in the Augustinian doctrine of "free grace," which was a core tenant of continental Protestantism. She held house meetings and persuaded many of the doctrine. The Puritans had themselves originated from Calvinism, but they had become maniacally focused on piety—the letter of the law—rather than the Augustinian doctrines of grace that undergirded it. The Puritans viewed the doctrine of free grace as the road to lawlessness and thus as an antinomian heresy.[133] They banished Anne Hutchinson and her followers in 1637.[134]

- The Quakers originated in England within the same milieu as the Puritans; however, they were a very different denomination.[135] They began evangelizing in the Massachusetts Colony around 1656.[136] The Puritan-led colony passed laws that banned Quakers from Massachusetts, threatening harsh corporal punishment if they remained. Many Quakers defied the ban, leading the Puritans to cut off the right ears of two Quakers in 1658.[137] But the Quakers continued evangelizing. The Puritans expanded the penalties to include capital punishment.[138] In 1659, three Quakers were sentenced to death for defying the ban. The two men in the group were hanged, but the third was a woman who was given a reprieve at the last possible moment. The spared woman, Mary Dyer (1611–1660), was not satisfied to have her life spared while the unjust laws persisted. She returned to Boston in the spring of the next year in defiance. She was promptly arrested and summarily hanged. Persecution, including horrific punishment of the Quakers, persisted among the Puritans even after the reinstated English King Charles II banned executions in 1661.[139]

Counterfeit Unity Today

The snapshots in this chapter of coercion, persecution, and intolerance should seem completely incompatible with our modern expectations of religious liberty. We might be tempted to dismiss this troubling history as a byproduct of the unenlightened and barbaric past. Indeed, Christians are not executing other Christians today for heresy. However, if we shift our focus from outcomes to beliefs that motivated those outcomes, it becomes clear that these stories are not just historical. The beliefs that motivated coercion, persecution, and intolerance are alive and well. Even today, some Christians leverage state authority to enforce Christian beliefs, and many Christians readily condemn others for heresy. Thus, there are cautionary insights we can learn and *apply* from the snapshots in this chapter.

Certainty of Being Right

One belief that motivated persecution, intolerance, and coercion by each alliance of church and state was the certainty of being "in the right." The certainty of "rightness" manifests itself today as the presumption of authority to define what is Christian and what is not. Without secular enforcement, these definitions do not translate into criminal punishment as they did in past centuries, but these definitions still cause harm in that they stigmatize and discriminate. We'll review three "true-Christian" litmus tests that are currently applied to various subgroups of Christians.

Trinitarian. When Michael Servetus published his book, he challenged Calvin's notions of predestination; however, this was not the inflammatory doctrine that led to his death. After all, Lutherans coexisted with Calvinists during that time and disagreed with Calvin about many aspects of predestination. Servetus's unforgiveable heresy was his rejection of the Nicene Creed and its doctrine of the Trinity. Although the preeminent Reformers rejected canon law coming from ecumenical councils, they did not challenge the bedrock doctrine of the Trinity established by the First Council of Nicaea. They would not or could not tolerate another Reformer challenging this doctrine. Consequently, well over 90 percent of today's Christians accept the Trinitarian doctrine of the Nicene Creed. Those that don't, non-Trinitarian denominations such as The Church of Jesus Christ of Latter-day Saints, Jehovah's Witnesses, Unitarians, Iglesia Ni Cristo, and others are viewed, like Calvin did Servetus, as heretics and non-Christians.

Faith Alone. Because of their Protestant heritage, evangelicals believe that salvation comes solely through faith and that denominations that require the "works" of sacraments for salvation, or that view salvation as a reward for obedience, are not Christian. According to this definition, about 80 percent of believers in Christ would not be true Christians. This is reflected in a Q&A response written by the founder of the Christian Apologetics and Research Ministry relative to whether Roman Catholics are Christian. Keep in mind that close to 50 percent of all believers in Christ are Roman Catholic:

> Notice that justification by faith alone is denied [in the Catholic canon established in Council of Trent], and heaven is the reward for doing good works. This is the problem. The RCC [Roman Catholic Canon] does not teach the biblical doctrine of justification by faith. It teaches justification by faith and works. . . . If a Roman Catholic believes in the official Roman Catholic teaching on salvation, then he is not a Christian since the official RCC position is contrary to Scripture.[140]

Cults. Pope Innocent III established the Inquisition and sanctioned bloodshed to eradicate a secretive heretical group known as the Cathars. Today, the Cathars would be considered a cult. The term *cult* may bring to mind visionary and apocalyptic "prophets" like David Koresh and the Branch Davidians, Jim Jones and the Peoples Temple of Jonestown, or Marshall Applewhite and the Heaven's Gate group.[141] However, the term is applied to much more mainstream denominations based on a broad definition usually offered by evangelicals. Search the Web for "what is the definition of a cult of Christianity" and you will find varying answers. Here's a sampling from multiple Christian websites (note that no single site used every example in the list):

- Cults are exclusive. They may say, "We're the only ones with the truth; everyone else is wrong, and if you leave our group your salvation is in danger."
- Cults are secretive. Certain teachings are not available to outsiders or they're presented only to certain members, sometimes after the members take vows of confidentiality.
- Cults are authoritarian. A human leader expects total loyalty and unquestioned obedience.
- Cults change the Bible or use sacred writings in addition to the Bible.
- Cults are groups that do not believe salvation is by faith alone.
- A cult is any group that deviates from the orthodox teachings of the historic Christian faith being derived from the Bible and confirmed through the ancient ecumenical creeds.

Take for example The Church of Jesus Christ of Latter-day Saints, often called the Mormon Church. It is often mentioned as a cult by evangelicals: the church believes it is the restored true church of Christ; it has nonpublic buildings called temples, in which salvific rituals are performed; it has an authoritative central figure considered to be a prophet; it believes in nonbiblical scripture; it believes that saving ordinances and obedience to commandments are necessary to qualify for grace; and it rejects the Trinitarian Nicene Creed. The tags of *cult* and *non-Christian* understandably make The Church of Jesus Christ of Latter-day Saints defensive, but this church is far from alone in meeting many or most of the "cult" criteria. In fact, about 65 percent of believers in Christ around the world belong to denominations that fail the "cult" test, including the Roman Catholic, Eastern Orthodox, Oriental Orthodox, and Anglican churches. All these denominations believe that their church is the embodiment of the one true catholic church established by Christ. Each has a priesthood hierarchy with a pope, patriarch, or archbishop, respectively, at their head. They accept as authoritative, on par with the words of scripture, the conclusions of church councils and the edicts of their leaders. They practice sacred sacraments and believe them to be necessary for salvation. Importantly, these patterns that are used as indicators of a cult are patterns common to God's people of the Old Testament, the Israelites. Clearly, the validity of criteria that would render the majority of today's Christians and ancient Israel as a cult must be questioned.

Litmus tests that judge the majority of believers in Christ to be non-Christian may seem demonstrably absurd, but they cannot be lightly dismissed. They are passionately taught over pulpits and divide Christians today. These litmus tests are clear evidence of the conviction of "rightness" held by many Christians. In the context of this chapter, we can see the parallels between the certainty of "rightness" that justified outright physical coercion in the past and the certainty of "rightness" that fosters Christian stigmatization and discrimination today.

Enforcing Moral Law

Since the time of Constantine, elements of Christian moral law have been enforced by state power. Without question, there is a legitimate secular interest in citizens obeying certain moral laws. As examples, "thou shalt not steal," "thou shalt not kill," and "thou shalt not bear false witness" are Judeo-Christian commandments, but they are also essential to a civil society. But what about religious laws with dubious secular purpose? What about the commandment to "keep the Sabbath day holy"? Or, what about blasphemy of the Christian God? What about laws constraining private sexual relations including polygamy, adultery, and sodomy? What secular benefits warrant the state enforcing these and similar Christian commandments?

We may shrug off the strict enforcement of moral conduct in Calvin's Geneva or in Puritan Boston as a thing of the past. But the central question of whether the state has an interest in enforcing moral law persists to this day. Let's look at several examples, including Sabbath worship, sexual relations, and school prayer.

Sabbath Day. Constantine was the first to mandate Sunday restrictions: no celebrations, circuses, or theatrical productions could take place (except a celebration of the emperor's birthday); all court actions, legal disputes, and debt collection was suspended on Sunday; those who skipped holy rituals on Sundays were to be regarded as sacrilegious.[142] Fast-forward to the English colonies in North America where church worship on Sundays was widely prescribed by law. Citizens were routinely fined and even whipped for missing church on Sunday.[143]

Fast-forward again to the Protestant religious fervor of the Second Great Awakening in the early nineteenth century. Protestant groups successfully lobbied for Sunday Sabbath laws, nicknamed "blue laws."[144] These laws varied from state to state but broadly restricted the sale of many things on Sundays, including alcohol, groceries, housewares, durable goods, and even automobiles. For the majority of Christians, these laws aligned with their religious practices and in that sense were unobjectionable. But consider the burden these laws placed on Seventh-day Adventists, Seventh Day Baptists, and Jews, who observe the Sabbath on Saturday.

Various court cases were fought relative to the Sunday laws. Interestingly, the Supreme Court of the United States did not strike down Sunday closure laws in a 1961 case, arguing that even though Sunday laws originated to foster Christian worship, the state had an interest in fostering a day of rest among its citizens.[145] Nevertheless, as

Sunday evolved into a day for sports, recreation, and shopping, state legislatures have whittled away and softened blue laws. Indiana, one of the final holdouts, didn't repeal its prohibition on the sale of alcohol on Sundays until early 2018.[146]

Sexual Relations. Nathaniel Hawthorne's *The Scarlet Letter* tells of the public consequences in Puritan New England America for sexual sin. Hester Prynne, an unwed young woman, became pregnant and was thus publicly shamed, forced to wear a scarlet "A." The notion that the government has a role in enforcing sexual propriety found its way into the laws of virtually every state in America. Adultery was criminalized in most states until the mid-twentieth century. As of the writing of this book in 2018, twenty U.S. states still criminalize adultery. Idaho, Oklahoma, Michigan, and Wisconsin still consider it a felony.[147]

Similarly, sodomy, including homosexual relations, was criminal in most states until the landmark Supreme Court case of *Lawrence v. Texas* in 2003, a ruling that decriminalized homosexual relations between consenting adults.[148]

Polygamy was outlawed by the United States Congress in the Morrill Anti-Bigamy Act in 1862, in response to the adoption of the practice by The Church of Jesus Christ of Latter-day Saints. The Supreme Court upheld the law in the 1878 decision of *Reynolds v. United States*, leading the church to stop the practice in 1890.

Contraceptives were often prohibited by state law. Married couples did not have the right to use contraceptives until that right was established in the Supreme Court ruling *Griswold v. Connecticut* in 1965.[149]

School Prayer. Up through the middle of the twentieth century, it was common in the Unites States for public school children to start each day with a prayer or recitation of Bible verses. Understandably, non-Christians including Jews and atheists found the practice objectionable. Even Catholics objected to the use of the Protestant King James Version of the Bible. A variety of lawsuits were adjudicated at the state level, and then in the early 1960s the United States Supreme Court weighed in. Steven Engel, a Jew, brought a lawsuit against the state of New York, attempting to stop the recitation of the state's Regents' prayer in the public schools. The Supreme Court ruled in *Engel v. Vitale* in 1962 that recitation of the state-sponsored prayer in public schools was unlawful.[150] Another landmark case soon followed. Two lawsuits, one brought by a Unitarian Universalist and the other brought by an atheist, challenged the required reading of the Bible and the recitation of the Lord's Prayer at their children's local schools.

The cases were joined before the Supreme Court in 1963, and in *Abington School District v. Schempp* the Court ruled that prayer and Bible reading in public schools were unlawful.[151] Many Christians strongly disagreed with the ruling. Billy Graham, for example, suggested that it was not right that the wishes of 80 percent of the country were ignored.[152] One of the most vocal opponents of the ruling was Jerry Falwell, who founded the Moral Majority in 1979. The group helped to elect conservative Ronald Reagan over the incumbent evangelical Christian Jimmy Carter, with the hope that Reagan would support their socially conservative agenda. In general, they were disappointed by Reagan's lack of interest in social issues, but the president did appoint the executive director of the Moral Majority as special assistant to the secretary of education in the Department of Education and supported a constitutional amendment reintroducing school prayer in 1982. However, in 1984, in spite of the majority of the Republican Senate voting in favor of the amendment, it failed to garner the required sixty votes to pass. Importantly, mainline Protestant denominations, including Methodists, Presbyterians, Episcopalians, and Lutherans joined Unitarian and Jewish groups in opposition to the amendment.[153]

These three examples are but illustrations of the very real connections between Christian belief and secular laws. These connections can range from the geopolitical, as in the support for Israel,[154] to the extremely personal, as in divorce laws[155] and the treatment of LGBTQ individuals.[156] Clearly, there is a balance that must be navigated between enforcing a moral code required for civility and enforcing a moral code for purposes of morality.

It may seem counterintuitive that a book dedicated to explaining the splintering of Christianity into denominations would have a chapter about the opposite—the attempt to restrict splintering. But these topics go hand-in-hand. Just as splintered Christianity is far from Jesus's aspired unity, the enforcement of counterfeit unity is far from Jesus's *invitation* to follow Him.

Hopefully, this chapter has given us some wisdom in the cautionary lessons of history when church and state are conjoined. However, it has left us with many difficult and nuanced questions: Surely, Jesus's aspiration for unity was not an idle wish, so what are the circumstances under which unity should be achieved? What role, if any, do governments play in preparing for Jesus's return? Is acceptance of a robust separation of church and state tantamount to endorsing the acceleration of general moral decay in society? These questions are for each of us to ponder so we can reach personal conclusions.

Finally, we would be wise to consider the history presented in this chapter when considering the size and dominance of major denominations of Christianity. The common wisdom that the majority is usually right is irrelevant when denomination size is in part the legacy of coercion.

Notes

---

[1] Matthew 11:28.

[2] Matthew 16:24.

[3] John 16:26.

[4] Philippians 1:27; 2:2–3, 12–13.

[5] See Leviticus 20:9.

[6] See Leviticus 20:10.

[7] See Leviticus 20:13.

[8] See Leviticus 20:15.

[9] The punishments within the Law of Moses first sought to restore what was lost to the victim by making "satisfaction." If that was not possible, the perpetrator would pay either through banishment from the community ("cut off from the people") or by death. Although the death penalty was prescribed, it was the ultimate, not the first, punishment.

[10] Exodus 32:27–28.

[11] Numbers 16:1–35.

[12] Numbers 21:4–9.

[13] Numbers 25:1–5.

[14] See Genesis 5:24 and Hebrews 11:5.

[15] See Exodus 33:11.

[16] Exodus 19:5–6, 8, 10–11 (emphasis added).

[17] Deuteronomy 23:14 (emphasis added).

[18] Isaiah 4:3–4.

[19] Isaiah 52:1.

[20] See Isaiah 47:13–14, Malachi 4:1, and Revelations 17:16.

[21] Matthew 13:24–30: "From whence then hath it tares? He said unto them, An enemy hath done this. . . . In the time of harvest I will say to the reapers, Gather ye together first the tares, and bind them in bundles to burn them."

[22] Luke 14:16–24: "So that servant came, and shewed his lord these things [rejection by the invited]. Then the master of the house being angry said to his servant, Go out quickly into the streets and lanes of the city, and bring in hither the poor, and the maimed, and the halt, and the blind. And the servant said, Lord, it is done as thou hast commanded, and yet there is room. And the lord said unto the servant, Go out into the highways and hedges, and *compel them to come in*, that my house may be filled."

[23] Moss 2010.

[24] Moss 2010.

[25] Blötzer 1910. (emphasis added).

[26] West, Imperial Laws and Edicts 2008.

[27] The Donatists are mentioned most frequently in the edicts followed by the Manicheans. Many other Christian offshoots are mentioned, including Eunomians, Phontinians, Montanists, Priscillianists, Encratitans, Saccoforians, Hydroparastantans, Macedonians, Pneumatomachi, Apotactites, Saccophori, Encratites, Apollinarians, Luciferians, Phrygians, Pelagians, Novatians, Sabbatians, Valentinians, Marcionites, Borborians, Messalians, Euchitans or Enthusiasts, Audians, Tascodrogitans, Paulianists, and Marcellians West, Imperial Laws and Edicts 2008.

28 Capital punishment was possible for carrying out pagan sacrifice or ritual (not just for being a pagan), disturbing the peace by conducting an unlawful assembly, refusal to destroy heretical books, outrage against a bishop, and attempting to convert a Christian to a heretical sect, pagan, or Jewish religion West, Imperial Laws and Edicts 2008.

29 Wikipedia, Priscillian 2018.

30 Wikipedia, Priscillian 2018.

31 Blötzer 1910.

32 P. Schaff, History of the Christian Church, Volume V: The Middle Ages. A.D. 1049-1294 1910, 394.

33 Lippold 2016.

34 Wikipedia, Edict of Thesselonica 2018. (emphasis added).

35 Lippold 2016.

36 Blötzer 1910.

37 Wikipedia, Vladimir the Great 2018.

38 Wikipedia, Forced Conversion 2018.

39 Wikipedia, Lombards 2018.

40 Wikipedia, Saxon Wars 2018.

41 Wikipedia, Charlemagne 2018.

42 Wikipedia, Charlemagne 2018.

43 Wikipedia, Saxon Wars 2018.

44 Wikipedia, Saxon Wars 2018. (emphasis added).

45 Madsen, Dickson and Others 2018.

46 Madsen, Dickson and Others 2018.

47 Madsen, Dickson and Others 2018.

48 Madsen, Dickson and Others 2018.

49 See the section Gnosticism in Chapter 5: The Age of Heresy

50 Wikipedia, Consolamentum 2018.

51 Wikipedia, Catharism 2018.

52 Wikipedia, Catharism 2018.

53 Wikipedia, Catharism 2018.

54 Peters and Hamilton 2016.

55 Blanchard 1844, 78.

56 Blötzer 1910.

57 Blanchard 1844, 78.

58 Blötzer 1910.

59 Peters and Hamilton 2016.

60 Blötzer 1910.

61 Wikipedia, Catharism 2018.

62 Wikipedia, Waldensians 2018.

63 Blötzer 1910. It was little solace to the deceased that the inquisitor was himself later tried and imprisoned for his harsh tactics.

64 P. Schaff, History of the Christian Church, Volume VI: The Middle Ages. A.D. 1294-1517 1910, 419.

65 P. Schaff, History of the Christian Church, Volume VI: The Middle Ages. A.D. 1294-1517 1910, 419.

66 P. Schaff, History of the Christian Church, Volume VI: The Middle Ages. A.D. 1294-1517 1910, 420-421.

67 Russell and Lewis 2016.

68 Russell and Lewis 2016.

69 Ryan 2017.

70 Ryan 2017.

71 Wikipedia, Tomas de Torquemada 2018.

72 P. Schaff, History of the Christian Church, Volume VI: The Middle Ages. A.D. 1294-1517 1910, 439.

73 Blanchard 1844, 79.

74 Ryan 2017.

75 Wikipedia, Alhambra Decree 2018.

76 The lower estimates come from Wikipedia, Alhambra Decree 2018. The higher estimates from Ryan 2017.

77 Ryan 2017.

78 Wikipedia, Pope Alexander VI 2018.

79 Christianity: Christianity in Latin America 1987.

80 Christianity: Christianity in Latin America 1987.

81 Wikipedia, Pope Alexander VI 2018.

82 Wikipedia, Economienda 2018.

83 Wikipedia, Economienda 2018.

84 Wikipedia, Jesuit Reduction 2018.

85 Wikipedia, Jesuit Reduction 2018.

86 Syncretism occurs when one religion adopts elements of another into its own, rendering it more palatable to those of the other religion.

87 Wikipedia, Catholic Church in Latin America 2018.

88 Wikipedia 2018.

89 Wikipedia, Affair of Sausages 2017.

90 Wikipedia, Huldrych Zwingli 2017.

91 Wikipedia, Swiss Brethren 2018.

92 Anabaptist means baptized again.

93 Wikipedia, Swiss Brethren 2018.

94 Editors, Anabaptist 2016.

95 Wikipedia, Swiss Brethren 2018.

96 Wikipedia, Balthasar Hubmaier 2018.

97 Wikipedia, Swiss Brethren 2018.

98 Wikipedia, John Calvin 2018.

99 Hillar 2010, 25. (emphasis added).

100 Wikipedia, John Calvin 2018.

101 See Revelations 3:12 and Revelations 21:2.

102 Hillar 2010, 21.

103 Calvin and Servetus 1847, 5.

104 Meaning bragging or boastful.

105 Hillar 2010, 12. (emphasis added).

106 Hillar 2010, 12.

107 Hillar 2010, 12.

108 Hillar 2010, 17.

109 Hillar 2010, 34-36.

110 Hillar 2010, 44.

111 Hillar 2010, 45-46.

112 Wikipedia 2018.

113 Wikipedia 2018.

114 Wikipedia 2018.

115 Grell 1996, 4.

116 Wikipedia, Thomas Müntzer 2018.

117 Wikipedia, Thomas Müntzer 2018.

118 Wikipedia, Thomas Müntzer 2018.

119 Wikipedia, Thomas Müntzer 2018.

120 Wikipedia, German Peasants War 2018.

121 Wikipedia, German Peasants War 2018.

122 Smalcald Articles Part III, Article IX. Of Excommunication. Written in 1537. Luther, Smalcald Articles 1537.

123 The Protestant Inquisition n.d.

124 Wikipedia, Cuius regio, eius religio 2017.

125 Wikipedia 2018.

126 Wikipedia 2018.

127 Ackroyd 1999, 299-306.

128 Marius 1999, 404.

129 This is a simplification. See Religious Turbulence in England in Chapter 7: The Reformation for a more complete history.

130 Wikipedia, Massachusetts Bay_Colony 2018.

131 A separatist Puritan was one who had concluded that the Church of England was corrupt to the point of being irredeemable. The pilgrims and early Baptists are examples of separatist Puritans Wikipedia, Puritans 2018.

132 After banishment, Roger Williams founded Rhode Island in 1636, establishing by law freedom of religious worship Editors, Roger Williams 2016.

133 *Antinomian* means "anti-law," a doctrinal controversy since Paul first criticized the law.

134 Wikipedia, Antinominianism 2018.

135 See an introduction to the Quakers in The Rise of Presbyterianism in Chapter 7: The Reformation.

136 Wikipedia, Mary Dyer 2018.

137 Wikipedia, Mary Dyer 2018.

138 Wikipedia, Mary Dyer 2018.

139 Wikipedia, Mary Dyer 2018.

140 Slick n.d.

141 Jim Jones and Marshall Applewhite both led their groups to mass suicide.

142 West, Imperial Laws and Edicts 2008.

143 J. Cox 2003.

144 Wikipedia, Blue Law 2018. The introduction of blue laws was not unique to the United States. For example, British Parliament passed the Sunday Observance Act of 1781 that prohibited many of the same activities as in the United States Lane 2012.

145 Wikipedia, Blue Law 2018.

146 Wikipedia, Blue Law 2018.
147 Wikipedia, Adultery 2018.
148 Wikipedia, Lawrence v. Texas 2018.
149 Wikipedia, Lawrence v. Texas 2018.
150 Wikipedia, School Prayer 2018.
151 Wikipedia, Abington School District v. Schempp 2018.
152 Wikipedia, Abington School District v. Schempp 2018.
153 Tolchin 1984.
154 In December 2017, President Trump officially recognized Jerusalem as the capital of Israel. The controversial move was strongly supported by evangelical Christians who see it as a critical step in ushering in the end-times Maza 2018.
155 Divorce is not recognized in the Catholic Church. Consider examples such as Argentina, which did not legalize divorce until 1987, or Brazil, which did not legalize it until 1977. Even today, the Philippines do not legally grant divorce Wikipedia, Divorce law by country 2019.
156 On July 26, 2017, the Justice Department filed a brief arguing that the Civil Rights Act does not apply to discrimination based on sexual orientation. On the same day, President Trump tweeted that the U.S. military will no longer accept or allow transgender individuals to serve The Discrimination Administration n.d. Surely, the administration's stand on LGBTQ issues is in response to the evangelical Christian influence of Vice President Pence and the evangelical leaders who had counseled Trump during the campaign. Yet, many Christian denominations fully accept LGBTQ Christians and perform gay marriages Wikipedia, List of Christian denominational positions on homosexuality 2018.

Chapter 12

Onward Christian Soldiers

As this book comes to a close, we are left to make sense of what we have learned. Hopefully, the book has helped each of us understand how our Christian heritage fits into the whole. Perhaps this is sufficient for you—like fitting a puzzle piece into a larger puzzle that was previously incomplete.

However, a primary purpose of this book is to help us mature our faith by prodding us to consider challenging questions arising from Christian history and its splintering. The book has offered few answers because the questions it has raised have no simple answers. Thus, there is a risk in its attempt to mature our faith—the risk that the messiness of Christian splintering actually undermines our faith.

The worst possible outcome of this book is that reading it has left you cynical and faithless. There is no denying that there is a credibility problem when a religion's founder characterizes the religion's path as a "narrow way" entered through a "strait gate,"[1] but the resulting religion has thousands of paths of all sizes and virtually no gate. There is no denying that Christianity has been used and abused for shameful purposes. And, yes, there are questionable actions by some Christians that cast a shadow on the whole religion. Nevertheless, Christianity's central truth remains untarnished and strikingly simple—Jesus came, was sacrificed, and rose again the third day. Through Him, the cruel bands of death were broken and a path to peace, renewal, and forgiveness—even a path to God—was provided. Nothing about the story of Christian splintering diminishes this truth. Please, do not let the story of splintering rob you of faith!

Our individual quest for a more mature faith requires sincere reflection and will undoubtedly be accompanied by some discomfort. It requires each of us to reconcile our denominationally learned convictions with the admirable Christian lives of others who do not share our denomination's doctrines, governance, or practices. Our quest for maturity requires us to find a way to frame Christian splintering that counters the discouraging reality that Christianity failed to fulfill Jesus's aspiration for unity—a framework that inspires hope and allows us to "be ready always to give an answer to every man that asketh . . . a reason of the hope that is in [us]."[2] Our quest for maturity requires us to wade through the confusion that history reveals without losing our personal convictions and willingness to act in faith. Our quest for maturity requires us to suspend the simple notion that God works His glory through only one denomination and replace it with open-mindedness, even though such open-mindedness may result in internal tension, even an unsettled feeling. In fact, it is expected that we finish this book feeling somewhat unsettled. After all, we have been challenged to juxtapose Jesus's aspiration for unity with the reality of a highly splintered religion—that juxtaposition can instill doubt that modern Christianity is what Jesus intended. We may find ourselves questioning Jesus Himself—wondering why He organized a church but left so much undefined. We can feel a tension between a desire to be respectful, civilized, and tolerant of others' beliefs while remaining committed to the convictions learned from our own denomination.

The rest of this chapter offers us a framework that, for simplicity, is called the Christian Army Framework. Remember the allies in World War II, gathered on ships singing "Onward Christian Soldiers" in an expression of hope for Christian unity?[3] This framework is inspired by them. They came from all sorts of backgrounds and denominations, yet they shared a faith and purpose that superseded their differences.

Like a prism that splits white light into a rainbow of colors, this framework has three facets. Through the first one, we see Christian denominations with all their differences. But these denominations, reflecting, as it were, off a second facet, can also be seen through a third facet as an amazingly unified religion, one in which we can rejoice and celebrate. The three facets of the Christian Army Framework are Christian truth, the nature of faith, and unity of purpose. We will explore these three facets and how they affect our view of Christianity in detail in the following sections.

Christian Truth

Many realms of human endeavor are independent of underlying truth. Our literature, fashion, consumer goods, and more are the fruits of human creativity and innovation, and our commerce and governments are founded on well-reasoned judgments and opinions. In contrast, underlying other realms, such as the laws of nature, are fundamental truths, and no amount of human opinion or debate will change them. Still, even in these realms the harsh reality is that humans can't be sure that they have fully discovered and understood the underlying truths, and thus these realms are also often overshadowed by human opinion and debate. Indeed, we may be convinced that we have grasped truth only to learn later that our convictions of the truth were mere theories or superstitions. To illustrate the point, consider the evolving beliefs about the truths of planetary motion within the solar system and the broader universe.

In about 150, Ptolemy (c.100–c. 170), a Greek mathematician and astronomer,[4] brilliantly described his observations of the sun, moon, planets, and stars in his work *Almagest and Planetary Hypotheses*.[5] The Ptolemaic system was so robust in its predictions and so harmonious with Hebrew and Christian scriptures that it was accepted as truth for more than fifteen hundred years! However, it was patently wrong. Ptolemy asserted that Earth was stationary and that all other celestial bodies orbited around it.[6]

Nicolaus Copernicus (1473–1543) first developed notions of a sun-centered (heliocentric) universe in the first decade of the sixteenth century, but it took another thirty or so years before he was willing to risk public scorn and in 1542 publish his work, *On the Revolutions of the Heavenly Spheres*.[7] Through the lens of our modern understanding of the universe, we can see that Copernicus's perception of truth was a massive step forward but was still terribly limited. Brave scientists including Galileo Galilei (1564–1642) picked up Copernicus's cause. However, the Roman Catholic Church continued to hold that Earth was the center of the universe, and Galileo was judged by the Roman Inquisition to be a heretic in 1616 and again in 1633. Consequently,

Galileo lived the final decade of his life under house arrest.[8] Johannes Kepler (1571–1630), a keen observer and another Copernican disciple, published observations of planetary motion and proposed elliptical orbits—again, an important step forward toward a more correct understanding of the truth.[9] In an ironic twist, Galileo rejected Kepler's elliptical orbits.[10]

Isaac Newton (1642—1727), one the greatest scientists and mathematicians of all time, developed an even more complete picture of the truths of planetary motion. Paradoxically, the math prodigy who had immersed himself in the rational world of natural philosophy also studied theology and the hermetic disciplines of alchemy and astrology.[11] Rational natural philosophy inspired his mathematics and led him to the invaluable tool of calculus. But it was the realm of hermetic mystery and magic that opened his rational mind to the notion of invisible "attractions" between objects. Step by step, observation by observation, he described mathematically the presence of an invisible yet consistent force between all objects, which he called *gravity*.[12] In his twenties, Newton first grappled with the concept of gravity and observed that Earth's gravity extended even to the moon. But it took prodding and encouragement from other eminent members of the Royal Society nearly two decades later to induce Newton to apply his notion of gravity to Kepler's observations of planetary motion. The result was a three-volume work known as *The Principia*, published in 1687, in which Newton proposed the "law" of universal gravitation. The law explained planetary motion with incredible accuracy, and it explained all sorts of other terrestrial phenomena, such as the tides. The invisible force of gravity became the foundation of Newton's laws of motion that are the bedrock of classical physics. Through our modern lens, we see that Newton was truly inspired and that his work took humankind another massive step closer toward fundamental truth. However, in Newton's time, gravity was not accepted by all. Many scientists scoffed at the notion of an invisible magical force acting across distance. Skeptics viewed the entire theory as a "retreat to medieval doctrines of 'occult forces.'"[13] Even Newton acknowledged that gravity described the "what" while the "how" remained an elusive mystery.

One obvious shortcoming of the understanding of truth in Newton's time was the limited understanding of the scope of the universe. To the people living then, the "universe" was our solar system. They didn't have the tools to see that our solar system is just one of many solar systems in just one galaxy of many galaxies in an incomprehensibly vast universe. With such a relatively limited view of the universe, Newton had no reason not to believe that gravity worked instantaneously across any distance. In other words, he believed that time did not affect gravity. In 1915, Albert Einstein published his general theory of relativity, which redefined gravity as a property of space *and* time. The theory's equations provided even more robust predictions of gravity. Again, we took another step forward in our understanding of the underlying fundamental truths.

Quantum physics began as the quest to understand the subatomic realm, but quantum scientists have set their sights on revealing the elusive "how" of gravity. Perhaps quantum science will be the portal to an even deeper understanding of gravity and planetary motion. However, there's a troubling quandary. Quantum physics is incompatible with general relativity. Thus, physicists continue to search for the holy grail, a unifying theory of truth, or the Theory of Everything, that describes the forces acting on celestial bodies as well as subatomic particles.[14] In short, in spite of all that modern people have learned, gaps remain in our understanding, and the search to reveal fundamental truths of planetary motion continues.

Importantly, the journey of revealing truth is not always forward. In spite of astronauts being sent to the moon using Newton's physics, the cumulative evidence of images from space of the globe we live on, and the successful orbiting of thousands of satellites, there is a burgeoning community, fed by social media, that believes Earth is a flat disc. The staunch beliefs of "flat-Earthers" in the face of cumulative evidence and collective wisdom is a cautionary example of the uneven progress toward understanding fundamental truths. It is a sobering reminder that living in "modern times" with access to unprecedented information does not insulate the gullible from tangents and falsehoods.

This story of humankind's attempt to describe some of the fundamental truths of the universe illustrates several important lessons.

Within each generation of philosophers and scientists, many have been convinced that they had uncovered the underlying truth. Nevertheless, some convictions are simply wrong, in spite of how many "authorities" have accepted them or how many centuries the convictions have gone unchallenged—Ptolemy's model. Other convictions approach the truth but are limited and incomplete—Kepler's model. The understanding of truth advances only because seekers are open-minded—Newton's openness to mysticism. But that same open-mindedness creates the risk of believing in falsehoods—flat-Earthers. Importantly, after all these centuries, the pursuit of truth continues! Yes, some scientists with hubris may be certain about one theory or another, but the collective wisdom of the scientific community recognizes that there is still much to discover relative to the fundamental truths of the universe.

The gospel of Jesus Christ at the core of Christianity claims truths of eternal significance, such as the existence and nature of God, humankind's purpose and destiny, the means of communicating with the divine, the path to God, the nature of evil, and so on. The gospel asserts truths that precede, supersede, and exceed human intelligence. Given its claims, the gospel is either the most important truth we can know or it is a deceitful fraud. The middle ground is not possible. The gospel cannot justifiably belong to the realms of human endeavor. It cannot be akin to art, business, fashion, or politics. Rather, it is either a massive fraud or akin to natural laws based on underlying fundamental truths that exist whether we understand them, agree with them, or believe in them. The existence and essential nature of underlying Christian truth exposes a critical reality—it is simply impossible that all Christian denominations are equally true! There are too many differences between beliefs and practices. This facet of Christian truth causes us to see the differences in denominations and evaluate their respective doctrines.

This reality is yet another reason why many readers may feel unsettled after reading this book. We want to respect others' beliefs while remaining committed to our own. But this creates tension because we know that two very different sets of beliefs cannot be equally true. It may be tempting to resolve this tension by framing Christian splintering with the virtue of diversity. After all, Christian denominations are usually the fruit of virtuous things: religious freedom, religious conviction, sincerity, courage, and human creativity. Furthermore, diversity in other contexts is usually a virtue, and Christian diversity is superficially no different. But we simply can't resolve Christian splintering without rejecting the very premise of Christian truth. To accept Christian splintering as diversity is to relegate Christianity to the realm of human creativity and innovation. It is to tacitly accept that there are no fundamental Christians truths—that "truth is in the eye of the beholder," "truth is relative," or the supreme truth is "your truth."

The story of the search for the natural laws governing planetary motion gives us a pragmatic approach to interpret Christian splintering and is key to the Christian Army Framework. The story reminds us that while truth exists and is the goal of our pursuits, it is essentially impossible for each of us to be certain that we know truth or that we know it *fully*. Thus, our commitment should be to the *pursuit* of truth and not to an unquestioning conviction that we personally already know it. Instead of rejecting others outright because of our own certainty, we can remain committed to the pursuit of truth while remaining open-minded to the possibility that our current convictions will yet be shaped by new insights. This facet of the framework encourages dialogue with sincere Christians of all denominations. We bring our convictions to the table, but we respectfully and sincerely ask, "What do you believe?" "Why do you believe it?" "How do your beliefs compare to my own?" And then, we humbly seek to discern truth. Of course, this raises the critical question, How can we possibly discern Christian truth?

The Gospel of John offers some "tools" to use on our quest to find Christian truth. Like Kepler's keen observations, one path to truth is empirical—try it and observe. Jesus said, "If any man will do his will, he shall know of the doctrine, whether it be of God."[15] Jesus emphasized the role that witnesses can play in establishing truth—both living witnesses and those recorded in scripture. In His time, He offered John the Baptist as a living witness: "There is another [John the Baptist] that beareth witness of me."[16] He also referred to witnesses who heard the voice of the Father at the time of His baptism: "the Father himself . . . hath borne witness of me."[17] Of course, these witnesses are no longer living, and their testimonies, along with many others, are now found in the scriptures. Thus, Jesus said, "Search the scriptures . . . they are they which testify of me."[18] However, it was arguably in Jesus's parting moments with His apostles that He promised the greatest key to discerning truth. Referring to the Holy Ghost, He said, "Howbeit when he, the Spirit of truth is come, he will guide you into all truth: for he shall not speak of himself."[19]

Many sincere Christians from myriad denominations have applied these tools and are convinced that they have gleaned Christian truth. Yet, using the same tools, Christians have reached strikingly different conclusions about gospel truth. We can only conclude that the Lord who gave us these tools is well aware of their limitations to lead all who use them to the same set of convictions. It is the pattern of God that the Holy Ghost rarely reveals truth as a completed mosaic. Rather, the Spirit nudges sincere seekers toward truth. His guidance is usually subtle and personal, which means that it is inherently subject to personal preparation, preconceptions, context, and biases.[20] The foundation of Christian faith is a personal conviction that Jesus is the Lord. If we take Paul's words at face value, then everyone who declares that Jesus is Lord—with no exception given for sect or denomination—can do so only because the Holy Ghost has planted that truth in their heart: "no man can say that Jesus is the Lord, but by the Holy Ghost."[21]

The Christian Army Framework does not ask us to ignore the differences in denominations' doctrines and convictions, but it does ask us to trust that God is revealing His truth to sincere seekers of it according to His divine wisdom and timing. It asks us to give the benefit of the doubt to fellow Christians, believing that God is at work leading them according to their sincerity to the portion of truth that he or she is prepared to receive and live. It asks us to be open-minded to truth through whatever channel God has revealed it—not by gullibly believing in every theory but by sincerely applying the tools that Jesus offered.

Nature of Faith

Jesus demonstrated the centrality of faith in the new religion in an exchange with Thomas, one of the apostles. Jesus's followers were bereft with grief at His death and did not understand that He would rise again.[22] But in the greatest miracle of all, He did rise again. He first appeared to Mary Magdalene[23] and then to other women.[24] But the news was too good to be true, and the gathered eleven apostles generally did not believe the first witnesses to the Lord's resurrection. As Luke records, "[the women's] words seemed to them as idle tales, and they believed them not."[25] Later that day, Jesus appeared to many of the apostles in a closed room, but Thomas was not present.[26] Thomas stubbornly resisted the cumulative witnesses, saying, "Except I shall see in his hands the print of the nails, and put my finger into the print of the nails, and thrust my hand into his side, I will not believe."[27] A week later, the disciples, including Thomas, were again gathered when the resurrected Lord appeared. He invited Thomas to touch His wounds to eliminate all disbelief, but He also gently rebuked Thomas: "be not faithless, but believing."[28] Then He added, "Thomas, because thou hast seen me, thou hast believed: blessed are they that have not seen, and yet have believed."[29] In these words, we see that God intends that belief rather than certain knowledge motivate Christians. Peter echoed the centrality of faith when he referred to believers' faith as "more precious than of gold."[30] He praised the saints of his day for loving the Lord, rejoicing with joy, and having every expectation in salvation in spite of *never having seen Jesus.*[31]

Paul helps us understand the nature of faith: "Faith is the substance of things *hoped for*, the evidence of things *not seen.*"[32] By its very definition, faith is uncertain! Nevertheless, faith can be compelling and can motivate action. Paul provided a lengthy list of scriptural examples of men and women taking action motivated by faith in spite of uncertainty. He offered the example of Abraham: "By faith Abraham, when he was called to go out into a place . . . obeyed . . . not knowing whither he went."[33] Abraham and his family acted based on "promises" because they were "persuaded of them, and embraced them."[34] In light of their uncertain journey, they "confessed that they were strangers and pilgrims."[35] Similarly, faith requires all Christians to act, believing in promises. We are persuaded that the promises are real, and so we embrace them and set out into uncertain and unknown territory as pilgrims, not knowing for certain "whither we go." Considering the inherent difficulty of fully knowing fundamental Christian truths, it is faith that allows us to press forward in spite of a humbling awareness that we are not yet certain of all underlying truths.

Faith motivates us to believe in and seek wisdom from an unseen God. James counseled those who lack wisdom to solicit God for answers: "Let him ask in *faith*, nothing wavering."[36] Was James equating wavering with doubting—telling us to push aside any glimmer of doubt? Indeed, at a basic level, we can imagine doubt and faith to be the opposing ends of a playground seesaw. When faith rises, doubt falls, and, conversely, when doubt ascends, faith subsides. This correlation of doubt and faith is reinforced by the story of Peter impetuously leaving the safety of a storm-stricken ship to join Jesus, who was approaching on the water. As Peter stepped onto the water, the boisterous wind and crashing waves sapped his confidence. "He was afraid; and beginning to sink, he cried, saying, Lord, save me." Jesus then said, "O thou of little faith, wherefore didst thou doubt?"[37] Implied in Jesus's words was the correlation between faith and doubt—we assume that if Peter had not doubted, he would have had the necessary faith to successfully walk on water. Not surprisingly then, Christians often conclude that the pinnacle of faith is to push aside all doubt.

James's words and Peter's story create a perception that *unwavering* faith is *undoubting* faith. From here, it is a small step to equate *undoubting* faith with *unquestioning* faith. Indeed, the ideal of faith was stretched in the earliest centuries of Christianity to mean unquestioning belief in and obedience to the doctrines of the church. The term *rule of faith* emerged, used by apologists, including Irenaeus and Tertullian in their fight against the blossoming heresies of their respective times. It was used to mean "orthodoxy in belief and practice."[38] Under this ideal of faith, unflinching commitment to orthodoxy became the litmus test for one's faith. For example, the Athanasian Creed states, "Whosoever will be saved, before all things it is necessary that he hold the Catholic Faith. Which Faith except everyone do *keep whole and undefiled, without doubt* he shall perish everlastingly."[39] The Baltimore Catechism, used by North American Catholics for nearly a century, expresses this same sentiment: "We ourselves need not seek in the Scriptures and traditions for what we are to believe. God has appointed the Church to be our guide to salvation and we must accept its teaching us our *infallible rule of faith*."[40]

Protestants also refer to the rule of faith, but usually in reference to the doctrine of *sola scriptura*, that is, the belief that the scriptures are the singular, complete, and infallible word of God.[41] Whether Catholic or Protestant, the common theme is that truth is fully defined in a denomination's creeds, confessions, and catechisms and that "faith" is the unquestioning acceptance of and unflinching obedience to them. Thus, paradoxically, *faith has come to connote certainty*! Arguably, it is this distorted ideal of infallible faith that fosters the persecution and discrimination described in the previous chapter. Christians who are certain of their own rightness are equally certain of others' wrongness.

Let's consider again James's counsel. Is unwavering faith unquestioning and doubt-free? Importantly, the person to whom James offers counsel is one *lacking* wisdom; that is, one with unanswered questions. Such a person is quite the opposite of one who is unquestioning, certain, or doubt-free! Immediately after the words "nothing wavering," he explains that "he that wavereth is like a wave of the sea driven with the wind and tossed" and then two sentences later adds, "a double-minded man is unstable in all his ways."[42] James assures us that such a person will not "receive any thing of the Lord."[43] It makes sense that James directly associated wavering with double-mindedness. Being tossed on the waves is an apt description of an uncommitted double-minded person. The term *double-minded* calls to mind the words of Jesus when He said,

> No man can serve two masters: for either he will hate the one, and love the other; or else he will hold to the one, and despise the other. Ye cannot serve God and mammon [riches].[44]

Arguably, then, James was telling us that a wavering person is a double-minded person: one who is not willing to give up the worldliness of riches or worldly pleasures, one who hedges bets by confessing God but does not actually obey Him, one of whom Jesus spoke, "Not every one that saith unto me, Lord, Lord, shall enter into the kingdom of heaven; but he that doeth the will of my Father which is in heaven."[45] If this interpretation is correct, James is *not* suggesting that *to waver* means "to question, have unbelief, or doubt." Quite the opposite, he invites those with questions and doubts—those who lack wisdom—to approach God.

The faith that Paul and James referred to is a mix of belief, hope, and action within the context of uncertainty. The nature of faith is reflected in the father who brought his very sick son to Jesus. The father's belief led to action—the request for healing. But he humbly recognized that his belief and hope were far from certain. Thus, he pled not only for his son but also for himself and "cried out, and said with tears, Lord, I believe; help thou mine unbelief."[46] It is a profound truth that faith and uncertainty can coexist—that is the inherent nature of faith.

This leads us to the second facet of the Christian Army Framework, which is an appeal to ground ourselves in the true nature of faith and set aside the distorted notion of infallible, certain "faith." When we shed our armor of infallible certainty and accept faith for what it is, it changes how we perceive other Christians. Instead of seeing other Christian behavior as "wrong" against the standard of our own convictions, we can see abundant examples of Christians acting in sincere but uncertain faith. We see Christians proceeding with holiness and godly purpose based on whatever wisdom they have. We see acts of faith worthy of honor and celebration, even though such acts are motivated by beliefs that we may not personally believe to be true.

If it was God's design that Christians believe and progress based on faith and not on certainty, as we saw with Thomas, then we must reasonably believe that God looks favorably on the exercise of faith by each Christian according to the understanding of truth that person has. Surely, a committed and diligent Christian life motivated by faith is beautiful to God, whether that person is a Southern Baptist, Catholic, Anglican, Pentecostal, Mormon, or whatever.

When we humbly recognize that our own convictions relative to Christian truths may or may not be perfectly correct or complete, we resist equating faith with infallibility, and we cease to judge other Christians on whether they believe and act as we do. Rather, we celebrate the virtue of each Christian acting in faith according to the understanding of truth that they have. This celebration of faith does not require us to diminish our conviction in the truthfulness of our own denomination or abandon the convictions we have formed from our own pursuit of truth, but it does leave us more open-minded to the worth of others' beliefs and helps us to be vulnerable to God's continued inspiration that nudges us individually toward a more accurate and complete understanding of truth.

Unity of Purpose

When sincere Christians of all denominations act in faith according to their best understanding, a reality emerges, namely, that the general desires and actions of Christians are strikingly similar. There is a common hope of life after death through Jesus Christ. Christians of all stripes pray, study scriptures, and worship to learn of and embrace the promises God has made to us through Jesus. Christians express a desire to live according to divine commandments and to resist the evil indulgences of the world. We attempt, albeit imperfectly, to love our neighbor and care for the needy. We seek to foster peace and liberty and to quell tyranny and oppression. In short, through the third metaphorical facet of unity of purpose, we see a much more homogenous body of Christ.

This is not to say that all who call themselves Christians are aligned with this unity of purpose. A compelling example to the contrary was introduced in chapter 2, which began by contrasting the unified Christian army of the Allied powers with the unified "Christian" army of the Axis powers. Many other chapters revealed how evildoers have used Christianity as an instrument of power or as a means of enriching themselves. Indeed, Christianity has too often been twisted and corrupted to serve ignoble goals. Jesus Himself prophesied that there would be convincing false prophets among believers.[47] He prophesied that some will feign Christian belief and even prophesy and claim to cast out devils, but they are corrupt workers of iniquity—unwilling or unable to actually live a Christian life.[48] Similarly, Paul warned of the grievous wolves among the flock[49] and prophesied to Timothy that the "latter times" would not be immune.[50] Surely, Christianity today has its share of corrupt, grievous wolves. It would be naïve for this book to suggest otherwise. Nevertheless, living a Christian life is demanding, and we can reasonably assume that the vast majority of Christians are sincere and well-intended.

Jesus gave the standard by which to discern the sincerity of Christians. Instructively, He lived at a time when there were many Jewish sects, and He undoubtedly knew that Christianity itself would splinter into many sects. Yet, the standard that Jesus gave us for discerning corruption has nothing to do with sects, credentials, or religious hierarchy. It is all about an individual's actions that stem from inner beliefs. In other words, it is about how faith is manifest! He said, "Every good tree bringeth forth good fruit; but a corrupt tree bringeth forth evil fruit. . . . Wherefore by their fruits ye shall know them."[51] The traits that Jesus offered in the Sermon on the Mount are surely many of the fruits to which Jesus referred: humble, meek, merciful, peacemaking, forgiving, faithful, honest, patient, generous, and so on.[52] Paul enumerated some of the fruits: "But the fruit of the Spirit is love, joy, peace, longsuffering, gentleness, goodness, faith, meekness, temperance."[53] Peter echoed many of these fruits: "Add to your faith, virtue; and to virtue knowledge; and to knowledge temperance; and to temperance patience; and to patience godliness; and to godliness brotherly kindness; and to brotherly kindness charity."[54] John encapsulated Christian fruits as the expression of love and the rejection of hate.[55] Collectively, these fruits are found in Christians all around the world from virtually all its denominations. As our Christian faith translates into these fruits, we are unified in purpose!

This broader type of unity was illustrated when John the Apostle told Jesus that the apostles had forbidden a person from using Jesus's name to cast out devils. Whoever this person was, he was evidently not actively following Jesus and by extension had not expressly been commissioned by Him. John said, "Master, we saw one casting out devils in thy name; and we forbad him, because he followeth not with us."[56] Jesus's answer was a little surprising. He said, "Forbid him not: for he that is not against us is for us."[57] We should not take His response as an endorsement of indiscriminate imitation of the duties and rights of the apostles. Jesus later emphasized to the apostles that He had done the choosing and that they had been ordained with authority.[58] Also, examples in Acts reinforce that authority matters.[59] Nevertheless, Jesus clearly wanted to teach a broader principle—if we are not against Him, then we are for Him. Thus, His answer is profoundly relevant to how we view fellow Christians not of our denomination.

Through the facet of unity of purpose, we see the possibility that Paul's description of spiritual gifts applies to Christianity in general. Indeed, there are "differences of administrations"[60] and "diversities of operations"[61] found in the multitude of Christian denominations, but there is just one Lord and one "body of Christ."[62]

Becoming an open-minded and humble seeker of truth, celebrating the uncertain nature of faith, and seeing unity of purpose give us a powerful framework through which to constructively perceive Christianity. We can continue to have hope in Christ and continue to believe in Christianity in spite of its many divisions. The Christian Army Framework asks us to set aside the appealing simplicity of whatever unquestioning conviction we may have had and replace it with a more mature faith—one that is necessarily nuanced and that requires a careful balance between extremes:

- Recognize and understand the differences between denominations, but don't lose sight of the common Christian purpose.

- Believe that truth exists, sincerely pursue it, and cling to the truth you have gleaned, but always be humbly cautious about a personal conviction that suggests you have found all truth or fully understand it.

- Believe that God is pleased when Christians proceed in faith. Therefore, act in faith, based on your personal convictions of Christian truth, but also celebrate the acts of faith of others, even if their motivating beliefs and expressions of faith are different than your own.

- Accept that not all denominations can be simultaneously true, given the vast differences between them, but trust the promise of God that He will impart wisdom to each sincere seeker of truth according to His divine wisdom and timing.

- Be open-minded toward the beliefs of others, but don't be gullible to charlatans and wolves. Use the tools offered by the Lord to seek truth, but know that others also legitimately use those tools and arrive at different convictions.

- Recognize that Christianity failed in the sense that it failed to preserve a unified church, but still believe that Jesus's actions in establishing His religion were done according to His divine omniscience and wisdom—what He instituted *and withheld* relative to doctrines, governance, and worship practices was done according to a perfect plan.

Through the prism of the Christian Army Framework we can respect and celebrate the faithful prayers of all Christians, whether they be a Catholic praying in front of an altar, a Charismatic swaying with outstretched arms, or a Messianic Jew praying to Jeshua, even if we disagree with the beliefs underlying their manner of prayer. Similarly, we rejoice when we see Christian worship, even if the worship services are very different from our own.

We can celebrate and support Christian charity in the relief work of Catholic Charities and similar denominational charities, in the community service rendered by missionaries from numerous denominations, and in the work performed by Christians of many stripes in the impoverished and disadvantaged neighborhoods of the world.

We can see individual Christians for their fruits, independent of their denominational alignment. We earn mutual trust and respect and discern the "grievous wolves" among us based on one's individual "fruits of faith," rather than on credentials or membership in "acceptable" denominations.

We can engage our fellow Christians in sincere two-way discovery and dialogue rather than taking up figurative arms in Bible bashes. We are willing to trust that God will gently nudge each sincere seeker toward greater understanding of truth according to the preparation and context of that person.

We can accept the uneasy reality that, in spite of sincere efforts to find and live by Christian truth, each of us may not know for sure if our personal convictions fully reflect Christian truth. Still, we remain committed to live a Christian life motivated by faith rather than certainty.

We are grateful that God inspires us, nudges us, and confirms our faith. When we experience a burst of understanding, feel a peace that calms our concerns, feel overwhelmed with awe at the miracle of creation, sense inexplicable hope and joy in a Savior we've never seen, feel an assurance that we are loved, or feel a rush of love toward others that far exceeds our own willful capacity to love, then we are experiencing subtle but very real evidence of the divine. Through these sacred moments, our faith is strengthened and we gain confidence that God lives and that the gospel's promise of salvation is real. Through these experiences, we feel God nudging us personally toward truth and inspiring us to live a Christian life. In the end, isn't that a primary purpose of this splintered but still glorious religion?

Notes

---

1 See Matthew 7:13–14.

2 1 Peter 3:15.

3 See Chapter 2: Unity—The Unfulfilled Aspiration.

4 Ptolemy lived in Alexandria, Egypt, one of the preeminent centers for Greek thought.

5 Jones 2008.

6 Jones 2008.

7 Wikipedia, Nicolaus Copernicus 2019.

8 Wikipedia, Galileo Galilei 2019.

9 Wikipedia, Johannes Kepler 2019.

10 Wikipedia, Galileo Galilei 2019.

11 Dolnick 2011, 227.

12 Westfall 2019.

13 Dolnick 2011, 303.

14 Wikipedia, Theory of everything 2019.

15 John 7:17; Abraham Lincoln captured the essence of this approach in his simple couplet, "When I do good I feel good, when I do bad I feel bad, and that's my religion." Lincoln n.d.

16 John 5:32.

17 John 5:37, referring to the words of the Father in Matthew 3:17.

18 John 5:39.

19 John 16:13.

20 The experience on the day of Pentecost was a very public event. See Acts 2.

21 1 Corinthians 12:3.

22 See John 20:9.

23 See John 20:11–18.

24 See Matthew 8:9.

25 Luke 24:11 (clarification added).

26 See John 20:19–22.

27 John 20:25.

28 John 20:27.

29 John 20:29.

30 1 Peter 1:7.

31 See 1 Peter 1:8–9 (emphasis added).

32 Hebrews 11:1 (emphasis added).

33 Hebrews 11:8.

34 Hebrews 11:13.

35 Hebrews 11:13.

36 James 1:6.

37 Matthew 14:29–31.

38 Wikipedia, Rule of Faith 2019.

39 Sullivan 1910.

40 Wikipedia, Rule of Faith 2019. (emphasis added).

41 See, for example, the Presbyterian Westminster Confession.

42 James 1:6, 8.

43 James 1:7.

44 Matthew 6:24.
45 Matthew 7:21.
46 Mark 9:24.
47 See Matthew 7:15.
48 See Matthew 7:21–23.
49 See Acts 20:29.
50 See 1 Timothy 4:1–3.
51 Matthew 7:17, 20.
52 See Matthew 5.
53 Galatians 5:22–23.
54 2 Peter 1:5–7.
55 See 1 John 2:9–11; 4:18–20.
56 Luke 9:49.
57 Luke 9:50.
58 See John 15:16.
59 See Acts 8.
60 1 Corinthians 12:5.
61 1 Corinthians 12:6.
62 1 Corinthians 12:27.

Bibliography

"1249. diakonos." *Bible Hub.* Accessed May 29, 2019.
https://biblehub.com/str/greek/1249.htm.

"1941: The Atlantic Charter." *United Nations.* Accessed December 14,
2017. http://www.un.org/en/sections/history-united-
nations-charter/1941-atlantic-charter/index.html.

"1985. episkopos." *Bible Hub.* Accessed May 29, 2019.
https://biblehub.com/str/greek/1985.htm.

"2016 Presidential Election Exit Polls." *CNN.* November 23, 2016.
https://www.cnn.com/election/2016/results/exit-
polls/national/president.

"2098. euaggelion." *Bible Hub.*
http://biblehub.com/str/greek/2098.htm.

"2099. euaggelistés." *Bible Hub.*
http://biblehub.com/str/greek/2099.htm.

"652. apostolos." *Bible Hub.* Accessed May 30, 2019.
https://biblehub.com/str/greek/652.htm.

"A brief history of Methodism." *Aberdeen Methodist.* Accessed May 31,
2018.
http://www.aberdeenmethodist.org.uk/AbriefhistoryofMeth
odism.pdf.

"A Question of Miracles." *YouTube.* January 27, 2014.
https://www.youtube.com/watch?v=JJfaaPdP0kI.

"ABC News PrimeTime Live (November 21, 1991)." *YouTube.*
December 4, 2016.
https://www.youtube.com/watch?v=m2In7tZsBHY.

Ackroyd, Peter. *The Life of Thomas More*. New York: Anchor Books. 1999.

"Affirming Denominations." *gaychurch.org*. 2018. https://www.gaychurch.org/affirming-denominations/.

American Council of Christian Churches "Statement on the Death of Billy Graham." *American Council of Christian Churches*. February 23, 2018. https://accc4truth.org/2018/02/23/statement-on-the-death-of-billy-graham/.

Anderson, Leith "Evangelical Does Not Equal Political." *National Association of Evangelicals*. Winter, 2017/2018. https://www.nae.net/evangelical-political/.

"Arius." In *The Columbia Encyclopedia, 6th ed.* https://www.encyclopedia.com/reference/encyclopedias-almanacs-transcripts-and-maps/arius.

"Athanasian Creed." *Christian Classics Ethereal Library*. Accessed December 8, 2017. https://www.ccel.org/creeds/athanasian.creed.html.

Augustinians Australia "1031 The Manichee." *Augnet*. Accessed March 10, 2018. http://augnet.org/en/life-of-augustine/growing-up/1031-the-manichee/.

— "1210 Pelagianism." *Augnet*. Accessed February 26, 2018. http://augnet.org/en/life-of-augustine/in-africa-again/1210-pelagianism/.

— "1211 Combating Pelagianism." *Augnet*. Accessed February 26, 2018. http://augnet.org/en/life-of-augustine/in-africa-again/1211-combating-pelagianism/.

Babcock, William S. "Pelagianism." *Believe Religious Information Source Web-Site*. July 24, 2017. http://mb-soft.com/believe/txc/pelagian.htm.

Bacon Jr., Perry, and Amelia Thomson-DeVeaux "How Trump And Race Are Splitting Evangelicals." *FiveThirtyEight*. March 2, 2018. https://fivethirtyeight.com/features/how-trump-and-race-are-splitting-evangelicals/.

Balmer, Randall "Billy Graham exemplified what evangelical Christianity could be — and too often was not." *NBC News*. February 23, 2018. https://www.nbcnews.com/think/opinion/billy-graham-exemplified-what-evangelical-christianity-could-be-too-often-ncna850461.

Banks, Adelle M., Emily McFarlan Miller, Yonat Shimron, Jerome Socolovsky, and Religion News Service "All the president's clergymen." *National Catholic Reporter.* September 5, 2017. https://www.ncronline.org/news/politics/all-president-s-clergymen.

Banks, Adelle "The key evangelical players on Trump's advisory board." *National Catholic Reporter.* September 5, 2017. https://www.ncronline.org/news/politics/key-evangelical-players-trumps-advisory-board.

Banwart, Doug. "Jerry Falwell, the Rise of the Moral Majority, and the 1980 Election." *Western Illinois Historical Review* (Spring 2013): 133-157. http://www.wiu.edu/cas/history/wihr/pdfs/Banwart-MoralMajorityVol5.pdf.

Baring-Gould M.A., Rev. S. *The Lost and Hostile Gospels.* London: Williams and Norgate. 1874.

Barraclough, Geoffrey "Holy Roman Empire." *Encyclopædia Britannica.* December 6, 2017. https://www.britannica.com/place/Holy-Roman-Empire.

Bartosi, Frantisek M., and Matthew Spinka "Jan Hus." *Encyclopædia Britannica.* January 30, 2019. https://www.britannica.com/biography/Jan-Hus.

BeDuhn, Jason. "'Not to depart from Christ' Augustine between 'Manichaea' and 'Catholic' Christianity." *HTS Teologiese Studies* 69 (1): 8. http://dx.doi.org/10.4102/hts.v69i1.1355.

Blair, Leondardo "Creflo Dollar Will Get $70 Million Gulfstream G650 Jet." *Christian Post.* June 2, 2015. https://www.christianpost.com/news/creflo-dollar-will-get-70-million-gulfstream-g650-jet-says-church-world-changers-board-says-it-is-necessary-for-ministry-139858/.

Blanchard, Amos. *Book of Martyrs.* Kingston: N. G. Ellis. 1844. https://books.google.com.

Blötzer, Joseph. "Inquisition." In *The Catholic Encyclopedia.* New York: Robert Appleton Company. 1910. http://www.newadvent.org/cathen/08026a.htm.

Blumenthal, Henry J., and A. Hilary Armstrong "Platonism." *Encyclopædia Britannica.* June 15, 2017. https://www.britannica.com/topic/Platonism.

Bonaiuti, Ernesto, and Giorigio La Piana. "The Genesis of St. Augustine's Idea of Original Sin." *The Harvard Theological Review* Cambridge University Press. 10, no. 2 (April 1917): 159-175. https://www.jstor.org/stable/pdf/1507550.pdf.

Bratcher, Dennis "Ba'al Worship in the Old Testament." *Christian Resource Institute.* May 20, 2016. http://www.crivoice.org/baal.html.

Bruce, Fredrick Fyvie, H. Grady Davis, and Others "Biblical Literature." *Encyclopædia Britannica.* October 2, 2018. https://www.britannica.com/topic/biblical-literature.

Burns, Evan. "Moravian Missionary Piety and the Influence of Count Zinzendorf." *Journal of Global Christianity* (2015): 19-34. https://trainingleadersinternational.org/jgc/27/moravian-missionary-piety-and-the-influence-of-count-zinzendorf.

Burton-Edwards, Rev. Taylor "Is the concept "saved, born-again" unique to evangelicals or Baptists? Does it apply to Methodists?" *United Methodist Church.* Accessed June 27, 2018. http://www.umc.org/what-we-believe/is-the-concept-saved-born-again-unique-to-evangelicals-or-baptists.

Butler, Anthea, Paul Freston, and Donald Miller "Moved by the Spirit: Pentecostal Power & Politics after 100 Years." *Pew Research Center.* April 24, 2006. http://www.pewforum.org/2006/04/24/moved-by-the-spirit-pentecostal-power-and-politics-after-100-years2/.

Cadbury, Henry J. "George Fox." *Encyclopædia Britannica* . June 29, 2017. https://www.britannica.com/biography/George-Fox .

"Calvin and Servetus." *the Christian Reformer* Sherwood, Gilbert, and Piper. III, no. 25 (1847). https://books.google.com/books?id=xxsEAAAAQAAJ.

Catholic Answers "Are Catholics Born Again?" *Catholic Answers.* Accessed June 20, 2018. https://www.catholic.com/tract/are-catholics-born-again.

Cave, William. *Primitive Christianity: Religion of the Ancient Christians.* London: Thomass Tegg. 1840.

https://books.google.com/books?id=te8tqdgr7g8C&newbks
=1&newbks_redir=0&dq=PRIMITIVE+CHRISTIANITY:
&source=gbs_navlinks_s.

Center for the Study of Global Christianity "Global Christianity."
Gordon Conwell Theological Seminary. April, 2018.
https://www.gordonconwell.edu/wp-
content/uploads/sites/13/2019/04/GlobalChristianityinfogr
aphic.pdfPg1_.pdf.

"Chalcedonian Creed (451 A.D)." *Christian Classics Ethereal Library.*
451. https://www.ccel.org/creeds/chalcedonian-creed.html.

Chapman, John. *Clementines.* Vol. 4, in *The Catholic Encyclopedia.* New
York: Robert Appleton. 1908.
http://newadvent.org/cathen/04039b.htm.

Chapman, John. "Monarchians." In *The Catholic Encyclopedia.* New
York, New York: Robert Appleton Compnay. 1911.
http://www.newadvent.org/cathen/10448a.htm.

Chapman, John. *Paul of Samosata.* Vol. 11, in *The Catholic Encyclopedia.*
New York: Robert Appleton Company. 1911.
http://www.newadvent.org/cathen/11589a.htm.

Chapman, John. *Pope St. Clement I.* Vol. IV, in *Catholic Encyclopedia.*
New York: Robert Appleton Company. 1908.
http://newadvent.org/cathen/04012c.htm.

Charisma Magazine "Benny Hinn Remembers Kathryn Kuhlman."
YouTube. July 31, 2015.
https://www.youtube.com/watch?v=1KYMQXm-ySM.

"Christianity: Christianity in Latin America." *Encyclopedia.com.* 1987.
https://www.encyclopedia.com/environment/encyclopedias
-almanacs-transcripts-and-maps/christianity-christianity-latin-
america.

Church Educational System. *Church History in the Fulness of Times.* The
Church of Jesus Christ of Latter-day Saints. 1993.

Church of the Nazarene "About Us." *Church of the Nazarene.* Accessed
February 27, 2019. http://nazarene.org/#.

Concordia Publishing House "An Introduction to the Lutheran
Church Missouri Synod." *The Lutheran Church Missouri Synod.*
Concordia Publishing House. 2009.
http://www.lcms.org/Document.fdoc?src=lcm&id=961.

Cory, Greiss. "Thomas Bradwardine: Defender of God's Sovereignty." *The Standard Bearer* 92/2016, no.3 (November 2015). https://standardbearer.rfpa.org/node/55264.

Covey, Stephen R. *7 Habits of Highly Effective People*. New York, New York: Simon & Schuster. 1989.

Cox, James. "Bilboes, Brands, and Branks." *Colonial Williamsburg* (Spring 2003). http://www.history.org/foundation/journal/spring03/branks.cfm.

Cox, Robert, and Daniel Jones "America's Changing Religious Identity." *Public Religion Research Institute*. September 6, 2017. https://www.prri.org/research/american-religious-landscape-christian-religiously-unaffiliated/.

Cplakidas. 2007. *The Roman Empire ca 400 AD*. https://commons.wikimedia.org/wiki/File:The_Roman_Empire_ca_400_AD.png.

Crossman, Ashley "What is a Religious Sect?" *ThoughtCo*. 4 2018, May. https://www.thoughtco.com/sect-definition-3026574.

Dias, Elizabeth "How Evangelicals Helped Donald Trump Win." *Time.com*. November 9, 2016. http://time.com/4565010/donald-trump-evangelicals-win/.

"Dionysus." *Greek Mythology*. November 26, 2018. https://www.greekmythology.com/Other_Gods/Dionysus/dionysus.html.

Dolnick, Edward. *The Clockwork Universe*. New York: Harper Collins. 2011.

Douglass, Jane Dempsey "What We Believe: Predestination." *Presbyterian Mission*. September, 1985. https://www.presbyterianmission.org/what-we-believe/predestination/.

Duffy, Eamon. *Fires of Faith: Catholic England Under Mary Tudor*. New Haven, CT: Yale University Press. 2009.

ECFA "About ECFA." *Evangelical Council for Financial Accountability*. Accessed July 18, 2018. http://www.ecfa.org/Content/About.

Eddy, Mary Baker "Science and Health." *ChristianScience.com.* 1875.
https://www.christianscience.com/the-christian-science-
pastor/science-and-health.

Editors "Anabaptist." *Encyclopædia Britannica.* February 17, 2016.
https://www.britannica.com/topic/Anabaptists.

— "Anglican Communion." *Encyclopædia Britannica.* March 13, 2013.
https://www.britannica.com/topic/Anglican-Communion.

— "Arianism." *Encyclopædia Britannica.* October 9, 2015.
https://www.britannica.com/topic/Arianism.

— "Arius Priest of Alexandria." *Encyclopædia Britannica.* April 9, 2014.
https://www.britannica.com/biography/Arius.

— "Athanasian Creed." *Encyclopædia Britannica.* October 11, 2007.
https://www.britannica.com/topic/Athanasian-Creed.

— "Augustinian." *Encyclopædia Britannica* . September 27, 2011.
https://www.britannica.com/topic/Augustinians.

— "Book of Concord." *Encyclopædia Britannica* . September 18, 2007.
https://www.britannica.com/topic/Book-of-Concord.

— "Charles Taze Russell." *Encyclopædia Britannica.* February 12, 2019.
https://www.britannica.com/biography/Charles-Taze-
Russell.

— "Contstantius II Roman Emperor." *Encyclopædia Britannica.*
September 15, 2008.
https://www.britannica.com/biography/Constantius-II.

— "Dionysus." *Encyclopædia Britannica.* September 21, 2018.
https://www.britannica.com/topic/Dionysus.

— "Docetism." *Encyclopaedia Britannica.* April 11, 2014.
https://www.britannica.com/topic/Docetism.

— "Donatist." *Encyclopædia Britannica.* July 20, 1998.
https://www.britannica.com/topic/Donatists.

— "Ebionite." *Encyclopædia Britannica.* January 04, 2007.
https://www.britannica.com/topic/Ebionites.

— "Episcopal Church in the United States of America." *Encyclopædia
Britannica.* January 15, 2016.
https://www.britannica.com/topic/Episcopal-Church-in-
the-United-States-of-America.

— "Jerry Falwell." *Encyclopædia Britannica.* May 11, 2018.
https://www.britannica.com/biography/Jerry-Falwell.

— "Jovian." *Encyclopædia Britannica.* April 1, 2014.
    https://www.britannica.com/biography/Jovian.

— "Ku Klux Klan." *Encyclopædia Britannica.* July 27, 2018.
    https://www.britannica.com/topic/Ku-Klux-Klan.

— "Logos." *Encyclopædia Britannica* . May 21, 2012.
    https://www.britannica.com/topic/logos.

— "Lollard." *Encyclopædia Britannica* . August 3, 2016.
    https://www.britannica.com/topic/Lollards.

— "Manichaeism." *Encyclopædia Britannica.* June 24, 2014.
    https://www.britannica.com/topic/Manichaeism.

— "Michael Cerularius." *Encyclopædia Britannica.* October 23, 2007.
    https://www.britannica.com/biography/Michael-Cerularius.

— "Moral Majority." *Encyclopædia Britannica.* February 12, 2018.
    https://www.britannica.com/topic/Moral-Majority.

— "Pergamum." *Encyclopædia Britannica.* June 17, 2013.
    https://www.britannica.com/place/Pergamum.

— "Peter Lombard." *Encyclopædia Britannica* . June 15, 2017.
    https://www.britannica.com/biography/Peter-Lombard.

— "Philo Judaeus." *Encyclopædia Britannica.* June 14, 2017.
    https://www.britannica.com/biography/Philo-Judaeus.

— "Presbyter." *Encyclopædia Britannica.* April 01, 2016.
    https://www.britannica.com/topic/presbyter.

— "Puritanism." *Encyclopædia Britannica.* January 3, 2018.
    https://www.britannica.com/topic/Puritanism.

— "Reformation." *Encyclopædia Britannica.* January 15, 2018.
    https://www.britannica.com/event/Reformation.

— "Roger Williams." *Encyclopædia Britannica.* July 1, 2016.
    https://www.britannica.com/biography/Roger-Williams-
    American-religious-leader.

— "Schism of 1054." *Encyclopædia Britannica.* August 22, 2017.
    https://www.britannica.com/event/Schism-of-1054.

— "Scopes Trial." *Encyclopædia Britannica.* April 12, 2018.
    https://www.britannica.com/event/Scopes-Trial.

— "The Return of the Spirit: The Second Great Awakening."
    Christian History Institute. 1989.
    https://christianhistoryinstitute.org/magazine/article/return-
    of-the-spirit-second-great-awakening.

— "Valens." *Encyclopædia Britannica.* May 15, 2013.
https://www.britannica.com/biography/Valens.

Elton, Geoffrey, and John Morrill "Henry VIII." *Encyclopædia Britannica.* January 15, 2018.
https://www.britannica.com/biography/Henry-VIII-king-of-England.

Eusebius. *The Church History Of Eusebius.* Edited by Phillip Schaff.
http://www.ccel.org/ccel/schaff/npnf201.html.

Fairchild, Mary "Eastern Orthodox Denomination." *ThoughtCo.* March 17, 2017. https://www.thoughtco.com/eastern-orthodox-church-denomination-700624.

Falaye, T A. "Polygamy and Christianity Africa." *Global Journal of Arts Humanities and Social Sciences* 4, no. 10 (October 2016): 18-28.
http://www.eajournals.org/wp-content/uploads/Polygamy-and-Christianity-in-Africa.pdf.

First Council of Nicaea (A.D. 325). Vol. 14, in *Nicene and Post-Nicene Fathers,* edited by Philip Schaff and Henry Wace, translated by Henry Percival. Buffalo: Christian Literature Publishing Co.1900. http://www.newadvent.org/fathers/3801.htm.

Fortescue, Adrian. *Patriarch and Patriarchate.* Vol. 11, in *The Catholic Encyclopedia.* New York: Robert Appleton Company. 1911.
http://www.newadvent.org/cathen/11549a.htm.

Fortescue, Adrian. *Theodosius I.* Vol. 14, in *The Catholic Encyclopedia.* New York: Robert Appleton Company. 1912.
http://www.newadvent.org/cathen/14577d.htm.

Fox, Tamar "Who Are Messianic "Jews"?" *My Jewish Learning.* Accessed December 15, 2017.
https://www.myjewishlearning.com/article/messianic-judaism/.

Gareloch, Karen "1988: Observer wins Pulitzer Prize for coverage of PTL, Bakkers." *Charlotte Observer.* February 15, 2018.
https://www.charlotteobserver.com/news/state/article200305089.html.

Gerson, Michael "The Last Temptation." *The Atlantic.* April, 2018.
https://www.theatlantic.com/magazine/archive/2018/04/the-last-temptation/554066/.

Gibney, Alex "The Deceptions of Ralph Reed." *The Atlantic.*
    September 26, 2010.
    https://www.theatlantic.com/politics/archive/2010/09/the-
    deceptions-of-ralph-reed/63568/.

Godbey, John Charles "Unitarianism and Universalism." *Encyclopædia
    Britannica,* March 22, 2017.
    https://www.britannica.com/topic/Unitarianism.

Gottschalk, Stephen "Mary Baker Eddy." *Encyclopædia Britannica.*
    March 28, 2017.
    https://www.britannica.com/biography/Mary-Baker-Eddy.

Gottschalk, Stephen, and J. Gordon Melton "Christian Science."
    Encyclopædia Britannica. August 18, 2016.
    https://www.britannica.com/topic/Christian-Science.

Grell, Ole Peter. "Introduction." In *Tolerance and Intolerance in the
    European Reformation*, edited by Ole Peter Grell and Bob
    Scribner. Cambridge: Cambridge University Press. 1996.

Grossman, Cathy "The megachurch boom rolls on, but big concerns
    are rising too." *Religion News Service.* December 2, 2015.
    https://religionnews.com/2015/12/02/megachurch-
    evangelical-christians/.

Gutierrez, Lisa "'Word from the Lord': Televangelist's ministry buys
    Tyler Perry's Gulfstream jet." *Kasas City Star.* January 21,
    2018. https://www.kansascity.com/news/nation-
    world/article195841759.html.

Hackett, Conrad, and Brian J. Grim "Global Christianity." *Pew
    Research Center.* December, 2011.
    http://assets.pewresearch.org/wp-
    content/uploads/sites/11/2011/12/Christianity-fullreport-
    web.pdf.

Hanegraaff, Hank. *Christianity in Crisis.* Nashville: Thomas Nelson.
    2012.

Harper, Michael "An African way: the African Independent
    churches." *Christian History Institute.* September, 1984.
    https://christianhistoryinstitute.org/magazine/article/african
    -way-independent-churches.

Harper, Steven. *The Way to Heaven: The Gospel According to John Wesley.*
    Grand Rapids, Michigan: Zondervan. 1983.

Herlihy, David, David Weinstein, and Others "History of Europe: The Emergence of Modern Europe, 1500-1648." *Encyclopædia Britannica.* July 19, 2016. https://www.britannica.com/topic/history-of-Europe/The-emergence-of-modern-Europe-1500-1648.

Hibbert, Christopher "Benito Mussolini." *Encyclopædia Britannica.* July 18, 2017. https://www.britannica.com/biography/Benito-Mussolini.

Hillar, Marian. "Servetus and Calvin." In *Thirty Letters to Calvin, Preacher to the Genevans: & Sixty Signs of the Kingdom of the Antichrist and His Revelation which is Now at Hand (from The Restoration of Christianity, 1553),* translated by Marian Hillar and Christopher Hoffman, 175. Lewiston, NY: Edwin Meller Press. 2010. http://www.socinian.org/files/Sevetus_and_Calvin_from_T hirty_Letters.pdf.

Holocaust Museum "Holocaust Timeline." *Holocaust Museum Learning Center.* https://hmlc.org/holocaust-history/timeline/.

Horowitz, Mitch "How Oral Roberts Changed Religion." *Politico.* December 30, 2014. https://www.politico.com/magazine/story/2014/12/oral-roberts-changed-religion-113886.

Hudson, Winthrop S. "Baptist." *Encyclopædia Britannica.* December 20, 2017. https://www.britannica.com/topic/Baptist.

Huff, James. "CALVIN AND CHURCH GOVERNMENT." *WRS Journal 16:2* (August 2009): 15-18. http://wrs.edu/Materials_for_Web_Site/Journals/16-2_Aug-2009/Huff--Calvin_Church_Government.pdf.

Huffman, Carl. "Pythagoras." Edited by Edward N. Zalta. *The Stanford Encyclopedia of Philosophy* (Summer 2014). https://plato.stanford.edu/archives/sum2014/entries/pytha goras/.

Hussey, Laura S., and Geoffrey C. Layman. "George W. Bush and the Evangelicals: Religious Commitment and Partisan Change among Evangelical Protestants, 1960-2004." In *A Matter of Faith? Religion in the 2004 Election,* edited by David E. Campbell. Brookings. 2007.

Hutchinson, Ian, and Others "When God and Science Meet Suprising Discoveries of Agreement." *National Association of Evangelicals.* 2015. https://www.nae.net/godandscience/.

IndependentConservative "Ole Anthony (Trinity Foundation) Shades of a Cult!" *Independent Conservative.* October 15, 2007. http://www.independentconservative.com/2007/10/15/trinity_foundation_cult/.

"Israel 2015 International Religious Freedom Report." *U.S. Department of State.* 2015. https://www.state.gov/documents/organization/256481.pdf.

"John Calvin Father of the Reformed Faith." *Christianity Today.* 2018. http://www.christianitytoday.com/history/people/theologians/john-calvin.html.

Johnson, Todd M, and Gina A Zurlo "Stauts of Global Christianity 2018." *Center for the Study of Global Christianity.* June, 2018. http://www.gordonconwell.edu/ockenga/research/documents/StatusofGlobalChristianity2018.pdf.

Johnston, Lori "Trump's evangelical advisory board violates the law, advocacy group argues in new filing." *Washington Post.* August 30, 2018. https://www.washingtonpost.com/news/acts-of-faith/wp/2018/08/30/trumps-evangelical-advisory-board-violates-the-law-advocacy-group-argues-in-new-filing/?utm_term=.ebfef2f34be2.

Jones, Alexander Raymond "Ptolemaic system." *Encyclopædia Britannica.* June 16, 2008. https://www.britannica.com/science/Ptolemaic-system.

Kelly, John "Nestorius." *Encyclopædia Britannica.* April 7, 2014. https://www.britannica.com/biography/Nestorius.

— "Patristic Literature." *Encyclopædia Britannica.* April 12, 2017. https://www.britannica.com/topic/patristic-literature/The-post-Nicene-period.

"Kenneth Copeland Ministries." *MinistryWatch.org.* Accessed July 18, 2018. https://ministrywatch.com/ministry.php?ein=751300831.

Kenneth Copeland Ministries "Kenneth Copeland Ministries: A Brief History." *Kenneth Copeland Ministries.* Accessed July 16, 2018.

https://www.kcm.org/kenneth-copeland-ministries-a-brief-history.

"Kenneth Copeland, Jesse Duplantis, defending their private jets." *YouTube.* December 30, 2015. https://www.youtube.com/watch?v=AdH2DGSXjss.

Kent, William. "Indulgences." In *The Catholic Encyclopedia.* New York: Robert Appleton. 1908. http://newadvent.org/cathen/07783a.htm.

Keteyian, Armen "Televangelists Living Like Kings." *CBS News.* November 6, 2007. https://www.cbsnews.com/news/televangelists-living-like-kings/.

Kirsch, Johann Peter. *Simon Magus.* Vol. 13, in *Catholic Encyclopedia.* New York: Robert Appleton. 1912. http://www.newadvent.org/cathen/13797b.htm.

Kirsch, Johann Peter. *Unam Sanctam.* Vol. 15, in *The Catholic Encyclopedia.* New York: Robert Appleton Company. 1912. http://www.newadvent.org/cathen/15126a.htm.

Klein, Christopher "The Atlantic Charter's Surprising History." *History.com.* August 9, 2016. http://www.history.com/news/the-atlantic-charters-surprising-history.

Kopff, E. Christian, and Stewart Henry Perowne "Julian." *Encyclopædia Britannica.* September 24, 2009. https://www.britannica.com/biography/Julian-Roman-emperor.

Kozar, Steven "Costi Hinn Pleads for His Uncle Benny Hinn to Repent of Prosperity Gospel." *YouTube.* March 21, 2018. https://www.youtube.com/watch?v=Hh0hGg4mF4Y.

Kurtzleben, Danielle "Are You An Evangelical - Are You Sure?" *NPR.* December 19, 2015. https://www.npr.org/2015/12/19/458058251/are-you-an-evangelical-are-you-sure.

Landes, Richard "Millennialism." *Encyclopædia Britannica.* January 5, 2018. https://www.britannica.com/topic/millennialism.

Lane, Christopher "On the Victorian Afterlife of the 1781 Sunday Observance Act." *BRANCH: Britain, Representation and*

Nineteenth-Century History. Edited by Dino Franco Felluga. May, 2012. http://www.branchcollective.org/?ps_articles=christopher-lane-on-the-victorian-afterlife-of-the-1781-sunday-observance-act.

Lausanne Global Analysis "Number of Evangelicals worldwide." *Lausanne Movement*. Accessed February 5, 2018. https://www.lausanne.org/lgc-transfer/number-of-evangelicals-worldwide.

Lausanne Movement "Number of Evangelicals Worldwide." *Lausanne Movement*. 2011. https://www.lausanne.org/lgc-transfer/number-of-evangelicals-worldwide.

Lechleitner, Elizabeth "Seventh-day Adventist Church emerged from religious fervor of 19th Century." *Seventh-day Adventist Church*. February 4, 2013. https://www.adventist.org/en/information/history/article/go/-/seventh-day-adventist-church-emerged-from-religious-fervor-of-19th-century-1/.

Lee, Timothy "40 maps that explain the Roman Empire." *Vox*. August 19, 2014. https://www.vox.com/world/2018/6/19/17469176/roman-empire-maps-history-explained.

Lincoln, Abraham "Abraham Lincoln Quotes." *Brainy Quotes*. Accessed March 29, 2019. https://www.brainyquote.com/quotes/abraham_lincoln_106095.

Lippold, Adolf "Theodosius I." *Encyclopædia Britannica*. August 30, 2016. https://www.britannica.com/biography/Theodosius-I.

"Liturgical Rites." In *New Catholic Encyclopedia*. https://www.encyclopedia.com/religion/encyclopedias-almanacs-transcripts-and-maps/liturgical-rites.

Llewellyn, Jennifer, Jim Southey, and Steve Thompson "Hitler and Mussolini." *AlphaHistory.com*. 2014. http://alphahistory.com/nazigermany/hitler-and-mussolini/.

Lobdell, William "TBN's Promise: Send Money and See Riches." *Los Angeles Times*. September 20, 2004. http://articles.latimes.com/2004/sep/20/local/me-tbn20.

— "The Price of Healing." *LA Times*. July 27, 2003.
http://articles.latimes.com/print/2003/jul/27/magazine/tm
-benny30.

Loughlin, James. "The Sixth Nicene Canon and the Papacy." *American Catholic Quarterly Review* Classic Media, Inc. 5 (1880): 220-239.
http://www.biblicalcatholic.com/apologetics/CouncilNicaea
SixthCanon.htm.

Lumen Learning "Crises of the Roman Empire." *ER Services*. Accessed January 17, 2019.
https://courses.lumenlearning.com/suny-hccc-
worldhistory/chapter/crises-of-the-roman-empire/.

— "Diocletian and the Tetrarchy." *ER Services*. Accessed January 16, 2019. https://courses.lumenlearning.com/suny-hccc-
worldhistory/chapter/diocletian-and-the-tetrarchy/.

Lumpp, David "Returning to Wittenberg: What Martin Luther Teaches Today's Theologians on the Holy Trinity." *Concordia Theological Seminary Fort Wayne*. 2003.
http://www.ctsfw.net/media/pdfs/lumppreturningtowittenb
erg.pdf.

Luther, Martin "Smalcald Articles." *Book of Concord*. 1537.
http://bookofconcord.org/smalcald.php.

Luther, Martin. *The Smalcald Articles*. Vols. Part two, Article 1, in *Concordia: The Lutheran Confessions Saint Louis*. Saint Louis: Concordia Publishing. 2005.

Macpherson, Ewan. *Flavius Valens*. Vol. 15, in *The Catholic Encyclopedia*. New York: Robert Appleton Company. 1912.
http://www.newadvent.org/cathen/15253b.htm.

Macur, Juliet "For Some Sports Figures, Opinions Have a Price." *New York Times*. May 11, 2011.
https://www.nytimes.com/2011/05/12/sports/olympics/ga
y-marriage-stance-costs-vidmar-olympic-role.html.

Madsen, Thomas, Gary Dickson, and Others "Crusades." *Encyclopædia Britannica*. May 31, 2018.
https://www.britannica.com/event/Crusades.

Marius, Richard. *Thomas More: A Biography*. Harvard University Press. 1999.

Marotta, Krisan "Chronology of the Apostle Paul." *Wednesday In the Word.* 2016.
http://www.wednesdayintheword.com/resources/Chronolo
gyofPaul.pdf.

"Martin Luther Passionate Reformer." *Christianity Today.* Accessed
June 7, 2018.
https://www.christianitytoday.com/history/people/theologi
ans/martin-luther.html.

Martin, Jennifer C. "Making Money Off Miracles: The Gospel of
Televangelists." *Gawker.* August 25, 2015.
http://gawker.com/making-money-off-miracles-the-gospel-
of-televangelists-1725330875.

Martin, Marty, Jan Pelikan Jaroslav, and Others "Roman
Catholicism." *Encyclopædia Britannica.* February 12, 2018.
https://www.britannica.com/topic/Roman-Catholicism.

Martínez, Jessica, and Gregory A. Smith "How the Faithful Voted."
Pew Research. November 9, 2016.
http://www.pewresearch.org/fact-tank/2016/11/09/how-
the-faithful-voted-a-preliminary-2016-analysis/.

Maschke, Timothy. "Philipp Spener's Pia Desideria." *Lutheran
Quarterly* 6 (1992): 187-204.
http://www.lutheranquarterly.com/uploads/7/4/0/1/74012
89/timelinespener.pdf.

Matthews, J.F., and Donald MacGillivray Nicol "Constantine I."
Encyclopædia Britannica. August 27, 2018.
https://www.britannica.com/biography/Constantine-I-
Roman-emperor.

Maza, Cristina "Trump Will Start the End of the World, Claim
Evangelicals Who Support Him." *Newsweek.* January 12, 2018.
https://www.newsweek.com/trump-will-bring-about-end-
worldevangelicals-end-times-779643.

McCumber, Mishel "Lost Notes from MorningStar." *Deception Bytes.*
April 25, 2012. http://deceptionbytes.com/lost-notes-from-
morningstar/.

McGeown, Martyn J. "A Critical Examination of the Amyraldian
View of the Atonement." *Covenant Protestant Reformed Church.*
Accessed May 23, 2018.

http://www.cprf.co.uk/articles/amyraldianexamination.htm #.WwW0r_ZFymQ.

McVicar, Michael J. "The Religious Right in America." *Oxford Research Encyclopedia of Religion.* February 26, 2018. http://religion.oxfordre.com/view/10.1093/acrefore/97801 99340378.001.0001/acrefore-9780199340378-e-97.

"Meletius of Lycopolis." *Encyclopædia Britannica.* November 6, 2006. https://www.britannica.com/biography/Meletius-of-Lycopolis.

Melton, J. Gordon "Jehovah's Witness." *Encyclopædia Britannica* . December 19, 2018. https://www.britannica.com/topic/Jehovahs-Witnesses.

Melton, J. Gordon, and Ernest R. Sandeen "Christian Fundamentalism." *Encyclopædia Britannica.* November 29, 2016. https://www.britannica.com/topic/Christian-fundamentalism.

Melton, John Gordon "Evangelical Church." *Encyclopædia Britannica.* July 29, 2016. https://www.britannica.com/topic/Evangelical-church-Protestantism.

Mikelionis, Lukas "Chinese officials burn bibles, close churches..." *Fox News.* September 10, 2018. http://www.foxnews.com/world/2018/09/10/chinese-officials-burn-bibles-close-churches-force-christian-to-denounce-faith-amid-escalating-crackdown.html.

Miller, A.G. "Black and White Race in American Denominations." *National Association of Evangelicals.* Spring/Summer, 2016. https://www.nae.net/black-white-race-american-denominations/.

Mokgobi, M. "Understanding traditional African healing." *Afr J Phys Health Educ Recreat Dance* (September 2014): 24–34. https://www.ncbi.nlm.nih.gov/pmc/articles/PMC4651463/.

Moravian Church "Brief History of the Moravian Church." *The Moravian Church.* Accessed February 15, 2018. http://www.moravian.org/the-moravian-church/history/.

Moss, Vladimir "Orthodoxy and Freedom of Religion." *Orthodoxchrisitanbooks.com.* April 16, 2010.

http://www.orthodoxchristianbooks.com/articles/308/orth
odoxy-freedom-religion/.

Muthengi, Julius K. "Polygamy and The Church in Africa." *Biblical
Studies.Org.* February 14, 1995.
https://biblicalstudies.org.uk/pdf/ajet/14-2_055.pdf.

NAE "Evangelicals Can Have Different Views on Creation Leaders
Say." *National Association of Evangelicals.* September, 2017.
https://www.nae.net/evangelicals-can-different-views-
creation-leaders-say/.

— "Evangelicals Leaders Don't Want Partisan Political Identity."
National Association of Evangelicals. January, 2018.
https://www.nae.net/evangelicals-leaders-dont-want-
partisan-political-identity/.

New England Historical Society "Way More Than the Scarlet Letter:
Puritan Punishments." *New England Historical Society.* 2018.
http://www.newenglandhistoricalsociety.com/way-more-
than-the-scarlet-letter-puritan-punishments/.

"New Report: The Battle for China's Spirit: Religious Revival,
Repression, and Resistance under Xi Jinping." *Freedom House.*
February, 2017. https://freedomhouse.org/article/new-
report-battle-chinas-spirit-religious-revival-repression-and-
resistance-under-xi.

Newport, Frank "Percentage of Christians in U.S. Drifting Down, but
Still High." *Gallup.* December 24, 2015.
https://news.gallup.com/poll/187955/percentage-christians-
drifting-down-high.aspx.

News Division "Jesse Duplantis, Kenneth Copeland: God Gave Us
Jets So We Could Have Private Prayer Time." *Pulpit and Pen.*
December 30, 2015.
http://pulpitandpen.org/2015/12/30/jesse-duplantis-
kenneth-copeland-god-gave-us-jets-so-we-could-have-
private-prayer-time/.

Noll, Mark A. "Antinomianism." *Believe Religious Information Source Web-
Site.* Accessed February 27, 2018. http://mb-
soft.com/believe/txn/antinomi.htm.

"Ockhamism." In *Encyclopedia of Philosophy*.2006.
    https://www.encyclopedia.com/humanities/encyclopedias-
    almanacs-transcripts-and-maps/ockhamism.

O'Donnell, James "St. Augustine." *Encyclopædia Britannica*. October 24,
    2017. https://www.britannica.com/biography/Saint-
    Augustine.

— "St. Augustine." *Encyclopædia Britannica* . January 3, 2019.
    https://www.britannica.com/biography/Saint-Augustine.

Openheimer, Mark "Peter Popoff, the Born-Again Scoundrel." *GQ*.
    February 27, 2017. https://www.gq.com/story/peter-
    popoff-born-again-scoundrel.

Ort, H Van. "Augustine and manichaeism: new discoveries, new
    perspectives." *Verbum Et Ecclesia* 27, no.2 (2006).
    https://verbumetecclesia.org.za/index.php/ve/article/view/
    172.

"Ousia." In *Encyclopedia of Philosophy*.2006.
    http://www.encyclopedia.com/humanities/encyclopedias-
    almanacs-transcripts-and-maps/ousia.

Pavlo, Walter "Fraud Thriving In U.S. Churches, But You Wouldn't
    Know It." *Forbes*. November 18, 2013.
    https://www.forbes.com/sites/walterpavlo/2013/11/18/fra
    ud-thriving-in-u-s-churches-but-you-wouldnt-know-
    it/#7b1405c1d9d4.

Peters, Edward, and Bernard Hamilton "Inquisition." *Encyclopædia
    Britannica*. August 10, 2016.
    https://www.britannica.com/topic/inquisition.

Pew "Global Survey of Evangelical Protestant Leaders." *Pew Research
    Center*. june 22, 2011.
    http://www.pewforum.org/2011/06/22/global-survey-
    beliefs/.

— "Religious Landscape Study." *Pew Research Center*. Accessed June
    26, 2018. http://www.pewforum.org/religious-landscape-
    study/.

— "The Global Religious Landscape." *Pew Research Forum*. December
    18, 2012. http://www.pewforum.org/2012/12/18/global-
    religious-landscape-exec/.

Pieper, Josef "Scholasticism." *Encyclopædia Britannica*. June 23, 2015. https://www.britannica.com/topic/Scholasticism.

Pinson Jr., William "Is Soul Competency the Baptist Distinctive?" *Baptist Distinctives*. 2017. https://www.baptistdistinctives.org/resources/articles/is-soul-competency-the-baptist-distinctive/.

— "Jesus is Lord." *Baptist Distinctives*. 2017. https://www.baptistdistinctives.org/resources/articles/jesus-is-lord/.

Pinson Jr., William M "Baptists: What Makes a Baptist a Baptist?" *Baptist Distinctives*. 2017. https://www.baptistdistinctives.org/resources/articles/what-makes-a-baptist-a-baptist/.

Pohle, Joseph. *Pelagius and Pelagianism*. Vol. 11, in *The Catholic Encylcopledia*. New York: Robert Appleton Company. 1911. http://newadvent.org/cathen/11604a.htm.

Pointer, Steven "American Postmillennialism: Seeing the Glory." *Christian History Institute*. 1999. https://christianhistoryinstitute.org/magazine/article/american-postmillennialism-seeing-the-glory.

Popper, Helen "Llama fetuses, dead cats on sale at Bolivian market." *Reuters*. July 16, 2007. https://www.reuters.com/article/us-religion-bolivia-witches/llama-fetuses-dead-cats-on-sale-at-bolivian-market-idUSL1646771620070716.

Rees, B. R. *Pelagius Life and Letters*. Woodbridge: The Boydell Press. 1998.

Renaud, Myriam "Myths Debunked: Why Did White Evangelical Christians Vote for Trump?" *Univeristy of Chicago Divinity School*. January 19, 2017. https://divinity.uchicago.edu/sightings/myths-debunked-why-did-white-evangelical-christians-vote-trump.

Rhodes, Philip, Douglas James Guthrie, and Others "History of medicine." *Encyclopædia Britannica*. October 25, 2017. https://www.britannica.com/science/history-of-medicine.

Ritchie, Mark S. "Augustine and the Pelagian Controversy." *THE STORY OF THE CHURCH - PART 2*. 1999. http://www.ritchies.net/p2wk6.htm.

Robinson, Bruce "World War Two: Summary Outline of Key Events." *BBC.* March 30, 2011. http://www.bbc.co.uk/history/worldwars/wwtwo/ww2_summary_01.shtml#two.

Roman Catholic Church "Charisms." *Catechism of the Catholic Church.* Accessed June 8, 2018. http://www.vatican.va/archive/ccc_css/archive/catechism/p123a9p2.htm#799.

— "Sacraments of the Catholic Church." *Catholic Online.* Accessed February 9, 2019. https://www.catholic.org/prayers/sacrament.php.

"Roman Emperor Constantine's conversion to Christianity." *Classic History.* February 6, 2018. http://www.classichistory.net/archives/constantine-christianity.

Rosin, Hanna "Oral Roberts and His Green Buick." *Slate.* December 16, 2009. http://www.slate.com/culture/2018/06/bill-clinton-and-james-pattersons-the-president-is-missing-is-a-fascinating-projection-of-clintons-inner-life.html.

Rosten, Leo, ed. *Religions of America.* New York, New York: Simon & Schuster. 1975.

Rowe, Sean "The Resurrection of Robert Tilton." *Miami New Times.* January 1, 1998. http://www.miaminewtimes.com/news/the-resurrection-of-robert-tilton-6377686.

Russell, Jeffrey, and Ioan M. Lewis "Witchcraft." *Encyclopædia Britannica.* August 22, 2016. https://www.britannica.com/topic/witchcraft.

Ryan, Edward A "Spanish Inquisition." *Encyclopædia Britannica.* December 18, 2017. https://www.britannica.com/topic/Spanish-Inquisition.

Saddleback Church "Be a Part of Our History." *Saddleback Church.* Accessed July 17, 2018. https://saddleback.com/visit/about/our-church.

Sander, Emilie T., Linwood Fredericksen, Seymour Cain, Coert Rylaarsdam, Frederick Fyvie Bruce, Grady Davis, Robert Faherty, Robert Grant, Nahum Sarna, and Krister Stendahl

"Biblical literature:New Testament." *Encyclopædia Britannica.* November 15, 2017. https://www.britannica.com/topic/biblical-literature/New-Testament-canon-texts-and-versions .

Schaefer, Francis. *Council of Chalcedon.* Vol. 3, in *The Catholic Encyclopedia.* New York: Robert Appleton Company. 1908. http://www.newadvent.org/cathen/03555a.htm.

Schaff, Peter. *Theological Controversies and Development of the Ecumenical Orthodoxy.* Vol. III, chap. IX in *History of the Christian Church,* by Peter Schaff. Oak Harbor, WA: Logos Research Systems. 1997. http://www.ccel.org/s/schaff/history/3_ch09.htm.

Schaff, Philip. *Ante-Nicene Christianity. A.D. 100-325.* Vol. 2, in *History of the Christian Church.* New York: Scribner. 1910. http://www.ccel.org/ccel/schaff/hcc2.v.xiv.i.html.

—. *Creeds of Christendom.* Vol. no. I. Harper & Brothers. 1877. http://www.ccel.org/ccel/schaff/creeds1.iv.iii.html.

Schaff, Phillip. *History of the Christian Church, Volume V: The Middle Ages. A.D. 1049-1294.* Grand Rapids: Christian CLassics Ethereal Library. 1910. http://www.ccel.org/ccel/schaff/hcc5.pdf.

—. *History of the Christian Church, Volume VI: The Middle Ages. A.D. 1294-1517.* Grand Rapids, MI: Christian CLassics Ethereal Library. 1910. http://www.ccel.org/ccel/schaff/hcc6.pdf.

Schmidt, William E. "Adultery as a Crime: Old Laws Dusted Off In a Wisconsin Case." *New York Times.* April 30, 1990. https://www.nytimes.com/1990/04/30/us/adultery-as-a-crime-old-laws-dusted-off-in-a-wisconsin-case.html.

Scott, Donald "Evangelicalism, Revivalism, and the Second Great Awakening." *National Humanities Center.* Accessed July 26, 2018. http://nationalhumanitiescenter.org/tserve/nineteen/nkeyinfo/nevanrev.htm.

— "Mormonism and the American Mainstream." *National Humanities Center.* Accessed July 26, 2018. http://nationalhumanitiescenter.org/tserve/nineteen/nkeyinfo/nmormon.htm.

Scott, George R. *PHALLIC WORSHIP*. T. WERNER LAURIE LTD. 1941. https://archive.org/details/B20442737.

Seventh-day Adventist Church "Beliefs." *Seventh-day Adventist Church.* Accessed March 1, 2019. https://www.adventist.org/en/beliefs/.

— "Holy Scriptures." *Seventh-day Adventist.* Accessed March 1, 2019. https://www.adventist.org/en/beliefs/god/holy-scriptures/.

Shahan, Thomas. *First Council of Constantinople.* Vol. 4, in *The Catholic Encyclopedia.* New York: Robert Appleton. 1908. http://www.newadvent.org/cathen/04308a.htm.

Shelley, Bruce "American Adventism: The Great Disappointment." *Christian History Institute.* 1999. https://christianhistoryinstitute.org/magazine/article/americ an-adventism-the-great-disappointment.

Shelley, Marshall "What's a Cult." *Ignite Your Faith.* Accessed January 19, 2018. https://www.christianitytoday.com/iyf/advice/faithqa/what -is-cult.html.

Shellnutt, Kate "Trump Elected President, Thanks to 4 in 5 White Evangelicals." *Christianity Today.* November 9, 2016. https://www.christianitytoday.com/news/2016/november/t rump-elected-president-thanks-to-4-in-5-white-evangelicals.html.

Sherwood, Harriet "Christians in Egypt face unprecedented persecution, report says." *The Guardian.* January 10, 2018. https://www.theguardian.com/world/2018/jan/10/christian s-egypt-unprecedented-persecution-report.

Slick, Matt "Are Roman Catholics Christian?" *CARM.* Accessed January 19, 2018. https://carm.org/are-roman-catholics-christian.

Smith, Joseph. "Joseph Smith - History." In *The Pearl of Great Price.* Salt Lake City: The Church of Jesus Christ of Latter-day Saints. 1981. https://www.lds.org/scriptures/pgp/js-h/1?lang=eng.

—. *The Doctrine and Covenants.* Salt Lake City: The Church of Jesus Christ of Latter-day Saints. 1981.

https://www.lds.org/scriptures/dc-testament/title-page.html?lang=eng.

— "The King Follett Sermon." *The Church of Jesus Christ of Latter-day Saints.* April 7, 1844. https://www.churchofjesuschrist.org/study/ensign/1971/04/the-king-follett-sermon?lang=eng.

Sotomayor, Sonia "Commonwealth Club." Jan 28, 2013. https://www.commonwealthclub.org/events/archive/transcript/justice-sonia-sotomayor.

Southern Baptist Convention "The Baptist Faith and Message." *Southern Baptist Convention.* June 14, 2000. http://www.sbc.net/bfm2000/bfm2000.asp.

Spalding, James C., and John C. Stillwell "Reformed and Presbyterian churches." *Encyclopædia Britannica.* September 6, 2011. https://www.britannica.com/topic/Presbyterian-churches.

Staff, BGEA "Is baptism necessary for salvation?" *Billy Graham Evangelistic Association.* June 1, 2014. https://billygraham.org/answer/is-baptism-necessary-for-salvation/.

Stefon, Matt "Iglesia ni Cristo (INC)." *Encyclopædia Britannica.* February 5, 2016. https://www.britannica.com/topic/Iglesia-ni-Cristo.

Stefon, Matt, and Hans J. Hillerbrand "Christology." *Encyclopædia Britannica.* August 26, 2016. https://www.britannica.com/topic/Christology.

Stefon, Matt, Ernst Benz, and Others "Christianity." *Encyclopædia Britannica.* November 30, 2017. https://www.britannica.com/topic/Christianity.

Stetzer, Ed "Defining Evangelicals in Research." *National Association of Evangelicals.* Winter, 2017/2018. https://www.nae.net/defining-evangelicals-research/.

Stewart-Sykes, Alistair. "The Original Condemnation of Asian Montanism." *The Journal of Ecclesiastical History* (January 1999): 1-22. http://journals.cambridge.org/abstract_S0022046998008434.

Sullivan, James. "Athanasian Creed." In *The Catholic Encyclopedia*. New York: Robert Appleton Company. 1910. http://www.newadvent.org/cathen/02033b.htm.

Synod of Laodicea. Vol. 14, in *Nicene and Post-Nicene Fathers*, edited by Philip Schaff and Henry Wace. Buffalo, NY: Christian Literature Publishing Co.1900. http://www.newadvent.org/fathers/3806.htm.

Tanabe, Rosie "Monophysitism." *New World Encyclopedia*. November 14, 2014. http://www.newworldencyclopedia.org/p/index.php?title= Monophysitism&oldid=985353.

— "Nestorianism." *New World Encyclopedia*. December 29, 2014. http://www.newworldencyclopedia.org/p/index.php?title= Nestorianism&oldid=986079.

— "Sethianism." *New World Encyclopedia*. September 9, 2015. http://www.newworldencyclopedia.org/p/index.php?title=S ethianism&oldid=990427.

"Taxonomy, History of." *Biology Reference*. Accessed February 5, 2018. http://www.biologyreference.com/Ta-Va/Taxonomy-History-of.html.

Terdiman, Daniel "Study: Wikipedia as accurate as Britannica." December 16, 2016. https://www.cnet.com/news/study-wikipedia-as-accurate-as-britannica/.

"THE BAPTIST CONFESSION OF FAITH." *RBList.org*. June, 1996. http://www.rblist.org/1689.pdf.

The Barna Group, Ltd "Survey explores who qualifies as an evangelical." *Barna*. January 18, 2007. https://www.barna.com/research/survey-explores-who-qualifies-as-an-evangelical/.

The Church of Jesus Christ of Latter-day Saints "The Convert Immigrants." *The Church of Jesus Christ of Latter-day Saints*. August 1, 2013. https://history.churchofjesuschrist.org/article/pioneer-story-the-convert-immigrants-?lang=eng.

The Clementine Homilies. Vol. XVII, in *Ante-Nicene Christian Library: Translations of the Writings of the Fathers Down to A.D. 325,* edited by Rev. Alexander Roberts and James Donaldson. Edinburgh: T & T Clark.1870.

The Clementine Recognitions. Vol. 3, in *Ante-Nicene Christian Library: Translations of the Writings of the Fathers Down to A.D. 325*, edited by Rev. Alexander Roberts and James Donaldson. Edinburgh: T and T Clark.1867.

"The Creed of Chalcedon." *Christian Classics Ethereal Library*. Accessed May 7, 2019. https://www.ccel.org/ccel/schaff/creeds1.iv.iv.html.

"The Discrimination Administration." *National Center for Transgender Equality*. Accessed November 15, 2018. https://transequality.org/the-discrimination-administration.

"The End of Charismatic Gifts." *Free Brethren House Church*. Accessed June 7, 2018. http://www.house-church.net/doctrines/charisma.html.

"The Phrase Finder." Accessed February 8, 2019. https://www.phrases.org.uk/meanings/absolute-power-corrupts-absolutely.html.

"The Protestant Inquisition." *Catholic Apologetics*. Accessed October 8, 2018. http://www.catholicapologetics.info/apologetics/protestantism/protin.htm.

"The Thalia of Arius." *Early Church Texts*. Accessed December 31, 2018. https://earlychurchtexts.com/public/arius_thalia.htm.

"The Worship of Baal." *Bible History Online*. Accessed November 29, 2018. https://www.bible-history.com/resource/ff_baal.htm.

Thesleff, Holger "Pythagoreanism." *Encyclopædia Britannica*. February 21, 2013. https://www.britannica.com/topic/Pythagoreanism.

Thumma PhD, Scott "Exploring the Megachurch Phenomena: Their characteristics and cultural context." *Hartford Institute For Religion Research*. 1996. https://web.archive.org/web/20151101100905/http://hirr.hartsem.edu/bookshelf/thumma_article2.html.

Tolchin, Martin "Amendment Drive on School Prayer Loses Senate Vote." *New York Times*. March 21, 1984.

https://www.nytimes.com/1984/03/21/us/amendment-drive-on-school-prayer-loses-senate-vote.html.

Toner, Patrick. "Communion under Both Kinds." In *The Catholic Encyclopedia*. New York: Robert Appleton Company. 1908. http://newadvent.org/cathen/04175a.htm.

Trinity Foundation "Frequently Asked Questions About Religious Fraud." *Trinity Foundation*. Accessed July 11, 2018. https://trinityfi.org/frequently-asked-questions/#1.

Ullmann, Agnes "Louis Pasteur." *Encyclopædia Britannica*. February 26, 2019. https://www.britannica.com/biography/Louis-Pasteur.

Voltz, Dan "Coptic Church." *New World Encyclopedia*. October 20, 2008.

http://www.newworldencyclopedia.org/p/index.php?title=Coptic_church&oldid=834650.

Weber, Timothy "Dispensational Premillennialism: The Dispensationalist Era." *Christian History Institute*. 1999. https://christianhistoryinstitute.org/magazine/article/dispensational-premillennialism-the-dispensationalist-era.

Weiland, Noah "Evangelicals, Having Backed Trump, Find White House 'Front Door Is Open'." *New York Times*. February 7, 2018.

https://www.nytimes.com/2018/02/07/us/politics/trump-evangelicals-national-prayer-breakfast.html.

"Wenceslaus." In *Encyclopedia of World Biography*.2004. https://www.encyclopedia.com/people/history/german-history-biographies/wenceslaus.

West, Aaron "Imperial Laws and Edicts." *Wisconsin Lutheran College*. May 7, 2008.

https://web.archive.org/web/20081026010432/http://www.fourthcentury.com:80/index.php/imperial-laws-chart.

— "Imperial Laws and Letters Involving Religion, AD 364-395." *Wisconsin Lutheran College*. July 18, 2008.

https://web.archive.org/web/20081025063840/http://www.fourthcentury.com:80/index.php/imperial-laws-chart-364.

— "Imperial Laws and Letters Involving Religion, AD 395-431." *Wisconsin Lutheran College*. July 18, 2008.

https://web.archive.org/web/20081025050453/http://www
.fourthcentury.com/index.php/imperial-laws-chart-395.

Westfall, Richard S. "Sir Isaac Newton." *Encyclopædia Britannica.* April
5, 2019. https://www.britannica.com/biography/Isaac-
Newton.

"What do Evangelical Christians think about televangelists?" *Qora.*
2015-2016. https://www.quora.com/What-do-Evangelical-
Christians-think-about-televangelists.

"What is the definition of a cult?" *Got Questions.* Accessed January 19,
2018. https://www.gotquestions.org/cult-definition.html.

White, Eileen "President Reagan Backs Constitutional Change on
Prayer in School." *Education Week.* May 12, 1982.
https://www.edweek.org/ew/articles/1982/05/12/0225003
3.h01.html.

Wikipedia "1689 Baptist Confession of Faith." *Wikipedia, The Free
Encyclopedia.* June 28, 2018.
https://en.wikipedia.org/w/index.php?title=1689_Baptist_C
onfession_of_Faith&oldid=787885285.

— "Abington School District v. Schempp." *Wikipedia, The Free
Encyclopedia.* October 29, 2018.
https://en.wikipedia.org/w/index.php?title=Abington_Scho
ol_District_v._Schempp&oldid=866227965.

— "Act of Uniformity 1662." *Wikipedia, The Free Encyclopedia.* May 24,
2017.
https://en.wikipedia.org/w/index.php?title=Act_of_Unifor
mity_1662&oldid=782037808.

— "Acts of Union 1707." *Wikipedia, The Free Encyclopedia.* May 6,
2018.
https://en.wikipedia.org/w/index.php?title=Acts_of_Union
_1707&oldid=839981941.

— "Adultery." *Wikipedia, The Free Encyclopedia.* November 11, 2018.
https://en.wikipedia.org/w/index.php?title=Adultery&oldid
=868356679.

— "Affair of Sausages." *Wikipedia, The Free Encyclopedia.* March 4,
2017.
https://en.wikipedia.org/w/index.php?title=Affair_of_the_S
ausages&oldid=768583596.

— "Alexander Campbell (clergyman)." *Wikipedia, The Free Encyclopedia.* April 28, 2018.
https://en.wikipedia.org/w/index.php?title=Alexander_Campbell_(clergyman)&oldid=838591652.

— "Alhambra Decree." *Wikipedia, The Free Encyclopedia.* August 22, 2018.
https://en.wikipedia.org/w/index.php?title=Alhambra_Decree&oldid=855970635.

— "Allopathic medicine." *Wikipedia, The Free Encyclopedia.* March 4, 2019.
https://en.wikipedia.org/w/index.php?title=Allopathic_medicine&oldid=886130798.

— "Animism." *Wikipedia, The Free Encyclopedia.* August 28, 2018.
https://en.wikipedia.org/w/index.php?title=Animism&oldid=856939190.

— "Antinominianism." *Wikipedia, The Free Encyclopedia.* February 16, 2018.
https://en.wikipedia.org/w/index.php?title=Antinomianism&oldid=826013885.

— "Apostolic Constitutions." *Wikipedia, The Free Encyclopedia.* March 14, 2018.
https://en.wikipedia.org/w/index.php?title=Apostolic_Constitutions&oldid=830319600.

— "Apostolic Poverty." *Wikipedia, The Free Encyclopedia.* May 18, 2018.
https://en.wikipedia.org/w/index.php?title=Apostolic_poverty&oldid=841839766.

— "Arius." *Wikipedia, The Free Encyclopedia.* December 23, 2018.
https://en.wikipedia.org/w/index.php?title=Arius&oldid=875014267.

— "Arminianism." *Wikipedia, The Free Encyclopedia.* December 27, 2017.
https://en.wikipedia.org/w/index.php?title=Arminianism&oldid=817269734.

— "Augustine of Hippo." *Wikipedia, The Free Encyclopedia.* February 12, 2018.
https://en.wikipedia.org/w/index.php?title=Augustine_of_Hippo&oldid=825196013.

— "Avignon Papacy." *Wikipedia, The Free Encyclopedia.* January 31, 2019.
https://en.wikipedia.org/w/index.php?title=Avignon_Papacy&oldid=881080398.

— "Balthasar Hubmaier." *Wikipedia, The Free Encyclopedia.* October 1, 2018.
https://en.wikipedia.org/w/index.php?title=Balthasar_Hubmaier&oldid=861978633.

— "Baptists." *Wikipedia, The Free Encyclopedia.* November 3, 2017.
https://en.wikipedia.org/w/index.php?title=Baptists&oldid=808551175.

— "Barton W. Stone." *Wikipedia, The Free Encyclopedia.* November 20, 2017.
https://en.wikipedia.org/w/index.php?title=Barton_W._Stone&oldid=811243694.

— "Benny Hinn." *Wikipedia, The Free Encyclopedia.* June 23, 2018.
https://en.wikipedia.org/w/index.php?title=Benny_Hinn&oldid=847178625.

— "Bill of Rights 1689." *Wikipedia, The Free Encyclopedia.* February 19, 2018.
https://en.wikipedia.org/w/index.php?title=Bill_of_Rights_1689&oldid=826417443.

— "Billy Graham." *Wikipedia, The Free Encyclopedia.* June 14, 2018.
https://en.wikipedia.org/w/index.php?title=Billy_Graham&oldid=845872160.

— "Bishops Wars." *Wikipedia, The Free Encyclopedia.* March 16, 2018.
https://en.wikipedia.org/w/index.php?title=Bishops%27_Wars&oldid=830749715.

— "Black Death." *Wikipedia, The Free Encyclopedia.* February 6, 2019.
https://en.wikipedia.org/w/index.php?title=Black_Death&oldid=882037652.

— "Blasphemy Act 1697." *Wikipedia, The Free Encyclopedia.* Accessed December 9, 2017.
https://en.wikipedia.org/w/index.php?title=Blasphemy_Act_1697&oldid=811452659.

— "Blasphemy Act of 1697." *Wikipedia, The Free Encyclopedia.*
November 21, 2017.

https://en.wikipedia.org/w/index.php?title=Blasphemy_Act
_1697&oldid=811452659.

— "Blue Law." *Wikipedia, The Free Encyclopedia.* September 24, 2018.
https://en.wikipedia.org/w/index.php?title=Blue_law&oldid
=860921797.

— "Bob Jones Jr." *Wikipedia, The Free Encyclopedia.* August 30, 2017.
https://en.wikipedia.org/w/index.php?title=Bob_Jones_Jr.
&oldid=797966848.

— "Bob Jones Sr." *Wikipedia, The Free Encyclopedia.* June 15, 2018.
https://en.wikipedia.org/w/index.php?title=Bob_Jones_Sr.
&oldid=846019343.

— "Book of Common Prayer." *Wikipedia, The Free Encyclopedia.*
February 28, 2018.
https://en.wikipedia.org/w/index.php?title=Book_of_Com
mon_Prayer&oldid=828009693.

— "Born Again." *Wikipedia, The Free Encyclopedia.* June 25, 2018.
https://en.wikipedia.org/w/index.php?title=Born_again&ol
did=847414468.

— "Brownist." *Wikipedia, The Free Encyclopedia.* January 24, 2018.
https://en.wikipedia.org/w/index.php?title=Brownist&oldid
=822118128.

— "Calvinism." *Wikipedia, The Free Encyclopedia.* March 1, 2018.
https://en.wikipedia.org/w/index.php?title=Calvinism&oldi
d=828318375.

— "Cambridge Platform." *Wikipedia, The Free Encyclopedia.* January 9,
2018.
https://en.wikipedia.org/w/index.php?title=Cambridge_Plat
form&oldid=819415186.

— "Cane Ridge Revival." *Wikipedia, The Free Encyclopedia.* April 8,
2018.
https://en.wikipedia.org/w/index.php?title=Cane_Ridge_Re
vival&oldid=835418355.

— "Carl McIntire." *Wikipedia, The Free Encyclopedia.* December 1,
2017.
https://en.wikipedia.org/w/index.php?title=Carl_McIntire&
oldid=812999211.

— "Catharism." *Wikipedia, The Free Encyclopedia*. September 24, 2018.
https://en.wikipedia.org/w/index.php?title=Catharism&oldi
d=860985608.

— "Catharsis." *Wikipedia, The Free Encyclopedia*. July 20, 2018.
https://en.wikipedia.org/w/index.php?title=Catharsis&oldid
=851233258.

— "Catholic Church in Latin America." *Wikipedia, The Free
Encyclopedia*. April 2, 2018.
https://en.wikipedia.org/w/index.php?title=Catholic_Churc
h_in_Latin_America&oldid=833812226.

— "Catholic particular churches and liturgical rites." *Wikipedia, The
Free Encyclopedia*. August 28, 2018.
https://en.wikipedia.org/w/index.php?title=Catholic_partic
ular_churches_and_liturgical_rites&oldid=856919179.

— "Charismatic Movement." *Wikipedia, The Free Encyclopedia*. May 29,
2018.
https://en.wikipedia.org/w/index.php?title=Charismatic_M
ovement&oldid=843500308.

— "Charlemagne." *Wikipedia, The Free Encyclopedia*. September 20,
2018.
https://en.wikipedia.org/w/index.php?title=Charlemagne&o
ldid=860441659.

— "Charles Darwin." *Wikipedia, The Free Encyclopedia*. June 14, 2018.
https://en.wikipedia.org/w/index.php?title=Charles_Darwin
&oldid=845836985.

— "Charles Grandison Finney." *Wikipedia, The Free Encyclopedia*. June
8, 2018.
https://en.wikipedia.org/w/index.php?title=Charles_Grandi
son_Finney&oldid=844950221.

— "Charles Taze Russell." *Wikipedia, The Free Encyclopedia*. July 1,
2018.
https://en.wikipedia.org/w/index.php?title=Charles_Taze_
Russell&oldid=848372226.

— "Christian Coalition." *Wikipedia, The Free Encyclopedia*. February 19,
2018.
https://en.wikipedia.org/w/index.php?title=Christian_Coalit
ion_of_America&oldid=826519562.

— "Christian Fundamentalism." *Wikipedia, The Free Encyclopedia.* May 18, 2018.
https://en.wikipedia.org/w/index.php?title=Christian_funda mentalism&oldid=841856014.

— "Christian Science." *Wikipedia, The Free Encyclopedia.* July 24, 2018.
https://en.wikipedia.org/w/index.php?title=Christian_Scien ce&oldid=851715372.

— "Christianity in Africa." *Wikipedia, The Free Encyclopedia.* September 4, 2018.
https://en.wikipedia.org/w/index.php?title=Christianity_in_ Africa&oldid=858014794.

— "Christianity in China." *Wikipedia, The Free Encyclopedia.* August 3, 2018.
https://en.wikipedia.org/w/index.php?title=Christianity_in_ China&oldid=853315451.

— "Christianity in India." *Wikipedia, The Free Encyclopedia.* September 1, 2018.
https://en.wikipedia.org/w/index.php?title=Christianity_in_ India&oldid=857507105.

— "Christianity in Iran." *Wikipedia, The Free Encyclopedia.* August 27, 2018.
https://en.wikipedia.org/w/index.php?title=Christianity_in_ Iran&oldid=856838788.

— "Christianity in Iraq." *Wikipedia, The Free Encyclopedia.* July 27, 2018.
https://en.wikipedia.org/w/index.php?title=Christianity_in_ Iraq&oldid=852294680.

— "Christianity in Israel." *Wikipedia, The Free Encyclopedia.* September 6, 2018.
https://en.wikipedia.org/w/index.php?title=Christianity_in_ Israel&oldid=858323644.

— "Christians in Egypt." *Wikipedia, The Free Encyclopedia.* September 2, 2018.
https://en.wikipedia.org/w/index.php?title=Christianity_in_ Egypt&oldid=857690989.

— "Christology." *Wikipedia, The Free Encyclopedia.* October 26, 2017.
https://en.wikipedia.org/w/index.php?title=Christology&ol did=807177428.

— "Church of Christ in the Congo." *Wikipedia, The Free Encyclopedia.* 29 March, 2018.
https://en.wikipedia.org/w/index.php?title=Church_of_Chr ist_in_the_Congo&oldid=833087166.

— "Church of Christ in the Congo." *Wikipedia, The Free Encyclopedia.* March 29, 2018.
https://en.wikipedia.org/w/index.php?title=Church_of_Chr ist_in_the_Congo&oldid=83308716"6.

— "Church of Christ, Scientist." *Wikipedia, The Free Encyclopedia.* February 14, 2018.
https://en.wikipedia.org/w/index.php?title=Church_of_Chr ist,_Scientist&oldid=825549937.

— "Church of God in Christ." *Wikipedia, The Free Encyclopedia.* June 7, 2018.
https://en.wikipedia.org/w/index.php?title=Church_of_Go d_in_Christ&oldid=844788720.

— "Churches of Christ." *Wikipedia, The Free Encyclopedia.* April 1, 2018.
https://en.wikipedia.org/w/index.php?title=Churches_of_C hrist&oldid=833643741.

— "Circumcellions." *Wikipedia, The Free Encyclopedia.* December 12, 2018.
https://en.wikipedia.org/w/index.php?title=Circumcellions &oldid=873241997.

— "Civilizing Mission." *Wikipedia, The Free Encyclopedia.* July 22, 2018.
https://en.wikipedia.org/w/index.php?title=Civilizing_missi on&oldid=851463244.

— "Clarence Darrow." *Wikipedia, The Free Encyclopedia.* June 12, 2018.
https://en.wikipedia.org/w/index.php?title=Clarence_Darro w&oldid=845491579.

— "Congregational Church." *Wikipedia, The Free Encyclopedia.* December 3, 2017.
https://en.wikipedia.org/w/index.php?title=Congregational _church&oldid=813374127.

— "Congregatonal Church." *Wikipedia, The Free Encyclopedia.* December 3, 2017.

https://en.wikipedia.org/w/index.php?title=Congregational
_church&oldid=813374127.

— "Consolamentum." *Wikipedia, The Free Encyclopedia.* May 7, 2018.
https://en.wikipedia.org/w/index.php?title=Consolamentu
m&oldid=839989810.

— "Convocation of 1563." *Wikipedia, The Free Encyclopedia.* January 30,
2018.
https://en.wikipedia.org/w/index.php?title=Convocation_of
_1563&oldid=823222309.

— "Council of Constance." *Wikipedia, The Free Encyclopedia.* February
10, 2019.
https://en.wikipedia.org/w/index.php?title=Council_of_Co
nstance&oldid=882657010.

— "Council of Trent." *Wikipedia, The Free Encyclopedia.* February 19,
2018.
https://en.wikipedia.org/w/index.php?title=Council_of_Tre
nt&oldid=826567810.

— "Council of Trent." *Wikipedia, The Free Encyclopedia.* April 30, 2018.
https://en.wikipedia.org/w/index.php?title=Council_of_Tre
nt&oldid=838915949.

— "Covenanter." *Wikipedia, The Free Encyclopedia.* March 22, 2018.
https://en.wikipedia.org/w/index.php?title=Covenanter&ol
did=831888264.

— "Creflo Dollar." *Wikipedia, The Free Encyclopedia.* July 13, 2018.
https://en.wikipedia.org/w/index.php?title=Creflo_Dollar&
oldid=850073587.

— "Cuius regio, eius religio." *Wikipedia, The Free Encyclopedia.*
November 27, 2017.
https://en.wikipedia.org/w/index.php?title=Cuius_regio,_ei
us_religio&oldid=812358324.

— "Cyril of Alexandria." *Wikipedia, The Free Encyclopedia.* December
19, 2018.
https://en.wikipedia.org/w/index.php?title=Cyril_of_Alexa
ndria&oldid=874542627.

— "David W. Bebbington." *Wikipedia, The Free Encyclopedia.* June 3,
2018.

https://en.wikipedia.org/w/index.php?title=David_W._Beb
bington&oldid=844173786.

—— "Daystar Television." *Wikipedia, The Free Encyclopedia.* June 21,
2018.
https://en.wikipedia.org/w/index.php?title=Daystar_(TV_n
etwork)&oldid=846924399.

—— "Decius." *Wikipedia, The Free Encyclopedia.* November 12, 2018.
https://en.wikipedia.org/w/index.php?title=Decius&oldid=
868412442.

—— "Deism." *Wikipedia, The Free Encyclopedia.* August 2, 2018.
https://en.wikipedia.org/w/index.php?title=Deism&oldid=
853060286.

—— "Development of the New Testament canon." *Wikipedia, The Free
Encyclopedia.* July 24, 2019.
https://en.wikipedia.org/w/index.php?title=Development_o
f_the_New_Testament_canon&oldid=907619154.

—— "Diet of Worms." *Wikipedia, The Free Encyclopedia.* October 1, 2018.
https://en.wikipedia.org/w/index.php?title=Diet_of_Worm
s&oldid=861947325.

—— "Diocletianic Persecution." *Wikipedia, The Free Encyclopedia.*
November 18, 2018.
https://en.wikipedia.org/w/index.php?title=Diocletianic_Pe
rsecution&oldid=869468376.

—— "Disciples of Christ (Campbell Movement)." *Wikipedia, The Free
Encyclopedia.* August 8, 2017.
https://en.wikipedia.org/w/index.php?title=Disciples_of_C
hrist_(Campbell_Movement)&oldid=794504777.

—— "Divorce law by country." *Wikipedia, The Free Encyclopedia.* March
13, 2019.
https://en.wikipedia.org/w/index.php?title=Divorce_law_b
y_country&oldid=887553584.

—— "Docetism." *Wikipedia, The Free Encyclopedia.* October 20, 2018.
https://en.wikipedia.org/w/index.php?title=Docetism&oldi
d=864925480.

—— "Donatism." *Wikipedia, The Free Encyclopedia.* February 14, 2018.
https://en.wikipedia.org/w/index.php?title=Waldensians&ol
did=826130467.

— "Economienda." *Wikipedia, The Free Encyclopedia*. Septebmer 22, 2018.
https://en.wikipedia.org/w/index.php?title=Encomienda&oldid=860562941.

— "Edict of Thesselonica." *Wikipedia, The Free Encyclopedia*. August 8, 2018.
https://en.wikipedia.org/w/index.php?title=Edict_of_Thessalonica&oldid=854090511.

— "Elizabeth I of England." *Wikipedia, The Free Encyclopedia*. March 24, 2018.
https://en.wikipedia.org/w/index.php?title=Elizabeth_I_of_England&oldid=832217349.

— "Ellen G. White." *Wikipedia, The Free Encyclopedia*. July 23, 2018.
https://en.wikipedia.org/w/index.php?title=Ellen_G._White&oldid=851627725.

— "Epiphanius of Salamis." *Wikipedia, The Free Encyclopedia*. November 26, 2018.
https://en.wikipedia.org/w/index.php?title=Epiphanius_of_Salamis&oldid=870627331.

— "Equal Rights Amendment." *Wikipedia, The Free Encyclopedia*. June 24, 2018.
https://en.wikipedia.org/w/index.php?title=Equal_Rights_Amendment&oldid=847254592.

— "Eusebius of Nicomedia." *Wikipedia, The Free Encyclopedia*. August 30, 2018.
https://en.wikipedia.org/w/index.php?title=Eusebius_of_Nicomedia&oldid=857292684.

— "Evangelical Church in Germany." *Wikipedia, The Free Encyclopedia*. May 22, 2018.
https://en.wikipedia.org/w/index.php?title=Evangelical_Church_in_Germany&oldid=842426054.

— "Evangelicanism." *Wikipedia, The Free Encyclopedia*. February 2, 2018.
https://en.wikipedia.org/w/index.php?title=Evangelicalism&oldid=823649910.

— "Fetter Lane Society." *Wikipedia, The Free Encyclopedia*. January 15, 2018.

https://en.wikipedia.org/w/index.php?title=Fetter_Lane_Society&oldid=820665235.

— "First Council of Constantinople." *Wikipedia, The Free Encyclopedia.* September 27, 2017.
https://en.wikipedia.org/w/index.php?title=First_Council_of_Constantinople&oldid=802645780.

— "First Council of Nicaea." *Wikipedia, The Free Encyclopedia.* January 14, 2019.
https://en.wikipedia.org/w/index.php?title=First_Council_of_Nicaea&oldid=878423621.

— "First Great Awakening." *Wikipedia, The Free Encyclopedia.* February 22, 2019.
https://en.wikipedia.org/w/index.php?title=First_Great_Awakening&oldid=884516434.

— "Five Articles of Remonstrance." *Wikipedia, The Free Encyclopedia.* February 11, 2018.
https://en.wikipedia.org/w/index.php?title=Five_Articles_of_Remonstrance&oldid=825126290.

— "Five solae." *Wikipedia, The Free Encyclopedia.* March 30, 2018.
https://en.wikipedia.org/w/index.php?title=Five_solae&oldid=833161581.

— "Forced Conversion." *Wikipedia, The Free Encyclopedia.* September 18, 2018.
https://en.wikipedia.org/w/index.php?title=Forced_conversion&oldid=860074437.

— "French Wars of Religion." *Wikipedia, The Free Encyclopedia.* October 1, 2018.
https://en.wikipedia.org/w/index.php?title=French_Wars_of_Religion&oldid=861974351.

— "Galileo Galilei." *Wikipedia, The Free Encyclopedia.* May 14, 2019.
https://en.wikipedia.org/w/index.php?title=Galileo_Galilei&oldid=897018167.

— "General relativity." *Wikipedia, The Free Encyclopedia.* June 3, 2019.
https://en.wikipedia.org/w/index.php?title=General_relativity&oldid=900093226.

— "George Blaurock." *Wikipedia, The Free Encyclopedia.* September 6, 2018.

https://en.wikipedia.org/w/index.php?title=George_Blauro
ck&oldid=858346840.

— "George Fox." *Wikipedia, The Free Encyclopedia.* May 26, 2018.
https://en.wikipedia.org/w/index.php?title=George_Fox&o
ldid=843086856.

— "George Whitefield." *Wikipedia, The Free Encyclopedia.* May 22,
2018.
https://en.wikipedia.org/w/index.php?title=George_Whitefi
eld&oldid=842471825.

— "German Peasants War." *Wikipedia, The Free Encyclopedia.* February
12, 2018.
https://en.wikipedia.org/w/index.php?title=German_Peasa
nts%27_War&oldid=825228509.

— "Germany." *Wikipedia, The Free Encyclopedia.* February 14, 2018.
https://en.wikipedia.org/w/index.php?title=Germany&oldid
=825630290.

— "Glorious Revolution." *Wikipedia, The Free Encyclopedia.* March 16,
2018.
https://en.wikipedia.org/w/index.php?title=Glorious_Revol
ution&oldid=830750404.

— "Gnosticism." *Wikipedia, The Free Encyclopedia.* December 1, 2018.
https://en.wikipedia.org/w/index.php?title=Gnosticism&ol
did=871436905.

— "Grand Remonstrance." *Wikipedia, The Free Encyclopedia.* January
25, 2018.
https://en.wikipedia.org/w/index.php?title=Grand_Remons
trance&oldid=822347092.

— "Heidelberg Disputation." *Wikipedia, The Free Encyclopedia.* January
21, 2018.
https://en.wikipedia.org/w/index.php?title=Heidelberg_Dis
putation&oldid=821597799.

— "Henry VIII." *Wikipedia, The Free Encyclopedia.* January 28, 2018.
https://en.wikipedia.org/w/index.php?title=Henry_VIII_of
_England&oldid=822816156.

— "Hillsong Church." *Wikipedia, The Free Encyclopedia.* July 11, 2018.
https://en.wikipedia.org/w/index.php?title=Hillsong_Churc
h&oldid=849803681.

— "History of the Calvinist–Arminian debate." *Wikipedia, The Free Encyclopedia.* January 31, 2018.
https://en.wikipedia.org/w/index.php?title=History_of_the
_Calvinist%E2%80%93Arminian_debate&oldid=823384378.

— "History of the Puritans from 1649." *Wikipedia, The Free Encyclopedia.* February 10, 2018.
https://en.wikipedia.org/w/index.php?title=History_of_the
_Puritans_from_1649&oldid=824975979.

— "History of the Russian Orthodox Church." *Wikipedia, The Free Encyclopedia.* September 4, 2018.
https://en.wikipedia.org/w/index.php?title=History_of_the
_Russian_Orthodox_Church&oldid=857948794.

— "Holiness Movement." *Wikipedia, The Free Encyclopedia.* May 31, 2018.
https://en.wikipedia.org/w/index.php?title=Holiness_move
ment&oldid=843736870.

— "Homeopathy." *Wikipedia, The Free Encyclopedia.* February 26, 2019.
https://en.wikipedia.org/w/index.php?title=Homeopathy&o
ldid=885222806.

— "Homoousian." *Wikipedia, The Free Encyclopedia.* November 15, 2017.
https://en.wikipedia.org/w/index.php?title=Homoousion&
oldid=810394923.

— "Huldrych Zwingli." *Wikipedia, The Free Encyclopedia.* October 12, 2017.
https://en.wikipedia.org/w/index.php?title=Huldrych_Zwin
gli&oldid=804996775.

— "Hussite Wars." *Wikipedia, The Free Encyclopedia.* February 1, 2019.
https://en.wikipedia.org/w/index.php?title=Hussite_Wars&
oldid=881261615.

— "Hydrotherapy." *Wikipedia, The Free Encyclopedia.* February 6, 2019.
https://en.wikipedia.org/w/index.php?title=Hydrotherapy&
oldid=882066746.

— "Hypostasis (philosophy and religion)." *Wikipedia, The Free Encyclopedia.* December 9, 2018.
https://en.wikipedia.org/w/index.php?title=Hypostasis_(phi
losophy_and_religion)&oldid=872808485.

— "Inquisition." *Wikipedia, The Free Encyclopedia.* September 18, 2018. https://en.wikipedia.org/w/index.php?title=Inquisition&oldid=860104831.

— "Interregnum (England)." *Wikipedia, The Free Encyclopedia.* January 17, 2017. https://en.wikipedia.org/w/index.php?title=Interregnum_(England)&oldid=786092174.

— "Investigative Judgment." *Wikipedia, The Free Encyclopedia.* July 8, 2018. https://en.wikipedia.org/w/index.php?title=Investigative_judgment&oldid=849339760.

— "Irenaeus." *Wikipedia, The Free Encyclopedia.* October 26, 2017. https://en.wikipedia.org/w/index.php?title=Irenaeus&oldid=807188092.

— "Irresitable Grace." *Wikipedia, The Free Encyclopedia.* December 4, 2017. https://en.wikipedia.org/w/index.php?title=Irresistible_grace&oldid=813555969.

— "Jacob Arminius." *Wikipedia, The Free Encyclopedia.* February 21, 2018. https://en.wikipedia.org/w/index.php?title=Jacobus_Arminius&oldid=826787899.

— "James Hutton." *Wikipedia, The Free Encyclopedia.* April 23, 2018. https://en.wikipedia.org/w/index.php?title=James_Hutton&oldid=837815741.

— "James II of England." *Wikipedia, The Free Encyclopedia.* May 21, 2018. https://en.wikipedia.org/w/index.php?title=James_II_of_England&oldid=842339694.

— "James son of Zebedee." *Wikipedia, The Free Encyclopedia.* August 16, 2018. https://en.wikipedia.org/w/index.php?title=James,_son_of_Zebedee&oldid=855250396.

— "Jan Hus." *Wikipedia, The Free Encyclopedia.* February 7, 2018. https://en.wikipedia.org/w/index.php?title=Jan_Hus&oldid=824524696.

— "Jehovah's Witnesses." *Wikipedia, The Free Encyclopedia.* July 23, 2018.
　　https://en.wikipedia.org/w/index.php?title=Jehovah%27s_Witnesses&oldid=851550415.

— "Jerry Falwell." *Wikipedia, The Free Encyclopedia.* June 2, 2018.
　　https://en.wikipedia.org/w/index.php?title=Jerry_Falwell&oldid=844133706.

— "Jesse Duplantis." *Wikipedia, The Free Encyclopedia.* July 5, 2018.
　　https://en.wikipedia.org/w/index.php?title=Jesse_Duplantis&oldid=848903952.

— "Jesuit Reduction." *Wikipedia, The Free Encyclopedia.* September 13, 2018.
　　https://en.wikipedia.org/w/index.php?title=Jesuit_reduction&oldid=859303456.

— "Jim Bakker." *Wikipedia, The Free Encyclopedia.* June 14, 2018.
　　https://en.wikipedia.org/w/index.php?title=Jim_Bakker&oldid=845873520.

— "Jimmy Swaggert." *Wikipedia, The Free Encyclopedia.* June 16, 2018.
　　https://en.wikipedia.org/w/index.php?title=Jimmy_Swaggart&oldid=846168384.

— "Joel Osteen." *Wikipedia, The Free Encyclopedia.* June 18, 2018.
　　https://en.wikipedia.org/w/index.php?title=Joel_Osteen&oldid=846442076.

— "Johannes Agricola." *Wikipedia, The Free Encyclopedia.* November 7, 2017.
　　https://en.wikipedia.org/w/index.php?title=Johannes_Agricola&oldid=809163677.

— "Johannes Gutenberg." *Wikipedia, The Free Encyclopedia.* February 15, 2018.
　　https://en.wikipedia.org/w/index.php?title=Johannes_Gutenberg&oldid=825748627.

— "Johannes Kepler." *Wikipedia, The Free Encyclopedia.* June 3, 2019.
　　https://en.wikipedia.org/w/index.php?title=Johannes_Kepler&oldid=900107058.

— "John Calvin." *Wikipedia, The Free Encyclopedia.* February 12, 2018.
　　https://en.wikipedia.org/w/index.php?title=John_Calvin&oldid=825308558.

— "John Gresham Machen." *Wikipedia, The Free Encyclopedia.* June 20, 2018.
https://en.wikipedia.org/w/index.php?title=John_Gresham _Machen&oldid=846755246.

— "John Knox." *Wikipedia, The Free Encyclopedia.* March 25, 2018.
https://en.wikipedia.org/w/index.php?title=John_Knox&ol did=832332060.

— "John Wesley." *Wikipedia, The Free Encyclopedia.* March 7, 2018.
https://en.wikipedia.org/w/index.php?title=John_Wesley&o ldid=829252226.

— "John Wycliffe." *Wikipedia, The Free Encyclopedia.* February 11, 2018.
https://en.wikipedia.org/w/index.php?title=John_Wycliffe& oldid=825167330.

— "Jonathan Edwards." *Wikipedia, The Free Encyclopedia.* June 1, 2018.
https://en.wikipedia.org/w/index.php?title=Jonathan_Edwa rds_(theologian)&oldid=843959758.

— "Jonathan Edwards." *Wikipedia, The Free Encyclopedia.* June 5, 2018.
https://en.wikipedia.org/w/index.php?title=Jonathan_Edwa rds_(theologian)&oldid=844579440.

— "Julian of Eclanum." *Wikipedia, The Free Encyclopedia.* September 26, 2018.
https://en.wikipedia.org/w/index.php?title=Julian_of_Eclan um&oldid=861331065.

— "Kenneth Copeland." *Wikipedia, The Free Encyclopedia.* June 13, 2018.
https://en.wikipedia.org/w/index.php?title=Kenneth_Copel and&oldid=845634527.

— "Kimbanguism." *Wikipedia, The Free Encyclopedia.* February 25, 2018.
https://en.wikipedia.org/w/index.php?title=Kimbanguism& oldid=827632585.

— "Klu Klux Klan." *Wikipedia, The Free Encyclopedia.* November 13, 2018.
https://en.wikipedia.org/w/index.php?title=Ku_Klux_Klan &oldid=868645765.

— "Latter Day Saint Movement." *Wikipedia, The Free Encyclopedia.* June 23, 2018. https://en.wikipedia.org/w/index.php?title=Latter_Day_Saint_movement&oldid=847125128.

— "Law and Gospel." *Wikipedia, The Free Encyclopedia.* December 18, 2018. https://en.wikipedia.org/w/index.php?title=Law_and_Gospel&oldid=815991197.

— "Lawrence v. Texas." *Wikipedia, The Free Encyclopedia.* October 7, 2018. https://en.wikipedia.org/w/index.php?title=Lawrence_v._Texas&oldid=862968778.

— "List of Christian denominational positions on homosexuality." *Wikipedia, The Free Encyclopedia.* November 13, 2018. https://en.wikipedia.org/w/index.php?title=List_of_Christian_denominational_positions_on_homosexuality&oldid=868569230.

— "List of Christian denominations by number of members." *Wikipedia, The Free Encyclopedia.* February 4, 2018. https://en.wikipedia.org/w/index.php?title=List_of_Christian_denominations_by_number_of_members&oldid=824034682.

— "List of Lutheran dioceses and archdioceses." *Wikipedia, The Free Encyclopedia.* March 2, 2018. https://en.wikipedia.org/w/index.php?title=List_of_Lutheran_dioceses_and_archdioceses&oldid=828475053.

— "List of megachurches in the United States." *Wikipedia, The Free Encyclopedia.* July 15, 2018. https://en.wikipedia.org/w/index.php?title=List_of_megachurches_in_the_United_States&oldid=850407602.

— "List of the largest evangelical churches." *Wikipedia, The Free Encyclopedia.* May 21, 2018. https://en.wikipedia.org/w/index.php?title=List_of_the_largest_evangelical_churches&oldid=842288261.

— "List of United States over-the-air television networks." *Wikipedia, The Free Encyclopedia.* July 3, 2018.

https://en.wikipedia.org/w/index.php?title=List_of_United _States_over-the-air_television_networks&oldid=848713340.

— "Liturgy." *Wikipedia, The Free Encyclopedia.* February 4, 2018. https://en.wikipedia.org/w/index.php?title=Liturgy&oldid= 823878049.

— "Lollardy." *Wikipedia, The Free Encyclopedia.* February 11, 2018. https://en.wikipedia.org/w/index.php?title=Lollardy&oldid =825059594.

— "Lombards." *Wikipedia, The Free Encyclopedia.* September 3, 2018. https://en.wikipedia.org/w/index.php?title=Lombards&oldi d=857912838.

— "Lutheranism." *Wikipedia, The Free Encyclopedia.* February 15, 2018. https://en.wikipedia.org/w/index.php?title=Lutheranism&ol did=825759640.

— "Manichaeism." *Wikipedia, The Free Encyclopedia.* March 8, 2018. https://en.wikipedia.org/w/index.php?title=Manichaeism&o ldid=829468609.

— "Manichaeism." *Wikipedia, The Free Encyclopedia.* December 3, 2018. https://en.wikipedia.org/w/index.php?title=Manichaeism&o ldid=871731031.

— "Marburg Colloquy." *Wikipedia, The Free Encyclopedia.* December 30, 2017. https://en.wikipedia.org/w/index.php?title=Marburg_Collo quy&oldid=817709992.

— "Marcion of Sinope." *Wikipedia, The Free Encyclopedia.* January 5, 2018. https://en.wikipedia.org/w/index.php?title=Marcion_of_Sin ope&oldid=818825406.

— "Marcionism." *Wikipedia, The Free Encyclopedia.* October 30, 2018. https://en.wikipedia.org/w/index.php?title=Marcionism&ol did=866528804.

— "Maronite Church." *Wikipedia, The Free Encyclopedia.* September 7, 2018. https://en.wikipedia.org/w/index.php?title=Maronite_Chur ch&oldid=858470411.

— "Martin Luther." *Wikipedia, The Free Encyclopedia.* February 14, 2018.

https://en.wikipedia.org/w/index.php?title=Martin_Luther
&oldid=825598046.

— "Mary Baker Eddy." *Wikipedia, The Free Encyclopedia.* July 11, 2018.
https://en.wikipedia.org/w/index.php?title=Mary_Baker_E
ddy&oldid=849841599.

— "Mary Dyer." *Wikipedia, The Free Encyclopedia.* October 10, 2018.
https://en.wikipedia.org/w/index.php?title=Mary_Dyer&ol
did=863421774.

— "Mary I of England." *Wikipedia, The Free Encyclopedia.* April 19,
2018.
https://en.wikipedia.org/w/index.php?title=Mary_I_of_Eng
land&oldid=837192580.

— "Massachusetts Bay Colony." *Wikipedia, The Free Encyclopedia.* April
3, 2018.
https://en.wikipedia.org/w/index.php?title=Massachusetts_
Bay_Colony&oldid=833911477.

— "Massachusetts Bay_Colony." *Wikipedia, The Free Encyclopedia.*
October 1, 2018.
https://en.wikipedia.org/w/index.php?title=Massachusetts_
Bay_Colony&oldid=861990593.

— "Meletius of Lycopolis." *Wikipedia, The Free Encyclopedia.* December
19, 2018.
https://en.wikipedia.org/w/index.php?title=Meletius_of_Ly
copolis&oldid=874397541.

— "Mennonite." *Wikipedia, The Free Encyclopedia.* March 13, 2018.
https://en.wikipedia.org/w/index.php?title=Mennonite&old
id=830282336.

— "Methodism." *Wikipedia, The Free Encyclopedia.* March 5, 2018.
https://en.wikipedia.org/w/index.php?title=Methodism&ol
did=828984862.

— "Miaphysitism." *Wikipedia, The Free Encyclopedia.* November 19,
2017.
https://en.wikipedia.org/w/index.php?title=Miaphysitism&
oldid=811077187.

— "Michael Servetus." *Wikipedia, The Free Encyclopedia.* October 31,
2017.

https://en.wikipedia.org/w/index.php?title=Michael_Servet us&oldid=808038937#Theology.

—— "Missouri Executive Order 44." *Wikipedia, The Free Encyclopedia.* February 18, 2019. https://en.wikipedia.org/w/index.php?title=Missouri_Execu tive_Order_44&oldid=884132765.

—— "Monarchianism." *Wikipedia, The Free Encyclopedia.* January 14, 2019. https://en.wikipedia.org/w/index.php?title=Monarchianism &oldid=878368943.

—— "Montanism." *Wikipedia, The Free Encyclopedia.* September 13, 2018. https://en.wikipedia.org/w/index.php?title=Montanism&ol did=859423503.

—— "Moral Majority." *Wikipedia, The Free Encyclopedia.* March 15, 2018. https://en.wikipedia.org/w/index.php?title=Moral_Majority &oldid=830587807.

—— "Moravian Church." *Wikipedia, The Free Encyclopedia.* April 6, 2018. https://en.wikipedia.org/w/index.php?title=Moravian_Chur ch&oldid=83513787"4.

—— "Nicolaism." *Wikipedia, The Free Encyclopedia.* November 18, 2018. https://en.wikipedia.org/w/index.php?title=Nicolaism&oldi d=869469547.

—— "Nicolaus Copernicus." *Wikipedia, The Free Encyclopedia.* June 4, 2019. https://en.wikipedia.org/w/index.php?title=Nicolaus_Coper nicus&oldid=900230652.

—— "Occam's Razor." *Wikipedia, The Free Encyclopedia.* December 7, 2018. https://en.wikipedia.org/w/index.php?title=Occam%27s_ra zor&oldid=874759644.

—— "Old Swiss Confederacy." *Wikipedia, The Free Encyclopedia.* January 11, 2018. https://en.wikipedia.org/w/index.php?title=Old_Swiss_Con federacy&oldid=819896245.

—— "Oneness Pentecostalism." *Wikipedia, The Free Encyclopedia.* May 3, 2019.

https://en.wikipedia.org/w/index.php?title=Oneness_Pente
costalism&oldid=895378676.

— "Onward Christian Soldiers." *Wikipedia, The Free Encyclopedia.*
November 21, 2017.
https://en.wikipedia.org/w/index.php?title=Onward,_Christ
ian_Soldiers&oldid=811365535.

— "Oral Roberts." *Wikipedia, The Free Encyclopedia.* June 14, 2018.
https://en.wikipedia.org/w/index.php?title=Oral_Roberts&
oldid=845772105.

— "Original Sin." *Wikipedia, The Free Encyclopedia.* January 30, 2018.
https://en.wikipedia.org/w/index.php?title=Original_sin&ol
did=823091938.

— "Original Sin." *Wikipedia, The Free Encyclopedia.* January 28, 2019.
https://en.wikipedia.org/w/index.php?title=Original_sin&ol
did=880539673.

— "Pact of Steel." *Wikipedia, The Free Encyclopedia.* July 28, 2018.
https://en.wikipedia.org/w/index.php?title=Pact_of_Steel&
oldid=852105889.

— "Pat Robertson." *Wikipedia, The Free Encyclopedia.* June 9, 2018.
https://en.wikipedia.org/w/index.php?title=Pat_Robertson
&oldid=845160418.

— "Patriarch of Antioch." *Wikipedia, The Free Encyclopedia.* September
4, 2018.
https://en.wikipedia.org/w/index.php?title=Patriarch_of_A
ntioch&oldid=858001402.

— "Paul the Apostle." *Wikipedia, The Free Encyclopedia.* October 14,
2018.
https://en.wikipedia.org/w/index.php?title=Paul_the_Apost
le&oldid=864079145.

— "Peace of Westphalia." *Wikipedia, The Free of Encyclopedia.* January
28, 2018.
https://en.wikipedia.org/w/index.php?title=Peace_of_West
phalia&oldid=822808144.

— "Pelagianism." *Wikipedia, The Free Encyclopedia.* September 26, 2017.
https://en.wikipedia.org/w/index.php?title=Pelagianism&ol
did=802498143.

— "Pelagius." *Wikipedia, The Free Encyclopedia.* December 3, 2018. https://en.wikipedia.org/w/index.php?title=Pelagius&oldid =871781590.

— "Pentecostalism." *Wikipedia, The Free Encyclopedia.* May 29, 2018. https://en.wikipedia.org/w/index.php?title=Pentecostalism &oldid=843554767.

— "Philip Melanchthon." *Wikipedia, The Free Encyclopedia.* February 23, 2018. https://en.wikipedia.org/w/index.php?title=Philip_Melanch thon&oldid=827237799.

— "Philipp Spener." *Wikipedia, The Free Encyclopedia.* February 9, 2019. https://en.wikipedia.org/w/index.php?title=Philipp_Spener &oldid=882298147.

— "Physis." *Wikipedia, The Free Encyclopedia.* February 28, 2019. https://en.wikipedia.org/w/index.php?title=Physis&oldid=8 85577147.

— "Pietism." *Wikipedia, The Free Encyclopedia.* May 19, 2018. https://en.wikipedia.org/w/index.php?title=Pietism&oldid= 842007573.

— "Pilgrim Holiness Church." *Wikipedia, The Free Encyclopedia.* December 14, 2018. https://en.wikipedia.org/w/index.php?title=Pilgrim_Holines s_Church&oldid=873730026.

— "Plague of Cyprian." *Wikipedia, The Free Encyclopedia.* December 27, 2018. https://en.wikipedia.org/w/index.php?title=Plague_of_Cypr ian&oldid=875572861.

— "Plato." *Wikipedia, The Free Encyclopedia.* August 17, 2018. https://en.wikipedia.org/w/index.php?title=Plato&oldid=85 5354791.

— "Polycarp." *Wikipedia, The Free Encyclopedia.* December 20, 2018. https://en.wikipedia.org/w/index.php?title=Polycarp&oldid =874623945.

— "Pope Alexander I of Alexandria." *Wikipedia, The Free Encyclopedia.* June 9, 2018. https://en.wikipedia.org/w/index.php?title=Pope_Alexande r_I_of_Alexandria&oldid=845104594.

— "Pope Alexander VI." *Wikipedia, The Free Encyclopedia.* September 30, 2018.
https://en.wikipedia.org/w/index.php?title=Pope_Alexander_VI&oldid=861907594.

— "Pope Dioscorus I of Alexandria." *Wikipedia, The Free Encyclopedia.* August 15, 2018.
https://en.wikipedia.org/w/index.php?title=Pope_Dioscorus_I_of_Alexandria&oldid=855060191.

— "Pope Urban VI." *Wikipedia, The Free Encyclopedia.* December 24, 2018.
https://en.wikipedia.org/w/index.php?title=Pope_Urban_VI&oldid=875126928.

— "Pope Victor I." *Wikipedia, The Free Encyclopedia.* November 27, 2018.
https://en.wikipedia.org/w/index.php?title=Pope_Victor_I&oldid=870857394.

— "Postmillennialism." *Wikipedia, The Free Encyclopedia.* March 29, 2018.
https://en.wikipedia.org/w/index.php?title=Postmillennialism&oldid=833095132.

— "Premillennialism." *Wikipedia, The Free Encyclopedia.* July 5, 2018.
https://en.wikipedia.org/w/index.php?title=Premillennialism&oldid=848962279.

— "Presbyterian Polity." *Wikipedia, The Free Encyclopedia.* April 8, 2018.
https://en.wikipedia.org/w/index.php?title=Presbyterian_polity&oldid=835354562.

— "Presbyterianism." *Wikipedia, The Free Encyclopedia.* March 23, 2018.
https://en.wikipedia.org/w/index.php?title=Presbyterianism&oldid=832095914.

— "Prevenient Grace." *Wikipedia, The Free Encyclopedia.* February 21, 2018. Wikipedia.

— "Priscillian." *Wikipedia, The Free Encyclopedia.* September 7, 2018.
https://en.wikipedia.org/w/index.php?title=Priscillian&oldid=858541932.

— "Prosopon." *Wikipedia, The Free Encyclopedia.* June 27, 2018. https://en.wikipedia.org/w/index.php?title=Prosopon&oldid=847754402.

— "Prosperity Theology." *Wikipedia, The Free Encyclopedia.* June 17, 2018. https://en.wikipedia.org/w/index.php?title=Prosperity_theology&oldid=846217467.

— "Protestantism." *Wikipedia, The Free Encyclopedia.* March 4, 2018. https://en.wikipedia.org/w/index.php?title=Protestantism&oldid=828821119.

— "Puritans." *Wikipedia, The Free Encyclopedia.* March 15, 2018. https://en.wikipedia.org/w/index.php?title=Puritans&oldid=831243286.

— "Quakers." *Wikipedia, The Free Encyclopedia.* March 30, 2018. https://en.wikipedia.org/w/index.php?title=Quakers&oldid=833306308.

— "Quakers." *Wikipedia, The Free Encyclopedia.* May 3, 2018. https://en.wikipedia.org/w/index.php?title=Quakers&oldid=839499182.

— "Quartodecimanism." *Wikipedia, The Free Encyclopedia.* July 26, 2018. https://en.wikipedia.org/w/index.php?title=Quartodecimanism&oldid=852133537.

— "Reformation." *Wikipedia, The Free Encyclopedia.* February 15, 2018. https://en.wikipedia.org/w/index.php?title=Reformation&oldid=825796751.

— "Reformation in Switzerland." *Wikipedia, The Free Encyclopedia.* January 4, 2018. https://en.wikipedia.org/w/index.php?title=Reformation_in_Switzerland&oldid=818616373.

— "Relic." *Wikipedia, The Free Encyclopedia.* January 27, 2018. https://en.wikipedia.org/w/index.php?title=Relic&oldid=822605366.

— "Remonstrants." *Wikipedia, The Free Encyclopedia.* February 4, 2018. https://en.wikipedia.org/w/index.php?title=Remonstrants&oldid=823964414.

— "Restoration (England)." *Wikipedia, The Free Encyclopedia*. May 13, 2018.
    https://en.wikipedia.org/w/index.php?title=Restoration_(E
    ngland)&oldid=841076303.

— "Restoration Movement." *Wikipedia, The Free Encyclopedia*. April 15, 2018.
    https://en.wikipedia.org/w/index.php?title=Restoration_Mo
    vement&oldid=836563259.

— "Restoration Movement." *Wikipedia, The Free Encyclopedia*. June 15, 2018.
    https://en.wikipedia.org/w/index.php?title=Restoration_Mo
    vement&oldid=846047070.

— "Restorationism." *Wikipedia, The Free Encyclopedia*. July 17, 2018.
    https://en.wikipedia.org/w/index.php?title=Restorationism
    &oldid=850732391.

— "Reynolds v. United_States." *Wikipedia, The Free Encyclopedia*. September 4, 2018.
    https://en.wikipedia.org/w/index.php?title=Reynolds_v._U
    nited_States&oldid=858029467.

— "Robert Tilton." *Wikipedia, The Free Encyclopedia*. June 17, 2018.
    https://en.wikipedia.org/w/index.php?title=Robert_Tilton&
    oldid=846277792.

— "Roger Williams." *Wikipedia, The Free Encyclopedia*. March 29, 2018.
    https://en.wikipedia.org/w/index.php?title=Roger_Williams
    &oldid=833076777.

— "Roman-Persian Wars." *Wikipedia, The Free Encyclopedia*. December 7, 2018.
    https://en.wikipedia.org/w/index.php?title=Roman%E2%8
    0%93Persian_Wars&oldid=872520161.

— "Rule of Faith." *Wikipedia, The Free Encyclopedia*. May 24, 2019.
    https://en.wikipedia.org/w/index.php?title=Rule_of_Faith&
    oldid=898595882.

— "Rule of St. Augustine." *Wikipedia, The Free Encyclopedia*. May 27, 2018.
    https://en.wikipedia.org/w/index.php?title=Rule_of_St._Au
    gustine&oldid=843247610.

— "Sacrament." *Wikipedia, The Free Encyclopedia.* February 21, 2018. https://en.wikipedia.org/w/index.php?title=Sacrament&oldid=826879447.

— "Sacramental Union." *Wikipedia, The Free Encyclopedia.* November 13, 2017. https://en.wikipedia.org/w/index.php?title=Sacramental_union&oldid=810156280.

— "Savoy Declaration." *Wikipedia, The Free Encyclopedia.* April 9, 2017. https://en.wikipedia.org/w/index.php?title=Savoy_Declaration&oldid=774641952.

— "Saxon Wars." *Wikipedia, The Free Encyclopedia.* August 10, 2018. https://en.wikipedia.org/w/index.php?title=Saxon_Wars&oldid=854368246.

— "Schleitheim Confession." *Wikipedia, The Free Encyclopedia.* January 18, 2018. https://en.wikipedia.org/w/index.php?title=Schleitheim_Confession&oldid=821129932.

— "Schmalkaldic League." *Wikipedia, The Free Encyclopedia.* December 13, 2017. https://en.wikipedia.org/w/index.php?title=Schmalkaldic_League&oldid=815226091.

— "Scholasticism." *Wikipedia, The Free Encyclopedia.* May 30, 2018. https://en.wikipedia.org/w/index.php?title=Scholasticism&oldid=843714219.

— "School Prayer." *Wikipedia, The Free Encyclopedia.* November 1, 2018. https://en.wikipedia.org/w/index.php?title=School_prayer&oldid=866846097.

— "Scots Confession." *Wikipedia, The Free Encyclopedia.* March 5, 2018. https://en.wikipedia.org/w/index.php?title=Scots_Confession&oldid=828871505.

— "Second Council of Ephesus." *Wikipedia, The Free Encyclopedia.* November 11, 2018. https://en.wikipedia.org/w/index.php?title=Second_Council_of_Ephesus&oldid=868363428.

— "Second Great Awakening." *Wikipedia, The Free Encyclopedia.* July 5, 2018.

https://en.wikipedia.org/w/index.php?title=Second_Great_
Awakening&oldid=848889660.

— "Semipelagianism." *Wikipedia, The Free Encyclopedia.* February 26,
2018.
https://en.wikipedia.org/w/index.php?title=Semipelagianis
m&oldid=827684156.

— "Sentences." *Wikipedia, The Free Encyclopedia.* March 3, 2018.
https://en.wikipedia.org/w/index.php?title=Sentences&oldi
d=828528557.

— "Seventh-day Adventist Church." *Wikipedia, The Free Encyclopedia.*
July 10, 2018.
https://en.wikipedia.org/w/index.php?title=Seventh-
day_Adventist_Church&oldid=849694942.

— "Simon Sudbury." *Wikipedia, The Free Encyclopedia.* September 25,
2017.
https://en.wikipedia.org/w/index.php?title=Simon_Sudbury
&oldid=802374171.

— "Smalcald Articles." *Wikipedia, The Free Encyclopedia.* May 24, 2018.
https://en.wikipedia.org/w/index.php?title=Smalcald_Articl
es&oldid=842781417.

— "Sola Fide." *Wikipedia, The Free Encyclopedia.* January 31, 2018.
https://en.wikipedia.org/w/index.php?title=Sola_fide&oldid
=823360632.

— "Sola Gratia." *Wikipedia, The Free Encyclopedia.* December 4, 2017.
https://en.wikipedia.org/w/index.php?title=Sola_gratia&old
id=813578233.

— "St. Thomas Christians." *Wikipedia, The Free Encyclopedia.* August
25, 2018.
https://en.wikipedia.org/w/index.php?title=Saint_Thomas_
Christians&oldid=856409995.

— "State_church_of_the_Roman_Empire." *Wikipedia, The Free
Encyclopedia.* September 18, 2018.
https://en.wikipedia.org/w/index.php?title=State_church_o
f_the_Roman_Empire&oldid=859833090.

— "Summa Theologica." *Wikipedia, The Free Encyclopedia.* January 28,
2019.

https://en.wikipedia.org/w/index.php?title=Summa_Theolo
   gica&oldid=880652800.

— "Swiss Brethren." *Wikipedia, The Free Encyclopedia.* 25 January, 2018.
   https://en.wikipedia.org/w/index.php?title=Swiss_Brethren
   &oldid=822319122.

— "Switzerland." *Wikipedia, The Free Encyclopedia.* February 12, 2018.
   https://en.wikipedia.org/w/index.php?title=Switzerland&ol
   did=825340918.

— "Syncretism." *Wikipedia, The Free Encyclopedia.* August 28, 2018.
   https://en.wikipedia.org/w/index.php?title=Syncretism&old
   id=856884290.

— "Ted Haggard." *Wikipedia, The Free Encyclopedia.* June 15, 2018.
   https://en.wikipedia.org/w/index.php?title=Ted_Haggard&
   oldid=845921613.

— "Televangelism." *Wikipedia, The Free Encyclopedia.* June 13, 2018.
   https://en.wikipedia.org/w/index.php?title=Televangelism&
   oldid=845712906.

— "Tertullian." *Wikipedia, The Free Encyclopedia.* November 13, 2017.
   https://en.wikipedia.org/w/index.php?title=Tertullian&oldi
   d=810185663.

— "The 700 Club." *Wikipedia, The Free Encyclopedia.* June 29, 2018.
   https://en.wikipedia.org/w/index.php?title=The_700_Club
   &oldid=848014351.

— "Theology of John Calvin." *Wikipedia, The Free Encyclopedia.*
   November 27, 2017.
   https://en.wikipedia.org/w/index.php?title=Theology_of_Jo
   hn_Calvin&oldid=812368992.

— "Theology of Martin Luther." *Wikipedia, The Free Encyclopedia.*
   February 21, 2018.
   https://en.wikipedia.org/w/index.php?title=Theology_of_M
   artin_Luther&oldid=826798936.

— "Theory of everything." *Wikipedia, The Free Encyclopedia.* June 6,
   2019.
   https://en.wikipedia.org/w/index.php?title=Theory_of_ever
   ything&oldid=900609648.

— "Thirty Years War." *Wikipedia, The Free Encyclopedia*. May 19, 2017. https://en.wikipedia.org/w/index.php?title=Thirty_Years%27_War&oldid=842049265.

— "Thomas Aquinas." *Wikipedia, The Free Encyclopedia*. February 27, 2018. https://en.wikipedia.org/w/index.php?title=Thomas_Aquinas&oldid=827900453.

— "Thomas Campbell." *Wikipedia, The Free Encyclopedia*. February 1, 2018. https://en.wikipedia.org/w/index.php?title=Thomas_Campbell_(minister)&oldid=823461039.

— "Thomas Müntzer." *Wikipedia, The Free Encyclopedia*. January 26, 2018. https://en.wikipedia.org/w/index.php?title=Thomas_M%C3%BCntzer&oldid=822468155.

— "Thomas Road Baptist Church." *Wikipedia, The Free Encyclopedia*. April 2, 2018. https://en.wikipedia.org/w/index.php?title=Thomas_Road_Baptist_Church&oldid=833893064.

— "Tomas de Torquemada." *Wikipedia, The Free Encyclopedia*. September 24, 2018. https://en.wikipedia.org/w/index.php?title=Tom%C3%A1s_de_Torquemada&oldid=860957845.

— "Trinity." *Wikipedia, The Free Encyclopedia*. May 2, 2019. https://en.wikipedia.org/w/index.php?title=Trinity&oldid=895137671.

— "Unam Sanctam." *Wikipedia, The Free Encyclopedia*. November 23, 2018. https://en.wikipedia.org/w/index.php?title=Unam_sanctam&oldid=870213289.

— "Universal Priesthood." *Wikipedia, The Free Encyclopedia*. March 21, 2018. https://en.wikipedia.org/w/index.php?title=Universal_priesthood&oldid=831526175.

— "Utraquists." *Wikipedia, The Free Encyclopedia*. March 9, 2018. https://en.wikipedia.org/w/index.php?title=Utraquism&oldid=829580320.

— "Valentinianism." *Wikipedia, The Free Encyclopedia.* November 11, 2018.
https://en.wikipedia.org/w/index.php?title=Valentinianism&oldid=868350624.

— "Valentinus (Gnostic)." *Wikipedia, The Free Encyclopedia.* November 18, 2018.
https://en.wikipedia.org/w/index.php?title=Valentinus_(Gnostic)&oldid=869339981.

— "Vestments Controversy." *Wikipedia, The Free Encyclopedia.* March 19, 2018.
https://en.wikipedia.org/w/index.php?title=Vestments_controversy&oldid=831250957.

— "Vladimir the Great." *Wikipedia, The Free Encyclopedia.* September 19, 2018.
https://en.wikipedia.org/w/index.php?title=Vladimir_the_Great&oldid=860319015.

— "Waldensians." *Wikipedia, The Free Encyclopedia.* February 17, 2018.
https://en.wikipedia.org/w/index.php?title=Waldensians&oldid=826130467.

— "Watch Tower Society presidency dispute (1917)." *Wikipedia, The Free Encyclopedia.* November 16, 2019.
https://en.wikipedia.org/w/index.php?title=Watch_Tower_Society_presidency_dispute_(1917)&oldid=926423399.

— "Watch Tower Society unfulfilled predictions." *Wikipedia, The Free Encyclopedia.* December 9, 2018.
https://en.wikipedia.org/w/index.php?title=Watch_Tower_Society_unfulfilled_predictions&oldid=872863008.

— "Western Schism." *Wikipedia, The Free Encyclopedia.* January 22, 2019.
https://en.wikipedia.org/w/index.php?title=Western_Schism&oldid=879705488.

— "Westminster Confession of Faith." *Wikipedia, The Free Encyclopedia.* February 27, 2018.
https://en.wikipedia.org/w/index.php?title=Westminster_Confession_of_Faith&oldid=827867833.

— "William III of England." *Wikipedia, The Free Encyclopedia.* May 16, 2018.

https://en.wikipedia.org/w/index.php?title=William_III_of_
England&oldid=841535295.

— "William Miller (preacher)." *Wikipedia, The Free Encyclopedia.* May
23, 2018.
https://en.wikipedia.org/w/index.php?title=William_Miller_
(preacher)&oldid=842606808.

— "William of Ockham." *Wikipedia, The Free Encyclopedia.* February
21, 2018.
https://en.wikipedia.org/w/index.php?title=William_of_Oc
kham&oldid=826784210.

— "Word of Faith." *Wikipedia, The Free Encyclopedia.* May 16, 2018.
https://en.wikipedia.org/w/index.php?title=Word_of_Faith
&oldid=841506188.

— "Zion Christian Church." *Wikipedia, The Free Encyclopedia.* August
23, 2018.
https://en.wikipedia.org/w/index.php?title=Zion_Christian
_Church&oldid=856240541.

Wikisource Contributors "Acts or Disputation Against Fortunatus the
Manichaean/Disputation of the First Day." *Wikisource.*
December 24, 2010.
https://en.wikisource.org/wiki/Nicene_and_Post-
Nicene_Fathers:_Series_I/Volume_IV/Manichaean_Contro
versy/Acts_or_Disputation_Against_Fortunatus_the_Manic
haean/Disputation_of_the_First_Day.

— "Acts or Disputation Against Fortunatus the
Manichaean/Disputation of the Second Day." *Wikisource.*
December 24, 2010.
https://en.wikisource.org/wiki/Nicene_and_Post-
Nicene_Fathers:_Series_I/Volume_IV/Manichaean_Contro
versy/Acts_or_Disputation_Against_Fortunatus_the_Manic
haean/Disputation_of_the_Second_Day.

"Wise Old Sayings." Accessed May 28, 2019.
http://www.wiseoldsayings.com/perception-quotes/.

World Council of Churches "Orthodox churches (Oriental)." *World
Council of Churches.* Accessed February 5, 2018.
https://www.oikoumene.org/en/church-families/orthodox-
churches-oriental.

Zoll, Rachel "Televangelists Escape Penalty in Senate Inquiry." *NBC News*. January 7, 2011.
http://www.nbcnews.com/id/40960871/ns/politics-capitol_hill/t/televangelists-escape-penalty-senate-inquiry/#.W0Z1tPZFyAg.

Zylstra, Sarah Eekhoff "Died: Jan Crouch, Cofounder of Trinity Broadcasting Network." *Christianity Today*. May 31, 2016.
https://www.christianitytoday.com/news/2016/may/died-jan-crouch-cofounder-trinity-broadcasting-network-tbn.html.

Index

D

N

O

P

Y

Yahweh · 42, 105, 150
Young, Brigham · 236

Z

Zinzendorf · 175, 213, 214
Zwingli, Ulrich · 13, 164, 178, 180,
    185, 186, 188, 230, 251, 304,
    305, 306

About the Author

Jeff Richards was born in Salt Lake City, Utah. As a young man, he served a church mission in Bolivia. He graduated from Brigham Young University with an engineering degree. After several years working as an engineer, he pursued a Masters of Business Administration from the Johnson School at Cornell University. His career culminated in 20 years of senior leadership within a division of a Fortune 500 firm. His profession allowed him to live and travel widely throughout the United States engaging with Christians of many denominations. His positive experiences and his hope for greater cross-denominational understanding motivated this book.